T·H·E C·O·M·P·L·E·T·E HEART RECOVERY GUIDE

T·H·E C·O·M·P·L·E·T·E
HEART
RECOVERY
G·U·I·D·E

NEIL GORDON, M.D., Ph.D., M.P.H.
LARRY GIBBONS, M.D., M.P.H.

1991
OXFORD UNIVERSITY PRESS
CAPE TOWN

Oxford University Press
Walton Street, Oxford OX2 6DP, United Kingdom

OXFORD NEW YORK TORONTO
DELHI BOMBAY CALCUTTA MADRAS KARACHI
PETALING JAYA SINGAPORE HONG KONG TOKYO
NAIROBI DAR ES SALAAM CAPE TOWN
MELBOURNE AUCKLAND
AND ASSOCIATED COMPANIES IN
BERLIN IBADAN

ISBN 0 19 570631 5

© 1990 Neil Gordon, MD, and Larry Gibbons, MD

OXFORD is a trademark of Oxford University Press

All rights reserved. No part of this publication may be reproduced, stored in a retrieval system, or transmitted in any form or by any means, electronic, mechanical, photocopying, recording or otherwise, without the prior permission of the copyright owner.

Published in the United States of America by Simon and Schuster as
The Cooper Clinic Cardiac Rehabilitation Program.

Published in South Africa by Oxford University Press Southern Africa, Harrington House, Barrack Street, Cape Town 8001, South Africa.

DTP conversion by Theiner Typesetting (Pty) Ltd
Printed and bound by Belmor Printing

This book is not a substitute for the medical advice and supervision of your personal physician. No medical therapy or cardiac rehabilitation exercise programme should be undertaken except under the direction of your physician.

To my wonderful wife, Tracey, and lovely daughters, Kim and Terri, for their patience, understanding, love, and support.

NEIL GORDON

To LaDawn, Jeff, and Jenny, who mean everything to me, and to my parents, brothers, and sisters, who gave me abundant love and a great example.

LARRY GIBBONS

CONTENTS

INTRODUCTION _____ 13
by Kenneth H. Cooper, M.D., M.P.H.

▪ **PART ONE**
UNDERSTANDING CORONARY HEART DISEASE

Chapter 1	Case History of a Cardiac Patient: "It Could Never Happen to Me!"	23
Chapter 2	Myths: What Isn't True about Heart Disease	29
Chapter 3	The Heart Attack: What It Is, How It Happens	43

▪ **PART TWO**
RECOVERING FROM A HEART ATTACK OR SURGERY

Chapter 4	"Why Do I Feel This Way? What Does It Mean?"	63
Chapter 5	"How Bad Was My Heart Attack?"	71
Chapter 6	Coming Home, Moving Forward	99

▪ **PART THREE**
THE EXERCISE PRESCRIPTION

Chapter 7	Why Exercise?	129
Chapter 8	Better Safe Than Sorry	146
Chapter 9	Safety and Effectiveness: Your Twin Exercise Goals	173
Chapter 10	The Right Exercise for You	178

▪ **PART FOUR**
GROWING HEALTHIER DESPITE HEART DISEASE

| Chapter 11 | Risk Factors: The Reason Why Exercise Isn't Enough | 205 |

Chapter 12	Cholesterol: A Key Factor in Restoring Your Health	212
Chapter 13	What to Do about Excess Kilograms	250
Chapter 14	The Insidious Effects of Stress on Your Body	269
Chapter 15	Reducing Your Other Risk Factors	290

■ PART FIVE
POINTING THE WAY TO BETTER HEALTH

| Chapter 16 | Introducing the Heart Points System | 321 |
| Chapter 17 | Your Weekly Heart Points Scorecard: What It Says about Your Recovery | 333 |

■ PART SIX
MEDICAL TREATMENT OPTIONS

| Chapter 18 | When Angioplasty or Bypass Surgery Becomes Necessary | 337 |
| Chapter 19 | Controversial Treatments | 354 |

■ AFTERWORD
MEETING THE CHALLENGE OF HEART DISEASE

RESOURCES SECTION

Appendix A	Formulas for Estimating Your MET Value during Exercise Testing	371
Appendix B	Estimating Your Energy Expenditure during Exercise	375
Appendix C	Sample Initial Cardiac Recovery Exercise Programmes	401
Appendix D	For CHD Patients: The Cooper Clinic Exercise Safety Quiz	409
Appendix E	The ABCs of Heart Medication	419

GLOSSARY	437
ACKNOWLEDGEMENTS	444
CHAPTER NOTES	445
INDEX	461

PREFACE

ANY book as comprehensive as *The Complete Heart Recovery Guide* must have an interesting story behind it, and this one certainly does. Our story first began exactly ten years ago, shortly after I completed my military basic training. Because of my keen interest in sports medicine—which was why I went to medical school in the first place—I eagerly volunteered to help Dr Van Myburgh and Dr Jones Cilliers establish a cardiac rehabilitation programme at 1 Military Hospital in Voortrekkerhoogte. To get the ball rolling, I decided to telephone heart patients who had recently been discharged from hospital. It was my very first call that planted the seed for writing a book that would set the record straight about heart disease and lead patients step-by-step down the road to recovery—and far beyond.

That telephone call was a real eye-opener for me, a novice in the field of cardiac care. The patient, an army colonel, bellowed into the phone: "Why are you trying to create more problems for me? Isn't it enough that I've been turned into an invalid for the rest of my life by a heart attack?" Fortunately, I kept my cool and convinced him to give it a try—after all, what did he have to lose? Within months, the colonel was "miraculously" transformed into a man with a new zest for life. Like the thousands of patients we have subsequently worked with both here in South Africa and in the United States, he had experienced first-hand the numerous physical and psychological benefits of cardiac rehabilitation.

Today, we know that a comprehensive heart recovery programme—such as the one outlined in this book—will not only improve your quality of life, but may also cause some reversal of your existing coronary heart disease and substantially lessen your risk of dying prematurely from it. But, alas, despite the many benefits that have unfolded through numerous research studies during the past decade, heart patients are often not much better informed than the colonel was prior to my telephone call back in 1981. Moreover, only a mere eleven percent or so of heart patients in the United States currently participate in such programmes. And the figure is unlikely to be much greater in South Africa, despite its exceptionally high standard of medical care.

Our book is meant to help fill this void by providing you with practical, easy to follow information for use in collaboration with your doctor. In so doing, we hope that it will give you renewed hope for a healthier, longer life, and supplement the Herculean effort that the Heart Foundation of Southern Africa is already making in its war against the modern-day plague of coronary heart disease. If it does, then the untold hours Dr Larry Gibbons and myself have spent preparing this book will have been well worth the effort.

Neil F. Gordon, M.B.B.Ch., Ph.D., M.P.H.
Dallas, Texas
(February, 1991)

Should you have any comments, suggestions, or queries about this book, please address your correspondence to:
Drs. Neil Gordon and Larry Gibbons
Institute for Aerobics Research
12330 Preston Road
Dallas, TX 75230
USA

INTRODUCTION
Kenneth H. Cooper, M.D., M.P.H.

People who know of my work may think a book devoted to a medical rehabilitation programme runs counter to my reputation as one who promotes prevention. In a way, they're right. My preference by far is to keep people from getting sick in the first place. This has been my focus for the past two decades since I completed studies at the Harvard School of Public Health. My earlier medical degree had turned me into a doctor who could treat illness. My master's degree in public health taught me that it's easier to *maintain* good health than it is to *regain* it once it is lost, and that *staying* well is certainly a lot cheaper than getting well.

For years, I and many others have been saying that the keys to preventing major illness such as heart disease are a combination of regular aerobic exercise, good nutrition, and a balanced, moderate lifestyle. Unfortunately, there are still a lot of people around the world who are not heeding this advice, or may never have heard it.

Heart disease is, by and large, a self-inflicted malady. You don't catch it, like you do smallpox or tuberculosis.

Heart disease, as any person who reads a newspaper or watches TV knows, is today's predominant killer in industrialized nations around the globe. Virtually unknown in 1900, coronary heart disease (or CHD) has skyrocketed in all of the westernized nations. And as third-world nations are becoming more developed, CHD is increasing there, too.

It's ironic that the richest countries are the world's coronary capitals (see Figure I-1). Ironic, but not surprising. CHD is largely caused by life-style factors. In so-called civilized countries, we smoke, overeat, drink too much, run errands in cars instead of on foot, watch sport on TV instead of participating in sport ourselves, and otherwise behave in ways that are detrimental to our health. In truth, many of us in advanced countries choose to ruin our health despite the fact that we have at our disposal far

DEATH RATES (PER 100 000 PERSONS)

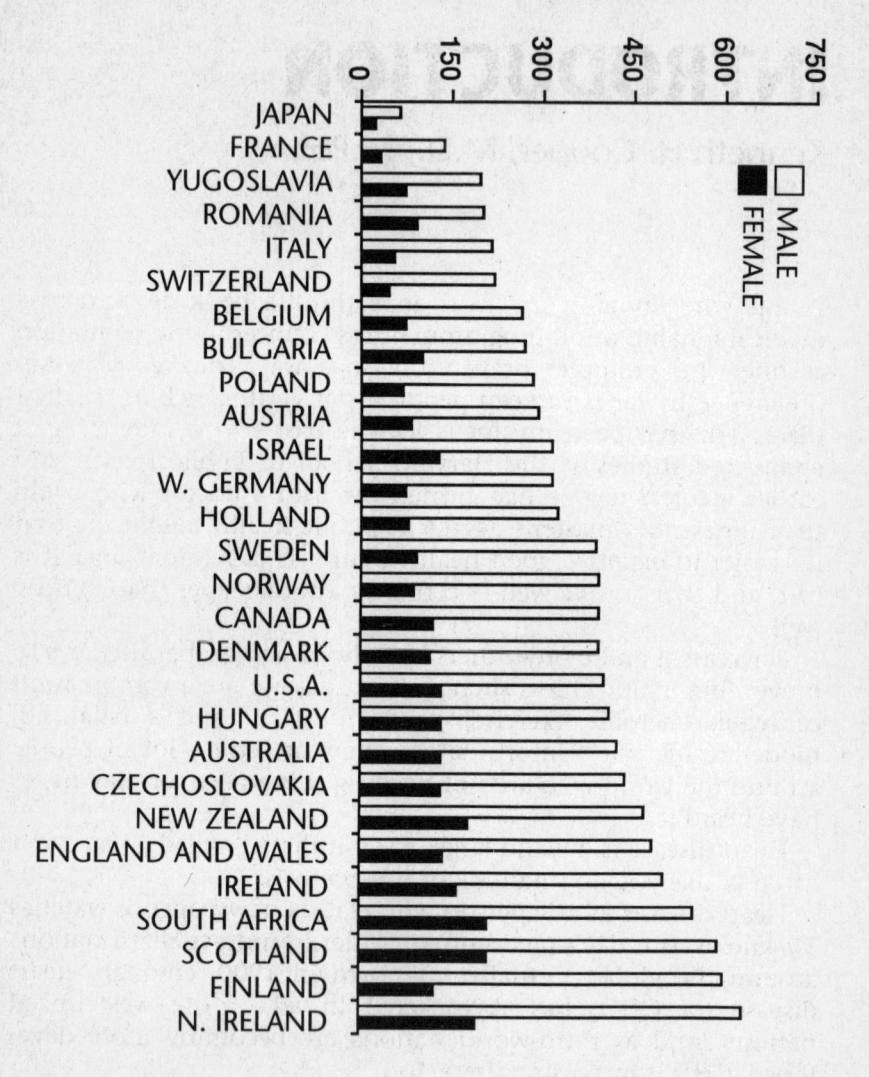

Figure I-1. Estimated international annual coronary heart disease death rates for men and women between the ages of forty and sixty-five. Death rates for South Africa are for whites only (accurate data are unavailable for blacks). (Adapted in part from L. A. Simons, "Interrelations of Lipids and Lipoproteins with Coronary Artery Disease Mortality in 19 Countries." *American Journal of Cardiology*, 57 [1986]: 5G–10G.)

more scientific knowledge about the human body and its functioning than did any previous generation. And certainly more than the people in less developed parts of the world where heart disease is almost unheard of.

Take South Africa. This country is a good example of the havoc civilization can wreak on the human heart, because it embodies within its borders a stark contrast between modern and primitive life-styles.

It's no accident that the world's first human heart transplant was performed in Cape Town in 1967 by Dr. Christiaan Barnard. White male South Africans have one of the highest CHD rates in the entire world. This is not the case for the black population, which has one of the lowest. Not surprising, as the black population's life-style bears little resemblance to that of the white Afrikaners—until they move to the cities, that is.

Fortunately, a great many people in Westernized societies have seen the light over the last twenty years (see the heart disease statistics in Figure I-2). In the United States, deaths from CHD increased relentlessly throughout the 1930s, 1940s, and 1950s, culminating in a situation that the World Health Organization termed "of the utmost urgency." But this headlong flight into personal self-destruction began to turn around somewhat in the 1960s. Today, regular exercise has become a way of life for millions of Americans and heart disease rates are down by almost 40 percent.

I predict that the exercise boom will grow stronger as the population ages and people become more attuned to health issues. According to a Gallup poll, in the early 1960s only about 24 percent of adults exercised regularly; by 1984, the figure had increased to 59 percent.

However, in my opinion, there are four other predominant reasons for the drop in the incidence of heart disease over the past two decades.

First, every year more and more people stop smoking. Second, hypertension detection and treatment have improved markedly. Third, many people now understand the harmful effects of stress and do what they can to combat it. And last, but perhaps most important, more people are eating healthier diets, eschewing many of the high-cholesterol fried foods and overly processed foods which are so disastrous for one's heart.

But despite all this good news, the Heart Foundation of Southern Africa still expects 48 000 South Africans to suffer heart attacks this year. A quarter of them will die instantly or soon

PERCENTAGE CHANGE IN DEATH RATES : 1970 TO 1980

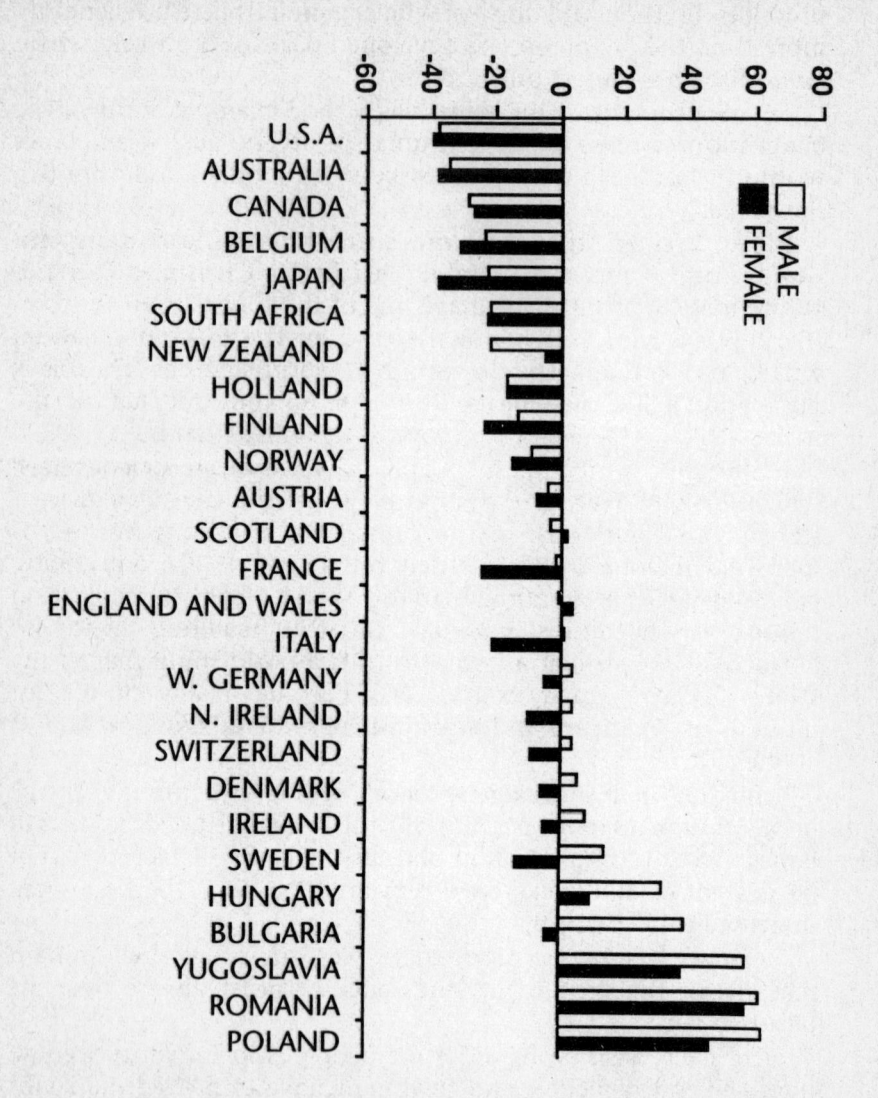

Figure I-2. Estimated percentage decline or rise in international annual coronary heart disease death rates between 1970 and 1980 for men and women aged forty to sixty-five. Percentage changes for South Africa are for whites only (accurate data are unavailable for blacks). (Adapted in part from L. A. Simons, "Interrelations of Lipids and Lipoproteins with Coronary Artery Disease Mortality in 19 Countries." *American Journal of Cardiology,* 57 [1986]: 5G–10G.)

thereafter. This means that 36 000 South Africans will live through this devastating personal health crisis and will need education in cardiac rehabilitation and prevention—prevention of another heart attack.

In the early 1970s, I resigned from the air force and founded the Aerobics Centre* in Dallas. For the first decade or so, my staff and I devoted ourselves almost exclusively to "primary prevention." This bit of medical jargon means promoting a healthy diet and life-style so that patients reduce their chances of developing serious ailments, especially self-induced conditions like heart disease. The goal is peak health—what I like to call "total well-being." It's not simply a matter of regular exercise. Eating correctly and emotional factors enter into the picture, too. I always stress this well-rounded approach when I counsel patients or talk on television.

More recently, I've turned my attention to "secondary prevention." This refers to doing all we can to prevent a recurrence of a health crisis; for example, preventing a follow-up heart attack after a middle-aged individual has suffered his or her first.

It has been my experience that in the wake of a cardiac bypass operation or some other life-threatening health crisis, the majority of people are transformed—ready, willing, and able to listen to reason, perhaps for the first time in their lives. The health advice they turned a deaf ear to for years now becomes music to their ears.

This book is directed to these highly motivated survivors.

If you're a cardiac patient recovering from a heart attack, angioplasty, or bypass operation, I believe you've got the right book in your hands, for I feel we at the Cooper Clinic have developed a truly sound cardiac rehabilitation programme.

Dr. Larry W. Gibbons and Dr. Neil F. Gordon, the authors of this book, are the two people most responsible for our programme. Allow me to introduce them:

---

* The Aerobics Centre is composed of the Cooper Clinic, a preventive and rehabilitative medicine facility; the Institute for Aerobics Research, where researchers study the role of exercise in the maintenance of health; the Guest Lodge, where people can stay when visiting the Aerobics Centre for extended periods of time; and the Aerobics Activity Centre, a health club in which all members' exercise efforts are supervised by a well-trained staff of health professionals.

Larry Gibbons joined the Cooper Clinic in 1974, not long after its founding. He came from a preventive medicine teaching post with the U.S. Army and has also held staff positions at the University of Texas Medical School at San Antonio and the Tulane University School of Public Health in New Orleans. He earned a medical degree from the University of Utah in 1970 and a master's degree in public health from Harvard University in 1978. He is a fellow of the American College of Preventive Medicine and of the American College of Sports Medicine.

Larry has been the Cooper Clinic's medical director since 1979. Patients appreciate very much his ability to speak succinctly on technical subjects that would otherwise be difficult to comprehend and his soft-spoken, comforting manner. Larry's energy level never ceases to amaze me. Despite caring for many patients and attending to his Cooper Clinic administrative duties, he still manages to lecture extensively to both lay and medical audiences in the United States and abroad.

Neil Gordon is a more recent addition to our staff. Neil relocated to the United States from South Africa in 1987 to become the director of exercise physiology at our Institute for Aerobics Research and the director of the Aerobics Centre Cardiac Rehabilitation Programme. He holds a medical degree as well as a Ph.D. from the University of the Witwatersrand, and a master's degree in public health from the University of California at Los Angeles. Neil is a fellow of the American Association of Cardiovascular and Pulmonary Rehabilitation and, like Larry, of the American College of Sports Medicine. Recently, he was elected as the physician-representative of the board of directors of the American Association of Cardiovascular and Pulmonary Rehabilitation.

Neil's scientific credentials are extremely impressive—and extensive. Despite his relative youth, he's been the principal author of more than thirty major scientific papers and has presented his research findings before scientific gatherings all over the globe. Neil has a tremendous grasp of state-of-the-art medical thinking, which comes through in this book.

In South Africa, where I met Neil on a speaking tour in 1985, he had established and served as the medical director of one of the country's finest inpatient and outpatient cardiac rehabilitation programmemes. He was also widely regarded as one of South Africa's leading authorities on exercise and health, and he is rapidly gaining a similar reputation in the United States. Since moving to the United States, Neil has already received major research awards from distinguished organizations such as the American Diabetes Association and the National Institutes of Health.

Anyone familiar with my books knows that I believe people need all the motivation they can get to break a bad health habit and replace it with a good one. Neil and Larry agree.

To provide you, the recovering heart patient, with a strong incentive to regain your health and prevent a recurrence, they've created the Heart Points System. It's a great system—and one of the cornerstones of this book. It represents a Herculean effort and I take my hat off to them.

The Heart Points System combines six of the controllable CHD risk factors into one workable—and easily understood—self-analysis programme. I think you'll like it. It will ease you into a healthier life-style and motivate you to keep going and persevere even on those days when you feel most tempted to backslide.

Our programme is based on a simple notion: rehabilitation is a two-part process. The first part involves education—helping a patient gain a thorough understanding of why change is crucial. The second part involves action—giving the patient the wherewithal to make change a reality. That's where our Heart Points System comes in.

I urge you to do more than just fill your head with the medical facts contained herein. I urge you to *act on what you learn*.

Good intentions are fine, but when it comes to cardiac rehabilitation, they amount to nothing unless you make them reality. You can't just talk about lowering the stress in your life, for instance; you must do it. You can't join an organized cardiac exercise group and then be absent all the time; you have to go there faithfully and work out.

Think of our cardiac rehabilitation programme as a means to two very worthwhile ends—prolonging your life as well as improving the quality of your added years. You, of all people, know how precious life is, because you've had a brush with death. We're sure you aren't eager to repeat that experience soon.

Please remember at all times that this superb book is intended for use only in close consultation and collaboration with your personal physician. By working closely with your own physician and adhering to our programme, you stand the best chance of improving both the quality and quantity of your years. Good luck. And the best of health to you!

PART ONE

UNDERSTANDING CORONARY HEART DISEASE

CHAPTER 1

CASE HISTORY OF A CARDIAC PATIENT: "It Could Never Happen to Me"

Granted, no two heart attacks are exactly alike, especially from the point of view of the sufferer; and the same can be said about people's bypass surgery operations and angioplasties. Still, as doctors, we sometimes come across a case that's more typical than unique, and contains lessons that would be instructive to others.

John Venter is one such case. John is a successful graduate of the rehabilitation programme described in this book and his story runs throughout the opening chapters. John has agreed to let his case history be printed because he hopes others can benefit from his experience—and his mistakes.

Unfortunately, John acquired the knowledge contained in this book only after he'd already suffered his heart attack. If he had known what precautions to take, he could probably have prevented what eventually happened.

To be sure, John Venter's heart attack was preventable. You could even say John caused his heart attack. He let circumstances transform the good health habits he had acquired earlier in his life into bad ones later on. Of his own volition, John tempted fate. He's lucky he's still around to tell the tale.

Before his sudden heart attack, John was a vigorous forty-five-year-old businessman. As so many of us do, he took his seeming good health for granted. He understood the concept of preventive medicine but he believed he didn't need a doctor to work out a health programme for him. Indeed, John was one of those people who refused to go to a doctor unless there was something obviously wrong that needed fixing—an ingrown toenail or an ear infection, for instance.

Occasionally John would hear about a middle-aged acquaintance who'd died of a heart attack. But it never crossed his mind that it could happen to him.

John thought of himself as a sportsman because he'd been one as a young man. He grew up on a farm in Stellenbosch and at busy times of the year would have to get up at dawn to help with the loading of grapes and other fruit. At high school he played flyhalf in the rugby team and was generally fairly fit.

John put himself through university and it was then that his exercise routine began its long downhill slide. He did train a little with weights. And he occasionally jogged to his job at a Stellenbosch steakhouse, where he worked for four years. John also ate in the steakhouse because free meals were a perk of the job.

By the time John had his heart attack twenty-five years later, he'd climbed up the business ladder to a senior-level position in a massive insurance company. Unfortunately, once he got near the top, the company found itself in grave financial difficulties. Although John knew he'd never be without a job, the implications of the crisis were grave. Eventually the danger was averted, but for years the pressure was intense and the hours were long.

Up to that point, John would have said that he maintained a moderate fitness level. He'd play a game of squash or a round of golf on Saturdays, and during the week he'd jog with his sons from time to time. But this began to peter out during the four years prior to his heart attack.

Nine months before the attack, John applied for a life insurance policy which required a medical examination. The check-up was by no means thorough. The doctor made him run on the spot for three minutes and then checked John's heart rate. The physician detected nothing out of the ordinary, except that John's blood pressure was 146/94, slightly elevated. He was also nearly twelve kilograms over his ideal mass.

The doctor's advice was pretty perfunctory: lose mass, cut back on salt, exercise more, and come back in three months for a more intensive check-up. John remembers the doctor mentioning that it would be good for him to have his cholesterol checked. The doctor said he'd run a blood cholesterol test during John's next visit.

John describes what happened next:

> I never had that second medical because work got too hectic. I was working twelve, sometimes fourteen, hours a day. I've always been a hard driver who enjoys business challenges, but the stress of trying to keep our institution solvent in the face of such enormous odds took the fun out of it. I felt tired and tense all the time. My

family started referring to me as "the phantom," the mystery man who appears out of nowhere late every night to catch a few winks of sleep and disappears just as silently the next morning.

Nonetheless, to preserve my sanity during this awful period, I always made time for squash once or twice a month. While I was playing, I began to notice something was different. It wasn't the usual me. I got winded easily. In fact, about a month before the attack, I actually experienced chest discomfort. I assumed I was just out of shape and forgot about it.

I'll never forget the Saturday morning when it happened. I'd put in two hours at the office and on the way home I'd stopped to pick up some groceries for my wife. The supermarket was so jammed I couldn't even get my car into the parking area. I remember losing my temper at the till because people were being so slow with their transactions.

It was raining when I got outside, so I ran with four heavy grocery bags all the way to the car, some distance from the supermarket. That's when I first noticed the tightness in my chest, just like the feeling I'd had on the squash court. I passed a hospital on my ten-minute drive home but it never occurred to me to stop.

My wife's greeting wasn't very encouraging. She took one look at me and asked in an alarmed voice, "What on earth is wrong with you? You look white as a sheet!"

I felt horrible. The tightness had turned into a feeling of being crushed, as if a horse were sprawled on top of me. Pain, starting in my neck, was running down the inside of both arms.

I didn't stop my wife when she phoned our family doctor. He said it sounded like a heart attack and to come to the hospital immediately.

What happened next is hazy. The excruciating pain and nausea are all I remember. I broke out in a cold sweat and started thinking about death for the first time in my life.

At the emergency entrance, I was rushed into an area specifically designated for cardiac patients, and an army of medical professionals descended on me.

While the physician was looking me over, he asked me some medical-history questions that I managed to answer despite the excruciating pain. Meanwhile, they'd hooked me up to an electrocardiograph and were administering oxygen. Someone drew a blood sample and punctured my arm with an intravenous line (IV).

Finally, the doctor made the announcement to his colleagues: "It's an MI, all right"—which I later learned stands for "myocardial infarction."

Since the nitroglycerin pills they'd placed under my tongue earlier hadn't relieved the pain, the doctor ordered a morphine infusion via the IV. He also ordered a drug called lidocaine, which he said would reduce my risk of developing heart arrhythmias, or irregular beats. Then he tried to reassure me:

"You're fortunate, Mr. Venter. Since you've only been experiencing pain for a little over an hour, we can try to limit the damage to your heart by infusing a medication called t-PA, or tissue-type plasminogen activator. If we're lucky, it will dissolve the blood clot in your coronary artery that's probably causing the heart attack. Do we have your permission?"

John remembers this direct question well because he says it shocked him into realizing that this was actually happening to *him*. He wasn't just a bystander. The life-and-death decisions were his—and his wife's. Like most people, they knew very little about heart attacks or coronary matters. But they did have the common sense to ask all the right questions.

First, they asked what the chances were that the t-PA would do the job. They learned that it's successful in nearly 80 percent of patients. If John fell into the unfortunate 20 percent category, he might have to go a step further and have an angiogram. This diagnostic test would be performed in a special room called a cardiac catheterization laboratory—or "cath lab." A cardiologist would insert a thin plastic tube, called a catheter, into an artery in his groin. That area of his body would be anaesthetized with a local anaesthetic and he'd be conscious throughout. After the doctor moved the tube up to the coronary arteries, he'd inject a dye into John's coronary arteries while an X-ray machine took a rapid series of pictures.

The next option would depend on the X-ray results. To limit further damage to the heart, John might have to have an angioplasty, a procedure in which the coronary arteries are dilated at those points where they've become narrowed by plaque. Once again, a catheter is used, but at its end there's a small, tough balloon. The doctor inflates this balloon within each of the blocked coronary arteries to flatten out the obstructions. An angioplasty is such a simple technique that general anaesthesia is not necessary.

Finally, John and his wife were told about the last resort— bypass surgery. The mere thought of it was terrifying. Anything seemed preferable to open-heart surgery. They asked what the chances were that bypass surgery would be needed.

The doctor said that from what he could see of John's condition, bypass surgery was only a very remote possibility.

Naturally, John and his wife were enormously relieved. But the immediate problem was the severe pain. John told the doctor to try the t-PA. Here's what he recalls about the next few hours:

Soon thereafter, they moved me into the coronary intensive care unit. About forty-five minutes later, the t-PA started to work and I began to notice my surroundings.

Long after my chest pain had completely disappeared, I was still hooked up to a monitor. I didn't like being so confined, or the atmosphere in that room.

Intensive care is not a place for rest and relaxation. People scurry about amid machines that are constantly buzzing and flashing and sounding alarms. All I could think of was ESCAPE. I was especially disturbed by the sound of the patients around me breathing on ventilators. It seemed like the last station before death.

I signalled to a nurse nearby and asked when I could be moved to my own hospital room. She explained that all the claptrap and apparatus was for my own good. My condition wasn't stable yet and the monitor enabled the ICU staff to detect any problems immediately. Wouldn't I want them to know and act on such information instantaneously?

I couldn't argue with the logic. So I tried to take my mind off my whereabouts and think happy thoughts. Happy thoughts were impossible. Gruesome images kept recurring.

One picture wouldn't go away. It was the stricken look on my father's face during his first heart attack at age fifty-one. He'd been working in the vineyards one day, when he suddenly collapsed. We'd known about his high blood pressure for a long time but nobody took that seriously. He was also a heavy smoker. Three years after his first heart attack, he had the fatal one. We always believed the smoking caused it. Because I never smoked, I thought it could never happen to me.

Lying there, it suddenly struck me. My older brother had angina. Maybe heart disease runs in our family.

I remember thinking: My brother is fortunate. Angina pain at least gives you a lot of advance warning. You've got time to do something constructive about your problem.

To my brother's credit, he had done everything the doctor said. He'd altered his diet radically, stopped smoking and started exercising. Because of this, his angina had improved considerably and he had yet to suffer a heart attack.

I was impressed with my brother's willpower. In comparison, what had I done after the warning signs on the squash court? I was angry with myself. I hadn't even had the good sense to go in for that second medical check-up.

I remember lying there thinking about the health and fitness principles my high school rugby coach used to drum into us.

Suddenly it dawned on me how far my health habits had really slipped from those days when I had 85 kilograms of muscle on my 1,85 m frame. Now I weighed 97 kilograms and much of it was flab!

There's good reason why John became a heart attack sufferer. In reality, John's problem started back at university when his diet went from wholesome, high-fibre foods to high-fat, high-cholesterol, high-sodium, over-refined fast foods. From his first year of college onward, John gained mass steadily.

His diet didn't improve much when he graduated from university and moved into the business world. Several times a week, he would entertain colleagues and clients at lunches or dinners in restaurants. Steak, often topped with rich sauces, was his favourite and he indulged frequently since the company was usually picking up the bill. Since he faithfully declined dessert, he mistakenly assumed he was making choices that would safeguard his health.

If John had been able to look inside his circulatory system, he wouldn't have felt so invincible. Little by little, fatty deposits, called plaque, were building up on the inner walls of most of his arteries, gradually reducing their internal diameter. John was suffering from a progressive condition known as atherosclerosis. The arteries to his heart muscle were also affected.

Clearly, John—like many people—was caught up in a game of denial. Over the preceding twenty-five years he had never stopped to reflect on his health status. He had other priorities, more pressing certainly than a body that appeared to be in good working order.

John finally had a heart attack because his coronary arteries had narrowed to the point where a small blood clot ("thrombosis") was enough to shut off the usual flow of nourishing blood to his heart muscle. This "coronary thrombosis" caused permanent damage to his heart muscle. That irreversible damage is the myocardial infarction, or "MI," John heard his doctor discussing in the emergency room.

CHAPTER 2

MYTHS: What Isn't True about Heart Disease

John Venter spent ten days in the hospital. The stay was uneventful except for his acute mental discomfort. Any physical discomfort had largely subsided after the first couple of days.

When John was awake and alone, he was thinking. More accurately, he was worrying. Like many heart patients, he held numerous misconceptions about heart disease and its implications for his future.

Here are some of the myths John harboured until his doctor set him straight during daily visits to his bedside, and during his predischarge evaluation the day before his hospital release:

> **"My heart attack means I'm at great risk for having another one soon."**

Not necessarily. All heart attacks are serious. No one disputes that. But some are more serious than others.

Using risk criteria and relatively simple tests that have been developed by researchers in recent years, medical professionals can now classify those who've had heart attacks into risk groups.

About 35 percent of all patients who survive a heart attack fall into the low-risk category (see Chapter 5). It's unlikely they'll suffer another one. In short, the first-year death rate among this group is less than 5 percent. Individuals in this group won't require as much medication, testing, or medical surveillance as their moderate- and high-risk counterparts.

At the other extreme is the high-risk category, which comprises about 25 percent of all heart attack survivors. Without appropriate treatment, more than 20 percent of these people are expected to die within their first year of recovery.

The moderate group in between—some 40 percent of heart attack survivors—contains individuals whose chances of dying within the first year after their attack run from 5 to 20 percent. John Venter falls into this group. These are individuals who, like high-risk patients, require in-depth evaluation by specialists and, in many cases, additional medical procedures such as bypass surgery or angioplasty.

What about the hundreds of thousands of people with heart disease who haven't had a heart attack but have angina or have undergone angioplasty or bypass surgery? What are their chances of developing more serious heart problems in the future?

Many of the same risk criteria which we apply to heart attack victims can be used for these individuals. This issue of "patient stratification" is discussed in Chapter 5.

> "I probably won't be able to resume my old life. Everything—from my work to my recreation and social life—will have to change."

John's negative outlook is typical of coronary patients recuperating in hospitals. If anything, depression is a normal reaction to such a frightening event. It even strikes patients who've had angioplasties or bypass surgery, although to a much lesser extent.

The famous Dr. Paul Dudley White, personal physician to US President Eisenhower, may have summed it up best when he said, "The heart may recover more rapidly [after a heart attack] than the depressed mental state [of the patient] which is so often a complication."

Sad to say, but the world is filled with heart attack patients who unnecessarily turn into "cardiac cripples". These are people who become depressed and fearful because they perceive their heart condition to be far worse than it really is.

In their defence, we have to admit that these patients' cardiologists are sometimes to blame. Some physicians don't outline for their patients what's normal and what isn't during the recuperation period. They don't tell patients that it's normal to feel a sense of chronic tiredness and fatigue during the initial weeks after they arrive home from the hospital. Naturally, many patients who aren't told this assume that their weariness means they'll be invalids forever. This frightening notion impedes their return to their regular occupational, recreational, and social pursuits.

In actuality, this fatigue usually has very little to do with their heart condition. It's caused by the extended bed rest patients get in the hospital. Even young athletes who suddenly find themselves flat on their backs in a hospital bed experience this fatigue during recuperation. Inactivity is the culprit, not heart disease.

Yes, high-risk patients will have to take it slower. And, indeed, some strenuous activities may be permanently off limits to them. But with appropriate therapy, evaluation, and guidance, most of even the high-risk patients should be able to return to a normal routine within a reasonable amount of time.

In contrast, low-risk patients have little excuse for feeling sorry for themselves. Studies show most of them recover quickly and are capable of taking up a normal, healthy lifestyle shortly after their hospital stay. In fact, preliminary research by Dr. Eric J. Topol and his colleagues at the University of Michigan Medical Centre suggests it may be safe for some low-risk patients to be discharged from the hospital as early as three days after their heart attacks.[1]

While additional studies are obviously needed before such a liberal strategy can be widely recommended, Dr. Topol's research does emphasize the fact that there is no evidence whatsoever that early resumption of most normal activities is harmful to low-risk patients.

"Now that I have heart disease, it's all downhill for my sex life."

This is one of the most enduring myths about heart disease. And, again, many physicians are to blame for not addressing this subject in a forthright manner. If a patient doesn't ask a direct question about sex, too often it's not mentioned at all.[2]

You'll no doubt be delighted to know that heart disease should have minimal negative impact on sexuality. The dangers of sex for heart patients have been grossly exaggerated.

As early as 1970, research by Dr. Herman K. Hellerstein and Dr. Ernest H. Friedman of the Case Western Reserve University School of Medicine in Cleveland showed that the average amount of energy expended during the sex act is equivalent to walking up a flight of stairs—which isn't an enormous amount of energy.[3]

A Japanese study conducted a little earlier also showed that sexual intercourse is, contrary to popular belief, only a very rare cause of sudden death.[4] In that study, researchers discovered that of some five thousand people who had died suddenly, only thirty-four—or a tiny 0,7 percent—had died during sexual intercourse. Furthermore, at the time of intercourse, thirty of the thirty-four victims were with someone other than their spouse. Their sexual partner was, on average, eighteen years younger than they were, and all those who died had elevated blood alcohol levels. In other words, you could interpret this study as an argument for marital fidelity. It suggests that sex with one's spouse is an extremely safe activity—in contrast to extramarital affairs, which could place a heart patient at some risk. We'll cover this subject in more detail in Chapter 6.

> **"If I'd cut out high-fat foods and improved my eating habits, maybe I could have lowered my blood cholesterol level and prevented this heart attack. But now that I have heart disease, it's too late to reduce the blockages in my coronary arteries by lowering my blood cholesterol."**

The first statement about prevention has a lot of truth to it. The landmark Lipid Research Clinic's Coronary Primary Prevention Trial results, published in 1984, demonstrated that an 8,5 percent reduction in blood cholesterol achieved by improved eating habits and medication produced a 19 percent reduction in the risk of developing—and/or dying from—heart disease.[5] In other words, this monumental $150 million study, which involved 3 806 men with no symptoms of heart disease at the start of the study, showed pretty conclusively that for every 1 percent you lower your cholesterol level, you lower your risk of developing and/or dying from heart disease by double that—or about 2 percent.

The findings of the recently completed Helsinki Heart Study are further proof of the benefits of a lower cholesterol level.[6] This is especially true if the lowered level is coupled with a significant increase in high-density-lipoprotein (HDL) cholesterol, which helps clear plaque deposits from the walls of blood vessels. In this five-year-long study involving 4 081 symptom-free men with elevated blood cholesterol levels, dietary changes and medication were accompanied by a 10 percent reduction in blood cholesterol and by an 11 percent increase in HDL cholesterol levels. The result: an amazing 34 percent reduction in heart disease risk.

The second half of John's statement—that blockages are already present in his coronary arteries and can't be reversed, so why try?—represents a common misconception.

Three major studies show that cholesterol-lowering drugs—when coupled with low-fat diets—can decrease overall blood cholesterol levels as well as increase the beneficial HDL cholesterol component. Not only that, coronary artery blockages were visibly reduced in some of the study participants.[7]

Dr J. E. Rossouw, a South African now working with the National Institutes of Health in Washington, recently published a report in the prestigious *New England Journal of Medicine*.[8] The report showed that more MIs would be prevented if one lowered the raised cholesterol levels of patients who had already had an MI than if one only reduced the blood cholesterol levels of patients who had never had an MI.

All these studies add up to a simple conclusion: lowering cholesterol is a good thing whether it happens before or after the onset of heart disease. Not only does it slow the deterioration, but it can also help unblock your blood vessels—reversing the degree of coronary artery narrowing that has already occurred.

"If I'd stuck with a prudent low-cholesterol diet all my life, my blood cholesterol level would be normal today and I wouldn't have heart disease."

Unfortunately, this is a myth for people who have inherited a high cholesterol level. Many people have a stubbornly high blood cholesterol level even though they're careful about what foods they buy. They can't understand what's wrong. Heredity may be one culprit. Their biological makeup, which they can't do much about, plays an important role in the way their body handles cholesterol. Still, even this biological predisposition to a high cholesterol count can be ameliorated with proper diet in most instances. But there is a second problem as well. Although many people are careful about what foods they buy, they are often misinformed—and food manufacturers don't help matters at all. The truth is that cholesterol is not the only thing to avoid. This is because it's the saturated-fat content of the food we eat more than the cholesterol content that has a negative influence on our blood cholesterol level. Some foods which can correctly be described as cholesterol-free are at the same time high in saturated fat. Examples are fried foods, non-dairy milk and cream substitutes, sweets, potato chips, and baked products such as biscuits, cakes, and crackers. Look for the Heart Foundation of Southern Africa "Heart Mark" to identify products approved as part of a heart healthy eating plan (see pages 267-8).

Some people also think that the words "contains no animal fat" are a blanket safety endorsement. While it's true that foods derived from plants contain no cholesterol and are usually rich in polyunsaturated and monounsaturated fats—the "good" fats—there are exceptions. The exceptions are coconut oil, palm oil and palm kernel oil—all loaded with saturated fats. Even though they originate from plants, they'll all raise the level of cholesterol in your blood. So too do hard vegetable fats.

"Low-fat" labels can also be misleading. For example, milk with 2 percent fat is usually advertised as "low-fat". That milk may be lower in fat than regular whole milk, but it's still not low-fat enough. Fat accounts for only 2 percent of that milk's mass, but about 35 percent of its kilojoules. As you'll discover in Chapter 12, in the ideal diet, fat should provide a maximum of only 30 percent of your daily kilojoule intake. Using that standard, 2 percent milk doesn't make the grade. Products labelled "fat free" are the ones that can contribute to a cholesterol-lowering diet.

> **"Everyone talks about exercise. I did get a reasonable amount of exercise until the last few years. It didn't prevent my heart disease. And I doubt there's any solid evidence that it will reduce my risk of dying now."**

Like many informed people, John knows that a sedentary lifestyle, devoid of physical activity, increases a person's chances of developing heart disease. But he seems to have forgotten that exercise can't be stored the way you can store money in a bank vault, for instance. Once you stop exercising regularly, you lose any protection that exercise offers against heart disease.

Since the 1950s, when researchers first began focusing on activity levels and accentuated risk for heart attacks, more than forty major studies have been completed in this area. What John and others don't always realize, though, is that our modern age has made physical inactivity a very common and serious problem.

In 1987, Dr. Kenneth E. Powell and his colleagues from the Centres for Disease Control in Atlanta scrutinized the findings of these forty or so earlier studies and came to the conclusion that inactivity is a strong risk factor for death from heart disease and can be compared to the traditional risk factors we hear so much about—cigarette smoking, high blood pressure, and a high cholesterol level.[9] Furthermore, since inactivity is often present, it can be viewed as an important health problem.

As you'll learn in Chapter 7, there is also now convincing evidence that exercise training can reduce the risk of dying from heart disease, even after a person has already had a heart attack. In other words, if John had continued his exercise regimen despite his newfound job pressures, he might have prevented his heart attack or, at least, he might have postponed it until a later date. And now that he has had a heart attack, a programme of regular exercise will still benefit him greatly.

> "Whenever I found time, I always exercised—albeit more for the enjoyment of it than for the health benefits. Maybe more strenuous exercise would have prevented my heart disease."

John is letting himself fall prey to the "no pain, no gain" myth. It's also referred to as the "weekend-warrior syndrome". People who subscribe to this way of thinking either exercise as if the Grim Reaper is their adversary or don't exercise at all because they don't like physical discomfort. They believe that if exercise has to be so agonizing in order to do any good, they'd rather not do it at all.

If this were true (which it isn't), who could blame them? Even though it's not true, a lot of people are still prey to this distorted notion of just what constitutes worthwhile exercise. As a consequence, millions of people miss out on the health-producing benefits of moderate, "fun" exercise.

A recent study conducted at the Aerobics Centre in Dallas by Dr. Steven N. Blair and his colleagues shows that moderate levels of physical activity are all that it takes to reduce the risk of dying from heart disease.[10] This important study tracked the health-related benefits that more than 13 000 men and women derived from moderate-intensity exercise such as a "brisk walk of 30–60 minutes each day". (A lot of us could reach or exceed that goal just by walking to and from work instead of driving or hopping onto public transport.) According to Dr. Blair, exceeding this moderate level of activity is unnecessary if protection from cardiovascular disease-related death is your goal.

The results of another major study—the Multiple Risk Factor Intervention Trial, or MRFIT (pronounced "Mr. Fit")—are in complete agreement with Dr. Blair's findings.[11] This study's huge sample of 12 138 middle-aged men enabled researchers to conclude that ordinary physical activities—such as gardening, dancing, and walking—when performed regularly and for at least thirty minutes non-stop, can bring about a 25 percent reduction in deaths from heart disease.

This MRFIT study also investigated the extremely energetic study participants who went beyond moderate activity levels. Were their chances of dying from heart disease even lower?

The answer, once again, was a resounding no.

When the results of these studies, which involved predominantly healthy persons, are extrapolated to heart patients, it is clear that you don't have to run marathons—nowhere near it—to benefit from exercise. Indeed, walking has emerged as the exercise of choice for a growing number of adults, particularly cardiac patients. You will obtain most benefit if you walk for at least thirty minutes and at least three or four times per week.

Dr. James M. Rippe and his fellow researchers at the University of Massachusetts concluded in a 1988 report that walking, if you do it consistently, will not only reduce your risk for heart disease, but may lessen any anxiety or tension you feel as well. In addition, it can help you lose mass, control high blood pressure, and slow the development of osteoporosis, or "brittle-bone disease."[12]

> **"Since heart disease runs in my family, my fate is out of my hands. I'm probably doomed to die young anyway, so why spend what's left of my life trying to prevent another heart attack?"**

This is another instance where John is deceiving himself. What John has to realize is that biology is by no means destiny. By altering his life-style, he—and others like him—can still overcome the biological hand they've been dealt. John need not be a victim of some inalterable fate.

Part of John's problem is psychological. John, like many people in his position, can't stand the idea of a disconcerting lifestyle change forced upon him by his heart condition. He views his heart ailment in the negative light of a handicap, rather than seeing it as a signal to alter his health habits for the better.

Change is hard for the best of us, even the most strong-willed. But John—and you—must realize that change can make a huge difference. In John's case, it can spell the difference between the possibility of a long, productive life and a premature death after an MI.

There's no doubt that genetic factors are a major factor in heart disease. Indeed, according to Dr. Joseph L. Goldstein and Dr. Michael S. Brown from the University of Texas Southwestern Medical Centre at Dallas, the risk of dying from heart disease is five to seven times greater in an individual with a close relative who died from a heart attack before the age of sixty.[13]

John is in that category. His father died at age fifty-four of heart disease.

Fortunately for John, and others like him, recent studies have shown that this blanket statement needs clarification. These studies indicate that this alarming increase in risk can be attributed, to a large extent, to the influence of genetic factors in the presence of such lifestyle risk factors as cigarette smoking, high cholesterol, high blood pressure, obesity, and diabetes.

For example, Dr. Kay-Tee Khaw and Dr. Elizabeth Barrett-Connor from the University of California at San Diego School of Medicine estimate that 68 percent of the excess deaths due to a family history of heart attacks are attributable to the interaction between cigarette smoking and genetic factors.[14] After they took other potentially modifiable risk factors into consideration, these researchers concluded that family history itself appears to have little effect on heart disease risk. They say that their study "suggests that risk of cardiovascular disease associated with an apparently inherited predisposition appears to be profoundly affected by modifiable behaviour".

The fact that heart disease runs in a family does not necessarily mean that the increased risk is genetic in origin. It can simply be a matter of passing unhealthy habits and life-styles around within a family. Following this hypothesis, researchers at the Centre for Inherited Diseases at the University of Washington in Seattle have shown that the wives of male heart disease patients are at greater risk for heart disease.[15] Why? Because men and women resembling each other in life-style are more likely to marry each other. Also, people who are close to each other are likely to mimic each other's habits, good and bad, during the many years of most marriages.

In other words, even acquired habits can be "inherited". If a parent smokes, the child is more likely to grow up to be a smoker, for example.

We don't want to leave you with the idea that we're underplaying the genetic factor. It's just that genetic traits, such as high cholesterol, high blood pressure, obesity, and diabetes, can be modified. The inheritor of such traits—in this case, John—is a person with free will who can resist smoking, exercise regularly, fight high cholesterol and high blood pressure, lose mass, and control diabetes. Neither John nor you need fall victim to a first-degree relative's fate if you're determined to take steps leading you in another direction and protecting you against genetic trends by means of a healthy lifestyle.

> **"At least I'll know when my heart condition worsens. I'll have chest pains."**

Don't count on it. You cannot rely on the absence of angina, which is chest pain or discomfort, to tell you anything conclusive once you've had a heart attack, an angioplasty, or bypass surgery. Unfortunately, you cannot assume that a lack of pain is indicative of health.

You may have heard the anecdote about the man who goes for a medical checkup, at which the doctor, after running a few tests, asks, "When did you have your heart attack?" The patient, of course, doesn't know what the physician is talking about. As far as he knows, he's never had a heart attack.

Our patient is in good company. Studies have shown that anywhere from 2,5 to 10 percent of all middle-aged men in the United States suffer from a condition called silent ischaemia, which is a temporary oxygen shortage to the heart due to obstruction or constriction of a coronary artery; there are no symptoms. Translating the percentages into numbers, there are anywhere from two million to six million American men between the ages of thirty-five and sixty who have significant heart disease and don't know it. They're "asymptomatic", to use medical terminology.

Fortunately, we have every reason to anticipate that a healthy lifestyle after an MI will also reduce silent ischaemia, since a reduced risk factor profile has also been shown to reduce true angina.

The Framingham Study, one of the most comprehensive and significant medical studies ever attempted, sheds additional light on this issue.[16] Of 708 heart attacks among 5 127 Framingham Study participants, more than 25 percent were discovered only through the detection of electrocardiogram (ECG) abnormalities during a routine physical examination. Upon careful questioning by researchers, it was found that these participants, who had discovered to their utter surprise that they had indeed suffered a heart attack sometime in the past, fell into two almost equal groups. About half had had heart attacks that were truly "silent": they couldn't pinpoint when an attack had happened because they were unaware that anything of the sort had occurred. The other half had experienced unusual, or atypical, symptoms, so a heart attack had never crossed their minds. Interestingly, the proportion of all heart attacks that were unrecognized was higher in women and in older men than in middle-aged men. However, the most unsettling finding of all was that these unrecognized heart attacks are just as likely as recognized ones to result in death, stroke, or heart failure.

The preceding misconceptions are typical of people who suffer unexpected heart attacks. There are others, too. Here are two that doctors hear over and over again from patients following rehabilitation programmes:

> "My worries about heart disease are over since my angioplasty (or bypass surgery). I'm cured."

"Cured" is not accurate terminology. These procedures are remedial measures. The same factors that drove you into the hospital in the first place can pull you back there again—or usher you into a cemetery plot. An angioplasty or bypass surgery represents another chance to alter the circumstances that caused your heart disease. That's all. The rest is up to you.

Each year thousands of bypass operations and angioplasties are performed in South Africa. Because both these procedures tend to have such a dramatic positive impact on the patient's quality of life, many are lured into believing that their heart disease is miraculously "cured". Before their hospital sojourn for these procedures, many couldn't even walk for short distances without developing angina. Not long after their discharge, many are able to exercise vigorously without any symptoms.

Unfortunately, there's a downside to these rapid recoveries: complacency. Too many patients think, "It's all behind me now. Back to the good life—smoking, rich foods, and lounging about." Today, we have convincing evidence from a number of studies that this back-to-the-old-routine approach can have a devastating effect on a patient's heart.

Take the study conducted by Dr. Lucien Campeau and his colleagues from the Montreal Heart Institute.[17] They examined eighty-two patients ten years after bypass surgery and found only 37.5 percent of the blood vessels used for bypass to be free from atherosclerotic disease. Of the coronary arteries that had not been bypassed, 47 percent had narrowed further from additional plaque buildup in the intervening ten years. And of those arteries which had been normal and clear at the time of surgery, they found that 47 percent now had obstructions. Those who had not developed further obstructions had lower cholesterol levels than those who developed obstructions. The researchers' conclusion: there is a close correlation between study participants' circulating blood cholesterol levels and their risk of developing atherosclerotic obstructions in both their bypass vessels and their natural coronary arteries.

More recent work at the same research institution further demonstrates that bypass patients who later suffer heart attacks have no greater chance of survival than any other heart attack victims.[18] The findings of this study, published in the October 1988 issue of the *Journal of the American College of Cardiology*, were so disconcerting that the journal also ran an editorial in the same issue. It carried the provocative title "Is There Any Long-Term Benefit from Coronary Artery Bypass Surgery?"[19]

In this editorial, Dr. Kanu Chatterjee from the cardiology division of the University of California at San Francisco concluded that there is considerable benefit provided bypass patients receive treatment with aspirin and dipyridamole—both drugs which prevent blood-clot formation—and control their blood cholesterol levels.

Follow-up studies on angioplasty recipients have a similar message. Not long after angioplasty, the coronary artery that was unblocked via the procedure often narrows again.[20]

All of this brings us full circle to our original point: if you've undergone an angioplasty or bypass surgery, don't rest assured. Do everything in your power to prevent your condition from deteriorating, by following the guidelines in this book.

> "I've smoked cigarettes all my adult life. They've already helped to cause my heart condition. So it's not going to do any good to stop smoking now."

This is what the confirmed smoker would like to believe. But it just isn't so. Despite its bad press, smoking is still an addiction plaguing South Africa, especially the white and "coloured" populations. According to a 1984 study by the Medical Research Council, over 100 000 potential years of life were lost in 1984 in this country in people of 35 to 65 years of age, through smoking. Smoking, after all, isn't just a risk factor for lung cancer. Together with an elevated blood cholesterol level and high blood pressure, it is widely regarded as one of the three most important risk factors for heart disease.

If you're a smoker and you really care about living to a good age, there's good news, thanks to recent study findings. While these studies show that the adverse effects of cigarette smoking are cumulative, they also show that stopping will have a positive impact on your health.

A Yale University School of Medicine study monitored data on 2 674 elderly smokers, aged sixty-five to seventy-four.[21] The researchers' goal was to determine if veteran smokers could still benefit from giving up in their later years. Their conclusions are enough to make smokers of any age stop immediately. They assert that people who continue to smoke after age sixty-five have a risk of death from heart disease that is 75 percent higher than that for their contemporaries who've had the good sense to stop. The best news of all: after only a few years of not smoking, these elderly ex-smokers' risk of death from heart disease is about the same as that of people who have never smoked.

A more recent study, dubbed the Coronary Artery Surgery Study, reported on the effects of cigarette smoking and its cessation in 1 893 men and women with known heart disease.[22] During the six-year study period, death rates were 70 percent higher among the people who smoked than among the 807 participants who stopped the year before enrolling in the study and abstained throughout. The beneficial effects of abstinence were the same for study participants of all ages, young and old; these effects were also felt by those who had previously undergone bypass surgery.

You may think that smoking is something you cannot live without. In fact, such studies should prove to you that it's something you cannot live with, no matter what your current age or health status. As these studies show, it's never too late for anyone to stop smoking and derive health benefits from that deliberate act of omission.

CHAPTER 3

THE HEART ATTACK:
What It Is, How It Happens

JOHN'S heart attack was caused by a disease known in the medical world as coronary heart disease, or "CHD".

It goes without saying that AIDS and such modern-day plagues as cancer are serious threats. But, at least in industrialized countries, none is more serious—in terms of sheer numbers or costs—than CHD. In the United States, for example, CHD and other circulatory disorders are currently responsible for more deaths annually than AIDS, cancer, accidents, lung diseases, and influenza combined. Indeed, it's America's number-one killer. It claims one life every thirty-two seconds. And it places a $50 billion annual burden on that country's economy.

The facts are startling. There are an estimated six million Americans with symptoms of CHD. About half of these people are at least partially disabled by the disease. Still, in a way, they're the lucky ones. There are countless millions of others who also have heart disease but don't know it—because they have no symptoms. Their first symptom could be sudden death.

Here in South Africa, one in four women and one in three men will have CHD by the time they are sixty years old. A total of 48 000 South Africans have heart attacks every year. Of these, 12 000 die and 36 000 survive. The latter require rehabilitation, but for various socioeconomic reasons, many of them are not receiving it.

The most tragic part about these statistics is the ages of the sufferers. Many CHD patients are in their most productive, middle-aged years. The ongoing Framingham Study, initiated in Framingham, Massachusetts, in 1949, underscores the fact that some 5 percent of all heart attacks occur in people under the age of forty, and a whopping 45 percent occur in those younger than sixty-five.

It's probably been a while since you learnt the basics of human anatomy or physiology at school. Maybe you've never heard of epidemiology. The discussion that follows is short and to the point. Be sure to read it carefully, for the more you know about your circulatory system and heart disease, the better able you'll be to understand the rationale for the protocols and Heart Points System that we outline later in the book.

THE HEART—YOUR BODY'S MOTORIZED PUMP

You've heard it hundreds of times, no doubt. Your heart is a kind of pump, a muscular one, which has a mass of 250 g to 500 g and is a little larger than your fist. It's surrounded by a tough, protective membrane known as the *pericardium*. It's situated behind your breastbone, a little to the left of mid-chest. As you continue reading, you might want to refer to the heart diagram, Figure 3-1.

The Chambers of Your Heart. Your heart, which is a hollow organ, is divided into left and right sides by a muscular wall called the *septum*. Each side has an upper chamber, known as an *atrium*, and a lower one, called a *ventricle*.

In reality, your heart is not one pump, but four separate pumps. There are the pumps of the two upper atria, the filling pumps that move the blood within the heart, and the two lower ventricular pumps, the powerful pumps that make the blood surge forward out of your heart and into your body.

Blood—the Lifeline to Your Body's Cells. Blood, of course, is the red, sticky fluid that transports oxygen and other substances through your body. You cannot live unless your bloodstream carries a constant supply of oxygen and other nutrients to your cells, which use them as food and energy sources. When oxygenated blood reaches your cells, they take what they need and give up carbon dioxide waste in return. You might think of carbon dioxide as the end product remaining after the energy-producing cycle in your cells has been completed.

Your Blood's Transport Network. Blood travels throughout your body via blood vessels, which are hollow tubes—very elastic and very muscular. These vessels have three layers. The inside layer has a

THE HEART ATTACK   45

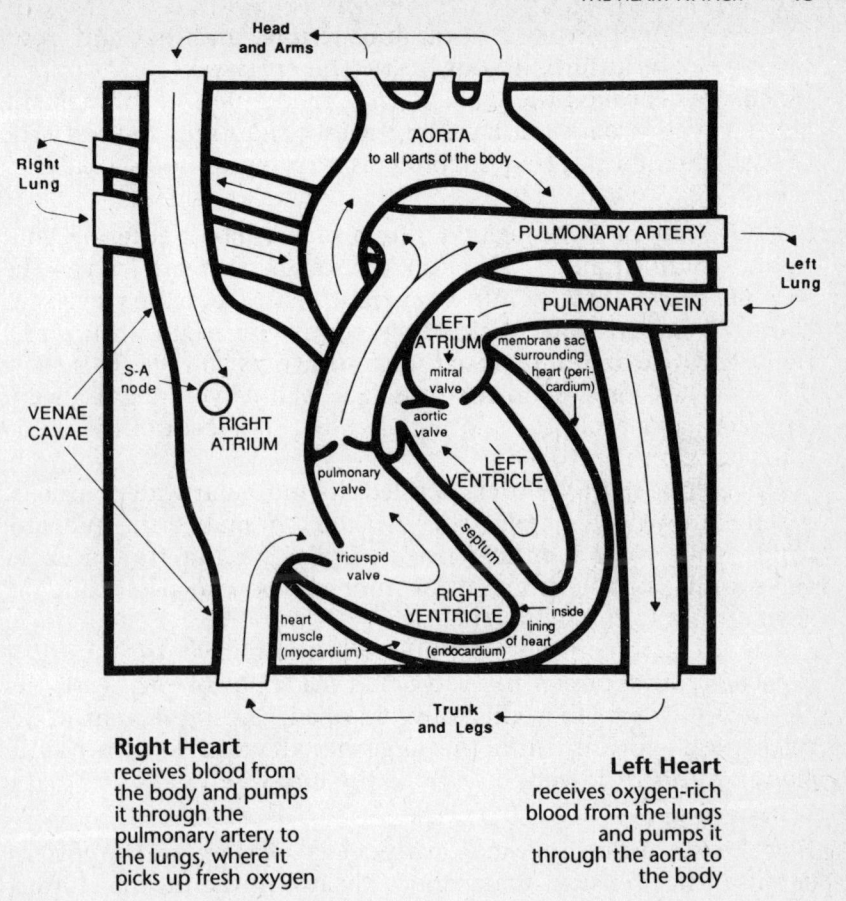

Right Heart
receives blood from
the body and pumps
it through the
pulmonary artery to
the lungs, where it
picks up fresh oxygen

Left Heart
receives oxygen-rich
blood from the lungs
and pumps it
through the aorta to
the body

Figure 3-1. The functioning of the heart. (Reproduced with permission. ©
Illustration and Symbols Kit, 1983. Copyright American Heart Association.)

smooth surface which allows blood to flow freely. The middle layer is muscular, contracting to help regulate the flow. And the outer layer anchors the vessels to the surrounding body parts.

Blood vessels are divided into *arteries* and *veins*.

In general, arteries carry bright red, oxygenated blood away from the left side of your heart. There's one exception—the *pulmonary artery*, which carries unoxygenated blood to the lungs.

Veins carry the dark red, carbon dioxide-laden blood from your body back to the right side of your heart. The exceptions are the pulmonary veins, which shunt oxygenated blood from your lungs back to your heart.

Blood Enters Your Heart. Blood, depleted of its life-giving oxygen and burdened with the toxic waste gas, carbon dioxide, returns to your heart from your head, arms, trunk, and legs and flows into the right atrium of your heart. The entryways are two large blood vessels called the *venae cavae*. Blood entering through the venae cavae is dark red in colour rather than crimson red. The dark shade indicates that the blood is carrying carbon dioxide.

Blood Is Pumped to Your Lungs. Much of the blood entering your right atrium immediately flows through a heart valve—the *tricuspid valve*—directly into your right ventricle, which swells to about 70 percent full. At this stage, both your right atrium and right ventricle are in a relaxed state known as *diastole*. This stage does not last long. Soon the muscular wall of your right atrium contracts, squeezing the additional 20 to 30 percent of the blood into your right ventricle.

Once your right ventricle is filled, its muscular wall contracts, a state known as *systole*. The contraction makes the pressure inside your right ventricle rise abruptly, forcing the tricuspid valve shut. For the moment, no more blood can pass from the right atrium to the right ventricle.

The pressure continues to build in the right ventricle until it eventually forces open the valve that leads out of the heart, the *pulmonary valve*. Once this valve is open, the right ventricular blood flows forward into the large blood vessel known as the *pulmonary artery*. It leads directly to the lungs.

Your Heart's Valve System. Clearly, heart valves are important because they ensure that blood always flows in the correct direction. They open when blood is pumped against them and close immediately afterward to prevent blood from flowing back.

Your heart has four such valves. We've just introduced you to the first two. The other two are situated in the left atrium and left ventricle and function in very much the same way as those we've described. They're called the *mitral valve* (between your left atrium and left ventricle) and the *aortic valve* (between your left ventricle and the large artery, the aorta, that carries blood away from the left side of your heart. When your doctor puts a stethoscope on your chest, he or she is listening to these valves. Their rhythmic sound can help tell your doctor if your heart is functioning properly.

The Lungs, Your Oxygen Source. We return now to the blood that flowed out of your right ventricle on its way to your lungs. Depleted of its oxygen stores, this darkish-looking blood is being pumped to your lungs for more oxygen. In the "filling station" of your lungs, a quick exchange takes place: the blood unloads its carbon dioxide waste, which you'll exhale from your body, and it receives a fresh supply of oxygen, turning a bright red in colour as a result.

From here the blood returns to the *left* side of your heart. The "tunnels" back to your heart are your pulmonary veins, and they lead directly from your lungs to your left atrium.

The Left Side of Your Heart. The oxygen-rich blood from your lungs reaches the left side of your heart at about the same time as that oxygen-poor blood moves into the right side. Thus, the contractions in both sides of your heart happen almost simultaneously.

In the same way that oxygen-poor blood moved from your right atrium into your right ventricle and onward, this newly supplied oxygen-rich blood surges into your left atrium and left ventricle, with the mitral valve regulating the flow in between.

The left side of your heart plays such a key role for this reason: the crimson blood exiting the left ventricle through the aortic valve will travel through your arteries to dispense oxygen to all parts of your body. Because the blood leaving your left ventricle makes the difference between life and death for your body's cells, your left ventricle is the most muscular of your heart's four chambers. It has to be strong since the blood leaving it will travel a long way before it finally returns, about ten to fifteen seconds later, devoid of oxygen, to the right side of your heart.

Clearly, your left ventricle holds the key to your body's peak functioning. This is why damage to that section of your heart causes the most serious problems after a heart attack.

Your Blood Pressure. As your blood is pumped out of your left ventricle and through your arteries, naturally it pushes against the arterial walls. This force that the blood exerts against the walls is called *blood pressure*.

Each time your ventricles contract—the systole part of your heart rhythm—a surge of blood enters your arteries, making your blood pressure rise. The level to which it rises is referred to as your *systolic blood pressure*. In contrast, each time your heart relaxes between beats, your blood pressure falls. Thus, your *diastolic blood pressure* reflects the lowest amount of pressure in your arteries at any given time.

Your Heart's "Electrical System". You're probably wondering how the chambers of your heart know when to contract and when to relax. The answer is by a kind of electricity. Your heart is endowed with a special electrical conduction system which generates rhythmical impulses. These impulses travel rapidly through your heart muscle and cause the chambers of your heart to beat rhythmically in the correct sequence.

The source of the impulses is the *sinoatrial node* (or "S-A node"), located near the top of your right atrium. The S-A node is your heart's natural pacemaker. It determines just how fast it beats. When the S-A node and the rest of your heart's conduction system are functioning normally, your atria contract about one-sixth of a second before your ventricles, which permits the extra filling of the ventricles before they push blood out of your heart.

These electrical impulses are crucial. Unfortunately, your conduction system is very susceptible to damage by CHD, and the consequence can be a bizarre heart rhythm, even to the extent of causing death. The electrical activity of your heart can be measured using a test called an *electrocardiogram,* or "ECG".

The cycle repeats continuously. It is estimated that about ten to fifteen seconds are needed for your blood to circulate, that is, make one complete trip through the heart–blood vessel network of your body. This network is termed your *cardiovascular system.*

When you're not exerting yourself unduly, your heart pumps blood, or beats, about 50 to 100 times a minute, circulating about 5 litres of blood. When you are exerting yourself or when you're under great stress, your body requires more oxygen and more nutrients than normal and your heart beats faster. During intense exercise, the kind performed by young, well-trained athletes, the heart may pump out as much as 30 to 35 litres of blood each minute in order to meet the energy requirements of the working muscles.

YOUR CORONARY ARTERIES

We've mentioned that your cell "factories", located alongside your bloodstream, keep running—that is, provided oxygen and other nutrient raw materials keep arriving. Your heart is made up of cells, too, and they're no different from their counterparts in other parts of your body. They also need oxygenated blood to survive.

You might assume that your heart, to stay energized, simply siphons off the oxygen it needs from the blood flowing through the left side of your heart. Not quite. Your heart muscle, or *myocardium,* is not capable of taking up oxygen directly from the blood inside its chambers. Instead, it has its own blood vessels, the *coronary arteries,* that branch off from the aorta shortly after it leaves your left ventricle.

There are two major coronary arteries. The *left coronary artery,* as you'd expect, supplies oxygenated blood to the left side of your heart, mostly the left ventricle. And the *right coronary artery* supplies both the right ventricle and part of the back of the left ventricle. Both coronary arteries lie on the surface of the heart and subdivide into a myriad of branches which penetrate into the myocardium.

You may have heard people say there are three, rather than two, major coronary arteries. This is because the left coronary artery, after running along the surface of the heart for only a short distance, divides in two. The initial portion of the left artery before this fork is called the *left main coronary artery.* Its two branches are referred to as the *left anterior descending coronary artery* (LAD) and the *circumflex coronary artery* (see Figure 3-2).

Myocardial Oxygenation. The coronary arteries provide your myocardium with a constant supply of freshly oxygenated blood, which ensures that your heart has enough energy to continue its vigorous pumping action.

At its resting level of beating, your heart muscle removes 65 to 70 percent of the maximum amount of oxygen that it is capable of extracting from the passing blood. But as your heart works harder, during vigorous exercise, for example, it needs more oxygen.

How much?

The precise amount of oxygen required by your myocardium depends on the product of your heart rate (the number of beats per minute) and your systolic blood pressure—the so-called *rate-pressure* product. (We use the word "product" in the mathematical sense of multiplying one amount by the other.)

Your Heart's Oxygen Needs Under Pressure. Under severe conditions—such as when John Venter, our heart attack sufferer in Chapter 1, sprinted to his car in the rain lugging heavy

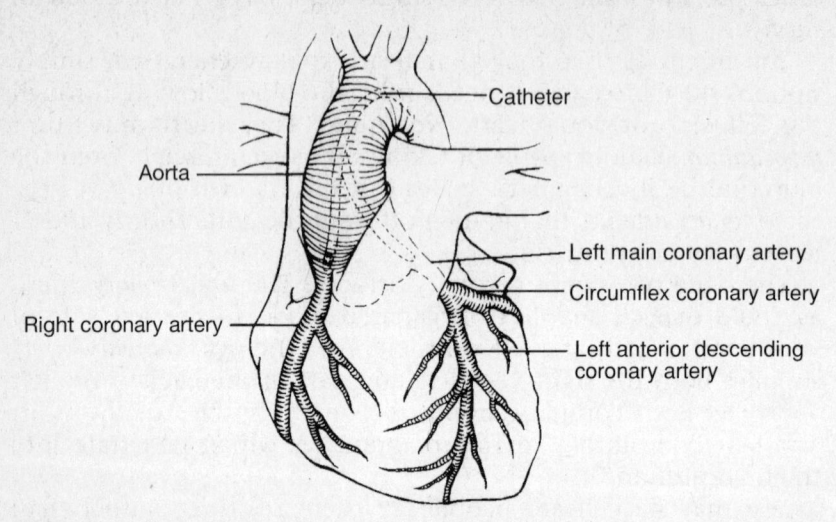

Figure 3-2. The major coronary arteries as visualized during coronary angiography. Both the right coronary artery and the left main coronary artery originate from the aorta. The left main coronary artery divides into the left anterior descending coronary artery (or LAD) and the circumflex coronary artery. (Reproduced with permission. © Illustration and Symbols Kit, 1983. Copyright American Heart Association.)

grocery bags—the rate-pressure product may increase as much as six- to eightfold. However, there's a limit to how much more oxygen the heart can extract from the blood flowing through the coronary arteries. At best, it can extract only another 20 to 30 percent more oxygen since, in the normal course of activity, it extracts almost 70 percent. Thus, little additional oxygen can be taken up by the myocardium unless the blood flow increases.

In healthy people, the blood flow does increase in proportion to their myocardial oxygen requirements. However, some people have obstructions in their coronary arteries—we'll describe these blockages in a moment—and these obstructions make it difficult (or impossible) for the blood flow to increase as much as is necessary to meet the increased oxygen requirements. When this happens, the oxygen supply available to the myocardium is inadequate; in other words, the heart's oxygen needs simply exceed the ability of the coronary arteries to fill them.

CHD—WHAT IT IS, WHAT CAUSES IT

CHD is progressive, and it is usually slow, extending over many years. Eventually, the coronary arteries fail to supply the heart muscle with adequate amounts of blood and, hence, oxygen.

The most common reason for this failure is the thickening of the arterial walls. This build-up in the walls can contain cholesterol and other fatty substances. Over time, these thickenings cause a narrowing of the *lumen* of the coronary arteries, the central channel through which your blood flows. The buildup is known as *atherosclerosis.* As we already mentioned, it's the condition that caused John Venter's heart attack.

This explanation sounds straightforward enough, but in actuality the buildup process is extremely complex, involving many factors. Exactly how it takes place is currently the focus of much research. Although full clarification may be years away, there are some interesting new hypotheses:

Fatty-Streak Formation. Researchers now believe that atherosclerosis begins very early in life. On the basis of existing evidence, Dr. Russell Ross of the Department of Pathology at the University of Washington in Seattle suggests that the process is initiated by injury to the inside lining (or *endothelium*) of the coronary arteries.[1] The damage enables blood cells called *monocytes* to penetrate this inner lining and burrow into the inner layer of the coronary artery walls. These monocytes release chemicals which not only attract more monocytes to the damage site, but also cause some of the muscle cells of the middle layer of the coronary artery to proliferate and move into the wall's inner layer. Both the monocytes and muscle cells start to fill up with cholesterol and other fats. The result: fatty streaks.

It may alarm you to learn that fatty streaks first begin appearing in the coronary arteries of many people sometime around the ages of ten to fifteen. Often there's a considerable increase between the ages of fifteen and twenty. At certain sites in the coronary arteries these fatty streaks may simply sit harmlessly for years. Over time, they may even regress. But in other places in the coronary arteries, in some people, these streaks may progress to form atherosclerotic plaques.

Atherosclerotic Plaque Buildup. In the presence of certain CHD risk factors, which we'll cover fully in Part 4, the injury to the endothelium may persist or even grow worse. More monocytes and muscle cells may accumulate in the inner layer of the coronary artery walls. In addition, another type of blood cell, called a *platelet,* may affix itself to the injured endothelium and worsen an already deteriorating situation. The result is something to be feared: the formation of atherosclerotic plaque, a condition referred to in common parlance as "hardening of the arteries". Atherosclerotic plaque is a hard mass containing monocytes, muscle cells, cholesterol and other fats, fibrous tissue, calcium, and certain other elements carried in the blood. Plaques are covered by a tough outer lining of cells and are yellowish in colour.

Dr. Russell Ross also suggests that atherosclerotic plaques may develop even when the damage to the endothelium isn't severe enough to permit the entry of monocytes into the inner layer of the coronary artery. He postulates that in this instance it's the injured endothelium itself which releases the chemicals that gradually result in atherosclerotic plaque buildup. Again, this tends to occur only when CHD risk factors—such as smoking, high blood cholesterol, obesity, high blood pressure, prolonged stress, etc.—are present.

The buildup of plaque has two deleterious effects: the coronary artery wall becomes so rigid that it can no longer effectively regulate blood flow, and the artery's lumen (in essence, the diameter of the inside part of the artery) is narrowed, thereby reducing the ability of this artery to supply your heart muscle with adequate blood and oxygen.

Autopsy Evidence. The results of international autopsy studies, including those performed on American soldiers killed in the Korean and Vietnam wars, prove that atherosclerotic plaque is present in the coronary arteries of many people as early as their late teens and early twenties. Of course, if these soldiers had lived and their life-styles had included CHD risk factors, this plaque would have continued to spread, perhaps even at a rate that would have meant additional coverage of approximately 2 percent or more of the inside surfaces of their arterial walls each year—a rate that is relatively common among CHD victims.

THE ROLE OF CHOLESTEROL

Cholesterol, as we've said, is a fatlike substance. What you may not know is that it plays an essential role in the production of cell membranes and sex hormones as well as aiding in the digestion of certain foods. Given its bad press of late, you may be surprised to learn that cholesterol is synthetized by all the cells in the body. In fact, the cells of your body would not be able to function without it. On the other hand, too much cholesterol is not a good thing because it predisposes you to CHD.

Of the total amount of cholesterol in the body, only about 7 percent or so circulates in the blood of a healthy person. In people with a high blood cholesterol level, the percentage of cholesterol in the blood can increase markedly. But this is the potentially dangerous cholesterol because it can accumulate in atherosclerotic plaques.

Where does the cholesterol in your bloodstream come from? Most of it is manufactured by your liver. The rest comes from the foods you eat that contain saturated fats and cholesterol. Thus, you could say the cholesterol level in your blood is determined partly by inheritance and partly by the fat and cholesterol content of your diet. Other factors, such as exercise, smoking, and obesity, play a role, too.

Lipoproteins: Transporters of Cholesterol. Cholesterol is not water soluble, so it needs an agent to transport it through the blood. That agent is protein. The circulating cholesterol-protein packages in your blood are called *lipoproteins*. There are four major classes of lipoproteins, ranked according to their density. They are, in order of increasing density: (1) the *chylomicrons;* (2) *very-low-density lipoproteins,* most commonly referred to as "VLDLs"; (3) *low-density lipoproteins,* or "LDLs"; and (4) *high-density lipoproteins,* or "HDLs".

There is now convincing evidence that each of these four major lipoproteins serves a specific function in cholesterol metabolism. While there's a lot we still don't know about them, it's clear that some are benign and some aren't.

The Chylomicrons. Chylomicrons, for instance, are synthesized in your intestine; their purpose is to transport dietary cholesterol and fats called *triglycerides* into the bloodstream. An enzyme in your blood called *lipoprotein lipase* breaks down your triglycerides. Either the breakdown products are used as fuel immediately by your cells or your cells store them for future use. With the triglycerides broken down, the remains of the chylomicrons are then removed from the bloodstream by your liver.

Chylomicrons aren't much of a threat because they are usually found in the blood in significant amounts only after meals. Because they're large, they don't fit through the endothelial lining of your coronary arteries, and thus they do not contribute to atherosclerotic plaque.

The VLDLs and LDLs. VLDLs are produced in your liver, where they're loaded with cholesterol and triglycerides. Like chylomicron triglycerides, VLDL triglycerides are broken down by lipoprotein lipase and then utilized by the various cells throughout your body.

While elevated VLDL and triglyceride levels in the bloodstream are associated with a higher risk for CHD, no one knows yet for sure whether VLDLs and triglycerides directly cause plaque buildup. What is known is that VLDLs retain their cholesterol even after they give up their triglycerides to the cells. The result is the formation of cholesterol-rich lipoproteins—the LDLs. These LDLs transport over 70 percent of your total blood cholesterol.

Some of the LDLs in your blood are removed by special receptors on the surfaces of cells. Dr. Michael S. Brown and Dr. Joseph L. Goldstein were awarded a Nobel prize for discovering these LDL cell receptors. Stated in simple "American" terms, they found that the receptors "reach out and grab cholesterol like a first baseman catching a ball thrown by a shortstop".[2] Your cell factories use the LDL cholesterol they've taken up from your bloodstream to produce, among other things, cell membranes.

You may suspect that the LDL cholesterol left in the bloodstream is the excess that eventually builds up in your coronary arteries. You're partly right. However, before it gets to that point, your liver's receptors do their best to seize the remaining cholesterol. The liver cells then convert the cholesterol into bile acids, which you eventually excrete.

You can probably guess what often happens. The liver, as hard as it tries, can't manage to get all the excess cholesterol out of your bloodstream. What's left is indicated by a rise in your blood's LDL level. Since LDLs are small particles, they can readily penetrate the walls of your coronary arteries and aid the process of plaque buildup. That's why LDLs are referred to as "bad" cholesterol.

The HDLs. In contrast, HDLs, which are produced primarily in your liver and intestine, are known as "good" cholesterol. HDL even made the cover of *Time* magazine on December 12, 1988, with the headline " 'Good' Cholesterol—Encouraging News for Your Heart".

There are several reasons for the celebration. First, HDLs are responsible for transporting cholesterol from the various cells in your body to your liver, where it's put to use and eventually disposed of. The other good thing that HDLs allegedly do—although nobody has proved it conclusively yet—is act as a kind of self-activated scouring pad, removing cholesterol from the walls of your coronary arteries.

Your Cholesterol Ratio. What all this means is that it's not just a matter of how much total cholesterol you have circulating in your blood; what's also important is the proportion of different types being transported. High LDL levels predispose you to CHD, whereas high HDL levels lessen your risk.

The long and short of it is this: the lower your LDL level and the higher your HDL level, the better off you are, despite what might appear to be an overly high total cholesterol level.

WHEN CHD BECOMES A HAZARD

CHD progresses over the years and eventually turns into a serious health hazard.

Myocardial Ischaemia. This disease usually advances for decades before symptoms or other problems appear. Typically, a coronary artery is at least two-thirds blocked, or "occluded", by atherosclerotic plaque before you become aware that anything is wrong. Symptoms may appear abruptly, or they may not appear at all—in which case CHD remains "silent".

Your body has the marvellous ability to compensate for defects and blockages in its vessels, such as one in a coronary artery. Your heart compensates by building a network of reserve blood vessels known as *coronary collaterals*, which are small vessels that branch off from your other arteries near the obstructed area for the sole purpose of compensation.

Even with a two-thirds occlusion, most people do not have any symptoms while they're at rest. (The exceptions are people who suffer from a condition called *coronary spasm*, which we'll discuss in a minute.) After all, at rest, your heart muscle doesn't need much oxygen because it's not working very hard. It's not being challenged to deliver extra blood to the body.

But consider what happens when you exert yourself—by running to make a train, for example. Despite these collaterals, parts of your heart may suddenly find they have an inadequate supply of blood. This temporary lack of oxygen to your heart is a condition known as *myocardial ischaemia*. "Ischaemia" means a local, often temporary, deficiency in the oxygen supply to some part of your body. As a general rule, myocardial ischaemia does not result in actual heart muscle damage, *provided* it lasts for only a short period of time (less than about twenty minutes). However, there can be times when myocardial ischaemia of even a very short duration triggers a heart rhythm disturbance called *ventricular fibrillation*. When this happens, the sufferer feels dizzy and passes out within a matter of seconds. If ventricular fibrillation isn't corrected within minutes of its onset, for example by the application of an external electrical current to the heart, it will kill you.

Angina Pectoris. In some people, myocardial ischaemia is accompanied by symptoms—temporary discomfort in the chest or adjacent areas. This is called *angina pectoris,* or simply angina.

The term comes to us from Dr. William Heberden, who used it in a report published in 1772.[3] He chose "angina", derived from the Latin root *angere,* meaning "to strangle", because he wanted to convey a sense of strangling. It's apt, for angina sufferers often describe their discomfort as "heaviness", "tightness", "pressure", "squeezing", "vicelike", "constricting", "suffocating", or "crushing". The site of the discomfort is usually across the centre of the chest, in the region of the breastbone, but sometimes it radiates to other nearby parts of the body—the neck, jaw, shoulders, or arms. In fact, in some people, the discomfort is felt only in these areas and not in the chest at all.

What else is typical?

Actually, angina symptoms vary greatly. But here are a few things that we can say definitively about angina. Angina lasts more than five seconds but usually less than twenty minutes. It's not brought on or worsened by taking a deep breath. Changes of posture won't alleviate it. It's a generalized pain; that is, it's not confined to a small area. And sufferers seldom use the words "tenderness of the chest wall" to describe it. The typical attack comes on with exercise or emotional stress. It builds up gradually in intensity over a couple of minutes, and then slowly subsides when the activity that precipitated it is stopped. In other words, it stops when the heart muscle once again gets the amount of oxygen it requires.

Should you suffer an angina attack while you're resting, a spasm of a coronary artery is often the culprit. This atypical form of angina is sometimes called *Prinzmetal's angina,* because it was Dr. Myron Prinzmetal who, in a 1959 article in the *American Journal of Medicine*, offered the first detailed account of it.[4] Other terms are "rest angina" or "variant angina". It occurs when the muscular wall of a coronary artery goes into spasm and clamps off the artery temporarily.

Silent ischaemia. In other people, myocardial ischaemia may produce symptoms, but not the kind you associate with your heart. You may simply feel breathless all of a sudden, or faint, fatigued, or nauseated. Or you might just start burping a lot. These symptoms could be anginal equivalents. They should raise suspicion when they occur during a stressful event or physical exertion.

As mentioned in Chapter 2, many ischaemia sufferers feel nothing untoward at all. Their CHD is "silent". It's likely that John Venter suffered from silent ischaemia for some time before the onset of his shortness of breath (an anginal equivalent) and chest discomfort (angina) on the squash court.

THE WORST FINALLY HAPPENS: THE HEART ATTACK

The chest discomfort you experience during a heart attack can be very similar to the symptoms of angina, except that the feeling lasts longer and is often more intense. During a heart attack, the discomfort often turns into severe pain that may be accompanied by shortness of breath, sweating, nausea, dizziness, and pallor. However, just as ischaemia may be silent, so, too, can heart attacks, as we've already mentioned.

Unstable Angina. Some people get ample warning of a heart attack. These are usually people with angina who, if they're observant, start to notice it's worsening. They're getting attacks more often. The attacks are more severe. They last for longer periods and it takes less exertion to precipitate one. Or angina attacks may even start occurring while they're at rest.

In recent years, the term *unstable angina*—coined in 1971 by Dr. Noble O. Fowler from the University of Cincinnati College of Medicine—has been employed by physicians to describe this worsening condition, which may herald a heart attack.[5] Unstable angina can be caused by a variety of factors, occurring alone or in combination. Such factors include the buildup of more atherosclerotic plaque or the rupture of existing plaque; coronary spasm; and thrombus (blood-clot) formation. Should you find your angina becoming unstable, regard it as a medical emergency that warrants an immediate consultation with your doctor.

Myocardial Infarction—the Heart Attack. Unlike angina, which does not cause permanent damage to the heart, a heart attack always does. You could think of a heart attack as ischaemia taken to extremes. Exactly when ischaemia crosses the line and causes a heart attack is hard to say. But we can say this: generally, if ischaemia persists for longer than about thirty minutes, the oxygen-starved portion of your heart muscle becomes injured and finally permanently damaged.

This damage to the myocardium is referred to as a heart attack, or *myocardial infarction*—"infarction" meaning, very simply, death of heart muscle cells. The resulting damage is irreversible, and healing takes place through the process of scar tissue formation.

Scar formation is evident by the third week after a heart attack. Depending on the extent of the damage, healing is usually completed within four to eight weeks after the event. The scar—which cardiologists can detect using sophisticated nuclear medicine tests—will be there always. It will never be replaced with new heart muscle cells.

"*What Caused My Heart Attack?*" It is likely to have been one of three things.

In over 90 percent of heart attacks, a blood clot superimposed on an underlying atherosclerotic plaque in the coronary artery is the cause. Plaque buildup disrupts the normal flow of blood because the arterial wall is no longer smooth the way it should be. As the flow of blood becomes increasingly turbulent, blood platelets stick together at the site of the plaque obstruction. This results in the formation of the blood clot, a gelatinous clump of blood called a *thrombus,* from which we get the other term for a heart attack: *coronary thrombosis.* The clot may remain where it is, attached to the plaque. Or part of it may break off and lodge somewhere else in the coronary artery. Either way, it causes a complete occlusion. Drugs, such as the t-PA that was administered to John Venter, are used to try to dissolve these blood clots. If they're given early enough after the onset of ischaemia, they can limit the amount of damage to the heart muscle.

Stoic people who already have CHD yet continue to deny its symptoms are the second class of candidates for heart attacks. These are people who stubbornly refuse to admit that they feel chest discomfort or pain or shortness of breath. Unlike John Venter, who got ischaemic symptoms during his squash game and stopped to rest, these people would continue playing—or jogging, or running, or whatever physical exertion it is they're engaging in. The whole time, they'd be starving their heart muscle of oxygen. And if they allowed their ischaemia to continue for longer than thirty minutes or so, they would suffer a heart attack, despite the fact that the coronary artery might not be completely occluded.

Coronary spasm, discussed earlier, is a third cause. When it cuts off the blood supply to the heart muscle completely and for more than about thirty minutes, it triggers a heart attack. Plaque plays a role here, too, because coronary spasm typically occurs at the site of a buildup of plaque. Coronary spasm also increases a person's predisposition to thrombus formation.

Heart Attack Timetable. While heart attacks can occur at any time of the day or night, studies have shown that the hours between 6 a.m. and 12 noon are the most probable.

Why?

No one really knows. However, here's a hypothesis: these are the hours when most people experience an increase in their body's—and their heart muscle's—energy needs. Also, there's an increase in the stickiness of blood platelets, a decrease in the blood's ability to dissolve clots, and an increase in susceptibility to coronary spasm.

It might not be a coincidence that John Venter suffered his heart attack in the morning.

Damage Defines Heart Attack Severity. As we discussed in Chapter 2, heart attacks vary both in kind and in degree. There are severe heart attacks and minor ones. The difference is defined by how much heart muscle is lost.

Three major factors determine the precise degree of permanent heart damage: (1) the site of the blockage in the coronary artery; (2) the amount of blood that is still reaching the affected heart muscle via the coronary collaterals; and (3) the duration of the ischaemic attack.

Here's the interesting thing about heart attacks: they don't do their damage all at once. Studies conducted on dogs whose coronary arteries were tied off and subsequently untied demonstrate that once an artery is completely blocked off, it takes about six hours for all of the heart muscle cells that receive this blood supply to die.

This is why it is of the utmost importance to get medical help immediately if you think you're having a heart attack. The sooner the ischaemic condition is stopped, the more likely it is that you will survive and the more likely it is there will be less heart muscle damage. Unfortunately, all too many heart attack victims deny what their body is screaming at them. The idea of a heart attack admittedly is frightening, calling up visions of imminent death. But look at it this way: if you don't accept what may be happening, the consequences could be *very* imminent. You could die—perhaps even within the hour.

THE MOST PERPLEXING QUESTION

To be quite honest, at the present time we still don't really know why atherosclerotic plaque builds up within coronary arteries. We do know this, though: there were a number of large heart disease studies initiated both in the United States and elsewhere as early as the late 1940s and on into the 1950s. All show quite convincingly that CHD does not simply occur randomly in a given population. On the contrary, the risk of developing CHD is clearly related to the presence or absence of certain CHD risk factors (which will be discussed in Part 4).

Some experts consider this risk-factor concept, which was first put forward by the Framingham Study's research team, to be the greatest breakthrough in medicine since the development of the germ theory back in the nineteenth century. In fact, we now view these risk factors as the "germs" for CHD.

PART TWO

RECOVERING FROM A HEART ATTACK OR SURGERY

CHAPTER 4

"WHY DO I FEEL THIS WAY? WHAT DOES IT MEAN?"

To many patients, it comes as a great surprise that recovery from their heart attack involves more than physical healing. In fact, getting their emotions back on an even keel may be one of their biggest challenges.

If they didn't know it beforehand, they soon learn that cardiac recuperation is a period when many feelings—sometimes contradictory, often unpleasant—well up and boil over. The worst of it is that this happens despite many patients' best intentions to keep their negative thoughts under wraps and their temper in check.

Here we'll outline the emotional landscape of cardiac recuperation. There's plenty to discuss, for the scenario we sketched in the above paragraph is not unusual. If it's happening to you, you might as well accept it and learn to live with it for a while, because it's normal. Indeed, it's highly unlikely that the three months following your MI will be placid. Rather, it may well be a time of heightened feelings as well as of vacillating, uncontrollable moods. You could find yourself ministering to festering psychic wounds long after your physical symptoms have disappeared.[1]

HOSPITAL DISQUIET

Like almost everything else about his case, John Venter's emotional reaction to his heart attack was fairly typical. He experienced initial panic and anxiety in the hospital that gradually evolved into a protracted depression that hung on for some two months after he returned home.

You've already glimpsed John's distress in the intensive care unit (ICU). To say his outlook was negative would be an understatement. John's anxiety was based on fear—fear of death, unease about his family's welfare, concern about changes in his ability to work and earn a livelihood. He also kept seeing mental pictures of his damaged heart. His knowledge of physiology was sketchy, to say the least, so the image that kept flashing through his mind was far from accurate. In fact, it was ludicrous: it was that of a large hunk of Swiss cheese, shaped like a heart, barely beating.

Of course, John's state of mind wasn't helped by his stubborn refusal to take the tranquillizers offered to him to ease his psychological distress and make him sleep off his troubles while in the ICU. He feared other prescribed drugs, too, thinking that he might become addicted (a fear that was completely unfounded).

Without the tranquillizers, John wore his troubling thoughts on his sleeve for all to see. His apprehension and restlessness were apparent. He was hyper-alert, startled by the least unexpected noise, and was sweaty and tremulous. And in fact it wasn't John's heart condition that was causing these outward physical responses. It was his inner turmoil and mental unease.

John's apprehension and sense of foreboding—and the physical manifestations that accompanied these feelings—continued for about three days. Fortunately, after he moved from the ICU into a hospital room, the pleasanter, more normal surroundings gradually calmed his jitters. The reassurances of his family, friends, and hospital care-givers also helped.

John then replaced nervousness with stoicism. What he was really doing was denying the gloomier aspects of his situation—another reaction that's commonplace. Although he kept it to himself, John kept thinking: This can't be happening to me. I don't deserve this fate. It's all a bad dream. I'll wake up soon and everything will be back the way it was.

John's mental litany also included a good measure of hubris, the notion that you're somehow superhuman and immune to the afflictions that plague mere mortals: I'm not like other people who have heart attacks, John secretly thought. This is a horrible mistake. God won't let me die. I need more time. I've got important things to do.

Denial is a healthy defence mechanism that is sometimes necessary to control MI patients' intense initial anxiety and stress.[2] Doctors and nurses encourage it, for without a certain amount of denial to help alleviate the various terrors that some patients conjure up, their hospital stays might be unbearably torturous. Encouraging denial, however, does not mean lying to a patient in the face of reality. Rather, it means emphasizing the positive instead of dwelling on the threat to life and health.

Between reassurances, the nurses and doctors dealing with John's case did try to impart some useful and sobering information as well. For example, they delivered very emphatic warnings about the fatigue John would feel in his early weeks recuperating at home. They advised him to measure his progress by comparing his condition to how he felt during and immediately after his heart attack, not to how he felt before his heart attack.

THE HOMECOMING LETDOWN

All things, including moods, come to an end sooner or later—including the somewhat inflated self-confidence that characterizes the denial phase after a heart attack. Denial seldom lasts beyond cardiac patients' release from the hospital. Returning home and settling into a daily pattern that's far from the active life they once enjoyed is a mental jolt that often ushers in a several-week-long period of depression. Few patients escape it completely. Coronary specialists call it the "homecoming blues". It's as if the far horizon, which appeared to be brightening for a while, suddenly darkened.

John was no different from the average. His new at-home routines underscored his lamentable situation and erased the optimistic thoughts he had harboured during much of his hospital stay. No, it was not business as usual. Far from it. John felt weaker than he ever expected, despite the doctors' and nurses' predictions. His endurance was nil, and his spirits were at rock bottom. On top of that, he was irritable, resentful of the solicitous gestures of family and friends, and stricken with self-pity.

Ironically, the fact that John tried so hard to be a model patient, following doctors' recommendations and guidelines to the letter, only served to deepen his already glum mood. If I'm doing everything right, he wondered, why is this recovery taking so long? What am I doing wrong? Why isn't my body responding?

Of course, John's body was responding, but not at the fast pace he wanted. Like all cardiac patients, John was discovering through firsthand experience that his body's schedule for healing didn't match his own rehabilitation hopes. And this triggered many of John's worst moods, bouts of self-pity, and the explosive outbursts he intermittently aimed at innocent family members and friends.

Later, after contemplative moments when John gained some perspective on his behaviour, he realized his emotions had been bouncing around wildly. They swung from hostility, rancour, and frustration to feelings of guilt, remorse, and self-hatred. He recognized that those around him had done nothing to deserve his enmity. How could he ever make amends?

While the worst of John's depression disappeared after two months, he had lingering problems with irritability, tension, and hostility—often triggered by excessive fatigue—for up to four months after his MI. In some patients, this syndrome lasts up to a year or more. Several studies indicate that about 50 percent of all heart attack sufferers have such residual emotional reactions.[3] Thankfully, most overcome them, no doubt to the enormous relief of family members who have their own mixed bag of emotions to deal with during this trying time.

RETURNING TO NORMAL—
WITH RELATIONSHIPS INTACT

As physicians, we can attest to the fact that coronary patients often push the patience and fortitude of those entrusted with their care to the limit. Certainly, given their sharp mood swings, this is understandable. Nor are we surprised when studies show that many cardiac patients' marriages deteriorate immediately following their attack. That's understandable, too.

It is the purpose of the chapters in this part of the book to help you avoid straining the important relationships in your life to the breaking point during your convalescence. In the next two chapters, we offer our remedies for reducing familial dissension and strife brought on by confusion and insecurity.

We've got no magic elixir. We think our prescription, in fact, will seem obvious to any intelligent person. It is based on the straightforward notion that patients who know where they stand and what to expect are patients better able to cope with whatever difficulties and emotional troubles convalescence may bring.

In short, we feel that in-depth knowledge of your condition coupled with some common sense and goodwill will go a long way toward keeping you from regressing into a prolonged state of anguish and despair. True, depression is normal. But its depth and duration vary greatly from one individual to the next. We feel there's no reason for you to let it get so out of hand that the depression controls you instead of you controlling it.

Unfortunately, about 20 percent of all heart attack sufferers do get caught up in a downward spiral of hopelessness and despair from which they can't seem to extricate themselves. We are referring to the minority of people who don't bounce back after three months of recuperation. Six months, eight months, even a year later, they still have psychological problems severe enough to warrant professional counselling.

Close questioning often reveals that these are patients to whom melancholia is no stranger. Often it turns out that they suffered from various affective or psychological disorders before their MI Perhaps they were never treated back then. Now, when they have a heart condition that gives them a tangible reason for pessimism, they're pessimistic all right. Perhaps it's the same gloom they've exuded, on and off, for years, only now it's magnified and constant because of this new and very real justification for their feelings.

We recommend psychiatric counselling for these people because their unhealthy state of mind and counterproductive attitude create a self-fulfilling prophecy. Their mind, figuratively speaking, administers a daily dose of "poison" to their ailing body. Thus, their body will remain weak and afflicted until this vicious cycle is broken through counselling and, possibly, drug treatment.

Getting such patients to undergo therapy can be difficult, for despite their protestations to the contrary, some seem to prefer sickness to health. We are confident that every doctor has a couple of patients just like this, who seem to prefer invalidism and self-pity to vitality and self-reliance. The majority, however, are ready and anxious to get the help they need.

EMOTIONAL AFTERMATH OF BYPASS SURGERY OR ANGIOPLASTY

If you're a surgery or an angioplasty patient, you may find your outlook remains relatively sunny throughout it all.[4] This is not uncommon. After all, no one forced you to undergo surgery or angioplasty. You consented to the procedure of your own free will because your doctor told you there was a good chance it would prolong as well as enhance the quality of your life. If you had angina or other annoying symptoms, you were told they, too, might be lessened, even eliminated. For all these reasons, you—in contrast to the unwitting victim of a heart attack—have far less cause to get mired in the darker side of things. For you, life is getting better and you're growing healthier every day.

However, this is not to say that you, as a surgery or angioplasty patient, will be free of all negative thoughts and feelings during your convalescence. We're afraid that is too optimistic. But we are predicting that, for you, the worst is already over. You undoubtedly experienced the bulk of your anxiety, perhaps even depression, before the fact, much like a patient of ours, Peter Sender. Peter says he'll never forget the agony he went through deciding whether or not to submit to bypass surgery.

Peter's case is somewhat unusual. Peter had been troubled by recurring discomfort in his neck and jaw for several weeks. Finally his wife called their doctor, who ordered him to go to the nearest hospital casualty department immediately. Not long after he arrived there, he had a heart attack right in front of the doctors' eyes. While the doctors managed to abort the MI, preventing major damage to the heart muscle, it was still apparent that Peter needed an angiogram at the very least, and probably much more. This is Peter's account.

> By the next day, Friday, I was resting comfortably and feeling no pain—except for the psychic pain of dealing with the ordeal in front of me. I'd already signed all kinds of papers giving permission for an angiogram early Monday morning. If necessary, it would be followed by an angioplasty and, if that didn't work, a bypass. I spent the weekend in the ICU, mulling it over.
>
> I wasn't afraid of the angioplasty. But open-heart surgery was something else. They'd explained the risks in great detail. I felt cornered and very scared. I was scared of the pain and the aftereffects, maybe even more than the idea of death.
>
> Finally I bit the bullet and said to myself, What choice do you really have? Once I acceded to my destiny and relaxed about it, everything was smooth sailing from there.

Peter got the full treatment—from an angiogram through to bypass surgery. Like others before him, he went into the operating theatre knowing there was a risk of failure. Thus, when he woke up hours later, still alive, with a heart muscle strengthened by what had just happened, he felt an overwhelming sense of gratitude and relief. His elation carried over well into his recuperation at home, which often occurs with surgery patients.

However, for six months after his hospital discharge, Peter continued to have the discomfort in his neck and jaw, reminiscent of the pain that had made him visit the casualty department to start with. The symptoms worried him. Desperate to get to the root of the problem, Peter underwent a treadmill exercise test during which a radioactive dye called thallium was injected into his veins. It offered reassuring evidence that his heart was free of any significant ischaemia. He says: "The doctor and I came to the conclusion that my own fear and anxiety were causing the pain. After that, lo and behold, it went away. Isn't it amazing what the mind can do, on both the plus and minus side of the health ledger?"

One thing Peter managed to escape is a transient condition medical researchers call *postcardiotomy psychosis*. This is a form of delirium following surgery that about 15 percent of all bypass patients experience.[5] It's characterized by disorientation, confusion, memory loss, and difficulty in concentrating and thinking. In a few cases, patients actually experience paranoid delusions and hallucinations. In a mild form, some or all of the above manifestations can last for several weeks.

We find bypass patients are the most alarmed by temporary intellectual dysfunction. Their minds seem to go a little haywire for stretches of time, ceasing to do their bidding. They have trouble with simple arithmetic; they can't concentrate; they're forgetful; their handwriting changes; and they may have vision problems and distorted perception of distances, which becomes apparent when they try to negotiate a furniture-filled room.

All we can say is that this too shall pass. These are annoying side effects of the major trauma your body has just endured, not permanent conditions, and should disappear completely within six to eight weeks.

We've had a number of bypass patients report memory loss immediately after surgery, but we're happy to report few seemed disturbed by it. On the contrary, most were amazed. Their families tell them how lucid and talkative they were a day or two after their operation, but they can't recall a thing about it. Whole conversations are lost in the ether of memory, never to return again.

DEPRESSION IN DISGUISE

We've been using the word "depression" to describe what many heart attack sufferers, and some surgery patients, endure in the weeks following their attack or surgery. But we should point out that many patients don't experience it as depression. Some patients wrestle with insomnia; they're tearful; they're slovenly in their grooming and dress; they can't keep their mind on anything for long; they've lost all desire for sex, or food, or things that usually arouse their interest. They even admit they feel vulnerable, withdrawn, and out of sorts much of the time. These are all manifestations of depression, yet patients still manage to sit on the other side of our desks and deny they're depressed—unhappy about their situation, perhaps, but never depressed.

It's become apparent to us that, in contrast to the 20 percent of patients who wallow in despair after a heart attack, others will do almost anything to keep us from uttering the dread word "depression" in their presence. What Shakespeare said about a rose, we say about depression. Call it what you want, it's still depression. While we're willing to tiptoe around the issue if it makes these patients feel better, we as doctors know it for what it is—and want to give it the attention and careful consideration it deserves.

Patients sometimes do strange things during periods of intense psychological distress. One of our patients who was feeling especially sorry for himself during his convalescence from a heart attack did what he now considers two "very stupid things". By way of being good to himself "before I die", he splurged on a massive motor yacht and a Mercedes 380 SL. He didn't die, but to this day he's embarrassed by the purchases: "It's not like me at all," he explains. You may not find this odd, certainly nothing out of the ordinary. But our patient does because he lives in a very conservative part of the country where such extravagance draws unflattering attention. He says it's something he would never have done under normal circumstances. He still feels silly about it.

Even grief ends sometime. *Grief?* Yes, grief. While the term "grief" may seem out of context to you here, it is what we mean because most heart attack patients are in mourning. They're mourning the loss of a part of themselves—their strength, their vitality, their independence. Men sometimes view a heart attack as a loss of virility. Middle-aged women who have heart attacks (often perfectionists and compulsive overachievers) may also be despondent over the loss of control it represents.

All we ask is that you take the long view.

The future used to hold happy associations for you, didn't it? It can again, if you recognize that your present focus on limitations and restrictions is a passing one. It will gradually give way to cheerier thoughts of freedom and hope. Just like your health, your former rosier outlook on life can be restored, too.

CHAPTER 5

"HOW BAD WAS MY HEART ATTACK?"
How Your Physician Decides

IN the last chapter, we jumped ahead a bit, covering your emotional reactions during the first three months of your recovery. Now we'll go back for a moment and focus on your physical status in the period right after your heart attack, surgery, or angioplasty.

Picture yourself in the hospital. You're worried because you still haven't had a satisfactory answer to that all-important question: just how bad is my heart condition? It's inevitable that before you're released from the hospital, your doctor will answer that question, giving you some good news about your prognosis, and possibly some bad.

The good news may be that your heart attack was mild and you'll be home and able to resume your normal activities soon—provided you alter the dubious health habits that aided and abetted your CHD. On the other hand, the first news you hear may be bad. It may be that your MI was severe. But there's good news, too: in this age of advanced medical technology, you have a good chance of living a long and productive life. However, you may have to follow a prescribed drug regimen and/or undergo angioplasty or bypass surgery, or some other kind of very specialized treatment. You'll also have to follow your doctor's orders to the letter and readjust your priorities and life-style in the future to safeguard your body.

No doubt you wonder how a cardiologist arrives at such critical conclusions. How does he or she decide, first, the severity of your coronary condition and, second, how to treat it? This chapter—one of the most vital in this book—will give you the answers to these basic questions.

THE RISK-STRATIFICATION CONCEPT

The medical community uses the term "risk stratification" to describe the coronary detective work that goes into deciding the severity of a heart attack and the best mode of treatment. It's detective work that must be performed under deadline pressure, because those who are at high risk for a second heart attack or other problem are likely to have it during the first six months of their recovery period—maybe even while they're still recuperating in the hospital. Thus, any preventive measures must be undertaken as soon as possible.

There are a battery of tests available to your doctor during the risk-stratification process. These tests range from a routine physical examination to sophisticated nuclear medicine probes. All are intended to identify the areas of your heart muscle that either are already severely ischaemic or potentially ischaemic, or are already damaged to the point where the functioning of your left ventricle is badly impaired. But we'll say more about this in a moment.

The risk-stratification search is an ongoing one. It starts in casualty, continues throughout your hospital stay, and culminates during the early convalescence period—that is, the first four to eight weeks after your heart attack. This is the time period we'll be covering in this chapter.

What makes risk stratification particularly challenging is the dynamic nature of the population of heart attack patients. Patients' conditions change constantly. A person can enter a hospital as a low-risk patient and, owing to some unexpected event, be transformed into a high-risk patient within a matter of minutes. The reverse is equally possible. Because heart patients' conditions are initially so unstable, most hospitals maintain a coronary intensive care unit (ICU) in order to monitor heart patients around the clock.

While it's all very well to discuss the ideal risk-stratification process, it may be more helpful to you as a typical coronary patient to know the reality of it. We realize that state-of-the-art thinking and practice on coronary matters are not available to people who live, as you may, in rural areas or out-of-the-way towns far from major medical centres.

In 1987, researchers from Duke University Medical Centre's Division of Cardiology did an exhaustive survey of more than five thousand cardiologists, internists, and family general practitioners randomly chosen from the membership of the American Medical Association.[1] Their goal was to ascertain the most widely used approach to cardiac patient care and risk stratification. Before hospital discharge, straightforward physical examinations coupled with exercise stress testing were the most common practice. Not surprisingly, the cardiologists were the major routine users of in-hospital, predischarge exercise tests— some 90 percent of them routinely perform such tests.

This is very reassuring, for we feel that exercise testing, correctly carried out, is a safe and cost-effective way for physicians to identify existing as well as potential heart problems before discharging their patients from the hospital. We should also point out that, of those physicians who do not routinely perform predischarge exercise testing, many bring their patients back about a week after discharge for such a test. This approach is equally acceptable.

THE HEART DAMAGE THAT IS CRITICAL

Before your doctor can answer the all-important question about the severity of your attack, he or she must know the amount of damage your heart muscle has sustained and how much heart muscle is still at risk for damage in the future. Specifically, cardiologists are looking for two things:

- The extent of residual myocardial ischaemia
- The degree of left ventricular dysfunction

Neither is a good thing, but the latter is worse than the former because it often reflects irreversible heart muscle damage.

It's taken years of research and many clinical studies for investigators to isolate these two variables as the key determinants of risk for heart attack sufferers. The term "risk" in this context means the risk of death (which is usually greatest within six months after the initial heart attack) or of future non-fatal heart attacks.

RESIDUAL MYOCARDIAL ISCHAEMIA

Let's consider some medical information for a moment as we bring you up to date on your heart's functioning in light of the heart attack it has just experienced.

As you know, ischaemia is an inadequate oxygen supply to some part of your body—in this case, to your heart muscle ("myocardial"). "Residual" simply means that it's left over after your heart attack. Although you've just had a heart attack, there may still be parts of your heart muscle that are at great risk for future damage.

The extent of such ischaemia is determined by a variety of factors, including (1) the site or sites of atherosclerotic plaques in your coronary arteries; (2) the number of coronary arteries involved; (3) the degree of obstruction the plaques are causing; and (4) the amount of blood that can bypass the plaque sites via coronary collaterals. In patients with residual myocardial ischaemia, an angiogram is the best test for assessing many of these factors.

As your cardiologist will tell you, the risk associated with residual myocardial ischaemia can be reduced, sometimes to almost zero, with appropriate therapy—often angioplasty or bypass surgery.

Left Ventricular Dysfunction: Why It's a Bad Omen

As you'll recall from Chapter 3, your left ventricle is the most muscular chamber of your heart because its job is to pump out oxygenated blood to the rest of your body. Thus, your left ventricle spells the difference between life and death for your body's cells, making it the most vital of your heart's four chambers.

After a heart attack, the condition of your left ventricle is dependent on two things: (1) the irreversible damage the attack caused to your myocardium and (2) the extent of any residual myocardial ischaemia. In the first instance, the greater the area of dead heart muscle, the greater the left ventricular dysfunction. Likewise, the greater the residual myocardial ischaemia, the greater the dysfunction. Left ventricular dysfunction resulting from irreversible damage to the myocardium is not improved by angioplasty or bypass surgery. Left ventricular dysfunction is a serious matter. The appropriate treatment depends upon the cause, which is not always easy to pinpoint.

To decide if the cause is residual myocardial ischaemia that is potentially correctable by angioplasty or bypass surgery, we recommend that coronary angiography be considered for patients with severe left ventricular dysfunction. And this recommendation applies even to patients without angina or obvious ECG evidence of ischaemia. This is our reasoning: some post-heart attack patients with left ventricular dysfunction have residual myocardial ischaemia, but you'd never know it. They experience none of the usual ECG changes or ischaemic symptoms, such as angina. This is because their heart is compensating. It's downgrading its left ventricular function in order to reduce the myocardium's oxygen requirement.

Dr. Shahbudin H. Rahimtoola, professor of cardiology at the University of Southern California, coined the term hibernating myocardium to describe this particular balancing act of the heart, which has perplexed many a cardiologist.[2] In the absence of symptoms or other clues as to the cause of your left ventricular dysfunction, angiography is the definitive test to sort out what your heart muscle is really experiencing.

If residual myocardial ischaemia turns out to be the cause of your left ventricular dysfunction, you're fortunate. Treating the ischaemia should eliminate the problem. To do that, an angioplasty or bypass surgery is often warranted. If for some reason neither is possible, appropriate drug therapy might be the next-best option.

There are certainly other causes of left ventricular dysfunction that can also be corrected by surgery. Among the most common are (1) a malfunctioning mitral valve; (2) an *aneurysm* (that is, an outward bulging of the damaged heart area during ventricular contraction); or (3) a defect in the muscular wall separating the left and right ventricles, known as a *ventricular septal defect*. In these instances, specialized surgery may be required. Like myocardial ischaemia, these disorders can also be detected during heart catheterization.

TRIED AND TESTED STRATIFICATION GUIDELINES

How do we recommend that cardiac patients be stratified after a heart attack?

Our methodology relies largely on a thorough predischarge physical examination and exercise test. It is based primarily on our own clinical experience and three sets of recently published recommendations: those of a panel of cardiac experts from twelve major American universities;[3] those of a joint task force of the American College of Cardiology and the American Heart Association;[4] and the protocol of Dr. John Ross, Jr., of the University of California at San Diego and an international group of his colleagues from the United States, Canada, Switzerland, and Denmark.[5]

However, before turning to specifics, we wish to sound these warnings. First, the precise treatment of heart attack patients is still evolving and some aspects are controversial. Angiography and the methods for risk stratification are perhaps the most debated. Our guidelines—and those of other respected authorities—will no doubt change as new studies are published.

Moreover, the term "guidelines" means just that—these are guides to modes of practice; they are not intended to be applied rigidly in every case. Each patient is an individual with his or her own mix of physical and emotional problems. Doctors must exercise judgment in how they arrive at a prognosis and decide on a course of treatment. That type of sensitivity and intuition about individual patients is, after all, what being a good physician is all about. Before he or she decides what's best for you, your doctor will no doubt be considering such matters as the local facilities and equipment, your family situation and occupational needs, and, of course, your preferences.

Finally, as we describe our risk-stratification process, we will be citing percentages of heart attack patients that fall into the three risk categories of low, moderate, and high and their actual risk of death. These are only estimates. To get precise values, one would have to do a large-scale scientific study that takes into account many other factors outside the bounds of what we considered in formulating our stratification protocol.

In short, we present these guidelines to give you insight into your future prognosis as well as to help you make informed consumer decisions about the medical care you receive during your recovery.

Using our own risk-stratification protocol, we estimate that for every 100 patients who survive their heart attack, about 35 will be discharged from the hospital at low risk for future cardiac problems; some 40 will be considered at moderate risk; and the remaining 25 will be at high risk.

Let's talk about a depressing subject for a moment—the chances of dying within the first year after your heart attack. Based on existing studies, the risk of death for heart attack patients during their first year after discharge is about 10 percent. Of those stratified into the low-risk group, fewer than 5 percent will die. In contrast, some 20 percent or more of those in the high-risk group may not live to see the year's end. And the death rate of the moderate-risk group is likely to be everything in between: 5 to 20 percent. As can be seen in Figure 5-1, our risk stratification utilizes these figures. For heart patients in all three groups, however, the time of greatest risk is the first six months after a heart attack. And for all three groups, but in particular the moderate- and high-risk ones, this risk of death can often be substantially reduced by appropriate treatment. This is why knowing where you stand is so vitally important.

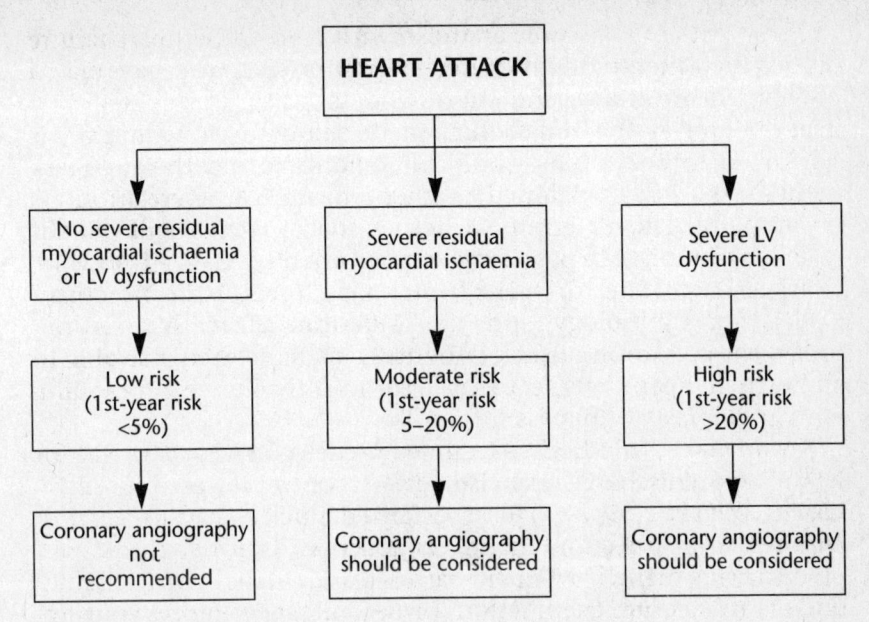

```
                    ┌─────────────────┐
                    │  HEART ATTACK   │
                    └─────────────────┘
         ┌─────────────────┼─────────────────┐
         ▼                 ▼                 ▼
┌─────────────────┐ ┌─────────────────┐ ┌─────────────────┐
│ No severe       │ │ Severe residual │ │ Severe LV       │
│ residual        │ │ myocardial      │ │ dysfunction     │
│ myocardial      │ │ ischaemia       │ │                 │
│ ischaemia       │ │                 │ │                 │
│ or LV           │ │                 │ │                 │
│ dysfunction     │ │                 │ │                 │
└─────────────────┘ └─────────────────┘ └─────────────────┘
         │                 │                 │
         ▼                 ▼                 ▼
┌─────────────────┐ ┌─────────────────┐ ┌─────────────────┐
│ Low risk        │ │ Moderate risk   │ │ High risk       │
│ (1st-year risk  │ │ (1st-year risk  │ │ (1st-year risk  │
│ <5%)            │ │ 5–20%)          │ │ >20%)           │
└─────────────────┘ └─────────────────┘ └─────────────────┘
         │                 │                 │
         ▼                 ▼                 ▼
┌─────────────────┐ ┌─────────────────┐ ┌─────────────────┐
│ Coronary        │ │ Coronary        │ │ Coronary        │
│ angiography     │ │ angiography     │ │ angiography     │
│ not             │ │ should be       │ │ should be       │
│ recommended     │ │ considered      │ │ considered      │
└─────────────────┘ └─────────────────┘ └─────────────────┘
```

Figure 5-1. Risk categories for post-heart attack patients. The above diagram outlines what cardiologists look for (1) to determine a patient's risk and (2) to decide if coronary angiography is warranted. The term "risk" in this context refers to a cardiac patient's chances of dying during the first year after a heart attack. "LV" in the chart stands for left ventricular. (*Source:* The Cooper Clinic, Dallas.)

PATIENTS WHO CAN'T BE EXERCISE TESTED

While we may be advocates of predischarge exercise testing, we also recognize that not everyone is a candidate. There are patients—usually 10 of every 100 non-fatal heart attack sufferers—who experience persistent or recurrent angina at rest twenty-four or more hours after their hospital admission. A good cardiologist doesn't need an exercise test to know that such patients should undergo coronary angiography as soon as possible. The goal of the angiogram is to find out if an angioplasty or bypass surgery is warranted.

A second group consists of those patients—also about 10 of every 100 sufferers—who go into a severe form of heart failure called *cardiogenic shock*. In ICUs, this is one of the phenomena the medical team is on guard for. It usually occurs during the first five days after an MI. The clinical manifestations are a dropping systolic blood pressure and abnormal breath sounds called *rales*. Through a stethoscope placed on your chest, a doctor can hear these sound alerts, which result from fluid buildup in your lungs.

These patients—as well as those with less severe heart failure during their first five days of hospitalization, but who have had a previous heart attack, and those who show clinical evidence of heart failure at the time when predischarge exercise testing is scheduled to take place—should be stratified into the high-risk group. As we mentioned earlier, heart catheterization is recommended to determine whether such patients will benefit from angioplasty, bypass surgery, or other specialized surgery. However, according to a 1987 joint task force of the American College of Cardiology and the American Heart Association, unless the condition of such patients is unstable, it's preferable to allow their heart muscle to heal sufficiently before proceeding with angioplasty or bypass surgery.[6]

An advanced method sometimes used to stratify patients for whom a predischarge exercise test is contraindicated is *radionuclide ventriculography*. This specialized nuclear cardiology test requires the injection of a radioactive isotope into your bloodstream, which, when it passes through the heart, enables doctors to measure the fraction, or percentage, of blood your left ventricle ejects when it contracts (which is termed the *ejection fraction*).

The normal resting left ventricular ejection fraction is about 60 percent. Any value less than 45 percent indicates severe left ventricular dysfunction, which places you in the high-risk category for future cardiac problems. In contrast, if your value is equal to or greater than 45 percent and predischarge exercise testing was not performed for reasons other than angina, resting ECG evidence of myocardial ischaemia, or heart failure, you can regard yourself as being at low risk.

In the Duke University survey mentioned at the beginning of this chapter, only 18 percent of the responding doctors practising in the United States routinely used radionuclide ventriculography to stratify their patients.[7] The technique is uncommon in South Africa—few institutions have the equipment. However, your heart's left ventricular ejection fraction can also be estimated via an *echocardiogram*. It's an ultrasound technique that bounces sound waves off the surface of your heart, and the results are converted into "pictures" that your cardiologist reads.

As we've emphasized, left ventricular dysfunction is a key indicator of severe heart problems. People with severe left ventricular dysfunction sometimes experience frequent irregular heartbeats, called *premature ventricular contractions,* or "PVCs". The combination of left ventricular dysfunction and frequent

PVCs places a patient at greater risk for future complications. Thus, when left ventricular dysfunction is suspected, we recommend twenty-four-hour ambulatory ECG monitoring in order to find out if the patient is experiencing frequent PVCs. This *Holter monitoring* requires that the patient wear at all times a small tape recorder, usually on a belt around the waist. The heart's electrical signals are magnetically recorded and played back later, using special equipment that helps single out those fleeting heart rhythm disturbances that aren't captured in most ordinary ECGs. Holter monitors may also be effective in detecting silent ischaemia in such patients before hospital discharge, according to a study performed by doctors at the Frances Scott Key Medical Centre and Johns Hopkins Hospital in Baltimore.[8]

PVCs generally don't cause patients discomfort and are often of no real significance. However, as we will discuss later in this chapter, certain types of PVCs do place patients at an increased risk, particularly those with left ventricular dysfunction. The treatment of PVCs is controversial. Some patients benefit from anti-arrhythmia drug therapy and, in rare cases, specialized surgery.

THE EXERCISE TEST

Ideally, it would be wonderful if heart patients could read this chapter before they take their first post-heart attack exercise test. It would erase a lot of their fears as well as enable them to get the maximum information from the medical team putting them through their paces.

Unfortunately, we know most of you will be well into your convalescence before you pick up this book. Nonetheless, we would like you to read through to the end of this chapter. The material we're about to cover will give you further insight into your prognosis, enable you to question your physician more intelligently at your next meeting, and give added meaning to any further exercise tests you undergo. As a heart patient, you probably have many exercise tests still ahead of you. In addition, many of the safety guidelines we'll be presenting in the exercise section (Part 3) are based on concepts we're about to introduce. To understand them, you must read to the end of this chapter.

Is Exercise Testing Safe for Coronary Patients?

Given the unstable condition of patients just after an MI, you probably wonder about the safety of placing such people on an exercise treadmill. In fact, you may wonder why it's not downright suicidal for patients to attempt even mildly strenuous exercise so soon. It's an obvious question and one we want to answer fully.

As we explained in Chapter 3, your heart, at rest, tends to compensate for any atherosclerotic obstructions in your coronary arteries. After all, when no undue stress is placed on your heart muscle, its oxygen requirements are not that great. This is why tests performed when you're resting may give you a clean bill of health. Despite patients' severe CHD, their ECG results, for example, may show no abnormalities. The obvious way around this problem is to make a patient's heart work harder during an ECG monitoring. That's where exercise comes in. Myocardial ischaemia may remain undetected during an ECG at rest, but it is unlikely to remain so during an exercise ECG test.

Careful monitoring of your heart responses during an exercise test can reveal a great deal to your doctor. For instance, observations can be made about the functioning of your left ventricle, and the test can also help your doctor determine your capacity to resume certain activities later, after you return home. It will also help him or her decide on a timetable for a safe and effective exercise programme for you.

You might want to look at it this way: a predischarge exercise test is reproducing—in a controlled, objective, monitored way—the kind of stress your heart is likely to undergo at various times after you return home. Wouldn't you rather test the limits of your heart's endurance under these circumstances, with a doctor and nurse standing next to you, than at home when you could be alone and too far away from a phone to call for help? This is precisely the point made in a 1981 editorial in the *Annals of Internal Medicine:* "Not to do an exercise test before discharge is to ask the patient to do the test at home".[9] In fact, most experts now believe that the exercise test results can tell a physician more about a patient's risk for future cardiac complications than the results of any other single procedure.

There's another, less talked about effect of predischarge exercise testing, and we think it's very important for the patient's smooth transition back into everyday life in the real world. This is a successful test's positive psychological effect on patients, not to mention on their spouses and loved ones.

In the early 1980s, a Stanford University study demonstrated that exercise testing—in this case, performed three weeks after a heart attack—can have a profoundly uplifting effect on patients' confidence in their ability to resume normal physical activities such as walking, climbing stairs, and sexual intercourse.[10] This is especially true if a physician interprets the test results for them and a nurse later reinforces the message.

In a second Stanford study, wives of men who had had heart attacks were introduced into the equation by comparing the reactions of thirty of them, all of whom had severe reservations about their husbands' conditions and abilities to withstand any exercise, after they had been divided up into three groups. Ten sat passively in the waiting room during their husbands' treadmill tests; ten were invited in to observe the tests; and the remaining ten not only observed but were also asked to walk on the treadmill for three minutes at the same peak work load that their husbands had just achieved.[11] The researchers found that the wives who not only watched the test but also tried it themselves "substantially increased their judgments of their husbands' physical and cardiac efficacy". In short, by going on the treadmill themselves, these women realized that their husbands weren't as fragile as they'd thought.

We've found that the opinion of a spouse or other close family member about a patient's health status is an extremely critical factor in the recuperation process. It never ceases to amaze us how the spouse's view of things can colour that of the patient, sometimes for better, often for worse. This is why we take the results of this second Stanford study seriously and always encourage spouses to participate in, or at least observe, exercise stress tests.

Having read all this, you're probably still not entirely convinced. What about the risk of dropping dead on an exercise test treadmill, even though there are doctors all around and all manner of medical devices within easy access?

In one major study, only one fatality occurred during 1 500 such tests.[12] An extensive review of the medical literature turned up only a few other examples of death on an exercise treadmill during testing shortly after a heart attack. This should put your mind at rest. After all, since the early 1980s predischarge exercise testing has come into its own worldwide as a recognized cardiac diagnostic tool. Thousands upon thousands of patients have undergone such tests anywhere from seven to fourteen days after their MI. There is seldom a problem with predischarge exercise testing if it is performed in an appropriate fashion.

However, what we mean by "an appropriate fashion" requires further explanation. As we have already mentioned, there can be problems if all coronary patients, regardless of the severity of their condition, are routinely pushed onto treadmills. One could also expect problems if doctors were to adhere to the wrong test protocol or if various other conditions were not met.

There are two ways of conducting an exercise test, and we feel only one is appropriate for assessing post-MI patients before their hospital discharge:

- Type 1 is referred to as a "submaximal" exercise test. This means that, even in the absence of abnormalities, the test is terminated the moment your heart reaches a predetermined rate or you've achieved an identifiable exercise exertion level.
- Type 2 is called a "symptom-limited maximal" exercise test. It's terminated only when specific abnormalities start showing up or you feel you've pushed yourself to your absolute fatigue limit. Clearly, this is the more stressful test.

Fortunately, present research data indicate that maximal testing before hospital discharge is not necessary to obtain an accurate assessment of a patient's condition. As early as 1980, Dr. Robert F. DeBusk and Dr. William L. Haskell, both from the Stanford University School of Medicine's Division of Cardiology, used a sample of 200 heart patients to measure the accuracy of the two forms of testing.[13] Although they found that a maximal test, performed three weeks after a heart attack, was a safe procedure, it was no more predictive than submaximal testing. In their study, they ended submaximal tests after a patient's heart rate reached 130 beats per minute.

More recently, physicians from the University of Alberta in Canada performed predischarge submaximal exercise tests on a representative sample of cardiac patients.[14] These tests, too, were terminated at 130 beats per minute. Later, six to eight weeks after their heart attacks, the same group underwent a maximal test. It revealed no further significant prognostic information.

There's no definitive answer to the question of whether maximal testing is safe for post-MI patients prior to their discharge from a hospital. However, since it doesn't seem to be necessary anyway, it's a moot point.

Our own stratification guidelines call for predischarge submaximal testing on appropriate patients. We recommend that, in the absence of specific abnormalities, testing be terminated the moment patients reach a heart rate of 130 beats per minute or complete an exercise level equivalent to 5 METs, whichever occurs first. The MET, or *metabolic equivalent unit,* is a key concept for convalescing coronary patients. This is a quantitative measure of human energy output. One MET equals the amount of energy you expend at rest, so five METs represents five times your resting energy expenditure. (Tables 6-1 and 6-2 in Chapter 6 give MET values for various common activities.)

The Borg Scale: Measuring Perceived Exertion

For patients on drugs which slow down the heart rate—beta-blockers, for example—a different exertion goal must be substituted for heart rate. In these instances, we recommend that the *Borg perceived exertion scale* be used to help determine when an exercise test should be stopped. In patients who are not receiving such drugs, both the heart rate and the Borg perceived exertion scale should be used.

The scale is named after a Swedish exercise physiologist, Gunnar Borg, who developed it in the early 1950s. The original Borg scale, used by cardiologists and medical centres around the world, helps a physician judge exertion level based on a patient's on-the-spot description of what he or she is feeling. This *rating of perceived exertion* (or RPE) is quantified by the patient on a scale from 6 to 20 (see Table 5-1 on page 84). For example, patients exercising at a level that they perceive as being fairly strenuous might assign themselves an RPE of 13. Those who are huffing and puffing would probably choose a rating of 17. On Borg's original scale we recommend termination when a predischarge patient reaches the 13 to 15 range, even if the heart rate is below 130 beats per minute.

More recently, Borg introduced a new rating scale, which goes from 0 to 10 (see Table 5-2). However, most physicians, including ourselves, still prefer the old scale. The Borg scale will be discussed in more detail in Part 3.

A Typical Exercise Test

It goes without saying that your physician should know your case thoroughly before he or she asks you to take an exercise test. In preparation for the test, medical personnel will instruct you to abstain from any strenuous activity on the day of the test. They'll also tell you not to eat for two or three hours beforehand, and they'll ask you to come dressed for a workout. If at all possible,

TABLE 5-1
Borg Perceived Exertion Scale[a]

Rating of Perceived Exertion (RPE)	Patient's Verbal Description of RPE
6	
7	Very, very light
8	
9	Very light
10	
11	Fairly light
12	
13	Somewhat hard
14	
15	Hard
16	
17	Very hard
18	
19	Very, very hard
20	

[a] The original Borg system for rating physical exertion is based on an open-ended scale running from 6 (equal to exertion at rest) to 20 (extreme effort).
Source: G. A. Borg, "Perceived Exertion: A Note on 'History' and Methods," *Medicine and Science in Sports and Exercise,* 14 (1982): 377–387.

we recommend walking, aerobics or running shoes and comfortable recreational wear such as a tracksuit.

You can expect to receive a brief cardiac examination and a verbal explanation of the benefits and risks of the exercise test that's to follow before you get anywhere near the exercise treadmill. In addition, you'll probably be asked to sign an informed-consent form.

If you have any questions whatsoever about the test—how it will be conducted or what you're supposed to do—be sure to get clarification before you begin. From our experience, the more detail we give patients, the more confidence they have during the test. This is also the time to ask if your spouse can observe. A wise doctor won't hesitate to grant permission.

It's rare for physicians to ask patients to stop their medications before a predischarge exercise test, although they might do so later when patients have recuperated more fully. While it's true that beta-blockers, nitrates, and calcium antagonists can lessen the chances of your doctor detecting an abnormality during the test, studies confirm that valuable risk-stratification information will still be obtained despite the drugs in your system. Indeed, one of the aims of the predischarge test is to assess whether

TABLE 5-2
Revised Borg Perceived Exertion Scale[a]

Rating of Perceived Exertion (RPE)	Patient's Verbal Description of RPE
0	Nothing at all
,5	Very, very weak
1	Very weak
2	Weak
3	Moderate
4	Somewhat strong
5	Strong
6	
7	Very strong
8	
9	
10	Very, very strong
—	Maximal

[a] The new Borg rating system for measuring physical exertion levels uses a scale from O to 10. Most physicians—including ourselves—still prefer the old scale (shown in Table 5-1).
Source: G. A. Borg, "Perceived Exertion: A Note on 'History' and Methods," *Medicine and Science in Sports and Exercise,* 14 (1982): 337-387.

you're on appropriate medication. What better way to find out than to test you while you're taking it?

In the exercise lab, a nurse or technician will apply discs, called electrodes, at various points on the front of your upper body, and sometimes on your back. First, however, your skin must be cleansed with alcohol and abraded ever so lightly with fine-grain emery sandpaper in the spots where the electrodes will make contact. There is no need for anxiety as this isn't painful—but it is important. Removing the oil and superficial dead layer of your skin before affixing the electrodes improves the quality of the ECG recordings.

Generally, ten or more electrodes are used to allow the heart's electrical activity to be monitored from various directions, referred to as leads. Ten electrodes are most commonly used, which actually allows twelve leads to be monitored during exercise.

Understanding Your ECG

Once the electrodes are in place, the technician connects them to a series of wires hooked up, via a long cable, to an electrocardiograph machine. At most hospitals, this machine has the capability of recording the electrical impulses emitted by your heart on a moving roll of graph paper while simultaneously displaying your heart pattern on a screen, or oscilloscope.

Each time your heart contracts and relaxes, a series of electrical events takes place. The events are recorded by the electrocardiograph machine as a series of straight and wavy lines. On the ECG tracing, each "wave" is labelled with a letter and represents a distinct myocardial electrical event.

As you can see in Figure 5-2, each heartbeat usually starts with the P wave, which is followed by the Q, R, S, T, and sometimes U waves. All of these waves constitute electrical events taking place during a single heartbeat. During a normal heartbeat, the spacing between beats is even (or regular) and the waves created by each individual heartbeat are identical (which is what is shown in Figure 5-2).

Before the test begins, the nurse or technician will take your blood pressure and an ECG reading in two positions—while you're lying down and while you're standing. Sometimes ECG irregularities occur simply because of a change in posture. Be assured that these types of irregularities have nothing to do with heart disease. However, it is important for your doctor to know about them and take them into account when interpreting your test results. Such irregularities, after all, increase the chances of a "false-positive" test—that is, a test that appears to be abnormal, but is not.

Some doctors ask patients to hyperventilate by breathing deeply and rapidly for at least twenty seconds, after which they record a resting ECG. Again, the purpose is to eliminate the

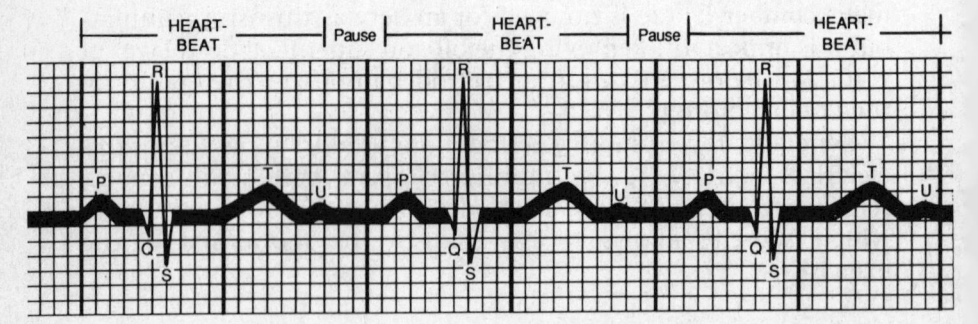

Figure 5-2. A normal ECG tracing. This drawing shows the heart muscle's electrical activity as it's recorded by an electrocardiographic tracing. Each heartbeat—three are shown in this example—results in P, Q, R, S, T, and sometimes U waves. There is a pause in the electrical activity of the heart muscle in between beats. (*Source:* The Cooper Clinic, Dallas.)

chances of a false-positive test. But this procedure is of questionable value during predischarge testing, which encompasses only low-level exercise. Of course, your doctor will take into consideration the many other factors that increase the chances of a false-positive test.

The Exercise Machine

It makes little difference whether the exercise machine used for the test is a treadmill or a stationary cycle. In South Africa, treadmills are more common.

There is a technique to maintaining your balance on a treadmill, so if you've never been on one before, be sure to let the technician and doctor know it. They will be glad to demonstrate how to walk on one, including how to step on and off. Also, be sure to ask your physician what treadmill test protocol is to be used. The two most popular for predischarge exercise testing are the modified Bruce and the Naughton protocols (see Table 5-3). After hospital discharge the standard Bruce protocol and the Balke protocol are also commonly used for exercise testing. The standard Bruce protocol starts out at a treadmill speed and grade that are the same as those for the third stage of the modified Bruce protocol; thereafter, the modified Bruce and standard Bruce protocols are identical. Specifics about the Balke protocol are outlined in Dr. Kenneth Cooper's book *Running Without Fear*.[15]

TABLE 5-3
Two Exercise Test Protocols: Naughton and Modified Bruce

	\multicolumn{6}{c}{Stages of Test}
	1	2	3	4	5	6
Naughton Protocol						
Duration (minutes)	3	3	3	3	3	3
Speed (km per hour)	3,2	3,2	3,2	3,2	3,2	3,2
Grade (% uphill slope in treadmill)	0	3,5	7	10,5	14	17,5
METs	2	3	4	5	6	7
Modified Bruce Protocol						
Duration (minutes)	3	3	3	3	3	3
Speed (km per hour)	2,7	2,7	2,7	4	5,4	6,7
Grade (% uphill slope in treadmill)	0	5	10	12	14	16
METs	2	3,5	5	7	10	13

The protocol tells your doctor how to conduct the test—how fast the treadmill should run, for what length of time, and at what grade. As you can see from Table 5-3, the protocol also indicates how many METs a patient is expending during each stage of the test. Each stage requires a change in speed and/or grade.

As the test proceeds, be communicative. Verbalize everything you're experiencing. Just don't look at your doctor while you're talking or you'll lose your balance. Keep looking straight ahead.

If your physician uses the Borg scale (Table 5-1 or 5-2), it will be posted in front of you where you can read it easily. You'll be asked to rate the level of your exertion at the end of each stage of the test, and possibly more often. Our advice is not to analyse the ratings too much before you respond. If you are uncertain about two numbers, pick the higher.

At the end of the test, your physician will tell you to hold on to the front bar of the treadmill as it slows down and levels off in grade. Even after the test is over, you'll be expected to walk at a slow pace for a while to cool down. When the machine is finally switched off, you'll lie down again, this time for six to ten minutes. The technician or nurse will continue to take your blood pressure and ECG at regular intervals during this recovery period. Even while you're resting, problems can develop, so stay communicative. Talk about what you feel happening inside your body.

The Test from Your Doctor's Perspective

A physician is using all five senses and a scientifically trained mind during your exercise test. He or she is observing your appearance, listening to your description of symptoms, monitoring your blood pressure, watching for aberrant ECG patterns, and making note of your endurance by the length of time you're capable of staying on the machine.

What specific abnormalities is your doctor looking for?

There are five major abnormalities: (1) angina during the test; (2) an inadequate rise or actual drop in your systolic blood pressure; (3) complex PVCs; (4) excessive depression or elevation of the ST segment as it appears on your ECG tracing; and (5) an inability to exercise at an energy expenditure of at least 4 METs without developing abnormalities that require the termination of the test.

Let's examine these signs of distress one by one:

Angina. The development of angina during low-level exercise—which is all predischarge patients are being subjected to—is suggestive of extensive residual myocardial ischaemia.

What we must emphasize here is that we are referring to angina, not atypical types of chest pain. This is why it is so important that you describe your symptoms accurately and fully. What is angina to you may, in your doctor's experienced opinion, be something else.

In the event that it is angina, your physician may ask you to grade its intensity using an angina scale such as the one shown in Table 5-4. The scale helps doctors decide when an exercise test should be terminated. The development of angina during predischarge testing indicates the need for angiography.

Blood Pressure Aberrations. As we've cautioned, patients with severe left ventricular impairment should be screened out long before the time comes for a predischarge exercise test. Unfortunately, this doesn't always happen. Don't worry about such an oversight, though. Once a patient is on a treadmill, a doctor can still detect signs of significant left ventricular dysfunction. The telltale sign is when the systolic blood pressure fails to rise in direct proportion to the level of the patient's physical exertion or even actually starts to fall.

Abnormal blood pressure responses occur in as much as 10 to 20 percent of all exercise tests conducted during the first three weeks after a heart attack. This percentage drops precipitously for tests done after four to eight weeks. It is for this reason that, although we take such responses seriously, we do not generally regard them as being indicative of the need for angiography, unless they occur during tests taking place six weeks or more after the attack.

TABLE 5-4
Angina Scale

1+	Light, barely noticeable
2+	Moderate, bothersome
3+	Severe, very uncomfortable
4+	Most severe pain you've ever experienced

Source: American College of Sports Medicine, *Guidelines for Exercise Testing and Prescription,* 3rd ed. Philadelphia: Lea and Febiger, 1986.

Complex PVCs. In Chapter 3, you learned about your heart's natural pacemaker—the S-A node. But under some circumstances, other parts of your heart take over as the pacemaker, giving rise to irregular beats, called *ectopic beats*. Usually, these occur for only a brief time and are of no real consequence. But in a cardiac patient, they can sometimes be of great consequence.

While ectopic beats can arise from the atria or the ventricles, those from the ventricles—called *premature ventricular contractions*, or "PVCs"—are potentially more dangerous because they can precipitate ventricular fibrillation. As we mentioned earlier, if ventricular fibrillation is not treated immediately, it can be fatal.

There are different kinds of PVCs, but they all have one thing in common: they form bizarre shapes on an ECG tracing (examples are shown in Figure 5-3).

The PVCs that are the biggest threat to heart patients are termed complex PVCs. These PVCs occur often; they originate from more than one site in the ventricles; and they occur even more prematurely than other PVCs, or they occur consecutively. The advent of three or more consecutive PVCs is referred to as *ventricular tachycardia*.

Abnormal ST Segment. Although all of the different waves in your ECG are important, the ST segment is the most important for revealing residual myocardial ischaemia. The ST segment is that portion of your ECG tracing between the end of the S wave and the start of the T wave.

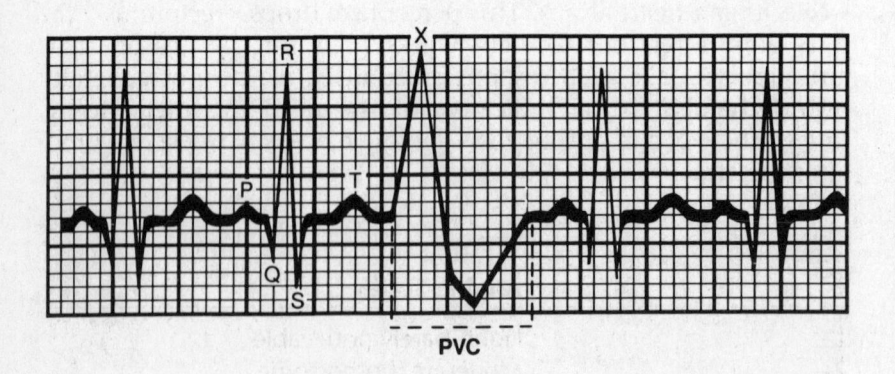

Figure 5-3. PVCs in an ECG tracing. This electrocardiographic tracing shows two PVCs. The R wave of the PVC—indicated here by an X—occurs earlier than would normally be expected. In other words, it occurs prematurely. (*Source:* The Cooper Clinic, Dallas.)

As the ECG diagrams in Figure 5-4 (see pages 92-93) show, in healthy people, the baseline between two successive heartbeats and the ST segment of each beat lie along the same straight line. During exercise, a healthy person's ST segment may slope sharply up toward the baseline. In contrast, when individuals with ischaemia exercise, their ST segment may drop below the baseline and be horizontal or slope downward. In some people, it may also become elevated above the baseline.

ST-segment depression or elevation that is more than one millimetre from where it should ordinarily appear on the ECG graph is abnormal and could indicate severe ischaemia. If the ST-segment depression or elevation does indeed result from ischaemia, then coronary angiography is recommended. (After a heart attack, ST-segment elevation sometimes occurs during exercise as a result of the heart muscle damage itself rather than ischaemia.)

Excessive Fatigue. Cardiac patients who can't withstand the effort required at 4 METs or less are people at greater risk for future heart problems. Four METs is usually achieved about three-quarters of the way through a predischarge exercise test. If abnormalities which require termination of the exercise test occur at this point or before, we would recommend an angiogram.

Of course, some patients have their exercise tests terminated on or before the 4 MET level simply because they've already achieved their heart rate goal. Such patients will want to consult Table 5-5 (on pages 94–95), which contains questions to ask re-

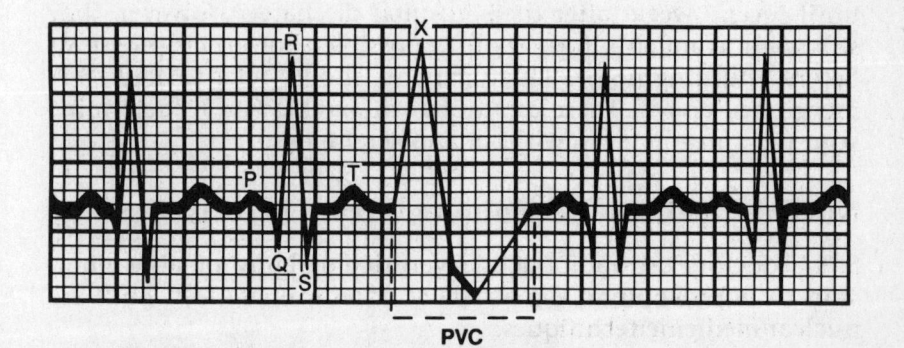

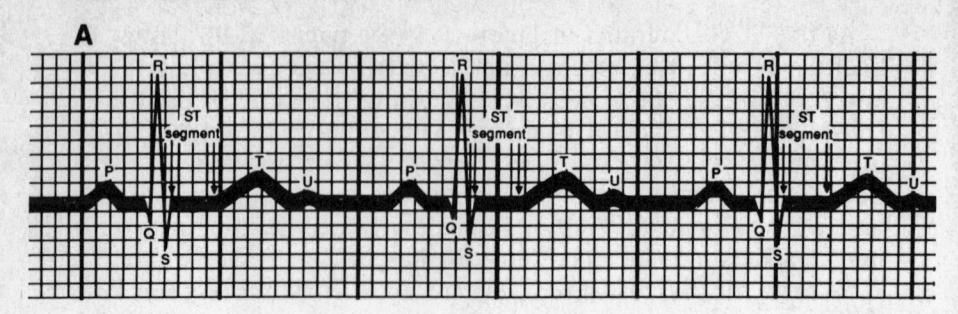

Figure 5-4. ST-segment abnormalities in an ECG tracing. The first of these two electrocardiographic tracings (A) shows a normal ST segment. The second (B) shows a depressed ST segment. A depressed ST segment is suggestive of myocardial ischaemia. (*Source:* The Cooper Clinic, Dallas.)

garding prognosis if the patient *did not* have an exercise test. Although these patients have had an exercise test, they haven't exerted themselves enough during the test for the results to be fully meaningful. That's why the answers to the questions in Table 5-5 are necessary to help determine whether these patients are candidates for an angiogram.

Interpreting Your Exercise Test Results

Most doctors are happy to share exercise test findings in detail with their patients. To help you glean the most information possible from your doctor, we've devised another chart, Table 5-6 (pages 96–97). Asking your doctor these questions should give you insight into your risk category if you're still confused about it.

Of course, many cardiac patients don't have an exercise test until several weeks after their hospital discharge. However, they still want as much information as possible about their prognosis before returning home. These patients should refer to Table 5-5, mentioned above. These questions will enable you to determine your risk category even without an exercise test.

Nuclear Medicine Techniques during Exercise Testing

Some doctors use radionuclide ventriculography or a thallium scan to improve upon the accuracy of an exercise test. Both are nuclear medicine techniques.

Radionuclide ventriculography, mentioned earlier, is mainly used to measure left ventricular function during exercise. The exercise thallium scan helps to assess the extent of residual myocardial ischaemia.

B

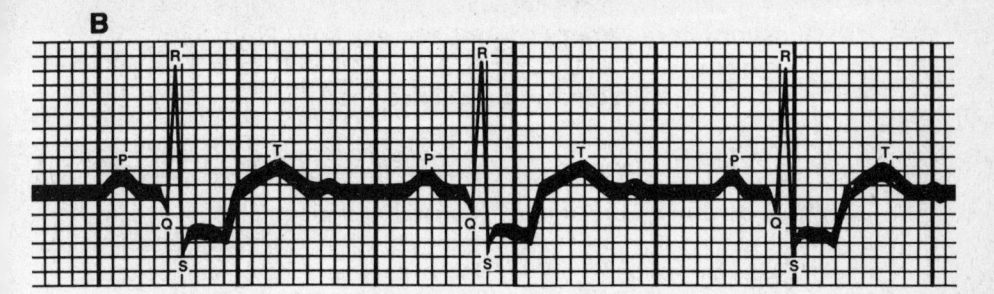

Here's how a thallium scan is conducted. Towards the end of an exercise test, the patient is injected with thallium-201, a radioactive isotope, through an intravenous line. Thallium's extraction from the blood flowing through the coronary arteries is then measured in the moments right after the patient stops exercising, and again three to four hours later.

Immediately after exercise, deficits in thallium uptake occur in regions of the heart where the blood supply is inadequate, as well as in those areas where the heart attack actually occurred. By remeasuring thallium uptake three to four hours after exercise, it's possible to distinguish ischaemic areas of the heart muscle from those that were irreversibly damaged during the heart attack. This is because the deficit in uptake observed immediately after exercise will no longer be present in the ischaemic areas. It is still present only in the damaged part of the heart muscle.

While both radionuclide ventriculography and thallium scans are very useful procedures, neither is widely used during pre-discharge exercise testing. In the Duke University survey we mentioned earlier, only 18 percent of the cardiologists in the USA said they use thallium scans on their cardiac patients during hospitalization, and only 7 percent reported regular use of exercise radionuclide ventriculography.[16] In South Africa both procedures are rare: they are found only in specialized hospitals which have the relevant equipment.

Subsequent Exercise Testing

This is our recommended timetable for post-heart attack exercise testing:
- Before hospital discharge
- During early convalescence (four to eight weeks after the MI)
- During late convalescence (six months after the MI)
- One full year after the MI
- Yearly thereafter

TABLE 5-5
Questions about Your Prognosis to Ask Your Physician before Hospital Discharge if You Did Not Have a Predischarge Exercise Test[a]

Question	Significance of a YES Reply
1. Did I have persistent or recurrent angina at rest 24 or more hours after hospital admission?	Coronary angiography is recommended to assess your suitability for bypass surgery or angioplasty. You are at MODERATE RISK.
2. Did I have cardiogenic shock or rales over more than 50% of my lung fields at some time during my first 5 days of hospitalization?	You probably had an extensive heart attack and have severe left ventricular dysfunction. Holter monitoring is recommended for you. Coronary angiography should be considered to assess your suitability for bypass surgery or angioplasty, but should be delayed to allow sufficient healing to occur, unless your condition is unstable. You are at HIGH RISK.
3. Did I have clinical evidence of significant heart failure at some time during my first 5 days of hospitalization?	If you have had a previous heart attack (besides the present one), significance of reply is similar to that for Question 2. You are at HIGH RISK.
4. Do I have clinical evidence of significant heart failure at present or was a predischarge exercise test contraindicated because of heart failure?	Significance of reply is similar to that for Question 3. You are at HIGH RISK.
5. Is my left ventricular ejection fraction less than 45%?	Significance of reply is similar to that for Question 3. You are at HIGH RISK.
6. Did I have contraindications to predischarge exercise testing besides angina, resting ECG evidence of myocardial ischaemia, or heart failure?	Your precise risk cannot be determined at present. Regard yourself for the moment as being at MODERATE RISK.

TABLE 5-5

Question	Significance of a YES Reply
7. Was an exercise test performed but terminated before I achieved 4 METs for reasons other than an abnormal symptom, sign, or ECG change?	If your left ventricular ejection fraction was not measured, your precise risk cannot be determined at present. Regard yourself for the moment as being at MODERATE RISK. If your left ventricular ejection fraction is equal to or greater than 45%, you are at LOW RISK.

[a]Patients whose exercise test was terminated before they achieved 4 METs for reasons other than an abnormal symptom, sign, or ECG change should also ask these questions. Choose the highest risk group assigned to you when using these questions to determine whether you are at low, moderate, or high risk. Coronary angiography is not recommended for low-risk individuals but should be considered where indicated for those at higher risk.
Source: The Cooper Clinic, Dallas.

We feel this schedule represents the minimum frequency for testing. Of course, we'd expect your doctor to order more frequent testing should there be any significant change in your condition.

We also recommend the more strenuous maximal type of exercise testing from early convalescence on because this is when you'll be starting a serious exercise programme.

During each exercise test, you can utilize the questions in Table 5-6 to re-evaluate your risk status. However, the time of greatest risk for any heart attack sufferer is the first six months after the event. Thus, the actual risk values presented in Figure 5-1 are no longer applicable from the six-month test onward.

Risk Stratification for Bypass and Angioplasty Patients. While it's true that medical researchers have yet to identify the precise factors that determine risk after bypass surgery or angioplasty, many of the same risk-stratification principles we've just outlined are applicable. The risk for future cardiac events in surgery and angioplasty patients, as with those who have suffered heart attacks, is largely dependent on the same two factors—the extent of residual myocardial ischaemia and left ventricular dysfunction.

What about exercise testing for such patients?

We approve of predischarge symptom-limited maximal testing for angioplasty patients, provided these patients have not had a recent heart attack. Symptom-limited maximal testing may also

TABLE 5-6
Questions to Ask Your Physician about Your Predischarge and Early-Convalescence-Period Exercise Test[a]

Question	Significance of a YES Reply or of Specific Value or Name Provided
1. Did I complete the test without developing any abnormal symptoms, signs, or ECG changes?	You are at LOW RISK.
2. a. What was the MET value of the last stage I fully completed? b. Was my test terminated prematurely because I achieved my target heart rate or for any reason other than an abnormal symptom, sign, or ECG change?	This value will be used for determining your prognosis and capacity to resume various activities. If the MET value is less than 4, coronary angiography is recommended to assess your suitability for bypass surgery or angioplasty, unless the reply to 2b is yes (in which case you should ask your physician the questions in Table 5-5). You are at MODERATE RISK if the MET value is less than 4.
3. If the answer to 2a is not known, then: a. For a treadmill test, what protocol was used and what were the speed and gradient for the last stage I fully completed? b. For a cycle test, what was the work rate (in watts or kilogram-metres per minute) for the last stage I fully completed?	If the modified Bruce or Naughton protocol was used, you can look up the MET value in Table 5-3. If not, the MET value can be calculated using the formulas in Appendix A. Significance of this value is the same as for Question 2.
4. What was the MET value of the stage before the one at which I first developed any significant symptom, sign, or ECG abnormality? If the MET value is not known, please provide treadmill speed and gradient, or cycle work rate. (If no abnormalities were noted, no reply is needed.)	This value will be used for determining your capacity to resume various activities and when formulating your exercise prescription.

TABLE 5-6 *(continued)*

Question	Significance of a YES Reply or of Specific Value or Name Provided
5. What was my heart rate when I first developed: a. any significant symptom, sign, or ECG abnormality; or b. in the absence of an abnormality, on completion of the test?	Regard this value as your symptom-limited heart rate. It will be used for determining your capacity to resume various activities and when formulating your exercise prescription.
6. Did I develop angina?	Coronary angiography is recommended to assess your suitability for bypass surgery or angioplasty. You are at MODERATE RISK.
7. a. Did I develop 1 mm or more (measured 0.08 seconds after the J point) ST-segment depression (in the absence of digitalis therapy or a left bundle branch block) or elevation (excluding lead AVR)? b. If it was only ST-segment elevation, was it in leads without significant Q waves?	You are at MODERATE RISK. Unless the answer to 7b is no, coronary angiography is recommended to assess your suitability for bypass surgery or angioplasty.
8. a Did I develop frequent PVCs (more than 30% of beats), multifocal PVCs, ventricular tachycardia, or R-on-T PVCs? b. Did I develop sustained ventricular tachycardia?	You are at MODERATE RISK. Coronary angiography to assess your suitability for bypass surgery or angioplasty is recommended only if the answer to 8b is yes.
9. Did my systolic blood pressure fall by more than 10 mm Hg following an increase in exercise intensity or fail to rise above my resting standing value?	You are at MODERATE RISK. (If the reply to this question is yes when testing is conducted 6 or more weeks after a heart attack, coronary angiography is recommended.)

[a]Choose the *highest* risk group assigned to you when using these questions to determine whether you are at low, moderate, or high risk. Coronary angiography is not recommended for low-risk individuals but should be considered where indicated for those at higher risk.
Source: The Cooper Clinic, Dallas.

be used before discharge in bypass surgery patients who have not had a recent heart attack. However, chest and leg discomfort often prevent such patients from exercising beyond 5 METs (the level at which predischarge testing is terminated for heart attack patients).

Bypass and angioplasty patients should use the guidelines we've outlined in Tables 5-5 and 5-6 to determine whether they're at high, moderate, or low risk for future complications. However, in the absence of a recent heart attack, the actual risk values we've assigned each of the three groupings in Figure 5-1 do not necessarily apply. Also, the indications for coronary angiography aren't necessarily valid. This is partly because these patients have already undergone this diagnostic procedure prior to their bypass or angioplasty.

SUMMARY

This chapter has given you more information about the practice of cardiology than most laypeople have access to. Our aim is to help you optimize the benefits you receive from the various diagnostic tests that you undergo while you're still in the hospital. It is not our intention to turn you into an amateur medical sleuth who second-guesses a doctor's every move and suggestion.

Be aware that the stratification guidelines we've outlined here are based on the latest research and clinical opinion. But also be aware that *there is no single correct approach to such a complex matter as risk stratification.*

Your physician may adopt a recovery plan more conservative—or even more liberal—than ours. If you've got questions about your doctor's approach, we advise you to discuss them frankly and openly. Share any reservations you may have. If what your doctor says makes good sense to you, fine. Follow his or her instructions to the letter. If you're unhappy, get a second opinion.

Remember, you need a good solid relationship with a local doctor if your recuperation is to proceed smoothly and on schedule. No book can take the place of a good, caring physician who is only a phone call away—and a few minutes by car from the nearest hospital.

CHAPTER 6

COMING HOME, MOVING FORWARD

MAKE no mistake about it: your early convalescence at home after a heart attack, bypass surgery, or an angioplasty can be a time fraught with much difficulty. We've already talked about the emotional difficulty—the topsy-turvy way you may react to life for a while. Here we'll discuss the physical hurdles you may encounter over this same time period, the first four to eight weeks after your cardiac hospitalization.

Following the advice in this chapter should help you smooth out the sometimes rocky transition from hospital to home. With the trend toward shorter hospital stays, comprehensive patient education isn't always possible. Books like this one are necessary to fill in the gaps in your knowledge about what to do and what to expect from your body during early convalescence.

There was a time not that many years ago when MI patients could expect to be in a hospital bed for six weeks. During most of that time, they would be "resting", prohibited from almost all physical activity.

Dwight Eisenhower, the president of the USA from 1953 to 1961, focused worldwide attention on cardiac care in 1955 when he suffered his heart attack. He spent seven weeks recuperating in a Washington, D.C., hospital. Two aides would carry him to and from his bed every day—that's how restrictive cardiologists were about activity then! South African doctors were as cautious.

The thinking back then was based on a historic 1939 article in the *American Heart Journal* by Dr. G. Kenneth Mallory, Dr. Paul D. White, and Dr. Jorge Salcedo-Salgar.[1] The article made the claim that any exertion before the scar tissue had completely formed—which can take up to two months—could extend the area of heart muscle damage. It suggested that premature exertion would increase the chance of a ventricular aneurysm forming. (An aneurysm is a weakened portion of the heart that bulges outward during myocardial contractions; aneurysms are dangerous because they can rupture.) The authors concluded: "To advise less than three weeks in bed is unwise, even for patients with the smallest of myocardial infarcts."

Three weeks in bed for cardiac patients today is unheard of. Long gone is the protracted hospitalization and sedentary, year-long convalescence before a patient is declared well enough to return to normal living or productive employment.

What prompted the change?

In 1952, several years before President Eisenhower's highly publicized infarct, two doctors from the Harvard Medical School questioned the conventional wisdom. Dr. Samuel A. Levine and Dr. Bernard Lown, in the *Journal of the American Medical Association,* discussed the results of their study of heart patients who had sat in comfortable chairs as early as the first day in the hospital.[2] Their theory was that, when the patient assumed an upright position, gravity lessened the amount of blood returning to the heart and thereby lessened its work load. Levine and Lown were, in effect, questioning the efficacy of bed rest as a mode of cardiac treatment. In addition to various negative physical effects, too much bed rest induced unnecessary "emotional disquiet and psychological tension", the researchers maintained.

Their more active approach to cardiac care found adherents. By the 1960s the hospital stay for uncomplicated heart attack was down to twenty-one days. By the 1970s it was averaging fourteen days, and in the 1980s it was anywhere from five to ten days. For bypass surgery patients the usual hospital stay is seven or eight days, and it's down to only two or three days for angioplasty patients—assuming neither category includes anyone who has had a recent heart attack. Complications, of course, mean a longer stay.

Even shorter stays for heart attack sufferers can be expected in the 1990s. In a recent study researchers from the University of Michigan Medical Centre in Ann Arbor documented the safety of discharging carefully selected MI patients after only three days.[3] While this one study is not sufficient to justify sweeping changes in the current treatment protocol of heart attack patients, it does demonstrate that the concerns of cardiologists in past decades were largely unfounded, at least regarding patients with uncomplicated heart attacks.

Today, it is well accepted throughout the medical community that prolonged bed rest is a bad thing. It's physically harmful, not to mention demoralizing. Research has shown that prolonged bed rest lowers fitness by reducing the pumping capacity of the heart as well as the capacity of the lungs; alters your heart rate and blood pressure when you shift positions; increases your predisposition to pneumonia, lung collapse, and blood-clot formation; changes your metabolism in a way that may adversely affect the healing of your damaged heart muscle; and creates musculoskeletal problems.

On the other hand, don't think we're champions of strenuous physical activity soon after a heart hospitalization. We are not, for this is potentially worse than too much bed rest. During the first four to eight weeks, when your heart is still in the process of healing, overdoing it can predispose you to a variety of adverse consequences, which we'll cover in a moment.

Moderation must be your watchword during your early convalescence at home. What you—with the advice of your doctor—must strive to achieve is the right balance between the two extremes of too much rest and far too little.

THE TRANSITION FROM HOSPITAL TO HOME

Before leaving the hospital, you must have certain information in order to feel secure about the unsupervised activities you'll be undertaking at home. First of all, make sure you're clear about the medications you'll be taking, how and when to take them, and any special precautions to follow or side effects to be on the lookout for. In fact, you should have all the medications you need before leaving the hospital. (We will discuss cardiac medications in more detail in Appendix E.)

Inquire about the date for your first appointment with your doctor. Generally, the first visit is between two and four weeks after discharge. Ask for a rundown of what will happen during this visit. During this postdischarge examination, many physicians perform a symptom-limited maximal exercise test to clear the way for the patient's return to work. You don't want to arrive at your doctor's rooms without being prepared for it.

After discharge, should you have any remaining questions or concerns, do not hesitate to contact your doctor. Many patients, particularly the stoic deniers, keep away from the phone for fear of raising a false alarm and looking silly. This attitude is foolish. After all, it's your life that could be at stake during this period.

By all means, investigate your local cardiac rehabilitation programme and ask your doctor for advice. Addresses for cardiac rehabilitation centres in South Africa are on page 165. These programmes are excellent sources of advice. In addition, many patients find these groups provide the social stimulus they need to start and remain committed to an exercise regimen. This is important, for regular exercise is the linchpin of your rehabilitation efforts, probably the best single thing you can do to set your feet on the pathway to a healthier life-style.

Perhaps the questions heart patients worry about most upon returning home are: How much is too much? When will it be safe for me to resume my customary self-care activities (pages 107-8) as well as my usual social, recreational, and occupational pursuits?

In our experience, physicians caring for heart patients often err in one of two ways. Either they're from the old school, still imposing severe restrictions, or they act almost blasé about the whole subject of appropriate activity. They wave away patients' questions with a cavalier "Don't worry so much—just don't overdo it", or an abrupt "Just take things easy".

Such responses tell a worried heart patient very little. They hardly constitute instructions. By offering few or no guidelines, these physicians are, in our opinion, making a serious mistake. They're leaving the decision-making entirely up to the patient. The result: patients either revert to self-imposed invalid status or attempt too much activity as a way to test themselves for continual proof that their heart attack was really just a bad dream.

Unfortunately, it takes very little exertion to impress upon overly energetic patients that their M.I was no dream. They discover immediately that they've got much less endurance than before the attack. After attempting an overly ambitious outing or workout, instead of feeling physically healthier, they end up feeling totally exhausted as well as depressed and discouraged, which may be even worse.

Minimal instructions are dangerous, for they leave patients confused. They also invite fights at home. One of the biggest sources of friction between heart patients and their spouses involves clashing interpretations of a doctor's instructions. When instructions are lacking or unclear, the spouse with the nurturing responsibility tends to become overly protective. The effect on the recuperating patient is not good. He or she resents the interference and bridles at being treated like a child. Harsh words may ensue.

Of course, sometimes there is squabbling despite wonderfully detailed medical instructions. We see this happen for a number of reasons. Some patients, to be sure, are overly demanding. But more often, they're simply so self-absorbed that they forget this is a stressful time for other family members too.

Spouses, especially, have a lot of newfound fears and uncertainties: Will I soon be the sole breadwinner in this large household, with four children to feed, clothe, and educate? I don't want to be single again and have to face the world alone. What will I ever do if the worst happens? How will we ever pay the medical bills that are mounting up?

You name it and your spouse may well be feeling it during your early convalescence. Your mate's emotions are likely to run the gamut from blaming you for disrupting the home life and usual daily schedule to feelings of guilt. Yes, we've known spouses who have actually thought that they somehow caused their mate's heart problem. We've also known angry spouses who ate themselves up with frustration at not being able to express any negative emotions at all during this time for fear a confrontation might trigger another heart problem.

Our best advice when either one of you seems overly irritable is to talk about it. Fears and grievances discussed openly, with empathy on both your parts, will go a long way toward relieving the pressure. We also suggest that your spouse do a little reading. A helpful book, by Rhoda F. Levin, the wife of a cardiac patient, is *Heart-Mates: A Survival Guide for the Cardiac Spouse*.[4]

Spouses may disguise their true feelings during times of family stress. But children are pros at it, especially teenagers. Adolescents often respond to either parent's major health problems with a combination of guilt, depression, and misbehaviour. To forestall such reactions, we recommend having a straightforward talk with them. Tell them what you know about your condition. Encourage them to express their feelings, fears, and concerns. And don't let your honest communication end at that. Try to capitalize on the situation by involving your children in your rehabilitation process. Not only will this bring you closer to them, but it may serve to improve their knowledge of what constitutes a healthy life-style—and lessen their chances of developing heart disease themselves someday.

Well-meaning friends can also be an annoyance during convalescence. In an effort to offer encouragement and be helpful, friends often tell stories about acquaintances' and other friends' heart problems. These tales can be riddled with misinformation that increases your anxiety and makes you question the care you're receiving.

The only protection against such meddling is to be well informed yourself. Reading this book will help. However, the knowledge you gain may also make you lose patience when you know that what your friends are saying is wrong. Before you snap back at them, though, remember that they do have your best interests at heart. You're probably more sensitive and quick to anger than usual right now. Count to ten and calmly tell them what you know to be correct. Then change the subject or try this: ask those of your friends who claim they really want to help to get in touch with your regional branch of the Heart Foundation of Southern Africa to learn cardiopulmonary resuscitation (CPR). (Some branches run CPR courses themselves; all can refer you to someone who does.) That way they may be able to save your own or someone else's life one day.

THE DANGERS OF OVERDOING IT

Depending on the extent of the damage and your own rate of healing, your heart will usually take anywhere from four to eight weeks to repair itself by forming scar tissue. Those early cardiologists were right about the time frame; they were guessing about what to do to promote the healing process, though. Bed rest is definitely not the answer.

In truth, however, we're still doing some guessing, for the precise effect of vigorous physical activity during this healing period is not really known even today. Two studies—one using animals and the other using humans—suggest that strenuous exertion during the period when the damaged heart muscle has not healed completely may interfere with scar tissue formation.[5,6] Of course, investigators have not fully tested the effect on human subjects for obvious reasons. So the question remains an open one.

In view of our lack of certainty about what will aid or interfere with heart muscle mending, coronary specialists recommend limited activity even for low-risk patients. With moderate- and high-risk patients, they're even more cautious. Inappropriate exertion could set off myocardial ischaemia, or heart rhythm disturbances, in these higher-risk individuals.

The cautions we've just expressed apply to anyone who has had a heart attack in the past eight weeks. However, if all you've had is an angioplasty, and you developed no complications during the procedure, you can resume your previous level of physical activity almost immediately after your release from the hospital. You may find you still have some discomfort where the catheter was inserted. But this will subside soon enough.

Bypass surgery patients can be assured that no disruption of their wounds is likely to occur after three weeks of healing. What bypass patients do have to worry about, even in subsequent weeks, is overdoing upper-body exercises, especially those concentrating on the chest, arms, and shoulders. This type of exercise, for up to eight weeks after surgery, could interfere with the healing of the sternum.

We aren't saying that you should avoid all upper-body exercise. On the contrary: if you don't maintain a sufficient level of regular movement in your upper body, you may end up having problems with the muscles in your chest wall. It is for this very reason that in many cardiac rehabilitation programmes, bypass patients—immediately after hospital discharge—are asked to perform upper-body exercises using light free weights of about 1,5 kilograms each. The exercises are continued for at least some six or eight weeks, with the weights increasing to up to 3,5 kilograms.

What we are saying, however, is that you should not pull, push, or lift heavy objects (over 4,5 kilograms) because such activities may place a lot of stress on your healing sternum.

Only about 5 percent of bypass patients are instructed to avoid almost all upper-body activity because of sternal instability, so you can see that it is a relatively rare condition. This is how you'll know if you have it: when you push gently on your sternum with your fingers, you will notice movement or a clicking or grating sound. Should this be the case, consult your doctor and be sure to avoid any upper-body exercise until at least a month after this problem disappears.

In some patients who have had bypass surgery, the doctors have transferred a saphenous vein from the inner side of the leg to the heart for use as a bypass around blocked coronary arteries. Any resulting leg discomfort should subside within four weeks. However, you might want to wear elastic stockings to lessen any leg pain and swelling during this period.

On the other hand, if the internal mammary artery, located in the chest, was used, it's likely that you'll experience more chest-wall discomfort than your saphenous-vein counterparts. The reason is obvious: you had more surgery in the chest and greater manipulation of the sternum. Expect this discomfort in the chest region to persist for up to two weeks after your operation.

ASSESSING HOW MUCH ACTIVITY IS RIGHT FOR YOU

Ideally, you'd like an activity programme during your early convalescence period that is geared especially to you. Fortunately, this is now possible, thanks to the concept of METs, to which you were introduced in the previous chapter.

Over the last several decades, there's been a lot of research in laboratories around the world aimed at pinpointing the exact energy requirements for performing various tasks. As a consequence, we now have scientific lists quantifying the strenuousness of activities ranging from the mundane to the sublime. These lists tell you how much effort is required to perform tasks such as vacuuming or light carpentry, or to do a specific type of exercise, such as walking. Such lists are a recuperating heart patient's lifeline.

You'll recall that one of the aims of the exercise test given to you before your release from the hospital—or of any exercise test you took shortly thereafter—was to determine, in METs, the maximum exercise intensity you are able to tolerate without adverse cardiac effects (see Question 4 or, in the absence of abnormalities, Question 2a of Table 5-6). Once you know how much this is, then it's simply a matter of taking that number and using it as a reference as you scan Table 6-1 (pages 107–108). It shows approximate energy expenditures (in METs) for various physical activities that are appropriate during early convalescence. With this list, you can easily see which activities are acceptable.

For those of you who were able to exercise at intensities above 5 METs without any problems, we still do not recommend participating in any activity that requires more than 5 METs during the first six weeks after your heart attack.

For bypass surgery and angioplasty patients who have not had a heart attack within the past six weeks, activities above 5 METs are acceptable, within these limits: refer back to the MET value your physician gave as the answer to Question 4 or, in the absence of abnormalities, Question 2a of Table 5-6. We recommend that you confine your exertion to at least 1 MET below the MET value you find there. For example, a bypass surgery patient who completes 7 METs would perform only those activities of 6 METs or below.

Let's suppose you had no exercise test upon which to base a judgment about your maximum MET level and you're classified as a high-risk patient. Our advice is this: *Do not perform any activities with a MET rating of more than 3 during the first four to eight weeks after your heart attack.* On the other hand, if you're a moderate-risk patient who did not have an exercise test, we recommend that you restrict yourself to 4 METs or less over the same period.

TABLE 6-1
Approximate Energy Expenditures for Various Physical Activities[a]

METs	Self-Care	Housework	Recreational	Occupational
1–2	Resting, lying down Sitting Standing, relaxing Talking Eating Dressing Undressing Washing hands and face	Sewing Knitting	Drawing, sitting Painting, sitting Playing cards Strolling (1,6 km/h)	Light desk work Using calculator
2.1–3	Bathing Showering	Polishing furniture Sweeping floor Scrubbing, standing Peeling potatoes Kneading dough Light laundering by hand Sewing with machine Using riding lawn mower Carrying light trays or dishes	Drawing, standing Billiards, non-competitive Level walking (3,2 km/h) Level cycling, away from traffic (8 km/h) Playing piano and many musical instruments Woodworking, light	Bakery, general Bookbinding Car repair, standing Radio repair TV repair Janitorial work Bartending Typing
3.1–4		Scrubbing floors Cleaning windows Making beds Vacuuming carpets Ironing, standing Mopping Wringing by hand Hanging washing	Croquet, non-competitive Fishing from bank Level walking (4,8 km/h) Level cycling, away from traffic (9,6 km/h) Slow social dancing Swimming, social	Bricklaying Plastering Machine assembly Welding, moderate load Cutting wood with power saw Stock clerk activities Locksmith

107

TABLE 6-1 (continued)
Approximate Energy Expenditures for Various Physical Activities[a]

METs	Self-Care	Housework	Recreational	Occupational
4.1–5		Stocking shelves Pushing light power mower Wallpapering Raking leaves Hoeing Weeding	Social dancing, energetic Level walking (5,5 km/h) Level cycling, away from traffic (12,8 km/h) Fly-fishing, standing, with waders	Light carpentry Paperhanging Painting Bricklaying
5.1–6		Garden digging Shovelling light earth	Stream fishing, walking in light current in waders Social dancing, more energetic Level walking (6,4 km/h) Level cycling, away from traffic (16 km/h)	
6.1–7		Shovelling, 10 per minute (4,5 kg) Splitting wood Hand lawn-mowing	Social dancing, very energetic Level walking (8 km/h) Level cycling, away from traffic (17,6 km/h)	

[a] The energy requirements of these tasks can be reduced by performing them less vigorously and by interspersing the activities with short rest periods.
Compiled from several sources: see N. F. Gordon, "Inpatient Cardiac Rehabilitation," *South African Medical Journal*, 65 (1984): 78–82.

But no matter where you fall in terms of risk category, we make this blanket recommendation concerning athletics: *avoid all competitive sports and physical activities during your early convalescence period.*

You can, however, participate in a sport if two conditions prevail: (1) You're doing it for purely social reasons—that is, no scorekeeping, which immediately turns exercise into competition—and (2) the sport's MET level doesn't exceed your acceptable MET level. Frankly, most sports probably will exceed this level, as you can see by consulting Table 6-2 on page 110.

JOHN VENTER'S EARLY CONVALESCENCE REGIMEN

Let's return to John Venter, whose case study we have been following. John, in his usual thorough fashion, followed our recommendations about his exercise test to the letter. You can follow the same process—provided you had an exercise test before discharge or soon thereafter.

John's predischarge test was based on the Naughton protocol. As we counsel patients to do, John asked his doctor the series of questions listed in Table 5-6, for he was determined to find out as much as he could about his condition and the restrictions it would impose on his life over the next few weeks. Table 6-3 (see page 111) shows the replies that John's doctor gave to his queries. Note that the reply to Question 1 was no. Thus, John knows that he did develop some abnormality during his test. For this reason, he used the value from Question 4—4 METs—as his maximum MET activity level. However, if the answer John had received to Question 1 had been yes, the MET value given in Question 2 (or determined from Question 3) would have been the value to use.

John's next step was to scan Tables 6-1 and 6-2 to pick out all the activities that require 4 METs of energy or less. That was the upper limit of his activity level over the eight weeks of his early recovery period.

We realize that some of our readers may wish to get involved in activities other than those included in Tables 6-1 and 6-2. In that case, your heart rate becomes the key to deciding whether a particular activity is appropriate or not. In fact, even if the activity you perform is listed in either of these tables, you should still use your heart rate response to verify that it is indeed appropriate for you.

Table 6-2
Energy Expenditures for Various Sporting Activities

Sport	Range (METs)
Backpacking	5–11
Badminton	4–9+
Basketball	3–12+
Bowling	2–4
Canoeing, rowing	3–8
Cricket	5–8
Dance, aerobic	6–9
Fencing	6–10+
Golf	
Using power cart	2–3
Walking (carrying bag or pulling cart)	4–7
Hiking (cross-country)	3–7
Horse riding	2–8
Hunting (bow or gun)	
Small game (walking, carrying light load)	3–7
Big game (dragging carcass, walking)	3–14
Running (1,5 km in 6 to 12 minutes)	9–16
Scuba diving	5–10
Skating, ice and roller	5–8
Skipping	9–12
Skiing, snow	
Downhill	5–8
Cross-country	6–12+
Soccer	5–12+
Squash	8–12+
Table tennis	3–5
Tennis	4–9+
Touch rugby	6–10
Volleyball	3–6

Source: American College of Sports Medicine, *Guidelines for Exercise Testing and Prescription,* 3rd ed. Philadelphia: Lea and Febiger, 1986.

The reason your heart rate response is so important is probably obvious: from a cardiac point of view, the safety of various activities is largely dependent on the oxygen demand they place on your heart muscle. Technically, this would be determined most accurately by multiplying your heart rate by your systolic blood pressure while you're in the middle of the activity. Since this isn't practical, monitoring your pulse rate will suffice. Even

TABLE 6-3
Case History: John Venter's Queries to His Doctor about His Predischarge Exercise Test and the Doctor's Answers[a]

Question (see Table 5-6)	Reply	Reason for the Reply
1	No	John developed 1,5 mm of ST-segment elevation during Stage 4 of the Naughton protocol.
2a	5 METs	Stage 4 corresponds to 5 METs. Although he developed an ECG abnormality during this stage, it was not severe enough to terminate the test, which he was able to complete.
2b	No	
3a and 3b	—	His physician knew the answer to Question 2a, so John didn't have to ask Question 3.
4	4 METs	The level of ST-segment elevation only became abnormal during Stage 4 of his test. During Stage 3, which took 4 METs' worth of John's energy, he had no significant abnormalities.
5a	114 beats per minute	This was John's heart rate when his ST-segment elevation first exceeded 1 mm. Because he developed an abnormality, he didn't have to ask Question 5b.
5b	—	
6	No	Although he developed ST-segment elevation, he did not experience angina.
7a	Yes	He developed more than 1 mm of ST-segment elevation. Because the reply was yes, he is at MODERATE RISK.
7b	No	His ST-segment elevation occurred in leads with significant Q waves.[b] (If the reply to this question had been yes, coronary angiography would have been recommended.)
8a and 8b	No	He did not develop any of these complex PVCs.
9	No	His systolic blood pressure increased as expected.
On the basis of these replies, John knows he is at MODERATE RISK		

[a] John Venter received a predischarge exercise test using the Naughton protocol (see Table 5-3). The questions John asked his doctor appear in Table 5-6 (pages 96–97)
[b] This means that his ST-segment elevation is probably a result of heart muscle damage itself rather than ischaemia.[7]

by itself, it's an excellent indicator of your heart muscle's oxygen requirement. We'll go into detail about how to take your pulse in Chapter 8.

You'll recall that one of a physician's goals during a predischarge exercise test is to determine the heart rate at which cardiac patients first develop cardiac problems or, in the absence of such problems, the heart rate upon completion of their exercise test. This is termed the *symptom-limited heart rate.*

During physical activity after your hospital release, you are at greatest risk for complications when you go beyond your symptom-limited heart rate. For this reason, *do not exceed 85 percent of your symptom-limited heart rate during your early convalescence.* If you completed your exercise test without any abnormalities, we still advise you not to exceed 85 percent of the peak heart rate reached during your test. To return to John Venter for a moment, his symptom-limited heart rate was 114 beats per minute, which meant that his heart rate could not exceed 97 beats per minute (85 percent of 114 beats per minute: $114 \times {}^{85}/_{100} = 97$ beats per minute).

In Chapter 5, we introduced you to the Borg perceived exertion scale. You can also use this as a guide in deciding on the right activity level. If you do, use Table 5-1 and *do not exceed a score that corresponds to "somewhat hard" on this scale.*

We hope it goes without saying that you must also apply some common sense to the process of working out which activities to pursue at what intensity. Charts and scientifically derived formulas are fine, but if an activity makes you feel exhausted, causes cardiac abnormalities, or otherwise sends out the strong message that you're overdoing it, immediately slow down and, if necessary, terminate that activity (see Table 6-4). Into this category may fall activities that are not physically strenuous but are stressful or emotionally taxing. Situations that induce anxiety, stress, fear, or excitement may be too much for you in your present condition. Examples are driving a car in heavy traffic, watching a tumultuous sporting event (such as the Currie Cup final!), or making a speech before a roomful of strangers.

Circumstances and situations like these require you and your doctor to use your best judgment. However, because we know this issue of "How much is too much?" is of major concern to coronary patients, we want to offer as much expert opinion on the subject as possible in order to set your mind at rest. To this end, we conducted a survey of twenty-one international authorities in the field of cardiac rehabilitation—all editors or editorial review board members of the *Journal of Cardiopulmonary Rehabilitation,* the official publication of the highly respected American Association of Cardiovascular and Pulmonary Rehabilitation. In our poll, we asked respondents to indicate how long

TABLE 6-4
Heart Alerts: What to Do When Symptoms Occur

This list outlines many of the symptoms and signs that could indicate all is not well with your body. It's meant to help you separate the false alarms from the true emergencies requiring immediate medical attention.

Is it Angina or Just Some Other Discomfort?

The patient most likely to have to make this distinction is someone who has had bypass surgery, which leaves many people sore in unexpected places.

To help you decide whether the discomfort you're feeling in the chest, neck, jaw, arms, back, or abdomen is really angina, ask yourself:

Does the discomfort get worse when I move my arms, neck, or shoulders?

Does the nature of the discomfort change when I change position?

Does pressing on the area of discomfort make it worse?

Did the discomfort last for only a second or two?

If you answer yes to any of these questions, then the discomfort probably is not angina.

On the other hand, if you decide it is angina, slow down or stop what you are doing immediately. The symptoms should subside within a minute or two, in which case you needn't be unduly alarmed. If not, your physician may have prescribed nitroglycerin tablets (or an oral spray) for just such an occurrence. Take one tablet or dose as directed.

If the discomfort is still present after another five minutes, take a second tablet. Again, wait for five minutes. If this doesn't work either, take a final nitroglycerin tablet and call your physician immediately.

(You might want to refer back to Chapter 3 for a full discussion of anginal pain.)

Shortness of Breath and Nausea

How alarmed you should be depends on whether either of these conditions was precipitated by exertion or undue stress. If they were, they may be anginal equivalents. Stop the activity that triggered the problem and rest completely for several minutes. If the symptoms persist, follow the above instructions for angina.

Shortness of breath occurring at rest is another matter. It is sometimes a sign of left-sided heart failure—that is, your left ventricle is not pumping as efficiently as it should. It's caused by blood backing up in the vessels in your lungs.

This surprise windedness is often experienced when patients are lying flat on their backs, sometimes when they're asleep. They wake up experiencing this somewhat frightening difficulty in breathing.

It can often be relieved by simply sitting upright on the side of your bed with your feet on the ground for several minutes, or by getting up

TABLE 6-4 *(continued)*

and moving about. Then, when you return to bed, prop up your upper body with several pillows before you attempt to go back to sleep. The effect of gravity lessens the backup of blood in your lungs.

However, if the symptom is not relieved by this procedure, don't wait until the morning to call your doctor. When excessive, the backup of blood in the lung vessels causes fluid to be forced out of the vessels and into the breathing spaces themselves, a condition called *pulmonary oedema*. It's serious.

Light-Headedness or Dizziness

We are not referring to the feeling a lot of us have when we stand up suddenly from a crouching or prone position. That's common. If you've ruled this out, the symptoms could be indicative of myocardial ischaemia or left ventricular dysfunction.

These symptoms can often be relieved by lying down. Even if they do disappear relatively quickly, be sure to let your doctor know about them.

Excessive Nighttime Urination; Swollen Feet, Ankles, or Legs; Mass Gain Without a Change in Your Eating Habits

All could be signs of right-sided heart failure, meaning your right ventricle is not functioning properly, which causes blood returning to the heart to back up in the veins. In turn, this causes fluid to be forced out of the blood vessels and into your tissues. Swelling of the lower extremities tends to occur because of the effect of gravity pulling the blood down to this region. An increase in urination occurs because your kidneys are attempting to remove the excess fluid buildup.

All of the above are symptoms that usually develop gradually. When they get bad enough for you to notice them, call your doctor.

Heart Palpitations

The ones to be concerned about are very rapid or irregular. They can signal that you have a heart rhythm disturbance that may or may not be serious. Be sure to let your physician know about it.

Pain, Swelling, Redness, or "Heat" in Your Calf

This could signal a blood clot or "deep venous thrombosis" in your leg.

To prevent this from occurring, don't sit for long periods of time. Get up every hour or two to walk around and revive the circulation in your body and legs, particularly during long drives or flights. Periodic motion reduces the risk of blood-clot formation, a problem more for some patients than others.

For Bypass Patients Only: Fever, Chills and Other Signs of a Wound Infection

Any redness around or draining from incisions must be reported to your physician as soon as possible.

Source: The Cooper Clinic, Dallas.

after a heart attack, bypass surgery, or angioplasty they generally advise patients in the various risk categories to wait before resuming various common stressful or emotionally taxing activities. Their answers are given in Table 6-5 on pages 116–117.

THE DELICATE MATTER OF SEX

Almost all heart patients have serious concerns about whether they will ever be able to return to an active sex life. Indeed, there are probably more myths about heart attacks and sex than about any other topic. Our very first recommendation to you is this: discount all the movies you've seen and novels you've read where a character dies during sexual intercourse. Death during intercourse may make for a dramatic fictional scene, but it doesn't correlate well with reality. In truth, sex does not place much strain on your heart.

As we mentioned briefly in Chapter 2, research conducted by Dr. Herman K. Hellerstein and Dr. Ernest H. Friedman shows that the physical demands of sexual intercourse are not as great as people assume.[8] In their study, which involved the use of Holter ECG monitors in married couples, the partners' heart rates rarely rose above 130 beats per minute at orgasm. The average value was 117 beats per minute. For the two minutes prior to orgasm, the average rate was 87 beats per minute, and heart rates tended to return to this level within about one minute after orgasm. In terms of METs, the average energy expenditure during sexual intercourse was 3,4 METs, with 4,6 METs at orgasm. These numerical observations led Dr. Hellerstein and Dr. Friedman to conclude that the energy output during intercourse is "similar to that of climbing a flight of stairs, walking briskly, or performing ordinary tasks in many occupations".

On the basis of this information and other corroborating findings in the medical literature, it's easy to see that sexual activity after a heart attack is not a particularly risky endeavour. To the contrary, it is normal, desirable, and healthy—provided it's with a familiar partner in surroundings that are inviting and familiar. In our survey of cardiac rehabilitation experts, they were asked to comment on this issue of when it is safe to resume your sex life, and their replies are included in Table 6-5.

To ease the transition back into a healthy and fulfilling sex

Table 6-5
The Experts' Opinions: Recommended Time Intervals before Resuming Various Activities after a Heart Attack or Major Cardiac Procedure[a]

Activity	Heart Attack Low Risk	Heart Attack Higher Risk	Bypass Surgery Low Risk	Bypass Surgery Higher Risk	Angioplasty Low Risk	Angioplasty Higher Risk
1. Minor dental surgery, requiring a local anaesthetic	4	8	4	6	1	4
2. Minor surgery, requiring a local anaesthetic	4	8	4	8	2	4
3. Surgery requiring a general anaesthetic	7	12	6	12	3	7
4. Driving a car short distances in light traffic	2	4	3	5	1	2
5. Driving a car short distances in heavy traffic	3	6	4	8	1	3
6. Driving a car long distances	4	8	4	8	2	4
7. Travelling as passenger during long-distance car trip	4	8	4	8	2	4
8. Riding a motorcycle	6	—	8	—	3	—
9. Taking a domestic flight on a commercial aircraft	3	6	3	6	1	3
10. Taking an international flight on a commercial aircraft	6	10	4	12	2	4
11. Going on an ocean cruise	6	10	6	12	2	4
12. Going on holiday	3	6	3	7	2	4
13. Attending a family member's wedding	2	4	2	4	0	2
14. Attending a family member's funeral	2	4	2	4	1	3
15. Attending a friend's wedding	2	4	2	4	0	1
16. Attending a friend's funeral	2	4	2	4	1	4
17. Making a speech in public	4	8	4	8	1	4
18. Going to the cinema	2	3	2	3	0	2

117

TABLE 6-5 (continued)

Activity	Heart Attack Low Risk	Heart Attack Higher Risk	Bypass Surgery Low Risk	Bypass Surgery Higher Risk	Angioplasty Low Risk	Angioplasty Higher Risk
19. Watching an exciting sporting event on television	2	4	2	4	0	2
20. Attending a live sporting event	3	6	3	6	1	3
21. Attending a live concert	3	5	2	4	1	2
22. Going to church or another place of worship	1	2	1	2	0	1
23. Engaging in sexual intercourse with your spouse	3	4	3	6	1	2
24. Engaging in sexual intercourse with an unfamiliar partner	6	10	6	10	4	8
25. Going shopping at a busy shopping centre	2	5	2	5	1	2
26. Returning to a sedentary occupation	4	8	4	8	1	2
27. Returning to a sedentary but stressful occupation	6	11	6	12	1	4
28. Taking a sauna	6	—	6	—	2	—
29. Swimming in the sea	4	8	6	10	2	4
30. Taking the grandchildren out for the afternoon without assistance	4	6	4	6	1	3

[a] This chart is based on the expert opinions of some twenty-one world-renowned authorities on cardiac rehabilitation. It is intended only to provide you and your physician with guidance. Different people respond differently to stressful and emotional events. The way in which you typically respond must be taken into consideration by your physician when making a final decision.

For the purpose of this chart, low-risk patients are defined in the same way as in Chapter 5. Higher-risk patients, on the other hand, include those we classified earlier as being at moderate and at high risk.

The numbers in each column refer to the number of weeks after your heart attack, bypass surgery, or angioplasty that the experts recommend you wait before resuming specific activities. Note that "0" means you may resume the activity immediately after hospital discharge and "—" means that the activity is inappropriate, at least during the first 12 weeks after your heart attack, bypass surgery, or angioplasty.

If you suffered a heart attack and then had angioplasty (within 6 weeks after your heart attack)—or if you suffered a heart attack during the angioplasty—it's critically important for you to follow the heart attack recommendations.

life, here are some guidelines:

Affection Is Always Possible. Simple acts such as hugging, touching, and caressing without the goal of orgasm require very little energy. Feel free to do so immediately after hospital discharge. At this time, affectionate gestures are a good way to express love and get back in touch with your sexual partner before moving on, a little later, to sexual intercourse.

We recommend that you gradually build up to intercourse over a few days or even weeks. Cuddling for a while without the added pressure of worrying about performance is important. Go slowly, for emotional and psychological reasons more than for safety ones. A successful first encounter is far more important than an early, awkward, misguided fumble.

Advice to Premenopausal Women. Younger female cardiac patients who might still be able to get pregnant should consult their doctor about appropriate contraception. Certainly this early recovery period is not the time to risk a pregnancy. As a heart patient, the Pill will probably be off limits to you forever because it increases your predisposition to blood-clot formation. When administered to postmenopausal women, oestrogen is usually given in doses lower than those contained in contraceptive pills. However, postmenopausal oestrogen should still be used with caution in CHD patients and only by those women for whom it is clearly needed. Interestingly, in women without CHD, postmenopausal oestrogen use is thought to reduce the risk of developing CHD.

Lower Your Expectations for a While. Even though you may have had a good sexual relationship with your partner before your heart attack, don't expect too much from each other sexually during your early convalescence. Remember, you've both been through a very stressful experience. During this period, open communication about any apprehensions either of you may have is far more important than sex. Indeed, if you rush into sex prematurely, before you're psychologically ready for it, problems will surely arise. On the other hand, if you're eager to resume your sex life because you feel sexual desire or frustration, go ahead and indulge. Avoidance in such an instance could place your heart at greater risk than the mild physical effort that intercourse requires.

We'll never forget one patient's reaction when he got the go-ahead to resume sexual activity. With his wife at his side, Mike beamed and said, "Doctors, you've just made my week! I'd say you've got two choices. Either end this visit right now so I can get home, or take me and my wife back into that examination room and lock the door behind you as you leave." Back home, Mike bathed, shaved, and splashed on his best cologne. He opened a bottle of wine, turned on soft music, and generally set the stage for a romantic evening of lovemaking. Mike didn't push. Still, it soon became clear that his wife was scared to death and wouldn't be able to respond with any real abandon. It dawned on Mike that he would have to get over this hurdle right then and there or the problem would simply fester and ruin what had always been a joyous sex life. We don't condone what Mike did next—or recommend that any of you try it—but it did work for this couple. During foreplay, Mike suddenly arched his back, grabbed at his chest, sucked in air, and fell off the bed, seemingly in great pain. His wife assumed it was another heart attack and instantly began administering CPR. At that point, Mike dropped the pretence and began kissing her passionately, finally blurting out, "It's about time you came to life!" Naturally, she was as outraged as she was relieved at his deception. Mike claims a lot of items got broken in their room that night as his wife vented her rage. But he's proud of the fact that they were able to laugh about it. And she never again treated him as if he were ready to break at the slightest touch.

Seek Out the Familiar. Convalescence is no time for sexual experimentation. Resume sexual intercourse in your usual surroundings at a time when both you and your spouse are rested and relaxed. Sex should be postponed if either of you is tense, angry, upset, or tired. Also, the room temperature should be at a comfortable level. Extreme temperatures place more stress on the heart. Because the process of digesting food also makes your heart work harder, it's best to wait about two hours or more after eating a heavy meal before having sex.

Reduce Alcohol Consumption. Ordinarily, small amounts of alcohol won't interfere with your sexual ability. However, alcohol is a depressant and the combination of even small quantities of alcohol with existing depression, which many post-heart attack patients feel, is not conducive to good sex. Even if you aren't depressed, we recommend you limit alcohol intake to no more than two drinks before any sexual encounter.

Don't Skip Over Foreplay. While it's never a good idea to do this, it's an especially bad idea during your early convalescence.

Besides creating a relaxed atmosphere and enhancing a couple's enjoyment, foreplay allows for a gradual increase in heart rate. It serves to prepare you for sexual intercourse in the same way that a warm-up prepares you for exercise. (You'll hear more about the theory behind pre-exercise warm-up in Chapter 8.)

Leave Out the Acrobatics. This is the wrong time to experiment with new positions. Stick with the tried and true. Although there is no research indicating that the top position is any more stressful to your heart than the bottom, what you should avoid is supporting your body on your hands, because this position amounts to isometric exercise. Isometrics is a passive form of exercise that involves tensing one set of muscles against another or against an immovable object. As you will learn later, such exercise is not advisable for moderate-risk, and especially not for high-risk, patients. Lifting a heavy object and changing a tyre are also isometric-type activities, which is why they're also potentially bad for higher-risk patients. So what's your alternative? We recommend that you partially support yourself on your elbows and forearms when assuming the top position.

While the position you choose for intercourse is up to you, it should be comfortable and permit unrestricted breathing. For bypass patients who have discomfort in the region of their chest incision, sex may be easier with both partners lying on their sides, either facing each other or with one behind the other. Such positions place less pressure on the chest wall.

It is a good idea to alert your partner to any tender areas. For example, angioplasty patients or those who have undergone an angiogram may experience tenderness in their groin at the site where the catheter was inserted.

Don't Misinterpret Normal Reactions. When you engage in intercourse after a heart attack or major cardiac procedure, you may find yourself monitoring your responses very closely. You may also find yourself becoming alarmed by responses that are actually normal.

This is what should happen, so don't worry when it does: as you become sexually aroused, your breathing usually becomes faster and deeper. You may sweat and your heart rate accelerates. As your excitement progresses, your heartbeat may be felt as a throbbing in your head or chest. Following orgasm, arousal gradually subsides over a period of several minutes.

These responses invariably accompany sexual intercourse, but go largely unnoticed. After a heart attack, though, you are likely to be more alert to such feelings and more apt to misinterpret their meaning. Unless any of them lasts more than five minutes after intercourse or you develop one or more of the abnormal symptoms we outlined in Table 6-4, none of these responses is cause for alarm.

Be Aware of Your Heart's Reaction. Should you experience any problems during sex that you think could be due to your heart condition, stop and tell your partner.

If you develop angina, for instance, follow the nitroglycerin instructions outlined in Table 6-4. In fact, during subsequent sexual encounters, you may want to take a nitroglycerin tablet or similar medication fifteen minutes or so before sex to forestall the development of chest discomfort during intercourse.

If any other heart-related problem occurs which does not subside after five minutes of resting, call your physician immediately. However, should the problem subside within that time, you can continue where you left off if you feel up to it. Should the problem then recur, stop any sexual activity for the rest of the day. At some convenient time, we advise you to call your doctor to discuss the matter. A small change in your medication may be all that is needed to rectify the problem.

Don't Discount the Dampening Effect of Medications. Be aware that many drugs, including some used by cardiac patients, can have an adverse effect on sexual desire and performance. At the head of the list are some tranquillizers and antidepressant drugs. Beta-blockers and diuretics don't normally interfere with sexual function, which is not to say that they won't in individual cases.

Should you experience sexual problems while taking any of the medications we just mentioned—or any others, for that matter—we encourage you to consult your physician. Sometimes the problem can be alleviated by scheduling sex when blood levels of a problem medication are low—some six to ten hours after taking the drug.

What about marijuana, amphetamines, cocaine, and other similar drugs? These aren't safe because they increase your heart's energy requirements and predispose you to heart rhythm disturbances. Amyl nitrite is something else to avoid. It could interact adversely with cardiac drugs you're taking.

Don't Be Embarrassed to Question Your Doctor about Sex. If you are unsure of or concerned about anything whatsoever related to your sex life, discuss it with your physician. While you shouldn't expect miracles, you should expect your sexual life to return to a level satisfactory to both you and your partner within three to six months. Otherwise, we would advise you to consider sexual counselling. There is no reason why patients should let unfounded fears about their heart condition blot out their sex life—and, as a consequence, cast a shadow over their marriage or a steady relationship. For more details about resuming sexual functioning after a heart attack or major cardiac procedure, you may want to consult a booklet called *The Sensuous Heart*.[9]

WHAT ABOUT ALCOHOL AND CAFFEINE?

As we've mentioned, our stance on alcohol is simple. We advise all our patients—heart patients as well as healthy patients—to limit their alcohol intake to no more than two drinks a day. We define one drink as any beverage containing two tots of 25 millilitres of 100-proof liquor, 150 millilitres of wine, or 300 millilitres of beer.

To date, there's conflicting evidence about caffeine's impact on CHD. It appears from existing studies that moderate caffeine consumption is probably not a major contributor to CHD risk. On the other hand, heavy caffeine intake—five or more cups of coffee a day—may cause a slight rise in risk.

What caffeine can do is predispose certain susceptible people to heart rhythm disturbances. Thus, patients with PVCs or episodes of palpitations should limit their intake of all caffeinated beverages. You and your doctor need to confer about the precise degree of restriction. Some patients may benefit from total abstinence.

Overall, we believe it's prudent for anyone with CHD to limit their daily caffeine intake to no more than 200 milligrams (one cup of coffee contains 100 milligrams; one 150 ml serving of tea, 50 milligrams; and one 300 ml soft drink, 50 milligrams). Where possible, decaffeinated beverages should be substituted for those with caffeine.

RETURNING TO WORK

Returning to work is another area fraught with misconceptions. In this section, we'll try to dispel them.

First of all, your major concern should not be *whether* you'll be able to return to work, but *when*. Many readers of this book will not be people whose work involves heavy physical labour. However, if you do engage in work of this kind, discuss your situation fully with your doctor.

Nor should you worry that the mental stress of white-collar work is more than you'll be able to endure now that you're a diagnosed heart patient. While the work environment is presumed to be more stressful, at least psychologically, than the home environment, you wouldn't know it from a random poll of where patients' heart attacks occurred: It's probably split about equally between home and work.

Also, we find there's plenty of self-imposed stress associated with recuperating cardiac patients' feelings of financial insecurity. Moreover, many patients find it hard to deal with their forced absence from familiar routines, not to mention the "withdrawal symptoms" they experience because of the disruption of their long-established work role.

In short, unless your work involves hard labour, there's no reason why you can't return to it after only a short delay. There can be no doubt that it is far healthier for the vast majority of heart patients to return to work rather than let their heart condition turn them into brooding invalids. Sixty to ninety days—some two or three months—is the average return-to-work time for patients with uncomplicated heart attacks. This average has not changed appreciably over the last two decades even though hospital stays have shrunk. And a recent study shows that low-risk patients who return to work earlier do not experience any more cardiac complications than their longer-recuperating counterparts.[10] In fact, the feeling of economic security that a fast return to work engenders may be extremely beneficial to many patients from a health standpoint.

In most cases, the most powerful determinants of when to return to work are doctors' recommendations combined with patients' own perceptions of their health. Physicians' advice is based, to a large extent, on subjective judgments. Physicians who are reluctant to let patients return to work within four to eight weeks often perceive a greater risk for repeat cardiac problems during recovery than there really is. The recommendations of our panel of cardiac rehabilitation experts with respect to returning to work also appear in Table 6-5.

We recommend that patients undergo a repeat exercise test before they return to work. In contrast to the predischarge test, which was submaximal, this one should be a symptom-limited maximal test. That means the test will continue until you either develop abnormalities or are too fatigued to go any further.

A recent study emphasizes the positive psychological effect such a test can have on insecure patients.[11] Subjects were divided into two groups. The first took symptom-limited maximal treadmill tests about twenty-three days after their heart attacks. Based on the results, they were told they could return to work anytime after the next two weeks. The second group, whose health status was similar, did not receive such an evaluation. The results demonstrate just how frightened many patients are. Those in the first group returned to work an average of fifty-one days after their heart attacks even though the doctors had recommended they return by around the fortieth day. It took patients in the second group some seventy-five days to work up the courage to go back to work, though they too had doctor's approval.

In general, we suggest that you return to work in accordance with your physician's recommendations. However, if they differ from the guidelines in Table 6-5, you should discuss the discrepancy with your doctor. And to satisfy yourself that you're well enough to go back, by all means have that symptom-limited maximal exercise test. From our own experience with patients, we view a symptom-limited maximal exercise test during convalescence as an important confidence builder as well as a key diagnostic tool.

If your job involves heavy manual labour or any other circumstances you think may place you at risk, it is *essential* that you discuss your situation fully with your doctor. One cardiac expert has come to the conclusion, though, that patients who display no symptoms or signs of exercise intolerance at 7 METs or higher "can safely withstand the physical component of most jobs held by men and women over age 45".[12]

However, should your job be an especially taxing one, particularly physically, you may have to find another line of work. In cases where there's a question, specialized work-simulation testing and on-the-job Holter monitoring may well be required. (Holter monitoring can be very effective, too, if your job involves a high degree of psychological stress.) Should you have a job involving manual labour, you may require a job reassignment if Holter monitoring detects abnormalities, or if a maximal exercise test reveals that you can only withstand a MET level below that required at work.

Bypass surgery patients are generally advised by their physicians to return to work after an interval similar to that recommended for heart attack patients. Angioplasty patients, on the other hand, are usually capable of returning to active employment almost immediately after their hospital release. The recommendations of our panel of cardiac rehabilitation experts for bypass surgery and angioplasty patients also appear in Table 6-5.

STARTING OUT ON A HEALTHY LIFE-STYLE

Think of your return home from the hospital as a new beginning. It's a golden opportunity to start afresh by practising a healthier life-style, perhaps healthier and more fulfilling than you've ever known. After all, as a cardiac patient, you've got a real incentive to change your health habits for the better. Unlike the average person, you know firsthand how precious—and fragile—life can be.

We think it's very important that you start leading a healthier life from the moment you return home. We don't want you to put it off, because once you allow yourself to resume old habits, you'll find it more difficult to make the necessary changes.

PART THREE

THE EXERCISE PRESCRIPTION

CHAPTER 7

WHY EXERCISE?

It was Hippocrates, the fifth-century B.C. Greek physician, who said: "All parts of the body which have a function, if used in moderation and exercised in labours in which each is accustomed, become thereby healthy, well-developed and age more slowly; but if unused and left idle they become liable to disease, defective in growth, and age quickly."

It's no wonder the ancient Greeks invented the Olympic Games. It was common for Greek leaders to extoll the virtues of sports as a way to sharpen the competitive instincts and athletic/soldiering abilities of their young men. Greek physicians also emphasized the value of exercise in health maintenance and longevity, as the above quote shows.

Taking their cue from the Greeks, medical practitioners ever since have endorsed exercise as a good health habit. However, not until the early 1960s did the idea of using exercise to prevent illness and rehabilitate the sick begin to take hold. In terms of cardiac rehabilitation, this notion—revolutionary when it was first broached—is considered mainstream today.

The growing interest in and acceptability of exercise as a medical tool becomes obvious when you scan the exercise citations in the annual Index Medicus, which lists all the articles published in major medical journals. Between 1943 and 1953, the average number of yearly exercise citations was 110; this rose to 328 in 1963, 798 in 1973, and 1 278 in 1983.

The trail that led the medical community to view too little exercise as a causal factor in heart disease was papered with numerous research studies, the most important of which we'll review here.

It was a British physician, Dr. Jeremy N. Morris, who did the research that laid the foundation for what has become known as the "exercise hypothesis". In the early 1950s, Dr. Morris and his colleagues from the London School of Hygiene and Tropical Medicine conducted a landmark study that provided the basis for subsequent well-controlled investigations of the relationship between coronary heart disease (CHD) and a sedentary life-style.[1] The study's subjects were men in a variety of well-defined occupations. The workers who captured Morris's attention, though, were London bus conductors. He was startled to discover that their risk for CHD was about one-half that of their bus-driver colleagues. Not only that, but when he compared the heart attack sufferers in the two groups, he found that the bus drivers were twice as likely as the conductors to experience fatal first heart attacks or to die during the initial two months after an infarction.

Morris theorized that the main difference between the two groups was their activity level. The drivers sat all day, while the conductors were constantly climbing up and down the steps of London's double-decker buses. He observed similar results when he compared the health of postmen, who moved about all day long, with that of such sedentary workers as telephone operators and office clerks. The result was the exercise hypothesis—the notion that people who exercise regularly are less prone to CHD than those who do not.

Later, Morris revisited his study, only to discover factors that made him question his earlier conclusions. Among them was the fact that the bus drivers, when they joined the London transport system, already had higher blood cholesterol levels, elevated blood pressures, and greater abdominal girths than the conductors. Presumably, the drivers started out at greater risk for CHD. Still, their curiosity piqued, Morris and his colleagues probed their exercise hypothesis further in a large-scale investigation of leisure-time activities.[2] It involved 17 944 middle-aged male office workers in six British government departments located around the country. During a follow-up period of eight and a half years, they found that the men who were physically active outside of work suffered approximately 50 percent fewer heart attacks than their less active colleagues. Moreover, these striking benefits persisted even when a variety of CHD risk factors—including hypertension, smoking, obesity, and a family history of CHD—were taken into account.

Another research physician who contributed significantly to the advancement of the exercise hypothesis is Dr. Ralph S. Paffenbarger, Jr., from the Stanford University School of Medicine. Paffenbarger conducted two major cardiac studies which bore out

Morris's pioneering work.[3] Paffenbarger's second study is his most famous.[4] Indeed, it's fair to say it's the most renowned of all the exercise-heart disease studies to date. Some 16 936 Harvard University alumni, thirty-five to seventy-four years old, made up the sample. Paffenbarger and his Stanford research group probed their physical activities, mainly those outside of work since most were in white-collar occupations. The exercise hypothesis stood the test. The physically active alumni were at reduced risk of death from CHD compared with their more sedentary fellow alumni.

Another interesting idea emerged from this study: sceptics have long suggested that the positive causal relationship that's emerged in the various exercise-CHD studies might be attributable to self-selection. In other words, it's likely that people with sound hearts will be among the most active, and that those with asymptomatic heart disease will prefer sitting it out on the sidelines. The Harvard study showed that the men who had been university athletes and later became inactive—just like our sufferer John Venter—had no carryover benefit. Years later, they were at higher risk for heart disease than those who had not been athletes at university but who had taken up regular exercise long after graduation. This observation argues strongly against the self-selection hypothesis.

Among the more recent and respected studies confirming the exercise hypothesis is the Cooper Clinic Aerobics Centre Longitudinal Study of over 13 000 male and female patients.[5] There's also the Lipid Research Clinic's Mortality Follow-up Study of more than 4 000 men[6]; the Multiple Risk Factor Intervention Trial (MRFIT) involving some 12 000 men[7]; and the US Railroad Study of 3 000 male railway workers.[8]

All this meticulous research, involving as it does many thousands of people, has led the majority of doctors today to conclude that a person's activity level does indeed play a key role in the progression of CHD. We believe that it's as important as high cholesterol, cigarette smoking, and high blood pressure. In westernized and industrialized countries, where machines perform most of the heavy labour, sedentary living is a way of daily life. This is why we feel that physicians could save more lives by simply persuading their patients to exercise than by modifying any other single CHD risk factor.

In short, we believe the exercise hypothesis has progressed well beyond the stage where it should be referred to as a "hypothesis".

EXERCISE AND THE POST-INFARCT PATIENT

The studies just cited show unequivocally that regular exercise can help prevent, or at least retard, the development of CHD. What about the readers of this book who already have heart disease? What can it do for them?

To date, no single study has yet included enough sufferers of heart attacks to adequately answer that question. However, one researcher, Dr. Neil B. Oldridge from the University of Wisconsin Medical School in Milwaukee, tried to find an answer by pooling the results of ten major studies involving 4 347 heart attack patients.[9] Oldridge's overview revealed an impressive 25 percent reduction in deaths from CHD in the 2 202 patients who participated in various cardiac rehabilitation exercise programmes. This happens to be about the same level of reduction in deaths as that attributed to cardiac patients' use of beta-blocker drugs, which are currently the most effective of all the many medications available for infarct sufferers. Thus, it's not surprising that in a recent American Medical Association study almost 90 percent of the medical experts polled felt that a prescribed regimen of exercise is a safe and effective treatment for people who've suffered a heart attack or undergone bypass surgery.[10]

Researchers still don't know the precise mechanism by which regular exercise does help lessen the risk of developing CHD or dying from it. But they have advanced a number of highly plausible theories to explain its protective effect. Their speculations—some partially verified by studies—include the following.

Regular Exercise Reduces Your Heart Muscle's Oxygen Needs. As we mentioned in our physiology discussion in Chapter 3, the heart's oxygen requirements are directly related to the rate-pressure product (the product of your heart rate and systolic blood pressure). Over time, exercise training reduces the rate-pressure product for each given level of exertion, and thus it lessens the heart's overall oxygen demand.

Why is this a good thing for a cardiac patient? Because it reduces the potential for further heart attacks and sudden death. It allows you to exert yourself more before you are likely to develop ischaemia, whether silent or symptomatic. And it enables angina sufferers to exert themselves more heavily before their chest discomfort sets in, a benefit first reported by Dr. William Heberden way back in 1802. Heberden wrote in his *Commentary on the History and Cure of Diseases* that he had little or nothing to advance for the treatment of angina. However, he then went on to cite the example of one patient "who set himself a task of sawing wood for half an hour every day and was nearly cured". A modern-day cardiologist spotted the mention and wrote in a 1988 medical article, "Heberden's observation that physical training can nearly cure angina in some patients has been confirmed in recent studies".[11]

Regular Exercise Improves Your Heart Muscle's Oxygen Supply. The flip side of the coin concerns your heart's oxygen supply. There is now some preliminary evidence to support the possibility that exercise increases the amount of oxygen that reaches your heart. How this happens is still the subject of debate. However, researchers think that exercise training may trigger the formation of coronary collaterals (those blood vessels that form to take over the function of blocked blood vessels). This has been shown to occur in monkeys, dogs, and rats after exercise training, but there is currently no direct evidence that it happens in humans.[12] This issue won't be clarified until a more adequate way to measure coronary-collateral growth in humans is found.

Regular Exercise Reduces Your Blood Platelets' Tendency to Stick. Platelets contribute to heart attacks in two ways. First, they foster atherosclerotic plaque buildup. Second, they can cause a blood clot to form at the site of the plaque obstruction in the coronary arteries. Recently, researchers from the University of Kuopio in Finland reported that moderate physical activity may reduce the aggregability—or stickiness—of platelets.[13] This is certainly welcome news given the problems that undue blood stickiness can cause.

Regular Exercise Enhances Your Body's Natural Ability to Dissolve Blood Clots. You'll recall that John Venter, like many heart attack patients, was injected with t-PA in casualty in an attempt to dissolve the coronary artery blood clot responsible for his infarction. In John's case, the injection was successful, obviating the need for an angiogram.

Since t-PA often does such an effective job, wouldn't it be useful if the human body had a natural source of it? In fact, it does. The endothelial cells lining your blood vessels are capable of producing their own t-PA. However, according to Dr. Edward R. Eichner, professor of medicine and chief of haematology at the University of Oklahoma, inactivity—from prolonged bed rest or a long car journey, for example—reduces your body's t-PA production. He pinpoints exercise as "a cardinal stimulus for release of t-PA into the blood".[14]

Regular Exercise Reduces the Chances of Developing Ventricular Fibrillation. As you learned in Chapter 5 when we discussed risk stratification, ischaemia can trigger ventricular fibrillation, which can cause death. This is another instance where human research is lacking. Instead, we have the work of Dr. Tim Noakes and his colleagues from the University of Cape Town Medical School which is, as we all know, the site of the world's first heart transplant in 1967.[15] Their research shows that the hearts of rats that undergo regular exercise training are more resistant to the development of ventricular fibrillation. The closest inference we can draw from existing human studies is the fact that the physically active participants in Paffenbarger's studies and the British civil servants in Morris's study had less chance of dying suddenly from heart disease.

Regular Exercise Has a Positive Impact on Other CHD Risk Factors. In addition to a person's physical activity level, there are six controllable risk factors for CHD. You'll be introduced to them in Chapter 11 and find out what to do about them in Chapters 12 to 15. The wonderful thing about regular exercise is that it tends to have a positive impact on these modifiable risk factors. Numerous recent studies have shown that regular exercise does the following:

- Increases the level of HDL cholesterol in the blood
- Reduces the ratio of total cholesterol to HDL cholesterol
- Lowers triglyceride levels
- Lessens the risk of developing high blood pressure
- Lowers both the systolic and diastolic blood pressures in hypertensive people
- Prevents obesity by reducing the amount of excess body fat
- Relieves stress and has a mollifying influence on Type A behaviour
- Helps prevent or control diabetes mellitus by aiding carbohydrate metabolism

There is even some evidence that exercise training can help offset some of smoking's detrimental effects. In the US National Exercise and Heart Disease Project, a study involving 651 heart attack patients enrolled in the rehabilitation programmes at five medical centres, the greatest relative effectiveness of exercise was observed in men who were cigarette smokers.[16] Among the smokers, the three-year death rate was 77 percent lower in those who exercised regularly than in those who didn't.

Exercise also influences the modifiable risk factors in an indirect way. Cardiac patients who start an exercise training programme and stick with it gain renewed self-respect. It's not long before they're telling themselves, "If I can stick with this, I can certainly do something about eating healthier foods, losing mass, throwing away cigarettes," etc. In effect, exercise becomes a visible and constant reminder of your perseverance, of your ability to make a commitment and stay with it. That is, exercise is a great health motivator.

There are few medical disorders that destroy a person's confidence as much as heart disease. Many coronary patients suffer from a minor physiological disability and a major psychological disability. Exercise is important because it allays patients' concerns and provides tangible proof of improving health. It also boosts self-esteem while reducing anxiety and depression, benefits you'll learn more about in Chapter 14. In other words, exercise tends to have a dramatic impact on the recovering cardiac patient's quality of life.[17]

True, we're enthusiastic exercise advocates. However, we realize our enthusiasm can be misinterpreted by frightened heart patients. They listen to our arguments in favour of regular exercise and arrive at what might seem to be a logical conclusion: If moderate exercise is good, then even more intense exercise must be better. It's the idea that "more is better". Indeed, some patients become so extreme in their thinking that they decide exercise must be the long-sought-after elixir of everlasting life.

The worst thing about this extremist position is that its adherents often assume that exercise, by itself, will solve their CHD problems. Thus, they ignore correct nutrition, keep smoking, and disregard the other essentials of a healthy life-style. This view, dubbed the "myth of invulnerability", was actually embraced by some highly reputable people in the late 1970s. For example, Dr. Thomas J. Bassler from the Department of Pathology of Centinela Hospital in Inglewood, California, put forward the notion, in both the lay and medical literature, that regular marathon-level exertion "confers virtual immunity from fatal heart attacks". This "Bassler hypothesis" was picked up by none other than Jim Fixx, the marathon runner who became world famous because of his best-selling *The Complete Book of*

Running. Fixx remarked, "Exercise can reduce, and in some cases nullify, the effects of everything from diabetes to a family history [of heart disease]."[18] Only it didn't in his case. Not many years after voicing this theory, Jim Fixx died of a heart attack during a daily run.

Indeed, long before Jim Fixx's fateful death, there was already plenty of evidence that ran counter to Bassler's belief that marathon athletes of any age are invulnerable to the ravages of heart disease. Autopsy reports published by Dr. Noakes and his colleagues at the University of Cape Town had demonstrated conclusively that marathon runners can indeed die from heart attacks,[19] and on the basis of Noakes's research, a 1979 editorial in the prestigious *New England Journal of Medicine* unequivocally destroyed the Bassler hypothesis.[20] Still, it took the surprise death of a popular figure like Fixx to discredit the myth in the eyes of the general public.

So, when it comes to exercise, more is not necessarily better. It's now quite clear that nothing—neither marathon-level athletic performance nor anything else—will provide total immunity from CHD. Exercise is not a panacea, but rather an important supplemental therapy; to be most effective, regular exercise must be combined with appropriate medical care as well as the positive life-style changes we outline in Part 4. We leave this subject by citing the findings of medical researchers in Heidelberg, West Germany. They have shown that this well-rounded approach to life after a heart attack can reduce a cardiac patient's myocardial ischaemia during exercise by more than 50 percent.[21]

EXERCISE IN THE CONTEXT OF CARDIAC REHABILITATION

The World Health Organization defines cardiac rehabilitation as "the sum of activities required to ensure cardiac patients the best possible physical, mental, and social conditions so that they may by their own efforts regain as normal as possible a place in the community and lead an active, productive life".[22] To achieve this return to normality, we feel strongly that most heart patients need to get involved in a comprehensive recovery programme—preferably formal—that encompasses exercise training, psychological counselling, vocational counselling, and CHD risk factor modification.

Not that long ago, most cardiac rehabilitation programmes

consisted almost entirely of exercise training. Today, most programme designers have realized the error of this one-dimensional approach and have instituted a multicomponent format. Still, exercise training, overseen by medical professionals, remains the central focus and core activity of most worthwhile cardiac rehabilitation programmes. As Figure 7-1 indicates, most recovery programmes involve four transitional phases. They're designed to restore a patient to optimal physiological and psychological health compatible with the extent of the person's heart problem. We'll describe briefly the scope of activities in each phase so you'll know what to expect during your own recuperation.

Phase 1: The Inpatient Programme

The recovery process begins as soon as the infarct, bypass, or angioplasty patient's condition stabilizes. Usually that's within twenty-four to forty-eight hours after the attack or procedure. However, complications can delay the start of the programme.

The goals of Phase 1's exercise efforts are threefold: (1) to

PHASE 1
Inpatient programme

↓

PHASE 2
Outpatient early convalescence programme

↓

PHASE 3
Long-term community-based programme

↓

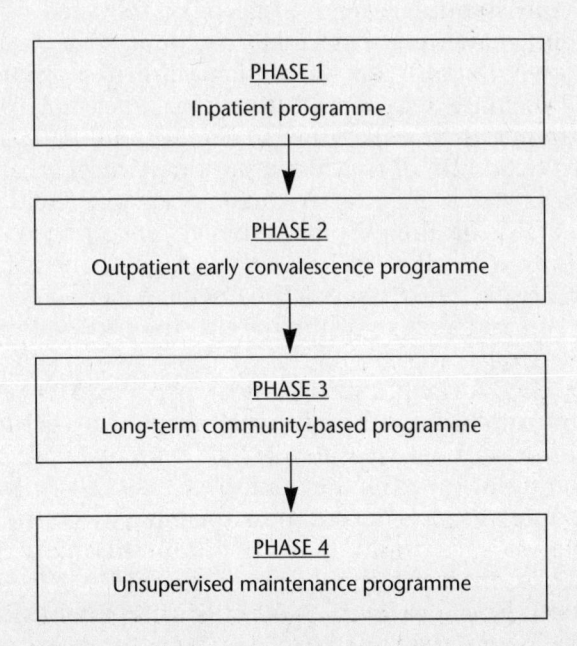

PHASE 4
Unsupervised maintenance programme

Figure 7-1. The four phases of cardiac rehabilitation. Some authorities consider Phase 4 to be a part of Phase 3, and therefore refer to only three (rather than four) phases of cardiac rehabilitation.

prevent the deleterious consequences of bed rest; (2) to provide medical surveillance while you gradually begin undertaking some semblance of normal daily physical activity; and (3) to prepare you for the more vigorous phases that follow after you return home from the hospital.

A good inpatient programme is one that's individualized to meet the very specific needs of each patient. It's also one that's completely medically supervised. *A patient should never take it upon himself or herself to embark on such a programme alone: there must be medical help and direction.* A nurse, physical therapist, exercise physiologist, or some other suitably qualified health professional should always be present for Phase 1's exercise sessions. One reason is that problems can develop that may require a temporary delay in the programme—or may even necessitate special treatment. There should always be ECG and blood pressure monitoring during cardiac patients' early attempts to exercise.

The exercise programme usually starts very early in the recuperation, while the patient is still in bed in the intensive care unit (ICU). The exercises are low-level, range-of-motion mobilizations with MET levels of 1 or 2.

Sitting and standing exercises are next, followed by walking. At this point, patients are normally encouraged to walk around on their own in addition to participating in a more formal, supervised exercise regimen. During the supervised portion of the programme, they walk either in the hospital hallway or on a slow-paced treadmill, or they use a stationary bicycle.

Since many patients, after their discharge, will have to negotiate stairs in their homes, they're encouraged to weave stair-climbing into their daily routine. A good format is to ask patients to walk, with one of the medical personnel, down a flight of stairs one day, returning by lift; then to walk up a flight the following day.

During the formal exercise sessions, patients eventually progress to exercising with light weights, starting gradually and building up to heavier weights. Two or more exercise sessions a day are common. Initially, the sessions are short—as little as five or ten minutes each. The duration increases over the patient's hospital stay to a maximum of thirty minutes in many cases.

The exercise intensity should never exceed 5 METs (see Tables 6-1 and 6-2). The idea is to make sure the patient's heart rate doesn't rise more than 20 beats per minute above its resting standing value. The Borg rating of perceived exertion, or RPE, should not exceed 13 (see Table 5-1).

The overall goal during Phase 1 is to keep the exercise intensity low throughout and gradually to increase the duration of exercise sessions.

Phase 1: For Bypass and Angioplasty Patients

Bypass surgery patients who have not experienced a recent heart attack usually commence with the exercise programme earlier than infarct patients. Typically, they also progress faster in both the intensity and the duration of exercise. Exercising your arms and upper body—unless specifically contraindicated—is emphasized. These types of exercises are helpful to prevent bypass patients from developing future chest-wall problems.

Because angioplasty patients are discharged very quickly, they receive only one or two days of inpatient rehabilitation. It's not as key an element in their recovery effort as it is for those who've had heart attacks or surgery.

Phase 2: The Outpatient, Early-Convalescence Programme

Phase 2 usually begins immediately after hospital discharge and lasts for four to twelve weeks. This time the goals are twofold: (1) to continue to reverse any of the reduction in fitness caused by hospitalization and bed rest and (2) to get patients used to a structured, medically directed exercise programme. It is hoped that by the end of this phase patients will be convinced of the value of a healthier life-style built around regular exercise.

As in Phase 1, the exercise intensity remains relatively low throughout. Heart attack and bypass surgery patients are not permitted to exceed a heart rate of more than 85 percent of the rate that they attained during their most recent treadmill exercise test. In most instances, this will be a pre-hospital discharge submaximal exercise test. This cautious level of exercise ensures that the patient's damaged heart muscle—and the surgical wounds in the case of a bypass patient—is given adequate time to heal.

Angioplasty patients—those who have not had a recent infarct—may progress faster because they don't have to worry about myocardial or sternal healing. Many of them, in fact, are moved directly to Phase 3, particularly if they're low-risk patients who have previously participated in a supervised cardiac rehabilitation exercise programme. Some may participate in Phase 2 for only a few weeks.

In terms of fast progress, after angioplasty patients, bypass patients are next. Behind them are heart attack sufferers, who have to be the most cautious of all.

Phase 2 patients undertake exercise three to five times a week in a hospital or some other local health facility. Ideally, there should be at least one health care staff member for every five exercising patients. This is important because of the close supervision that is often required at this early stage of recovery. Sessions usually last thirty to sixty minutes and include such activities as stretching exercises, calisthenics, light weight training, walking, and stationary cycling.

After six weeks, patients considered at low risk on the basis of their symptom-limited maximal exercise test can sometimes begin jogging. However, more often such patients are simply advanced into Phase 3.

Low-risk patients in remote areas where there is no organized programme can implement their own programme at home. However, this should not be attempted by their moderate- or high-risk counterparts. We do not recommend that higher-risk patients carry on without appropriate on-site professional supervision, at least during the early weeks following their hospital release, when the chance of complications remains relatively high.

In fact, no matter what your risk status or the degree of access you have to formal programmes, we feel you must undertake exercise under the tutelage of a physician knowledgeable about your condition. Convalescence is no time to become a paragon of self-reliance. Your medical condition requires at least a modicum of humility—and a willingness to follow directions.

Phase 3: The Long-Term, Community-Based Programme

Phase 3's goal is to maintain the fitness gains achieved during Phase 2, and to move even further down the road to normality. As a rule, no infarct or bypass patients, no matter how splendid their progress, are admitted into a Phase 3 programme until at least six weeks have passed from the time of the attack or surgery. Phase 3 generally begins, though, between six and twelve weeks after hospitalization.

Some centres offering Phase 3 programmes in South Africa are listed, with full addresses, on page 165. They all offer different facilities, depending on staff and equipment. One of the largest and most sophisticated rehabilitation centres in the world is the one run by the Johannesburg City Health Department. The referral of a physician is required to join the programme, and patients also need to show the results of a recent symptom-limited maximal exercise test. As you can see, Phase 3 sites are not necessarily clinical facilities. You should make sure the programme is run by qualified health professionals who have the ability, at the very least, to screen participants' ECGs at rest and handle any emergencies that may arise. The patient-to-staff ratio varies from programme to programme.

The number of exercise sessions per week varies. Just as in Phase 2, Phase 3 patients have an exercise intensity ceiling of 85 percent of the heart rate that was determined during their last exercise test. However, since the last test was a maximal (rather than submaximal) one, their actual heart rate limit should be higher.

The forms of exercise are usually similar to those in Phase 2, except that they may include such noncompetitive endurance team sports as volleyball. In most programmes, patients at lower risk who have been participating for three months or longer are given more and more freedom to regulate their own exercise.

According to the Heart Foundation of Southern Africa, none of these exercise programmes should be excessively expensive.

Phase 4: The Unsupervised Maintenance Programme

Ideally, we don't like to see patients advance to Phase 4 until they have spent at least three months in a medically supervised rehabilitation programme. However, this isn't always possible. In reality, participants in a Phase 4 programme are often people who have dropped out of a Phase 3 programme because of individual preference, economic concern, geographic isolation, or reasons related to convenience rather than to health.

We want to emphasize that "unsupervised" does not mean you're free to do whatever exercise strikes your fancy. Rather, it means that you are exercising without any on-site medical supervision. However, the exercises you're doing are still those that were approved by your doctor, who knows the intimate details of your case. In short, although "unsupervised", your programme is "medically directed" (this important distinction is discussed in more detail in Chapter 8).

Phase 4 isn't that different from Phase 3. Indeed, some experts feel that Phase 4 is actually a part of Phase 3 and therefore refer to only three—rather than four—phases of cardiac rehabilitation. Participants should be exercising three to five days each week for thirty to sixty minutes each time. However, because a health professional is no longer present, it may be desirable for the heart rate limit to be set slightly lower than it was during Phase 3. The forms of exercise in Phases 3 and 4 are virtually identical. (We'll discuss the pros and cons of unsupervised exercise as well as specific exercises in the remaining chapters of Part 3.)

PERSEVERING IN YOUR EXERCISE PROGRAMME

When you exercise, your body and its various organ systems are being exposed to potent physiological stimuli. If you exercise on a regular basis at an appropriate intensity and duration, these stimuli result in specific adaptations that both enhance your ability to exercise and, at the same time, improve your health status. In other words, you'll be the happy recipient of all the benefits of a physically active life-style—benefits we outlined earlier in this chapter.

Unfortunately, these benefits can't be stored up for a rainy day. They're reversible, and all it takes to start this reversal is abstinence. If you stop training or reduce your level of physical activity below your required level, your body's systems soon readjust themselves in accordance with this diminished number of physiological stimuli. The end result is that those exercise-related gains that you worked so long and hard to achieve are lost.

This "reversibility concept" is best illustrated by Paffenbarger's study of Harvard alumni, which we mentioned at the start of this chapter.[23] You'll recall that many of the former university athletes had become inactive adults. As a consequence, they were in worse shape and at greater risk for CHD than their contemporaries who had not participated in sports in college but who had started exercising later in life. We do not know how long it takes after you stop exercising for the health benefits you had gained to be lost. We do know that a rapid decline in fitness occurs during the first twelve to twenty-one days of inactivity and that the training benefits are almost totally lost after about two or three months.

In view of this, it's imperative that you stick with your exercise programme once you get started. Regrettably, this is easier said than done. A number of studies focusing on exercise compliance after a heart attack show that half or more of all patients drop out of their exercise programme within a year and that the critical dropout period is the first three to six months. What you need to get you through this critical time are motivators. The following suggestions will help keep you huffing and puffing even when you'd rather be home in bed or watching television.

Make Sure You Fully Understand the Costs of Not Exercising versus the Benefits of Exercising. Those of you who let reason guide your life should find the research studies we cited earlier sufficient inducement to stick with your exercise programme. The evidence that exercise confers significant protection against heart ailments is no longer in dispute. You ignore this exercise-CHD link at your own peril.

If at All Possible, Join a Formal Cardiac Rehabilitation Programme for at Least Three Months. This should help you get through the critical dropout period as well as help you with long-term exercise adherence. A British study has highlighted the importance of an organized programme.[24] The study focused on exercise compliance in the year after a heart attack or major cardiac procedure. Of the patients who did not participate in a formal cardiac rehabilitation programme, only 2 percent were still exercising regularly six to nine years later. On the other hand, 19 percent of those who had developed the exercise habit during a three-month organized programme stuck with it.

Start Exercising Slowly and Progress Gradually. In Chapter 9 we tell you precisely how often, for how long, and at what intensity you should start off exercising. We caution you against a burst of enthusiasm in the beginning that you will not be able to sustain. It's far better to approach exercise the way the turtle approaches the race—slowly and steadily.

Be Happy with the Cardiac Rehabilitation Programme You Join. Ideally, the programme should be within easy access and offer exercise sessions at a time that suits your body clock as well as your schedule. However, there are not many programmes to choose from in South Africa.

Nevertheless, it is essential to make the effort, even if it seems a little inconvenient: your life may be at stake.

Addresses for rehabilitation programmes in South Africa are given on page 165. You can contact your local branch of the Heart Foundation of Southern Africa for further information.

Choose a Form of Exercise That's Convenient as Well as Enjoyable. The appropriate forms of exercise for heart patients are described in Chapter 10. Ideally, exercise should not be a trial, but a joy.

Granted, it may take a period of adjustment before you view it this way. However, we say this with a great deal of certainty: the longer you persevere, the more likely you are to come to a full appreciation and sense of satisfaction with exercise.

Find a Role Model. Identify someone—a friend, a relative, or an acquaintance—who leads a physically active life and loves it. Talk to that person and find out why—what made them don running shoes or take up swimming. Such a chat may well introduce you to dimensions of exercise it might otherwise take you months to discover.

Learn from Your Past Exercise Experiences. It's unlikely this will be your first brush with exercise. Maybe you attempted to start a programme several years ago and were determined to stick with it, but failed. Think back over such experiences and try to work out where you went wrong—and how you can avoid the same mistakes this time around.

Obtain as Much Support for Your Exercise Programme as Possible. Going it alone isn't easy. Try to avoid this lonely fate during your convalescence by enlisting the company—or, at the very least, the moral support—of those closest to you. If your spouse or children are willing to go for walks with you, all the better.

We've known patients who find an exercise partner and seal the deal with a written contract. It states their short-term exercise goals, how they'll be accomplished, and how the parties will be rewarded for fulfilling them.

Take Your Body to Your Place of Exercise Even if Your Mind Is Temporarily on Strike. Just make yourself do it, even on the days when it seems a horrible chore. Nothing stays the same in this world. You'll have bad days, but you'll also have just as many—probably more—really good days. Look at it this way: you can't really tell how you're going to feel on a given day until you start exercising. Not to exercise simply because you suspect you won't enjoy it is a foolish way to conduct your life. After all, you're making decisions based on guesswork rather than on firsthand experience.

Special Occasions Are No Excuse. You may be on holiday—or visiting your daughter in Durban. This does not excuse you from your exercise programme. You'll notice we keep referring to it as a "programme", not just "exercise". A programme is something that is formal and institutionalized. It's carefully planned and understood by the parties involved. As a cardiac patient, you have an exercise *programme*. Just as you need to take your medication every day, you must exercise, based on a set of parameters you'll learn about in the next two chapters. In fact, thinking of exercise as a form of heart *medication* may in itself be a motivator.

EXERCISE IS FOREVER

Physical activity is a lifelong commitment. We exhort you to do everything in your power to keep from becoming a cardiac rehabilitation dropout, especially during the crucial initial months. Once you've passed the six-month mark and tasted some of the superb benefits of an active life-style, we think there will be much less of a chance that you'll ever revert to your old unhealthy inactivity.

CHAPTER 8

BETTER SAFE THAN SORRY

IN the early 1970s, a cartoon appeared in Mad magazine which just about summed up the medical profession's approach to prescribing exercise for patients at that time. It showed a middle-aged man in a doctor's examination room. The patient's complaint was that he'd been feeling tired and run-down. Because the doctor could find nothing wrong, he advised the patient to take up jogging. The startled patient replied that he'd been jogging for the past several years. What was the doctor's reply? There are no prizes for guessing: to stop jogging.

Fortunately, advances in the field of exercise science in the two intervening decades have enabled today's physicians to prescribe exercise for patients on a more rational basis. The guesswork has largely disappeared from the process. That's why we're now able to prescribe exercise just as we prescribe medications. It's also why we named this part of the book "The Exercise Prescription."

We know you're concerned about whether it's really safe to exercise, in light of your heart condition. Of course, we'd be lying if we claimed vigorous exercise can never trigger a heart attack. It can in certain susceptible people. The key question is: which people are susceptible?

Several recent studies help to provide an answer. A study spearheaded by Dr. David S. Siscovick and his colleagues from the University of North Carolina at Chapel Hill focused on the risk of cardiac-related death in sedentary versus physically active individuals between the ages of twenty-five and seventy-five.[1] They found that a sedentary man who engages in vigorous exercise is about fifty-six times more likely to die of a heart attack during the exercise session itself than if he had simply stayed home and done nothing. Relatively fit men are also at a slightly elevated risk when they go out for a workout. However, had these relatively fit men not exercised, their overall risk of a cardiac-related death—both during workouts and at rest—would have been 60 percent higher. The conclusion is fairly obvious: in a physically active person, although the risk of death is transiently increased during vigorous exercise, it is far outweighed by the marked reduction in the risk of dying when such a person is at rest. In short, the risk-benefit ratio is definitely tipped in favour of exercise.

Another study, by Dr. Paul D. Thompson and his associates, further demonstrates that the actual risk of dying during exercise is in fact extremely small for the general male population between the ages of thirty and sixty-four, with only one death per 396 000 hours of jogging.[2] In their study, the risk applied almost entirely to people who, like you, already have heart disease. Many other similar studies have reached the same conclusion.

In summing up these studies, we'd like you to note that it is not exercise itself that is problematic. It's the combination of injudicious exertion and significant pre-existing heart disease.

Thus, we feel confident in making this rather extreme statement: *when performed with the appropriate precautions, exercise training is exceptionally safe, even for cardiac patients.* We base what we say only partially on our more than ten years of clinical experience supervising cardiac rehabilitation exercise sessions—we've never had a fatality during exercise in all that time. Rather, this assertion is based primarily on the results of a comprehensive study of supervised outpatient cardiac rehabilitation programmes by Dr. Steven P. Van Camp and Dr. Richard A. Peterson from San Diego State University and Alvarado Hospital Medical Centre.[3] They analysed cardiac complications experienced by patients undergoing exercise training at 167 randomly selected cardiac rehabilitation centres in the United States between January 1980 and December 1984. The sample comprised some 51 303 patients involved in almost 2,4 million hours of exercise. Their risk of developing cardiac complications while engaging in exercise was as follows:

- 1 per 111 996 exercise hours for arrhythmias requiring defibrillation and/or CPR
- 1 per 293 990 hours for a heart attack
- 1 per 783 972 hours for sudden death

It is evident from these findings—and those of Dr. Thompson's study mentioned above—that the risk of death during supervised cardiac rehabilitation exercise training may in fact be even less than that experienced by joggers from the general adult male population. In the first instance, the risk is 1 per 783 972 exercise hours; in the second, it's 1 per 396 000 jogging hours. No doubt this is partly because the health professionals who run cardiac rehabilitation exercise programmes are such careful observers and act quickly and skilfully to deal with any potentially fatal arrhythmias.

You may be saying to yourself: all this is fine, but I can't stay on a supervised programme forever. What risk am I under when I start exercising on my own? We can't cite a comprehensive study like the one just mentioned to allay your fears. However, recent studies by Dr. Robert F. DeBusk and his colleagues from the Stanford University School of Medicine suggest that carefully prescribed exercise training can be performed safely at home by selected cardiac patients, with no medical supervision.[4]

At the Aerobics Centre in Dallas, all patients with CHD who wish to work out are required to participate in the medically supervised cardiac rehabilitation programme, at least until we are comfortable with their knowledge of exercise safety and their ability to self-monitor their training. This usually takes about twelve weeks. Patients who are at low risk for cardiac complications may then exercise at the centre without medical supervision. Granted, there are physicians on the premises who can be at a person's side within minutes should there be any problem.

GUIDELINES FOR EXERCISE SAFETY

To minimize your risk of developing an exercise-related cardiac problem we've developed a set of guidelines that we urge you to follow, in consultation with your physician. They are:

Guideline 1: Obtain medical clearance before you begin an exercise programme.
Guideline 2: Establish when and for how long you need on-site medical supervision.
Guideline 3: Determine your training heart rate limit and never exceed it.
Guideline 4: Know the warning signs of cardiac problems, and what to do should you experience them.
Guideline 5: Eliminate the factors that place you at greater risk during exercise, and know when not to exercise at all.

Guideline 1: Obtain Medical Clearance

There can be no doubt that there are certain cardiac patients for whom the risks of exercise training, even with medical supervision, outweigh the potential benefits. In Chapter 5 we mentioned conditions that made it too risky for certain patients even to undergo an exercise test conducted by a doctor in a hospital. Those factors, as well as some abnormalities that a doctor may have detected during an exercise test, could rule out exercise training for certain patients in the highest-risk category. However, if you've recently had an exercise test and "2 METs or more" was the reply to Question 4 or, in the absence of abnormalities, Question 2a of Table 5-6, then it's likely that your physician will clear you for participation in a medically supervised exercise programme.

We hope you are not among those unfortunate cardiac patients whose physicians, even in this advanced era of modern medicine, are excessively cautious. If you feel your physician is wrong in telling you not to participate in a supervised exercise programme, use the checklist in Table 8-1, on page 150, to ask your doctor to check off any medical conditions that apply to you. If none is applicable and your physician still balks at the notion of exercise, we strongly advise you to seek a second opinion.

Guideline 2: Establish When and for How Long You Need On-Site Medical Supervision

Participation in a cardiac rehabilitation programme with a doctor present has several advantages. Such programmes invariably do the following:

- Improve fitness
- Educate you about other CHD risk factors you should also be controlling
- Motivate you to stick with your programme
- Make you feel more secure about exercise
- Increase your chances of surviving any cardiac problem induced by exercise

Despite all these advantages, there is a current trend toward encouraging cardiac patients to engage in an exercise programme developed especially for them by their doctor and undertaken at home or at a health club where there's no on-site physician

TABLE 8-1
Do NOT Exercise If Your Physician Answers Yes to Any of These Statements[a]

Condition	Yes	No

I have...
1. Unstable angina pectoris.
2. Recent significant change in my resting ECG that has not been fully investigated.
3. A recent embolism.
4. Thrombophlebitis.
5. Active myocarditis or pericarditis.
6. Symptomatic heart failure.
7. Moderate to severe aortic stenosis.
8. Clinically significant hypertrophic obstructive cardiomyopathy.
9. Suspected or known dissecting aneurysm.
10. Uncontrolled atrial or ventricular arrhythmias that are considered to be clinically significant.
11. Resting heart rate greater than 100 beats per minute.
12. Third-degree heart block.
13. Uncontrolled hypertension with resting systolic blood pressure above 200 mm Hg or diastolic blood pressure above 100 mm Hg.
14. Recent fall in systolic blood pressure of more than 20 mm Hg that was not caused by medication.
15. Uncontrolled metabolic disease, such as diabetes mellitus, thyrotoxicosis, or myxoedema.
16. Acute systemic illness or fever.
17. Significant electrolyte disturbances.
18. Orthopaedic problems that prohibit exercise.
19. Major emotional distress (psychosis).
20. Any other condition known to be a contraindication to exercise.

[a]There are cardiac patients with specific medical conditions and illnesses that preclude aerobic exercise. According to the American College of Sports Medicine, patients with one or more of these conditions should not exercise until therapy or the passage of time controls or corrects their problem(s). Ask your cardiologist if you suffer from any of the conditions listed in this table.

supervision. The reasons for this growing trend have as much to do with finances and geography as they do with medicine. Only large communities tend to have medically supervised cardiac rehabilitation programmes. Moreover, even when such a programme is available, it may be too expensive or may be scheduled at an inconvenient time.

While we understand this trend, which makes a book like this one a necessity, we still advise all patients who are able to do so to exercise with on-site medical supervision for the first twelve weeks of their training programme (see Table 8-2 on pages 152–153). This initial on-site medical supervision—usually in a Phase 2 cardiac rehabilitation programme (see Chapter 7)—is especially important if you've recently been discharged from the hospital after a heart attack or bypass surgery and the healing of your heart muscle and/or sternum is still incomplete. The medically supervised programme will help you acquire the skills you need to self-regulate your exercise prescription later on when you're on your own.

If you cannot take our advice and get involved in a medically supervised programme for the full twelve weeks, we urge you to get involved for a shorter period. Even a single medically supervised session is better than none.

After the initial twelve weeks of exercise training, it would be ideal if the on-site medical supervision continued as part of a Phase 3 cardiac rehabilitation programme. However, we realize this isn't always possible. In that case, we urge you to make sure your medical status is such that an unsupervised exercise programme is acceptably safe for you (again, see Table 8-2).

Should you have no access whatsoever to a programme with on-site medical supervision, an alternative is a programme supervised by well-trained paramedical personnel. This is definitely preferable to totally unsupervised exercise. Today, many nurses, exercise physiologists, people trained in physical education, biokineticians and physiotherapists are perfectly capable of supervising the exercise efforts of coronary patients, particularly those who are at lower risk. While it is highly unlikely you'll need it, make sure such a programme has fast access to emergency care.

Continuous ECG Monitoring. By "continuous ECG monitoring" we mean use of the various technological devices that can continuously transmit your ECG to a recorder-receiver while you work out in a cardiac rehabilitation facility. This technology is an integral part of some advanced medically supervised rehabilitation programmes.

The most common form of this technology is *telemetry*, which is controversial for financial reasons. There's often a fivefold increase in cost when continuous ECG monitoring is introduced into a rehabilitation programme, and many health insurers balk at paying for it.

Still, in a 1987 American Medical Association survey, some 87

TABLE 8-2
Medically Supervised vs. Medically Directed Exercise Training: Which Is Right for You?[a]

You need on-site medical supervision, with continuous ECG monitoring, for at least 12 weeks if you have one or more of the following (your heart rate during exercise should not exceed 85% of your symptom-limited heart rate):

1. Severely depressed left ventricular function as evidenced by an ejection fraction below 30%
2. Resting complex PVCs
3. PVCs appearing or worsening with exercise (as evidenced by a "Yes" reply to Question 8a or 8b in Table 5-6)
4. Decrease in systolic blood pressure during exercise (as evidenced by a "Yes" reply to Question 9 in Table 5-6)
5. Marked exercise-induced myocardial ischaemia (as evidenced by a reply of "less than 4 METs" to Question 4 and a "Yes" reply to Question 7a in Table 5-6)
6. History of a cardiac arrest
7. History of a heart attack complicated by heart failure, cardiogenic shock, and/or serious ventricular arrhythmias

You need on-site medical supervision only if you have one or more of the following (your heart rate during exercise should not exceed 85% of your symptom-limited heart rate):

1. Prior participation in a programme with continuous ECG monitoring necessitated by any of the conditions outlined above
2. Fixed-rate pacemaker
3. Two or more heart attacks
4. Clinical evidence of heart failure
5. Symptom-limited exercise capacity of less than 5 METs (see the reply to Question 4, Table 5-6)
6. Symptom-limited heart rate below 120 beats per minute and you are not taking a beta-blocker (see the reply to Question 5, Table 5-6)
7. Presence of any significant abnormality during exercise testing (as evidenced by a "No" reply to Question 1 of Table 5-6), and an inability to self-monitor your own heart rate during exercise
8. Inadequate knowledge of exercise safety as evidenced by a score of less than 90% on the Exercise Safety Quiz at the end of the book (see Appendix D)
9. Heart attack or bypass surgery within the previous six weeks, unless symptom-limited maximal exercise testing has been performed and no significant abnormalities occurred (as evidenced by a "Yes" reply to Question 1 of Table 5-6)

TABLE 8-2 (continued)
Medically Supervised vs. Medically Directed Exercise Training: Which Is Right for You?[a]

You can get by with on-site supervision by health professionals OTHER THAN PHYSICIANS if you have NONE of the conditions listed above and meet ALL of the following criteria (your heart rate during exercise should not exceed 80% of your symptom-limited heart rate):

1. Clinically stable condition (especially no resting angina or heart failure)
2. Symptom-limited exercise capacity of at least 5 METs (see your reply to Question 4 of Table 5-6)
3. Ability to self-monitor your heart rate during exercise
4. Adequate knowledge of exercise safety as evidenced by a score of 90% or higher on the Exercise Safety Quiz at the end of the book (see Appendix D)

You can exercise on your own, following a medically directed programme, if:

1. You've met all the criteria listed in the previous part of this table.
2. You have a symptom-limited exercise capacity of at least 7 METs.
3. Your heart rate during exercise training does not exceed 80% of your symptom-limited heart rate.

---

[a]The distinction between a "medically supervised" and a "medically directed" exercise programme is an important one. When your exercise effort is medically supervised, there's a doctor at the ready in case you need emergency assistance—or just need to have your vital signs checked before and after exertion. If your programme is medically directed, it's been prescribed by a doctor but no physicians are present when you work out. The guidelines listed in this table are to be used as "talking points" with your doctor. Get his or her opinion before you proceed with your exercise programme.

percent of cardiovascular specialists considered continuous ECG monitoring to be "essential to the safety and efficacy of a prescribed regimen of exercise in coronary rehabilitation".[5] However, this is based on their clinical impressions and not on any controlled studies. To date, there have been no comprehensive studies comparing the safety of medically supervised exercise training with and without continuous ECG monitoring.

Dr. Philip Greenland and Dr. Paul V. Pomilla of the University of Rochester Medical Centre have reviewed the existing research in this area and are skeptical.[6] They feel only 5 percent or less of cardiac patients are, in fact, likely to derive substantial safety-related benefits from continuous ECG monitoring during exercise.

In light of the available evidence, we do not advocate the

indiscriminate use of continuous ECG monitoring over the long term. Indeed, we would like to see it restricted largely to those few patients who are at high risk for cardiac complications during exercise (see Table 8-2). However, we do acknowledge that if lower-risk patients can afford it and have access to it, continuous ECG monitoring during the early weeks of rehabilitation exercise training—and at intermittent periods thereafter—may be of real value in fine-tuning an exercise prescription. At the very least, using it during your first few exercise sessions may shed more light on your condition and your response to exercise training.

Tips for Exercising on Your Own. If you do decide to exercise without medical supervision—and your doctor concurs in your decision—here are some recommendations:

- If available and affordable, you might consider trans-telephonic ECG monitoring—a form of continuous ECG monitoring in which your ECG is transmitted via your telephone to a local cardiac rehabilitation centre while you work out at home. It will enable you to exercise by yourself, yet still enjoy some of the benefits of medical supervision. However, this is not at all common in South Africa.
- Assuming you've just completed twelve weeks in a medically supervised programme, you should try to return to that rehabilitation facility for a workout at least once every three months—or more often if possible. Use the session as an opportunity to review your self-regulated training programme with the professional staff members.
- Try to maintain regular telephone or mail contact with the facility. You'll be glad you kept this channel of communication open when you have questions or concerns, or just need motivation to continue your programme.
- Exercise with other people. Group participation, even when unsupervised, increases the likelihood you'll stick with it and gives you peace of mind that help will be summoned should you ever need it. Just make sure you haven't picked companions who are competitive and will cause you to overdo it.
- See your doctor at least every six months, even if you think you're doing fine. Be sure to have an exercise test once every year.

Guideline 3: Determine Your Training Heart Rate Limit and Never Exceed It

You'll recall that one of the goals of an exercise stress test is to increase your heart rate to the point where abnormalities, if present, start to appear. Angina and ST-segment depression are examples of such abnormalities. Each cardiac patient has a different threshold heart rate (or symptom-limited heart rate) after which the risk of a cardiac problem increases significantly. This is why we—indeed, most cardiac authorities—consider heart rate monitoring the key to safe exercise.

In aerobic exercise books directed at the lay public, a formula for estimating your target heart rate based on your age is usually given. *Such formulas are totally inappropriate for heart patients.* Before starting an exercise programme, you must have your training heart rate limit determined through an exercise test (to have been taken no later than three months beforehand). If anything major has changed in the interim—if you've had another cardiac problem or have begun taking new medication—then you need another exercise test.

Here are the crucial questions and answers a cardiac patient must commit to memory before he or she begins exercising:

What Should My Heart Rate Limit Be during Exercise? In order to give yourself a safety margin, we recommend you never exceed 85 percent of your symptom-limited heart rate. If you're exercising alone, even more leeway is desirable. (See our specific recommendations in Table 8-2.)

How Do I Measure My Heart Rate during Exercise? The same way you'd do it at rest—by taking your pulse. If you've never taken your pulse before, see the box on pages 156-157, which tells you how.

How Do I Calculate My Heart Rate per Minute? Your heart rate equals the number of times your artery pulses per minute. To illustrate: if you count your pulse for 60 seconds, that number is your heart rate. If you count for only 30 seconds, then you must multiply by 2; if for 10 seconds, then multiply by 6. There is a chart at the end of the box on pages 156-157 that has already calculated what your heart rate would be for 10-second pulse values between 12 and 31.

How Often during Exercise Should I Calculate My Heart Rate (Beats per Minute)? Initially, you may need to check your heart rate as often as every five minutes. Once you are familiar with your appropriate exercise intensity, though, you may need to do it

HOW TO TAKE YOUR PULSE AND WORK OUT YOUR HEART RATE

You have two pulse points to choose from—the radial artery in your wrist and the carotid artery in your throat. Your radial artery is the preferred place because the reading is usually more accurate.

Your two carotid arteries are located on either side of your windpipe. While these arteries are large and you should be able to locate them easily by gently pressing just to the right or left of your Adam's apple, there are several things you must keep in mind. Don't press hard; press on only one carotid artery at a time; and do not press too near the jawbone. Doing any of these things may cause your heart rate to slow down excessively and may lead to potentially harmful consequences, not to mention an inaccurate reading.

Taking your pulse is a two-step process. The third step is working out your heart rate if you haven't counted for 60 seconds. Here we give you instructions for taking a wrist pulse reading. Resort to your carotid artery only if you absolutely cannot locate the radial artery in your wrist.

1. Locate the pulse in your wrist. The hand of your wristwatch arm is the one you will use to monitor the pulse in your opposite wrist. Your "sensors" are the pads of your fingers, not your fingertips.

Place your index and middle fingers at the base of the outer third of your wrist, the side on which your thumb is located. If you feel your wrist's tendons, you need to move your fingers closer to the outside of your wrist. Do this incrementally, changing the location of your fingers by about half a centimetre until you finally locate a pulsation. Don't press too hard, as this may obliterate your pulse. A light but firm pressure is all that is needed. You should be able to feel your pulse each time your heart beats, making your pulse rate equivalent to your heart rate.

2. Count your pulse. To determine your resting heart rate, count for a minimum of 30 seconds, maybe even 60. (If you count for only 30 seconds you must, of course, multiply by 2.) Your heart rate varies with your breathing. It slows down when you exhale and speeds up when you inhale. Thus, if you count your pulse for shorter periods, you won't get a good average reading.

The situation is different when taking a reading during exercise. Then your pulse rate is faster, so a 10-second count is sufficient. If you're exercising in a stationary position—on a cycle ergometer, for example—you can count your pulse easily without stopping. However, if you're moving—walking or jogging, for example—you'll need to stop, but not completely. Keep your legs moving while you take your pulse, which you must do immediately. If you wait for more than a second or two, your heart will already have slowed down. This is particularly true if you are fit and is another reason why you should not count for longer than 10 seconds. If you do, you run the risk of greatly *underestimating* your heart rate.

Count as "one" the first pulsation you feel after your watch's second hand hits a digit. Do not count as "one" any pulsation that occurs at the same time as the hand hits the digit. Continue the count until your watch registers 10 seconds. If a pulsation occurs at the same time as the second hand hits the 10-second point, count it, but none thereafter. The same principle applies for digital watches.

3. *Work out your heart rate.* After you have counted your pulse for 10 seconds, multiply that number by 6 to get your heart rate (beats per minute). Here's a chart with the calculations already done for 10-second pulse counts of 12 to 31:

12 = 72	17 = 102	22 = 132	27 = 162
13 = 78	18 = 108	23 = 138	28 = 168
14 = 84	19 = 114	24 = 144	29 = 174
15 = 90	20 = 120	25 = 150	30 = 180
16 = 96	21 = 126	26 = 156	31 = 186

only a few times during each workout. At the very least, we recommend that you check your rate at the following times:

1. Before starting to exercise. If it is above 100 beats per minute and remains this high after fifteen minutes or so of rest, don't exercise at all. Call your doctor and discuss your elevated rate.
2. After you complete your warm-up. If your heart rate is above your heart rate limit at this point, slow down until it drops below the limit. Your problem is simple: you performed your warm-up at too high an intensity. Start off more slowly next time.
3. After you've been exercising at your peak intensity for about five minutes. If your heart rate is above your limit, slow down and recheck it within five minutes.
4. At the point when you stop the aerobic phase and begin your cool-down.
5. When you complete your cool-down. If your heart rate isn't below 100 beats per minute, rest until it reaches this level. Only then should you have a shower or drive off in your car.

Why Is Checking My Pulse and Staying Below My Prescribed Training Heart Rate Limit So Important? After all we've said, you should be able to answer this question without our help. However, we'd like to share with you the findings of a long-term University of Washington study involving 2 464 cardiac patients in a medically supervised rehabilitation programme.[7] During the study period of thirteen years, 25 male participants developed cardiac arrhythmias severe enough to require defibrillation. When the investigators reviewed these patients' treadmill test results and exercise logs, they discovered that 15 of the 21 patients for whom information was available had failed to comply with their prescribed training heart rate limit during 25 percent or more of their exercise sessions. The investigators concluded: "Recording of exercise heart rates at each session is advised, and monthly evaluation to detect persons who consistently exceed the training heart rate range should be carried out, *because such persons are at greatest risk*." (italics added)

Can I Rely on a Portable Heart Rate Monitor Instead of Checking My Heart Rate Manually? Commercially available meters are generally worn on the chest and provide continual monitoring of your heart rate by transmitting electrical signals to a special wristwatch or computer that is also worn on the chest. Usually, you can programme your heart rate limit into the device and it will set off an alarm if you exceed it.

Unfortunately, wearing one of these monitors will not completely free you from the task of taking your pulse manually. These monitors can't always be relied on to give an accurate reading, particularly during exercise in which you move a great deal. They're usually fine for patients who exercise on stationary bicycles or walk, but are of limited value during such activities as jogging.

We advise you to consult a rehabilitation programme staff member or your doctor before purchasing one. Ask them which model they think is reliable for accuracy. Then before you actually purchase a specific one, verify its accuracy by wearing it while you're undergoing continuous ECG monitoring. We would prefer not to recommend specific models.

Guideline 4: Know the Warning Signs of Cardiac Problems, and What to Do Should You Experience Them

Death induced by exercise is rare, and it's seldom unheralded. There are usually warning signs ahead of time.

In a review of twenty-eight cases of heart attack or sudden death in marathon runners with CHD, Tim Noakes found that twenty had definite warning symptoms prior to experiencing the cardiac complication.[8] Despite these signs, though, the majority of them stubbornly persisted in their exercise. Four of them had even completed marathon races feeling the symptoms of heart disease. One runner was participating in a 90-kilometre race and actually ran more than 28 kilometres after the onset of discomfort. Many other researchers have also documented the frequent occurrence of warning signs in runners who simply deny them and then die suddenly in mid-activity or shortly thereafter.

Here is a list of the signs which indicate all is not well with your exercise programme. Should you experience any of them, discuss them with your physician or, if you're enrolled in a rehabilitation programme, with the programme's doctor. *Under no circumstances should you undertake another workout until you've consulted a doctor.*

- **Pain or discomfort in your chest, abdomen, back, neck, jaw, or arms.** You should never exercise to the point where you develop even a mild form of these symptoms of myocardial ischaemia. Even a rating of 1+ ("light, barely noticeable") on our angina scale (see Table 5-4) is an indication you've overstepped the bounds of safe exercise. Upon experiencing these symptoms, slow down immediately and notify a rehabilitation programme staff member. If you're exercising alone and the discomfort doesn't subside within two or three minutes, follow our nitroglycerin guidelines outlined in Table 6-4. Remember, if ischaemia continues for a prolonged period of time, you run the risk of sustaining permanent damage to your heart muscle.
- **Unaccustomed shortness of breath during exercise.** For example, if you've always been capable of walking 5 kilometres in forty-five minutes with no breathlessness, then you should be alarmed if suddenly you can't anymore. Notify your doctor.
- **A nauseous sensation during or after exercise.**
- **Dizziness or fainting.** During or immediately after exercise, if you get very dizzy and feel as if you're about to faint, it is usually best to lie down flat on your back with your head level with or below your feet. (We'll talk about this in more detail later when we discuss the importance of an adequate cool-down.)
- **An irregular pulse, particularly when it's been regular in past exercise sessions.** If you notice what appear to be extra heartbeats or missed beats, you may be experiencing PVCs. Once again, summon a staff member or tell your doctor.

One final word of caution: we've known patients who experienced these and other symptoms while at rest and, unwisely, decided to use an exercise session as a way of determining whether the symptoms were significant or not. *Don't ever do this!*

It's foolhardy, not to mention extremely dangerous. You're running the risk of exacerbating any problems that are indeed present. We cannot stress this point enough. Over the years, we've probably prevented several potentially tragic consequences by educating adherents to our rehabilitation programme about this point.

Guideline 5: Eliminate the Factors that Place You at Greater Risk during Exercise, and Know When Not to Exercise at All

There are ten that you should pay particular attention to:

1. Failing to warm up or cool down adequately
2. Overdoing it to the point of inducing hyperthermia
3. Exercising in excessive heat and high humidity, especially when you're not used to these conditions
4. Having an illness or taking a medication that interferes with your body's temperature regulation
5. Wearing inappropriate clothing
6. Exercising in cold weather without adequate protection
7. Exercising when the air is highly polluted
8. Exerting yourself at high altitudes
9. Exercising competitively
10. Working out infrequently

We discuss each factor in detail below.

DO Warm Up and Cool Down Adequately. If you were an exerciser before your heart attack, angioplasty, or bypass operation, you're probably already aware of the importance of an adequate warm-up before you begin exercising at full intensity and of a gradual cool-down before you stop. Now that you're a heart patient, these transitions become doubly crucial. In one major study, it was found that of the sixty-one cardiac complications that occurred during rehabilitation exercise workouts, forty-four occurred either at the beginning or at the end of a session.[9]

Other research conducted in the early 1970s by investigators at the UCLA School of Medicine demonstrated that sudden strenuous exercise without a prior warm-up may in fact elicit ST-segment abnormalities and/or PVCs in as much as 70 percent of apparently healthy men.[10] In this study, subjects were asked to do five deep knee bends just before running on a treadmill. This did not prevent the occurrence of abnormal responses. But a low-level warm-up, consisting of jogging in place for two minutes, either eliminated or reduced the abnormal ECG responses in most cases.

It is well known that an adequate warm-up enables patients with angina to exercise at greater intensity without developing symptoms. This is because a good warm-up provides your circulation with sufficient transition time to adjust to the increased oxygen demands of your heart muscle during exercise.

We also know that approximately half of all exercise-related cardiac complications occur just after exertion, during the transition period when the body is just starting to cool down. There's nothing new about the phenomenon of post-exercise death. Ironically, the idea of the marathon race was based on such a death. In 490 B.C. Pheidippides dropped dead minutes after finishing a forty-two kilometre run from the Plains of Marathon to Athens to deliver the news that his Greek countrymen had just defeated the Persians. In memory of Pheidippides' supreme effort, the "marathon" was added to the programme of the Olympic Games.

Why is this post-exercise transition period more dangerous? During exercise, not only does your heart pump more blood, but that blood is diverted to your hardest-working muscles—your legs if you're walking, running, or cycling. After the blood unloads oxygen and other nutrients to your leg muscles, it returns to the right side of your heart. The return of the blood to your heart is largely accomplished by the rhythmic contraction and relaxation of your leg muscles. When you stop vigorous exercise abruptly, the cessation of these rhythmic contractions, coupled with the force of gravity, prevents the large amount of blood in your legs from returning to your heart. Consequently, the amount of blood available for your heart to pump to other parts of your body, including the heart muscle itself, drops precipitously. And so may your systolic blood pressure, which could cause you to become dizzy or even to faint.

The other troublesome physiological mechanism involves adrenaline-like hormones called *catecholamines*. Catecholamines, which are released from the adrenal gland into the bloodstream during exercise, continue to rise during the first few minutes after you stop exercising abruptly.[11] Catecholamines are natural cardiac stimulants. Not only do they increase the myocardium's oxygen requirement, but they may also predispose you to heart rhythm disturbances. The end result of all this is an inadequate supply of blood and oxygen to the heart muscle at a time when

162   THE EXERCISE PRESCRIPTION

its energy requirement is high and its susceptibility to rhythm disturbances is exaggerated. We think the cause of Pheidippides' death was probably the mechanisms we just outlined—not simple exhaustion, as most people might assume.

We'll describe what we consider to be good warm-up and cool-down routines in Chapter 10. For now let it suffice to say that you should never stop exercising suddenly and stand motionless. When you check your pulse, keep moving even if this simply means walking or running in place. Likewise, don't come to a complete halt at a robot to let cars pass. In the event that you still become dizzy after exercise and feel faint despite following our advice to keep moving, immediately lie flat on your back. This removes the effect of gravity and helps return blood to your heart more effectively.

UNDERSTAND and AVOID the Dangers of Hyperthermia. As you well know, the human body's temperature cannot fluctuate beyond a narrow range—several degrees above or below 98,6 degrees Fahrenheit, or 37 degrees centigrade—without the risk of death. If your body's temperature rises above 105°F (40,6°C), for example, a condition called heat stroke can occur. The result is damage to many of your body's organs, and even death. While a rise in body temperature above normal (called *hyperthermia*) poses a danger to everybody, it's of particular concern for people with CHD. The reasons why are somewhat similar to those we just described when we discussed your body's reaction to an inadequate cool-down.

When you engage in strenuous activity, heat is one of your body's by-products. In fact, as much as 70 percent of the total chemical energy you use when you exercise is released as heat rather than being channelled into further exertion. Blood is the agent that picks up heat from your working muscles and transfers it to the blood vessels near the surface of your skin. Provided you're wearing the right clothing while you exercise and it's not too hot or humid, sweat should evaporate off the surface of your skin relatively quickly. This evaporation of sweat removes heat from your blood and transfers it to the environment.

The more you exert yourself, of course, the more heat your body produces, and the greater the accumulation of heat-transporting blood near the surface of your skin. This means there's less blood available to return to your heart and recirculate around your body.

There's another aspect to hyperthermia. The more you sweat, the more fluid is removed from your blood. If it's not replaced, the end result is dehydration, which further reduces your circulating blood volume. This reduction causes the heart to beat faster in an attempt to pump out enough blood to your working muscles and other parts of your body.

If the above conditions continue for a long enough period of time, your heart's demand-supply ratio for oxygen may eventually be totally disrupted, causing myocardial ischaemia, among other adverse consequences. The physical signs of hyperthermia are listed in Table 8-3.

To avoid dehydration when you exercise, especially on hot, humid days, we recommend that you drink approximately 250 ml of cold water some fifteen minutes before you begin exercising (cold water is absorbed more quickly than tepid). If your workout lasts longer than thirty minutes, take a drink (250 ml) about every twenty minutes—without completely stopping your motion, as we explained. In our opinion, water is still the best thing to drink during cardiac rehabilitation exercise training, despite the claims made by the producers of drinks with added electrolytes.

Regular sponging of the exposed parts of your body with cool water can also be of some benefit if you exercise in the heat.

TABLE 8-3

The Ten Warning Signs of Hyperthermia

1. Headache
2. Light-headedness or dizziness
3. Mental confusion
4. Disorientation
5. Clumsiness or stumbling
6. Nausea or vomiting
7. Muscle cramps
8. Change in behaviour
9. Hallucinations
10. Cessation of sweating or its opposite—excessive sweating

NEVER Overexert Yourself When It's Very Hot and Humid, Especially If You're Not Used to These Conditions. There are two major causes of heat stroke and lesser heat-related problems during exercise: (1) high temperature and humidity and (2) a lack of acclimatization to them ("acclimatization" refers to the physiological adaptations that your body makes after repeated exposure to new environmental conditions).

Assuming you're acclimatized to hot, humid weather, there's still a point beyond which you shouldn't exercise. The degree of heat stress a person experiences during exercise is a function of, listed in order of importance, the humidity, the amount of radiant heat from the sun, and the air temperature. Learn to listen to your body and to know when it is too hot for you to exercise safely.

Should you still begin to experience any of the signs of hyperthermia (see Table 8-3), stop exercising—but do so gradually, keeping in mind that this is the safest way. You'll be compounding your problem if you stop exercising abruptly while you're experiencing the early symptoms of hyperthermia. If your symptoms are more severe, an alternative is to stop exercising and immediately lie flat on your back indoors or in the shade.

DON'T Exercise If You Have an Illness or Are Taking Medication That Affects Your Body's Temperature Regulation. Certain illnesses and medications also predispose you to hyperthermia during exercise because they interfere with your body's natural ability to regulate its internal temperature. Among the illnesses with this effect are chronic diseases such as certain brain disorders, an overactive thyroid gland, and diabetes mellitus. People with such diseases need to pay particular attention to hyperthermia-prevention strategies during exercise. Transient ailments falling into this category are gastroenteritis, sunburn, and influenza—indeed, any illness that gives you a fever.

Exercising while you've got the flu is especially foolish. Viral infections such as influenza tend to attack the cells of muscles throughout your body. Your heart is one of those muscles. Available evidence suggests that 2 to 5 percent of a virus-infected population generally experiences some degree of cardiac involvement. In some viral epidemics, these estimates can go as high as 12 percent. Viral infection of heart muscle cells causes an inflammatory condition known as *viral myocarditis*. Fortunately, it's usually mild, completely asymptomatic, and disappears spontaneously. When serious, however, irreversible heart damage and even death can result. There is now evidence that strenuous

SOME CARDIAC REHABILITATION CENTRES IN SOUTH AFRICA

The Head
Rehabilitation Unit
St Augustine's Hospital
107 Chelmford Road
DURBAN
4001
Tel (031) 21-1217

The Head
Physiotherapy Department
Wentworth Hospital
Private Bag
JACOBS
4026
Tel (031) 48-4311

Dr A. G. Digenio
Cardiac Rehabilitation Unit
City Health Department
PO Box 1477
JOHANNESBURG
2000
Tel (011) 777-1111 ext 3284

The Head
Rehabilitation Unit
Heart Foundation of SA
PO Box 27334
GREENACRES
6057
Tel (041) 33-8113

Mr P. Joul
Taiton Street
Trichardt Park
BLOEMFONTEIN
9301
Tel (051) 22-3332 (h)

Mr I. J. Gelderblom
63 Petrus Street
El Toro Park
KIMBERLEY
8300
Tel (0531) 39-1608 (h)

The Head
Physiotherapy Department
Addington Hospital
DURBAN
4001
Tel (031) 32-2111

The Head
Physiotherapy Department
R. K. Khan Hospital
CHATSWORTH
4092
Tel (031) 43-3223

Sr L. Kirton
Rehabilitation Unit
28 Foundation Shopping Centre
Main Road
RONDEBOSCH
7700
Tel (021) 686-6436

The Head
Rehabilitation Unit
PO Box 7650
EAST LONDON
5200
Tel (0431) 2-0601

Prof J. Loots
Sports Bureau
Institute for Sport Research and Training
University of Pretoria
0001
Tel (012) 43-7711/15

Sr E. Goosen
Rehabilitation Unit
Dept of Cardiology
Tygerberg Hospital
TYGERBERG
7505
Tel (021) 938-5781

Dr Jones Cilliers
Lifestyle Management Building
Clifton Arcade
Lyttelton Manor
Verwoerdburg
Tel (012) 664-0946

exercise can both predispose you to and exacerbate the severity of viral myocarditis.[12]

Our recommendation: do not exercise when you're suffering from flu or any other illness which raises your body temperature. Before resuming exertion, wait until your body temperature has been normal for at least twenty-four hours. Then return to your usual level of activity gradually over the course of a week or two. As a cardiac patient, never, ever attempt to "sweat out" a fever!

Medications such as atropine (included in some cold and cough remedies) interfere with your ability to sweat off heat during exercise and thereby place you at risk for hyperthermia. Beta-blockers, which many heart patients take, are another group of drugs that require special consideration. A series of our own studies showed that beta-blockers may cause excessive sweating and an exaggerated rise in body temperature during exercise.[13] If you're being treated with beta-blockers, you must pay strict attention to our temperature, fluid-replacement, and clothing recommendations.

DO Wear Appropriate Clothing. The clothing that you wear when exercising in hot or even warm weather should promote heat loss. A recent study indicates that this is best achieved by wearing light, porous clothing, such as "fishnet" or mesh T-shirts.[14] They allow as much free movement of air over the skin surface as possible.

Some overmass people purposely work out in heavy clothing, such as sweat suits, even on warm days. They mistakenly think this will induce greater loss of mass. It does cause more sweating, but because the sweat on their skin is trapped and can't evaporate properly, all they're really doing is predisposing themselves to hyperthermia and dehydration. (The same, by the way, applies to saunas, steam baths, and whirlpools, none of which should be entered until at least ten minutes after your workout. They should be avoided altogether by CHD patients in the moderate and high-risk groups.)

Clearly, wearing heat-entrapping clothing is the last thing you should do during hot- or warm-weather workouts. If mass loss is one of your goals, you should be trying to expend more energy during exercise, perhaps by working out for a longer period, while making sure your heart rate stays within the limit for you.

Our next piece of advice is of no importance as far as cardiac complications are concerned. But we urge you to heed it anyway in order to prevent musculoskeletal injuries. For walking and jogging—both weight-bearing forms of exercise—wearing the right shoes is crucial to prevent injuries. Recent technological advances have created shoes that not only are specifically designed for particular sports, but are also engineered to suit different types of feet. For example, some people have feet that rotate inward (or "pronate") too much on striking the ground. There are now shoes that adjust for this excessive foot motion and foster stability. Other people's feet do just the opposite—they don't pronate enough. Because a certain degree of pronation is needed for adequate shock absorption, these people need shoes with good shock-absorbing properties.

To ensure that you buy the best shoe for your particular needs, we recommend that you consult the staff at your rehabilitation facility. Also, patronize a shoe store where the sales staff is truly knowledgeable about athletic footwear. Finally, joggers and runners should consult the shoe evaluations that appear annually in the various runners' magazines and should read the sections on footwear in *Lore of Running* by Tim Noakes or in *Running Injuries* by Tim Noakes and Stephen Granger (both published by Oxford University Press).

BE CAUTIOUS about Exercise in Cold Weather. About one-third of all patients with heart disease report a worsening of their angina during workouts in cold weather. Not only that, but it takes less exertion to trigger discomfort. Why should this happen?

Researchers from McMaster University in Canada postulate that exposure to cold temperatures causes the skin's blood vessels to constrict in an effort to conserve body heat. This, in turn, increases a person's myocardial oxygen requirements because the heart has to work harder to pump blood through these narrowed blood vessels.[15] A more recent study, conducted at the Montreal Heart Institute, further demonstrated that a reduction in myocardial oxygen supply, possibly as a result of coronary artery spasm, could be an important precipitating factor of angina.[16]

Although our cold is not as severe as Canada's, do consult the weather report on radio or TV before you venture out. Winter temperatures in the morning in the interior of South Africa can be very low.

Clothing is an important issue for cardiac patients who exercise in cold weather. A mistake many cold-weather exercisers make is to dress too warmly. Remember, your body temperature rises when you exert yourself, so you should dress to be comfortable in mid-workout, not when you first begin. When you overdress, you trap your body heat and cause excess sweating. This is bad because your sweat-drenched clothing may cause your body temperature to drop at an alarming rate. Water, after all, is a relatively good conductor of heat.

When dressing for a cold-weather workout, aim for adequate insulation while avoiding excess sweat buildup in your garments. It sounds like a contradictory proposition, we realize. But there is a way to resolve it—by wearing multiple layers of clothing. Layered clothing has two advantages. You can shed layers at will if you become too hot, and the layers have the effect of trapping air in between, thereby allowing you to take advantage of its insulating effect. (Air is not a particularly good conductor of heat, in contrast to water.)

Your innermost clothing layer should serve to soak up excess sweat and carry it away from your skin. Polypropylene or cotton fabrics are recommended. Your middle layer should be specifically chosen to provide adequate insulation. For really bitter weather, wool or down garments are ideal. On rainy days, water-resistant materials, such as Gore-Tex and nylon, are the best solution for an outer layer. If you get too warm in the middle of your workout, you may only need to unzip or unbutton your outer layer to gain the desired cooling effect.

We hope it goes without saying that you should wear a hooded sweatshirt or woollen cap since a lot of your body's heat is lost through an uncovered head. In contrast to the blood vessels near the surface of most parts of your body, those in your head do not constrict in the cold to conserve heat.

Be sensible about cold-weather exertion. South Africans are so accustomed to thinking of this country as a warm, sunny part of the world that they tend to forget how cold it can get. Cardiac patients in the Transvaal and Free State particularly should use caution and commonsense when it comes to exercising in winter.

AVOID Exercising in Polluted Air. Hot and cold weather aren't the only environmental hazards to consider. The quality of the air we breathe also has a measurable impact on any person's ability to work out in safety.

The major sources of air pollution are vehicles, electric power plants which burn coal or oil, and factories (steel, metal, oil, and paper mills are the worst offenders). The seven most common pollutants, as defined by the U.S. Environmental Protection Agency, are total suspended particulates, sulphur dioxide, carbon monoxide, nitrogen dioxide, ozone, hydrocarbons, and lead.

While breathing excessive amounts of any of these pollutants is dangerous, we want to concentrate on the one that poses a special threat to heart patients. That pollutant is carbon monoxide, thrown off by vehicle exhausts and cigarette smoke. In people with CHD, oxygen delivery to the heart is already reduced by atherosclerosis. In such people, exercise combined with carbon monoxide exposure may be sufficient to trigger myocardial ischaemia.

A 1972 study conducted by cardiologists at the Long Beach Veterans Administration Hospital in California underscores this point.[18] Their sample consisted of ten angina patients. The subjects underwent exercise testing before and after they had been exposed to ninety minutes' worth of heavy freeway traffic in Los Angeles. After breathing this polluted air, the subjects experienced angina earlier than usual during their exercise test. The same patients were then put through the same drill after ninety minutes of breathing specially purified air during freeway travel. Predictably, their angina did not occur earlier than usual this time around. The moral of the story is: avoid running along heavily travelled roadways at rush hour. Even in lighter traffic, try to stay at least twenty metres away from exhaust-emitting vehicles.

You'll learn more about the dangers of carbon monoxide and of breathing in other people's cigarette smoke in Chapter 15.

BE CAUTIOUS about High-Altitude Exercise. At the higher altitudes in the interior, the air pressure—or barometric pressure—decreases, which causes a reduction in your body's ability to filter oxygen out of the air. For cardiac patients this is a potentially harmful situation because less available oxygen could mean a disruption in the supply of oxygen their hearts need.

While any workouts you undertake at a moderate altitude—1 000 to 3 000 metres above sea level—will affect you, the increased risk is generally only minimal. Dr. Bruno Balke, who conducted years of research with cardiac patients in Aspen, Colorado, which is 2 408 metres above sea level, states: "Patients referred by their personal physicians because of hypertension, angina, MI, post-coronary artery bypass graft surgery, or multiple (CHD) risk factors not only survived the testing and training period at high altitude without incidents or aggravation of symptoms, but left for home in better health and well motivated to continue a regular physical activity programme."[19]

If your holiday or travel plans include a higher-altitude destination, here are some tips:

- Obtain clearance from your physician. If your condition is unstable, travel to even a moderately high altitude is not advisable.
- Keep careful track of your heart rate during any high-altitude exercise sessions. Expect your heart rate to be higher at higher altitudes. According to Dr. Ray W. Squires of the Mayo Clinic in Rochester, Minnesota, you can expect your heart rate to be about 8 percent higher for a given exercise intensity at moderate altitudes.[20] This means you'll have to reduce the pace of your workout and take frequent pulse counts so you don't exceed your prescribed training heart rate limit.
- Until you've become acclimatized to the altitude, consider dividing your workout into two shorter daily exercise sessions rather than doing a single long one.
- Be aware of the symptoms of two altitude disorders, one transient and nothing to worry about, the other very serious. Acute mountain sickness is the more common of the two, and is the transient one. Symptoms, which assert themselves during the first four to ninety-six hours after a rapid ascent, include headache, insomnia, loss of appetite, and nausea. They should not be confused with cardiac symptoms. The symptoms are usually the most severe during the first few days at the new altitude, and subside within the week. The problem can usually be avoided simply by making a gradual ascent—that is, spending time at intermediate altitudes before proceeding to the peak. Medication to treat this temporary malady is available. High-altitude mountain sickness is another matter. Its symptoms include severe shortness of breath, excessive fatigue, chest tightness, and a cough which produces a pink, frothy sputum. This illness requires immediate medical attention; fortunately, though, it is very rare. Only about 0,4 percent of people ascending to altitudes of up to 3 600 metres are affected.
- Avoid long evening entertainment, especially during the initial few days at high altitude. Heavy eating and drinking, particularly when coupled with less sleep than usual, are a potent and unwise mix for the recuperating heart patient.

DON'T Exercise Competitively. Approach cardiac rehabilitation workouts in a recreational rather than a competitive manner. If you do get involved in group games or sports, it should only be if the emphasis is on fun, not on winning. Should you ignore our advice, your hormonal system may create problems for you.

The pressure and excitement of competition cause the release of catecholamines, the adrenaline-like hormones we mentioned earlier in this chapter. This state of heightened readiness for physical activity is often termed the *fight-or-flight reaction* because an animal in this state decides almost instantly whether to stay and fight or run away. Unfortunately, these hormones also speed up your heart rate, increase your myocardial oxygen requirements, and can lead to coronary artery spasm, potentially fatal heart rhythm disturbances, and blood clots. In a study of ours published in 1980, we identified competition as one of the major factors that increase the risk for cardiac complications during exercise training.[21]

Competition during the first six months after a heart attack, bypass surgery, or angioplasty is very unwise. Thereafter, these guidelines, issued by an American College of Cardiology task force, should be followed.[22] The task force recommended that unless a person with a cardiovascular problem can meet these criteria, he or she should not compete. A person must have:

1. Normal, or near normal, left ventricular function.
2. A normal, or near normal, exercise capacity of at least 7 METs if under fifty years of age; 6 METs if fifty to sixty-five; and 5 METs if over sixty-five.
3. No evidence of myocardial ischaemia during exercise testing—or the presence of ischaemia at high exertion levels only.
4. No exercise-induced ventricular tachycardia (three or more consecutive PVCs during exercise testing).

Exercising Infrequently Is a Mistake. At the beginning of this chapter we cited a study performed by Dr. David S. Siscovick and his colleagues which showed that a person who exercises only infrequently is at far greater risk of having a cardiac complication during exercise than someone who exercises regularly.[23] In the 1980 study of ours that we just mentioned above, infrequent exercise was also pinpointed as an important risk factor for cardiac complications during exercise.[24]

In short, don't become a "weekend warrior". Strive to work out at least three times a week.

TAKE IT SLOWLY

We would like to leave you with one final thought: in our rehabilitation programme we tell new patients they should leave their first few exercise sessions feeling that the programme is so easy that they may, in fact, be wasting their time. Even some of our patients who, months later, began running marathons started out in this leisurely fashion.

There are a couple of reasons for a gradual entry into this new world of frequent exercise. First, a gradual start helps prevent musculoskeletal injuries because you're giving your bones and joints a chance to adapt slowly to the new-found stresses of exercise. (For more on how to avoid exercise injuries—and what to do about them should they occur—we recommend two of Dr. Kenneth Cooper's books: *The Aerobics Programme for Total Well-Being* and *The New Aerobics for Women*.[25])

Second, to use a cliché, "Rome wasn't built in a day." It took you decades to develop CHD. You can't expect to reverse its adverse effects in a matter of weeks. So slow down and enjoy yourself.

CHAPTER 9

SAFETY AND EFFECTIVENESS:
Your Twin Exercise Goals

Safety and effectiveness are your twin exercise goals. As a CHD patient, you must strike a fine balance between the two. Each patient is different and each needs an individual exercise prescription to derive optimum health-related benefits with the minimum of risk.

When you're sick and you visit your doctor, he doesn't simply ask a few questions, scribble out a drug prescription, and send you home. You'd be forgiven for thinking such a doctor was totally incompetent.

On the contrary, your doctor takes a medical history, then examines you thoroughly, possibly even performing specific tests. He's trying to determine what ails you and how severe it is. Certainly, before your doctor writes out a prescription, he makes sure you have no contraindications for the drug in question, advises you about side effects or any specific precautions for that drug, and tells you the dosage and the schedule you are to observe.

You might want to think of exercise as a form of cardiac "medication". It is, in fact. Thus, before prescribing exercise-as-medication, your doctor will be—or should be—just as meticulous as if he were prescribing a drug.

HOW MUCH IS ENOUGH EXERCISE?

This is a key question for any exerciser, but it is especially important for recovering heart patients. To answer this question, Dr. Steven N. Blair, director of epidemiology at the Institute for Aerobics Research in Dallas and the principal investigator of the

Aerobics Centre Longitudinal Study,[1] reviewed the findings of the major epidemiological exercise-heart disease prevention studies, including the British civil servants and Harvard alumni studies and the Multiple Risk Factor Intervention Trial we discussed in Chapter 7. He also looked at the other major studies focusing on energy expenditure and health. After this exhaustive literature review, Dr. Blair reached the following conclusion:

> Exercise training that results in a weekly energy expenditure of approximately 85 kilojoules per kilogram of body mass will bring about the major cardiovascular health benefits.

To unscramble this statement, we have to define some of these terms for you. Here's what you need to know:

- 1 kilogram (kg) = approximately 2,2 pounds.
- A kilojoule is a basic unit of heat measurement. It is also commonly used as a measure of energy expenditure.

Here are two examples: a cardiac patient weighing 165 pounds (75 kilograms) would need to expend 6 375 kilojoules (or 75 × 85) during exercise each week. In contrast, a second patient weighing 220 pounds (100 kilograms) would need to expend 8 500 kilojoules (or 100 × 85) each week (see Appendix B for ways to determine the kilojoules you expend).

It also appears from the studies Dr. Blair reviewed that energy expenditures above this level do not provide substantially more benefit in terms of heart disease prevention.

So how little exercise can you get away with?

After reviewing the available studies much as Dr. Blair did, Dr. William Haskell (Stanford University), Dr. Henry Montoye (University of Wisconsin), and Dr. Diane Orenstein (Centres for Disease Control in Atlanta) concluded that the minimum weekly energy expenditure goal for adults who are otherwise sedentary should be approximately 60 kilojoules per kilogram of body mass.[2]

For our person weighing 165 pounds (75 kilograms), this means exertion equivalent to 4 500 kilojoules per week (or 75 × 60). For our 220-pound (100-kilogram) person, it means 6 000 kilojoules per week (or 100 × 60). These researchers' figures represent the absolute minimum weekly energy expenditure anyone exercising for health reasons should aim for, although less exercise will still result in considerable benefits.

The conclusions drawn by Dr. Blair and Dr. Haskell and their colleagues are based largely on studies involving healthy persons. However, we and most other authorities believe that their conclusions are also applicable to cardiac patients. In view of this, we feel that the best way for you to reconcile the need for safety with the need for cardiovascular benefits is to attain a weekly energy expenditure during exercise of between 60 and 85 kilojoules per kilogram of body mass, *without exceeding your training heart rate limit in the process.*

Weekly energy expenditure during exercise depends largely on four factors, namely, the *type, frequency, intensity,* and *duration* of your exercise sessions. It's your doctor's job to use these four major considerations to tailor a safe weekly exercise regimen for you. Keeping both your medical condition and your personal preferences in mind, your doctor must help you do the following:

1. Choose a suitable aerobic exercise
2. Decide on the number of times you should work out each week
3. Determine the appropriate intensity at which to perform exercise
4. Establish how long each exercise session should last

We tackle the issue of which exercise is right for you in Chapter 10, but before we get to that you need to understand how the last three concepts intertwine. They're embodied in the concept of FIT, which is an acronym for Frequency, Intensity, and Time. If you exercise regularly, you're undoubtedly familiar with this notion already. "Frequency" refers to *how often* you exercise. "Intensity" refers to *how hard* you exert yourself. "Time" refers to each exercise session's *duration*. These quantifiable factors are all connected to each other. An equation showing their interrelationship would look like this:

Frequency + Intensity + Time = Kilojoule Energy Expenditure
= Cardiac Benefit

Clearly, if the amount on the right-hand side of the equation—that is, kilojoule energy expenditure and cardiac benefit—remains constant and you cut down on, say, two elements on the left-hand side of the equation, the third element on the left-hand side must increase to make up the difference. For example, if you exercise at a low to moderate intensity three days a week, each exercise session may have to last a relatively long time if you're to get enough exercise to do your heart very much good. On the other hand, you may choose instead to exercise at the same low to moderate intensity but for a shorter length of time each session. In this instance, you'll have to increase the number of times per week that you exercise in order to achieve the desired weekly energy expenditure.

Here are our recommendations concerning each of these elements:

Frequency. For cardiac patients, we think exercising three to five times per week is ideal. Less probably won't produce significant cardiac benefits; more predisposes you to musculoskeletal injuries.

Time or Duration. As we discussed, the higher the intensity or frequency, the shorter the time needed to attain the desired weekly energy expenditure. Moderate-intensity aerobic exercise of longer duration is preferable to high-intensity exercise of shorter duration for coronary patients since this lessens the risk of cardiac complications. Workouts of thirty to forty-five minutes are ideal for most patients. Once again, longer workouts may predispose you to injury.

Intensity. For heart patients, it's crucial to get the intensity right. It's a fallacy to assume that you must exercise at high intensities in order to derive health-related benefits. In short, the "no pain, no gain" axiom is wrong, as we pointed out in Chapter 2. In the case of heart patients, it can be downright dangerous. Recent research on cardiac patients has clearly shown that major benefits can occur even at heart rates substantially below each patient's training heart rate limit.

One such study came out of two North Carolina schools—the Duke University Medical Centre in Durham and the Bowman Gray School of Medicine in Winston-Salem.[3] The joint research team studied the effects of exercise training on forty-five male heart attack sufferers. One group exercised at approximately 60 percent or less of their symptom-limited heart rates. The other group trained at about 80 to 90 percent of their symptom-limited heart rates. The men exercised three times a week for twelve consecutive weeks. Their exercise sessions consisted of ten minutes of warm-up exercises, then thirty to forty-five minutes of continuous walking or jogging, covering approximately three miles, followed by a ten-minute cool-down consisting of stretching and relaxation exercises. The results: both groups improved their exercise tolerance to the same degree, derived similar improvements in their heart rate and blood pressure responses to submaximal exercise, and experienced the same increases in HDL cholesterol levels.

WHAT EXERCISE INTENSITY IS RIGHT FOR YOU?

We currently advise our patients to exercise at an intensity that will raise their heart rates above 60 percent of their symptom-limited values. We find that an exercise heart rate in the range of 60 to 75 percent of the symptom-limited value—the *training target heart rate zone*—is ideal for most cardiac patients, particularly those who exercise without direct medical supervision. While it is usually unnecessary to go beyond 75 percent to achieve sufficient cardiac benefits, patients enrolled in medically supervised rehabilitation programmes may go higher; however, as we mentioned in Chapter 8, they should never exceed 85 percent of their symptom-limited heart rates. Although exercise performed at less than 60 percent of your symptom-limited heart rate may result in cardiac benefit, you will probably miss out on optimizing your fitness level if you exercise at such low intensity. Moreover, you'll probably have to exercise for well over an hour at each workout to attain our weekly energy expenditure recommendation.

Of course, those of you who choose to exercise less frequently and/or for shorter durations will have to exercise at the upper limit of your training target heart rate zone. In contrast, those who exercise more frequently and/or for longer durations will be able to exercise at the lower end of this zone.

CHAPTER 10

THE RIGHT EXERCISE FOR YOU

In the last three chapters, you learned about exercise's recuperative benefits and about the safety factors for cardiac patients. In this chapter, we get down to specifics. We explain how to tailor an exercise programme to suit your life-style and personal preferences, keeping in mind that you've had some heart problems and certain restrictions accompany this status. Specifically, we will (1) introduce you to the best forms of cardiac exercise; (2) acquaint you with stretching and strength training, two non-aerobic forms of exercise that are important nonetheless; and (3) offer precautionary advice to those of you who suffer from special medical conditions beyond your cardiac problems.

We are not—we emphasize *not*—suggesting that you read what we have to say here and ignore your doctor's advice. Not at all. For those of you who are enrolled in a formal cardiac rehabilitation programme, this chapter will help explain the rationale for the exercise you are already doing. Those of you who are not in a programme and don't plan to be can use this chapter to help formulate your own programme *in consultation with your physician.*

A CARDIAC PATIENT'S EXERCISE MENU: A POTPOURRI OF CHOICES

There are two basic forms of exercise: aerobic and anaerobic. Since an understanding of the root word "aerobic" is central to an understanding of each of these exercise categories, we'll start with a basic definition. Dr. Ken Cooper actually coined the term "aerobics" in 1968 when his first book, *Aerobics,* was published.[1] Indeed, if you'd looked up the word "aerobic" in the dictionary before 1968, it would have been described as an adjective meaning "growing in air or in oxygen". It was commonly used to describe bacteria that need oxygen to live. Dr. Cooper, however, used the word "aerobics" as a noun to denote those forms of endurance exercises for which the body requires increased amounts of oxygen for prolonged periods of time.

In the 1986 edition of the *Oxford English Dictionary* "aerobics" is defined as "a method of physical exercise for producing beneficial changes in the respiratory and circulatory systems by activities which require only a modest increase of oxygen intake and so can be maintained".

No, aerobic exercises don't require excessive speed or strength, but they do require that you place demands on your cardiovascular system. Examples are brisk walking, running, swimming, and cycling.

In contrast, "anaerobic", as the prefix implies, means "without oxygen". Sprinting is an anaerobic activity. It involves an all-out burst of effort and relies on metabolic processes that do not require oxygen for energy production. Such processes result in fatigue within a relatively short period of time.

Aerobic exercise is far better for cardiac patients for these reasons: energy expenditure is related to how much oxygen your working muscles use during exercise. Aerobic exercise obviously uses up more oxygen than anaerobic exercise. Also, because it's more moderate and you can do it for a longer time, aerobic exercise allows you to expend far more energy than anaerobic exercise. Furthermore, when you exercise aerobically, you can more easily monitor your heart rate and keep it within your prescribed limit. Anaerobic exercise is more likely to push your heart rate above that limit.

In sum, since your aim is to expend a large number of kilojoules while staying within your heart rate limit, aerobic exercise is the only way to go.

The ideal aerobic exercise for you has three basic characteristics:

1. It's pleasant. An exercise you enjoy is one you're more likely to stick with.
2. It should be practical and fit into your life-style. In short, it should be something you can perform conveniently all year round.
3. And, from a cardiac point of view, it should use large muscle groups. Why? Because the larger the muscle groups involved in your exercise effort, the greater your body's oxygen uptake will be, and hence the greater your energy expenditure for a given heart rate. Exercises involving large muscle groups enable you to

expend as much energy as possible without exceeding your heart rate limit (see Appendix B for ways to determine your energy expenditure).

The aerobic exercises that are most commonly used in cardiac rehabilitation programmes are walking, jogging, and stationary cycling. But there are other possibilities—swimming, outdoor cycling, arm-cycle ergometry, skipping, rebounding (running in place on a minitrampoline), aerobic dancing, circuit weight-lift training, and certain recreational sports, to name but a few.

Your Exercise Choices: The Pros and Cons

Walking. Most experts, including ourselves, consider walking the most appropriate aerobic activity for CHD patients for these reasons. The intensity is easy to control, so even those in the high-risk category can walk and get the desired conditioning effect.[2] It's simple and straightforward, requiring no special skill, setting, or equipment except a good pair of shoes. It is one of the least likely to cause musculoskeletal problems. And the findings of a recent study suggest that at fast speeds the energy expenditure for walking approaches that for jogging.[3]

Walking with Light Hand-Held Weights. This has become a popular form of exercise and we understand why. Studies show that carrying 0,5 to 1,5 kg hand-weights can increase the energy expenditure during walking—*provided* you move your arms more vigorously than normal.[4]

Unfortunately, these exaggerated movements may tend to elevate your heart rate excessively, which could cause you to exceed your limit. This is why we do not recommend that cardiac patients starting out on an exercise programme include hand-weights in their walking regimen. We might also add that this practice can disrupt your normal walking biomechanics and predispose you to injury.

If you're having trouble attaining your desired weekly energy expenditure during walking, we suggest you walk faster or for a longer duration rather than resort to hand-weights. However, if you're determined to try hand-weights, be sure that you have your physician's approval, particularly if you're prone to musculoskeletal problems.

Treadmill Walking. In inclement weather, treadmill walking is a useful alternative to outdoor walking. With most treadmills, you can change the speed and/or grade (incline) until you achieve your desired exercise intensity. In fact, a major advantage of using a treadmill is that it enables you to fine-tune your energy expenditure.

Jogging. The advantages of jogging are similar to those for walking. The catch is that jogging generally requires greater exertion—or intensity—than walking, thus often inducing a heart rate in excess of your designated limit. However, if you're enthusiastic about jogging despite the greater risk of musculoskeletal injury that accompanies it, we recommend that it be preceded by a walking programme, then by a walk-jog regimen.

A number of our cardiac patients have progressed to the stage where they have run forty-two kilometre marathons. Some, believe it or not, have even completed ultra-marathons such as the Comrades Marathon without any complications. But they all worked up to these milestones slowly.

We do not routinely recommend marathons for cardiac patients primarily for these reasons: (1) Very few CHD patients can take up marathon running successfully. Only 13 of 623 CHD patients—or 2 percent—attending one cardiac rehabilitation programme ever completed one or more marathons.[5] (2) The safety of this activity, from a cardiac standpoint, has yet to be fully clarified. (3) Marathon running requires exertion far in excess of that needed to derive optimal health benefits. (4) Marathon running greatly increases the chances of musculoskeletal injury.

If you eventually decide to take up marathon running, though, you may want to read two books: Dr. Terence Kavanagh's *The Healthy Heart Program*[6] and Tim Noakes's *The Lore of Running.*[7] Both include specific information on marathon running.

Stationary Cycling. This is an activity busy people love. While you're pedalling away, you can do other things—read a book or watch TV, for example. Stationary cycling gives you no excuse should the weather make outdoor cycling impossible, and it causes less wear and tear on the musculoskeletal system than jogging.

There is a disadvantage, though. During a long ride, you may find that you develop sore buttocks. This is why we often have our heart patients combine stationary cycling with walking. The two go well together.

You might think we'd highly recommend those stationary cycles (also called cycle ergometers) that electronically monitor your work rate via a built-in computer. Unfortunately, some aren't very accurate. If you are interested, ask your physician to recommend one.

Some stationary cycles are a variation on the usual theme. They help you achieve higher energy expenditures by working your arms and legs simultaneously. You pump your legs up and down while you're moving your arms forward and back. The result is a more thorough upper- and lower-body workout. We endorse these machines for our CHD patients, especially those who use their arms a lot while pursuing their occupation or for recreation. However, bypass surgery patients should avoid using their arms during stationary cycling until at least six weeks after their operation, when sternal healing is well under way.

Arm-Cycle Ergometry. This is another alternative for patients who use their arms a lot in their jobs or for recreation. Paraplegics, who can't use their legs for cycling, and people with musculoskeletal disorders or leg claudication (painful ischaemia of the legs) will also benefit from arm-cycle ergometry.

Outdoor Cycling. In our opinion, outdoor cycling is more enjoyable and exhilarating than pedalling away indoors. The disadvantage is that roads tend to go up and down. An unexpected incline could cause an excessive elevation in your heart rate. Also, too many downhill stretches and excessive delays while you wait for traffic and at robots may lessen your energy expenditure considerably and force you to increase your workout durations in order to meet your goal. Then, of course, there is the problem of traffic and the danger it poses.

Still, we feel if you can eliminate some of these drawbacks, outdoor cycling is very good—provided, of course, you don't need on-site supervision of your exercise sessions.

Swimming. This is an excellent aerobic activity because it incorporates both the upper- and lower-body musculature. And because it's a non-weight-bearing activity, the chances of a musculoskeletal injury are extremely low. We find swimming is especially valuable for CHD patients with lower-back problems and arthritis.

However, swimming is seldom high on the list of exercise choices of cardiac rehabilitation programmes for the following reasons. The amount of energy a swimmer expends is highly dependent on his or her skill and varies markedly from one person to the next. Swimming, even performed at slow speeds, may cause some cardiac patients to exceed their training heart rate limit. Moreover, swimmers in temperate water often fail to monitor their body's reactions as well as they would on land, thus overlooking such ischaemic symptoms as angina. In really cold water, myocardial ischaemia is a relatively common occurrence, whether or not it's accompanied by symptoms.

Cross-Country Skiing. For those fortunate enough to have holidays in places where skiing is possible, this is excellent aerobic exercise. You have more muscles involved than just the legs, and whenever you have more muscles involved, you get more aerobic benefit. In addition, the heavier clothing you wear and the weighty equipment you must carry further enhance the aerobic effect (that is, the energy expenditure) over that of walking or jogging at similar speeds. There's a drawback, though. The total exertion is greatly affected by variations in skill, snow surface, terrain, temperature and weather conditions, and altitude. Also, it's difficult to take your pulse in the middle of this activity.

Skipping. This is a practical, enjoyable, and easily accessible aerobic activity. However, it's not a popular choice for cardiac patients because it's relatively strenuous and results in excessively high heart rates. Even so, for a given heart rate, the energy expenditure is not as high as that for some other strenuous aerobic exercises such as jogging. Skipping does, however, expose you to the risk of musculoskeletal disorders; this is a significant drawback.

Rebounding. This refers to running in place on a minitrampoline. The advantage of rebounding is the reduced risk of injury. The problem, however, is that your energy expenditure probably won't be great. The trampoline serves as too much of a helpmate, causing your legs to spring up almost without any exertion on your part. This may be a suitable activity during the very early phase of rehabilitation, but it may have to be abandoned in favour of something more vigorous later on.

Aerobic Dancing. Aerobic dancing is steady, rhythmic movements done to the beat of relatively fast music, usually rock.

Unfortunately, this is not something we can recommend for cardiac patients unless the class is specially designed for them, and, frankly, you are not likely to find one. Aerobic dancing is very strenuous and will probably cause you to exceed your training heart rate limit. Moreover, you'll find it hard to quantify your energy expenditure.

Circuit Resistance Training. This is a combination of aerobics and strength training. Typically an exerciser would use a series of resistance training machines and move from one to another with very short rest periods, usually fifteen to thirty seconds, in between. Performed correctly, circuit training improves the cardiovascular system, builds and tones muscles, and burns kilojoules during one carefully constructed workout.

It *sounds* wonderful.

We didn't want to dismiss this exercise option out of hand, so we reviewed the medical literature and did our own study of its possible rehabilitation benefits. The catch is this: the primary benefit is enhancement of muscular strength, not improvement in the cardiovascular system. Thus, we do not recommend it for the recovering heart patient unless it's performed in conjunction with other forms of aerobic exercise.

Recreational Sports. Granted, games such as volleyball and tennis are likely to increase a cardiac patient's enjoyment, and hence compliance. But they don't afford much opportunity to self-regulate the amount of stress placed on the heart. It's more likely that during a sports match you'll find yourself responding to the pressure placed on you by your opponents or other team members. In the heat of competition, it's doubtful your heart rate will be your first concern.

As we mentioned earlier, once activities turn competitive, the risk of cardiac complications goes up. If you engage in recreational sports, you may have to modify the rules in order to minimize the competitive aspects and thus keep your heart rate within the designated limit. When performed in such a way, recreational sports can be—and often are—a very valuable component of a cardiac rehabilitation exercise programme.

STARTING ON YOUR AEROBIC EXERCISE PROGRAMME

From our and other doctors' experience with thousands of heart patients, we can make this sweeping generalization: *aerobic exercise performed for twenty to sixty minutes per workout three to five days each week at an intensity which raises the heart rate above 60 percent of the symptom-limited value will result in an energy expenditure that brings about the desired recuperative benefits.*

This still leaves open the question of how to determine your actual energy expenditure for each exercise session. You'll find the answer in Appendix B in the Resources Section at the back of this book. There you'll find charts for various exercises. These charts offer a rough estimate of your energy expenditure per workout in terms of your Heart Points. (You'll learn all about our Heart Points System in Chapters 16 and 17.) However, we caution you that these Heart Points Exercise Charts are rough estimates. To get a more accurate idea of your energy expenditure during each workout, we also include formulas for each form of exercise. Those of you who have calculators and who demand precision in all that you do may want to skip the charts and use the equations.

In Appendix C, you'll find guidelines for initiating a walking or stationary cycling exercise programme—or a combination of the two. We recommend these forms of exercise to cardiac patients because they're a good way to slowly ease into the routine of regular exercise over an eight-week period. Later, you may want to try some of the other forms of exercise we talked about earlier.

STRETCHING AND STRENGTH TRAINING

We depict what happens during a typical cardiac rehabilitation exercise session in Figure 10-1 on page 186. You'll note that stretching (or "flexibility training") and strength building (or "muscular conditioning") are included at the beginning and stretching is again included at the end of the workout.

What's the rationale for doing these other forms of exercise?

The aerobic portion of the workout is aimed squarely at your heart. It's definitely the most important. But stretching and strengthening your muscles shouldn't be overlooked. After all, without well-functioning muscles, you wouldn't be able to undertake aerobics and many other recreational, occupational, and self-care activities. And without strong, flexible muscles, you're more likely to experience a musculoskeletal injury.

Stretching is part of a good exercise protocol. It should always precede an aerobic exercise session, whether or not you're a heart patient. It won't take you long to appreciate the value of stretch-

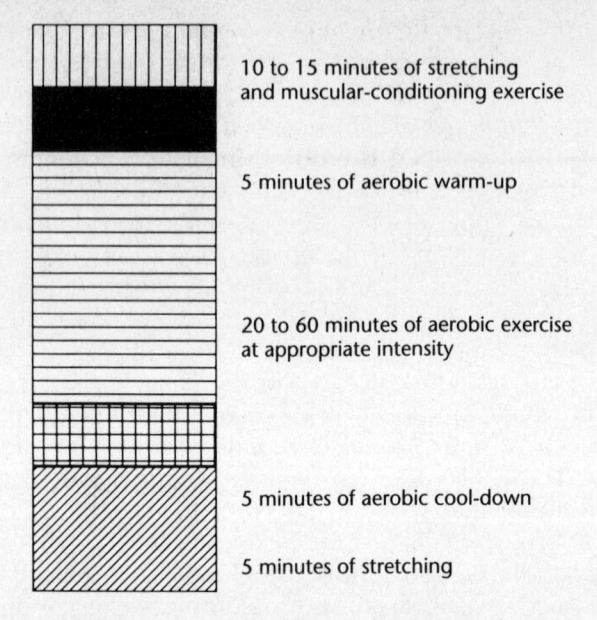

Figure 10-1. Structure of a typical cardiac rehabilitation exercise session. Your exercise sessions should follow the conformation we depict visually here. In a formal cardiac rehabilitation programme, before each workout patients are put through a pre-exercise assessment, which usually consists of measuring the blood pressure, taking the pulse, doing an ECG screening, and asking questions about any symptoms experienced recently. If you're exercising alone at home, you should do two things before you begin: (1) count your resting pulse rate and (2) assess, in your own mind, whether there's been any recent change in your condition that could be worsened by exercise. (*Source:* The Cooper Clinic, Dallas.)

ing. It relaxes you mentally and physically and probably helps prevent injuries by increasing your flexibility and widening your freedom of movement.

At the beginning of an exercise session and, if you have time, at the end (and we encourage you to make time), do several of the stretches shown and described in Figures 10-2A to 10-2E (see pages 187–188). Over the years, we have found these to be particularly useful.

Strength training is definitely a touchier issue for heart patients than is stretching. Although several recent studies have documented the safety of strength training for many cardiac patients, we'd like to add a few words of caution:

- Isometric exercise—a strength-building exercise in which a muscle remains contracted for more than a few seconds without relax-

ing—can elicit adverse cardiac responses in patients with left ventricular dysfunction. Even patients who don't suffer from this problem should *never hold a contraction for more than about three to five seconds.*
- A Valsalva manoeuvre during lifting—that is, pretending to exhale forcefully without releasing the air from the lung—is also ill-advised. In short, *avoid holding your breath,* because it places increased stress on your heart.
- *Do not undertake activities in which you must hold weights above your head for more than a few seconds.* Such movements place an excessive load on your myocardial oxygen requirement.
- Finally, *substitute lighter weights for heavier weights and do more repetitions.* Do not use the heavier weights with the idea that you'll just exercise for a shorter time.

We've developed an easy home muscular-conditioning programme based on the use of light hand-held weights, ranging from a beginning weight of 0,75 kg to 2,5 kg to a top weight of 5,5 kilograms. The programme works all the major muscles of the body and takes the above cautions into account. It is outlined in Figures 10-3A through 10-3K (see pages 189–195). Please note that our programme is specifically designed for home use *after* the first six weeks following a heart attack or bypass surgery.

Figures 10-2A to 10-2E. Exercises for stretching. Open your exercise session with several of the stretches we depict here and you'll help prepare your muscles for the more strenuous exercise to come. Each stretch should be held for 10 to 20 seconds with no bouncing. Do not stretch to the point where the exercise becomes painful. Remember to keep breathing regularly—do not hold your breath. (*Source:* The Cooper Clinic, Dallas.)

Figure 10-2A. Shoulder and back stretch. Lift your right elbow toward the ceiling and place your right hand as far down your back between the shoulder blades as possible. Allow your chin to rest on your chest. If possible, using your left hand, gently pull your right elbow to the left until a stretch is felt on the back of the right arm and down the right side of the back. Hold. Repeat with the left arm.

Figure 10-2B. Inner thigh stretch. Sit on the floor, place the soles of your feet together, and pull your heels in as close to the buttocks as possible. Gently press the knees down toward the floor.

Figure 10-2C. Lower back and hamstring stretch. Sitting on the floor with legs straight out in front and hands on thighs, bend forward slowly, reaching toward your toes. Keep head and back aligned as you move into the stretch. If necessary, you may bend your knees slightly.

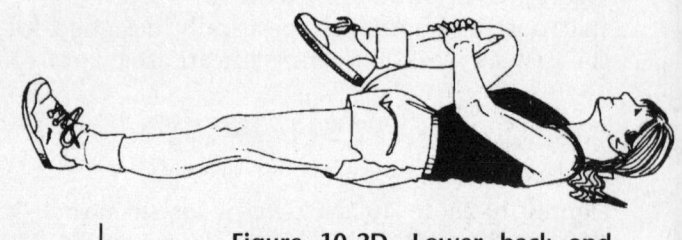

Figure 10-2D. Lower back and thigh stretch. Lie flat on your back with your legs extended on the floor, then pull the right knee up to your chest. Press your back to the floor. Hold the position and then repeat with the left knee.

Figure 10-2E. Calf stretch. Stand facing a wall, approximately one metre away. Place your palms on the wall and keep feet flat on the floor. Keep one foot in place and step forward with the other foot. Keep the back leg straight and gently bend the front knee forward toward the wall. Repeat with the opposite leg.

Most cardiac rehabilitation centres today have gyms equipped with free weights and/or other resistance-training equipment carrying a wide variety of brand names. The question is: at what point should you give this equipment a try and embark on a serious strength-building programme, if at all? Dr. Phillip B. Sparling of the Georgia Institute of Technology and Dr. John D. Cantwell of the Georgia Baptist Medical Centre in Atlanta have some answers for this question based on close patient observation and research.[8] Here are their recommendations in checklist form:

Do not embark on a serious strength-training programme—beyond our low-exertion home muscular-conditioning programme—unless you:

- Have been a regular participant in a cardiac rehabilitation programme, preferably medically supervised, for at least twelve weeks (four weeks for angioplasty patients).
- Have undergone a recent exercise stress test.
- Have let four months intervene from the time you had your heart attack or bypass surgery (four weeks for angioplasty patients).

(continued on page 192)

Figures 10-3A to 10-3K. Our Home Muscular-Conditioning Programme. These are strength-building routines that many heart patients are able to do at home by themselves with little risk of adverse consequences. However, we still suggest that you discuss our programme with your doctor and obtain his or her approval. We recommend that you perform these exercises three days a week on alternate days:

- Begin with hand-held weights no heavier than 2,5 kilograms each, then gradually progress to weights of a maximum of 5,5 kilograms each if you can tolerate it.
- Do 10 to 16 complete and continuous executions (that is, repetitions) for each exercise. Each repetition should take no longer than 3 to 5 seconds. It should not be necessary to rest for more than 2 to 3 seconds between repetitions.
- Perform all these exercises one or two times with anywhere from 15 to 60 seconds of rest between sets. Once you've reached the point where you can perform two complete sets (2×16 repetitions for each exercise) with relative ease, you may want to move up to heavier weights. However, keep in mind that it's more important to do the exercises correctly than to increase the amount of weight.
- Do not hold your breath during these repetitions. If you feel inclined to do so, the weight may be too heavy. You may be straining too much.
- Maintain good posture throughout each exercise set.

(*Source:* The Cooper Clinic, Dallas.)

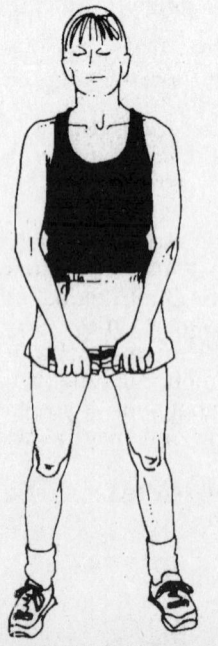

Figure 10-3A. Side shoulder raise (conditioning of the outer portion of the shoulders). Start with arms hanging in front of thighs, elbows slightly bent, and palms facing each other. Raise both dumbbells outward simultaneously to shoulder height, keeping elbows slightly bent. Lower dumbbells to starting position and repeat.

Figure 10-3B. Front shoulder raise (conditioning of the front portion of the shoulders). Begin with arms hanging in front of thighs and palms facing thighs. Raise one dumbbell straight in front of you to shoulder height. Lower dumbbell to starting position and repeat using other arm. Alternate arms.

Figure 10-3C. Bent-over shoulder raise (conditioning of the rear portion of the shoulders and upper back). Bend over until torso is roughly parallel to floor. Keep knees slightly bent. Start with arms hanging down toward floor, palms facing inward, and elbows slightly bent. Raise both dumbbells outward simultaneously to shoulder height, keeping elbows slightly bent. Lower dumbbells to starting position and repeat.

Figure 10-3D. Upright row (conditioning of shoulders, neck, and upper back). Stand with arms hanging in front of thighs, palms facing thighs, and dumbbells close together. Keeping palms close to the body, raise dumbbells simultaneously to the chin. Lower dumbbells to starting position and repeat.

192 THE EXERCISE PRESCRIPTION

- Have a systolic blood pressure below 150 mm Hg and diastolic blood pressure below 100 mm Hg.
- Have an exercise capacity of at least 7 METs (see your answer to Question 4 or, in the absence of abnormalities, Question 2a of Table 5-6).

Nor should you embark on such a programme if your heart condition has worsened recently. If you meet these conditions, there's still one final proviso: you should not proceed unless an adequately trained health professional who is familiar with your case and the equipment is willing to instruct you until you fully understand each specific exercise.

We urge our patients to keep track of their exercise efforts, at least in the beginning, via a training log. Once you're in the habit of exercising as a form of CHD therapy and as a means to work out daily stresses, a diary may no longer be necessary. But initially,

Figure 10-3E. Biceps curl (conditioning of the biceps, or front of the arm). Commence the exercise with arms hanging at sides and palms facing away from your body. Keeping the elbows close to your sides, curl both dumbbells upward to the shoulders. Lower and repeat.

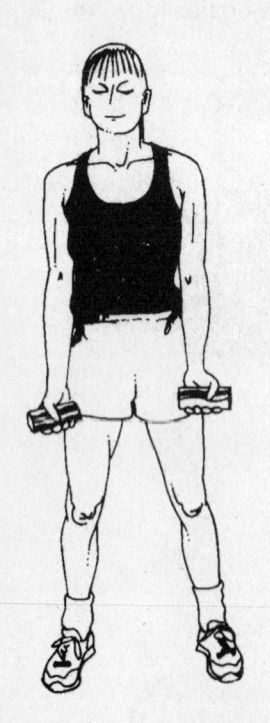

THE RIGHT EXERCISE FOR YOU   193

Figure 10-3F. Triceps extension (conditioning of the triceps, or back of the arm). Place one foot about a step in front of the other and bend the front knee slightly. Lean forward and rest your free hand, palm down, on the knee of the front leg. Place the hand holding the dumbbell against your hip (palm of hand facing the hip). Keeping the elbow still, straighten the arm fully behind you. Then bend the arm until it returns to your hip and repeat. After completing the desired number of repetitions, repeat with the other arm.

Figure 10-3G. Supine fly (conditioning of the chest muscles). Lie faceup on the floor with knees bent or straight, whichever is more comfortable. With dumbbells in your hands, place your arms on the floor at right angles to your body. Raise both dumbbells above your chest to meet in the centre. Lower dumbbells out to the side and repeat.

Figure 10-3H. Pullover (conditioning of chest and back). Lie faceup on the floor with knees bent. Begin with dumbbells held together directly above the centre of the chest, with the elbows slightly bent. Lower dumbbells to floor behind your head, keeping the elbows bent. Raise dumbbells back to starting position and repeat. Keep lower back pressed into floor as you move your arms.

Figure 10-3I. Sit-ups (conditioning of the abdominal muscles). From a horizontal position with knees bent at a 90-degree angle and the palms of your hands resting on your thighs, lift your shoulders off the floor and slide your fingers up toward your knees. Return to the starting position and repeat.

THE RIGHT EXERCISE FOR YOU   195

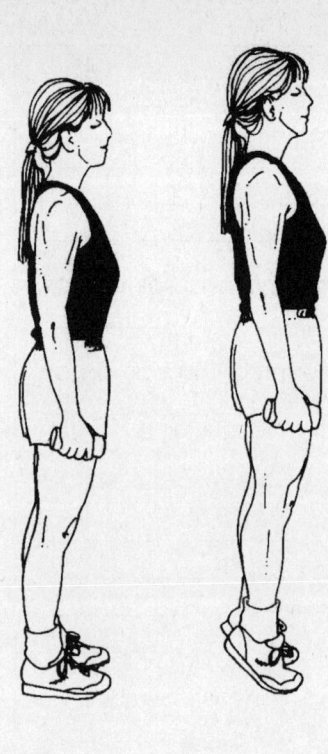

Figure 10-3J. Calf raises (conditioning of the calf muscles). Stand with arms hanging at sides, dumbbells in hands, and feet only slightly apart. Rise onto the balls of both feet. Lower heels to the floor and repeat. Do not bend the knees.

Figure 10-3K. Lunges (conditioning of the thigh muscles and buttocks). Stand with arms hanging at sides, dumbbells in hands, and feet apart. Take a step forward with one foot and bend the front knee slightly while keeping the back leg straight. Step back to starting position and repeat with opposite leg.

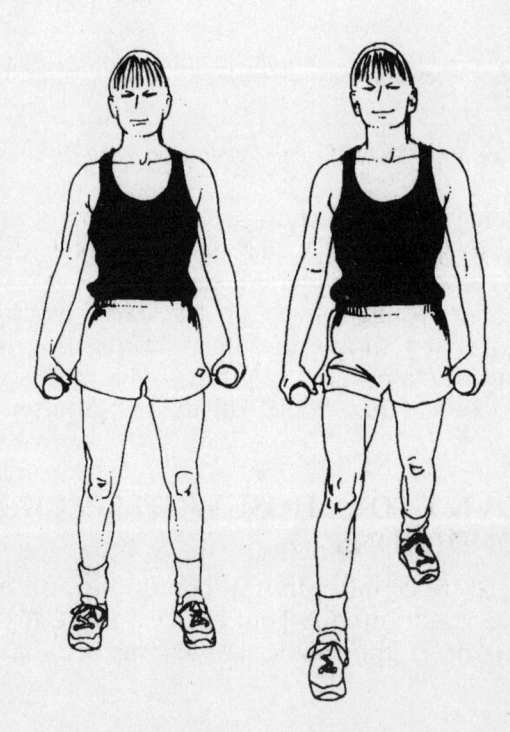

```
DATE: _____   TIME OF DAY: ____·_____   BODY MASS: _____
WHERE I EXERCISED: _____
ENVIRONMENTAL CONDITIONS: _____
RESTING PULSE: _____
BLOOD PRESSURE (if measured): _____

DURATION OF STRETCHING & STRENGTH-CONDITIONING PORTION OF
SESSION: _____

PULSE RATE AFTER STRETCHING & STRENGTH-CONDITIONING PORTION OF
SESSION (in beats per minute): _____

AEROBIC PORTION OF SESSION:
    Duration (in minutes): _____
    Distance covered or work rate/load: _____
    Highest heart rate during session: _____
    Borg RPE (at most Intense part of session—see Table 5-1) _____
    Any symptoms I experienced: _____

    ENJOYMENT RATING CHECKLIST:     _____   1  Not at all enjoyable
                                    _____   2  Not enjoyable
                                    _____   3  Tolerable
                                    _____   4  Enjoyable
                                    _____   5  Very enjoyable

    EXERCISE HEART POINTS I EARNED (see Chapter 16)
```

Figure 10-4. Daily exercise training log. (*Source:* The Cooper Clinic, Dallas.)

when you're still trying to get the hang of it, we strongly urge you to keep one. A diary is also a good idea because it provides your doctor with helpful data. Moreover, it will help you to be consistent and to stay on track with your exercise programme. Figure 10-4 shows an empty training log page. We suggest that you make a number of photocopies of this page and put them in a loose-leaf notebook. Fill in a page after each day's worth of exercise.

ADVICE FOR THOSE WITH SPECIAL CARDIAC CONDITIONS

There are certain physical conditions and medications that may force you to modify your exercise effort. If you have a pacemaker or a heart transplant, are taking beta-blockers, are elderly or obese, or suffer from peripheral vascular disease, osteoarthritis, rheumatoid arthritis, chronic obstructive pulmonary disease, or diabetes mellitus, read on. There are things you should know about how your body may react to exercise.

Pacemaker

The heart's natural pacemaker is the S-A (sinoatrial) node. When it is not able to do its job adequately, a pacemaker often becomes necessary. Over the last thirty years, pacemakers have evolved from simple devices capable only of causing the heart to beat at one preset rate (fixed-rate pacemakers) to more sophisticated, flexible models that increase the heart rate in accordance with a person's level of physical exertion (rate-responsive pacemakers). You should know what kind of pacemaker you've got and review the manufacturer's recommendations with your physician before embarking on an exercise programme.

We recommend that you allow eight weeks for a new pacemaker to settle firmly in place before performing any excessive upper-body exercise. Then continue to be cautious about this form of exercise. Always avoid any pressure over the area where your pacemaker battery is located.

If you have a rate-responsive pacemaker, follow our heart rate recommendations during your exercise training. Unfortunately, if you have a fixed-rate pacemaker, you won't be able to use your heart rate as a guide to exercise intensity. Instead, you'll have to monitor intensity based on your blood pressure response and Borg RPE (see Table 5-1).

We urge wearers of fixed-rate pacemakers to exercise in a medically supervised cardiac rehabilitation programme. In case you worry that even this relatively safe exercise setting may be too risky, we mention a study by Dr. Robert Superko that showed that wearers of fixed-rate pacemakers can definitely benefit from medically supervised exercise training.[9]

Heart Transplantation

Nobody had ever heard of a heart transplant until the 1960s when the first one was performed in Cape Town by Chris Barnard. Since then, heart transplantation has become an accepted treatment for very advanced cardiac disease, and survival rates get better every year. Currently the survival rates are greater than 60 percent for the first five years after surgery.

Medically supervised exercise training is definitely a possibility and a plus for people with heart transplants, according to a recent two-year collaborative study of thirty-six male recipients.[10] The study pointed out that heart transplant recipients have higher resting heart rates and lower maximal heart rates than normal subjects. They also have a delayed heart rate response at the start of exercise and get fatigued sooner. But the benefits they can realize from controlled exertion are impressive.

Overall, transplant recipients can follow our cardiac exercise training guidelines, as long as they exercise under medical supervision at first. However, because their heart rate does not respond to exercise in the expected fashion, particular emphasis must be placed on their Borg RPE (see Table 5-1). They should also pay special attention to the warm-up and cool-down phases and follow the sternum-healing guidelines for bypass surgery patients mentioned in Chapter 6.

In case you have any doubts, you may be surprised to learn that some heart transplant patients have pursued rigorous endurance exercise to the point where they've eventually run forty-two kilometre marathons. However, there are few doctors who would routinely encourage this course of action.

Heart transplants alone were once thought miraculous, but we've now graduated to combined heart-lung transplants for people with very advanced pulmonary vascular and lung diseases. Even for these recipients, exercise training is possible and beneficial, according to a 1989 study by researchers from the Cardiothoracic Unit at Haresfield Hospital in Britain.[11]

Beta-Blockers

These popular heart drugs slow the heart rate during exercise by 20 percent or more. For this reason, it's essential that patients taking a beta-blocker be on this medication when they take their exercise stress test. Otherwise, their heart rate calculations will be wrong and they won't be able to follow our exercise training guidelines.

Even when you do have an exercise test under the influence of beta-blockers, the test's accuracy depends on the time that's elapsed since you took your last dose. That time interval is key. Ideally, you should allow the same amount of time to pass between taking beta-blockers and exercising. Since this is not always practical, we urge all our patients who take beta-blockers to monitor, *very carefully*, their fatigue response via the Borg RPE scale (see Table 5-1).

Whenever your drug therapy changes in any way—say you switched brands or types of beta-blocker, or ended therapy—you must have another exercise test to determine your new target heart rates.

Because beta-blockers may also increase the risk for heat injury during prolonged and/or strenuous exercise, be careful to follow our advice in Chapter 8.

Elderly (Age Seventy and Over)

Because elderly people's physiological responses to exercise are slower, they must spend more time warming up and cooling down. Make sure the transition between warming up and exercising and that between exercising and cooling down are very gradual. Senior citizens must also avoid exercising in the heat since their bodies tend to have impaired heat-loss mechanisms.

Obese

Like the elderly, the obese must concentrate on the warm-up and cool-down. Overmass people must also pay special attention to the footwear guidelines we outlined in Chapter 8 because they are at greater risk for exercise injuries during walking and jogging. They are also especially susceptible to the problems associated with abrupt exercise cessation and to heat disorders.

Peripheral Vascular Disease

This refers to atherosclerotic disease of the peripheral arteries. In people with this problem, exertion may trigger ischaemia of the legs, a condition known as intermittent claudication. However, there's no evidence that this form of exercise-induced ischaemia, unlike myocardial ischaemia, results in damage.

The pain or discomfort from claudication may be mild, moderate, intense, or excruciating and unbearable. Patients should continue to exercise until the pain or discomfort reaches the intense stage. Once it reaches this stage, you should reduce your exercise intensity or, if necessary, gradually slow to a halt and sit down or rest completely. Those who suffer from this problem may have to alternate rest periods and exercise bouts. Another option is arm ergometry, if you're unable to attain your desired weekly energy expenditure with leg exercise alone.

Osteoarthritis or Rheumatoid Arthritis

Osteoarthritis refers to degenerative changes in the joints. In some people with osteoarthritis, weight-bearing exercise can be painful. You should not give up on exercise completely, however. To lessen the stress on osteoarthritic joints, our recommendation is to exercise for shorter periods of time, but more often, or to stay with non-weight-bearing activities like stationary cycling or swimming.

Rheumatoid arthritis is a chronic inflammatory disease of the joints. Exercise training is thought to be capable of retarding its progression. The American Rheumatism Association classifies people with this disease as follows:

Class 1: You're able to carry on all your usual duties without a handicap.
Class 2: You carry on your normal activities despite your handicap, discomfort, or limited motion in one or more joints.
Class 3: Your ability is limited. You cannot carry on all your usual occupational duties, or attend to self-care.
Class 4: You're incapacitated—perhaps bedridden or confined to a wheelchair. You cannot take care of yourself.

Patients in Classes 1 and 2 should be able to adhere to our exercise guidelines. Those in the latter two classes obviously can't. For rheumatoid arthritis patients, we also suggest trying non-weight-bearing exercises such as stationary cycling, arm ergometry, and swimming. Vigorous exercise should be avoided during episodes of severe pain.

Obstructive Pulmonary Ailments

The most common forms of chronic obstructive pulmonary disease (COPD) are chronic bronchitis and emphysema. Exercise is important for those who suffer from these diseases. While regular exercise may not improve their lung functions, it can improve their overall fitness and ability to perform their daily activities. Still, we urge COPD sufferers to consult their lung specialist before they begin.

If shortness of breath develops only with *strenuous* exercise, training can be carried out in the usual manner. However, if your shortness of breath develops early, when your exercise intensity is still low, you have more of a problem and will have to keep the intensity low throughout. Indeed, if your COPD is severe enough, you might consider the possibility of using supplemental oxygen during your exercise sessions. Talk to your doctor about it.

For COPD patients, especially during the initial stage of exercise training, we advise frequent exercise sessions of short duration rather than endurance training. Try two fifteen-minute workouts each day—or even three ten-minute sessions—rather than a single thirty-minute workout. Lower-body exercise—such as walking and cycling—is preferable to arm ergometry because, for a given level of energy expenditure, arm ergometry produces greater shortness of breath than does lower-body exercise.

No matter how severe your condition is, we urge you to keep exercising. Even a sufferer of severe COPD will find his or her tolerance and endurance improving.

Diabetes Mellitus

Type I diabetes results from a deficiency in the amount of insulin produced by the pancreas, whereas Type II means you have a reduced sensitivity to insulin, often as a consequence of obesity. Either type of diabetic can benefit greatly from regular exercise—*however, that statement pertains only to diabetics whose condition is under control.* Rushing ahead with exercise before your diabetes is under adequate control may cause your blood glucose level to increase and your condition to get worse.

Even after your diabetes is controlled, you must be alert to the possibility that your blood glucose level could drop precipitously during or right after exercise. Be especially vigilant if you're being treated with insulin. The warning symptoms of a low blood glucose level are shakiness, light-headedness, headache, visual disturbances, confusion, nervousness, an unsteady gait, hand tremors, inappropriate sweating, or hunger.

The American College of Sports Medicine has developed guidelines to help diabetics exercise safely. They recommend the following to diabetics embarking on an exercise programme:

1. Monitor your blood glucose level frequently.
2. Reduce your insulin dose—usually by 1 or 2 units or as recommended by your physician. Or take carbohydrates prior to and

during exercise—10 to 15 grams for every thirty minutes of exercise. Indeed, you should also carry a carbohydrate source with you.
3. Prior to exercise, if possible, do not inject insulin into sites on any limbs you'll be working vigorously.
4. Avoid exercise at the time of the peak insulin effect.
5. Stop exercising immediately should you experience the aforementioned symptoms of low blood glucose.
6. Exercise with a partner.
7. Be aware that a drop in blood glucose may occur as late as forty-eight hours after you stop exercising.

Type I diabetics should try to exercise daily to help establish a regular pattern of diet and insulin dosage. Type II diabetics should exercise at least five days a week to maximize their kilojoule energy expenditure. They need to expend kilojoules to control their mass as well as to achieve cardiac benefits.

Diabetics have to be especially careful to buy good footwear since long-standing diabetes can interfere with the peripheral circulation and cause foot problems. Exercising in the heat is another concern because diabetes predisposes you to heat disorders.

Diabetics with retinal problems must avoid activities that elevate their blood pressure significantly, such as heavy weight-lifting, and activities that cause excess jarring. For them, swimming is a good choice.

PART FOUR

GROWING HEALTHIER DESPITE HEART DISEASE

CHAPTER 11

RISK FACTORS: The Reason Why Exercise Isn't Enough

YOU'VE started exercising—which means you've taken a giant step toward your goal of reducing your chances of another heart attack. While this is an achievement to be proud of, you can't stop now. There are other steps you must also take, because of the following seeming contradiction: people who are aerobically fit still can be stricken by an unexpected heart attack, and can even die without ever knowing what happened to them.

It happened to Jim Fixx, after all. Here was a middle-aged man whose name was virtually synonymous with running. In 1977, his *Complete Book of Running*[1]—full of his own and other people's testimonials about the benefits of jogging—hit the best-seller lists. It stayed there for two amazing years. He was a legend in his own time, with millions of readers around the globe newly converted to exercise.

When Jim died in July 1984 after a solitary run on a rural road in Vermont, the world was shocked. Exercise enthusiasts were scared. If it could happen to him at the relatively early age of fifty-two, maybe they were next?

Dr. Ken Cooper, of the Cooper Clinic, was puzzled, too, and wanted answers. Many feel Ken was responsible for igniting the exercise boom of the last two decades owing to his 1968 groundbreaking book *Aerobics*.[2] If anybody wanted an explanation of Jim Fixx's death, he did. After his own thorough investigation, which he described in a book called *Running Without Fear*,[3] Ken laid out his findings: Jim Fixx may have run 16 kilometres daily, but that didn't mean he was free of CHD. In fact, his heart was far from healthy. An autopsy showed scar tissue from three previous myocardial infarctions, and a congenitally enlarged wall between his heart's two ventricles. His father had died of a heart attack at age forty-three, an early death by any standards.

Another problem was Jim's aversion to doctors and medical checkups. Jim felt a daily jog was all he needed to stay healthy and avoid his father's fate. Indeed, Jim's faith in running was almost religious. His fervor was evident in his books: "Exercise can reduce, and in some cases nullify, the effects of everything from diabetes to a family history (of heart disease)", he wrote.

There is abundant evidence that thousands of avid exercisers—some of them even convalescing heart attack sufferers—tend to overestimate what exercise can achieve in the same way that Jim Fixx did. Unfortunately, the "myth of invulnerability" is just that —a myth. It's the unfounded belief that an aerobic exerciser is more or less immune to coronary illness just because he or she works out faithfully.

What this thinking totally disregards are the other risk factors for CHD. There are ten in total. And a sedentary life-style, devoid of exercise, is only one of them, albeit an important one. (This does not dispute the value of exercise. It is possible that Jim may have died even earlier had he not exercised— after all, his father was nine years younger than Jim when he died.)

THE TEN RISK FACTORS

Coronary heart disease has no one cause. Unlike many other medical conditions, CHD is a multifactorial disease. One risk factor, even optimally controlled, won't completely offset the impact of the other nine.

"Risk factors" are hereditary traits, personal habits or behaviours, or environmental factors that increase your chances of getting certain diseases—or, if those diseases are already present, the likelihood of disease progression. In this case, the disease is CHD. Here's the CHD risk factor equation[4]:

3 Biological Traits (or Uncontrollable Risk Factors)	+ 7 Unwise Life-style Choices (or Controllable Risk Factors)	= 10 CHD Risk Factors
Age Sex Family history	Inactivity—sedentary life-style High blood LDL cholesterol and/or low HDL cholesterol Smoking Hypertension (high blood pressure) Excess mass in form of body fat Aggressive reaction to stress (Type A behaviour) Diabetes mellitus (glucose intolerance)	

As you can see, CHD risk factors fall into two categories: those you can control and those you can't.

The risk factors of age, sex, and heredity can't be altered. However, you should understand their implications, which we'll explain in a minute.

The other risk factors—such as smoking, obesity, hypertension, and high blood LDL cholesterol—are modifiable. They involve decisions you've made, consciously or unconsciously. With determination, you can change every one of them. So, naturally, that's where your energies should be concentrated.[5]

THE THREE UNALTERABLE RISK FACTORS

Age

As you know, CHD is a progressive disease involving the buildup of atherosclerotic plaque (see Figure 11-1 on pages 208–209). Thus, it stands to reason that as time passes and more plaque accumulates, you're at greater risk for a coronary artery blockage. Then there's the fact that the older you are, the more likely you are to develop one of the medical conditions—such as high blood pressure or diabetes—that constitute CHD risk factors. As people mature, they're also more likely to gain excess mass in the form of body fat, another risk factor.

While none of us can turn back the clock, we can strive to eliminate the factors that generally accompany ageing, such as inactivity, extra mass, higher blood pressure, and higher LDL cholesterol. These factors are far from inevitable, as you'll soon learn.

Sex

You could say that being born male rather than female is a major risk factor for CHD, for the conventional wisdom holds that men are more prone to heart problems than women. That's true to some extent. Women prior to menopause tend to have higher levels of the good HDL cholesterol than men and a relative immunity to CHD. Of course, men can help to offset some of their sex-related increase in risk by working to have as high an HDL cholesterol as possible.

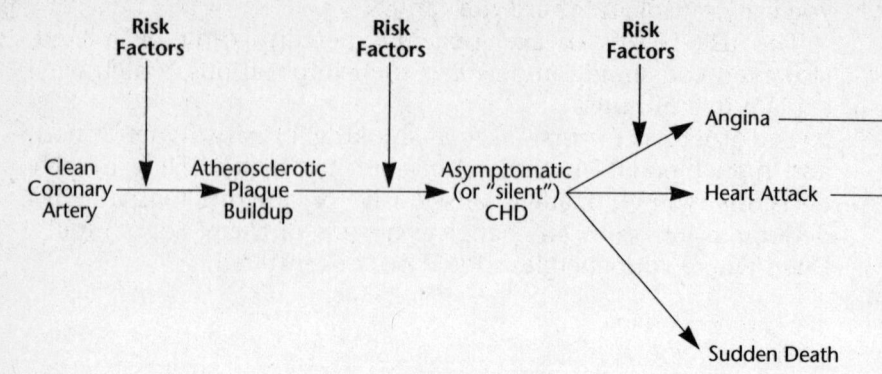

```
    Risk              Risk              Risk
   Factors           Factors           Factors
      │                 │                 │
      │                 │                 │
      ▼                 ▼                 ▼           ──► Angina ──
   Clean          Atherosclerotic     Asymptomatic
  Coronary ──►      Plaque      ──►   (or "silent") ◄
   Artery            Buildup              CHD         ──► Heart Attack ──
                                                      
                                                      ──► Sudden Death
```

Figure 11-1. Coronary artery disease: before and after your heart attack. This flowchart depicts the factors and events in the progression of coronary artery disease (CHD). It also offers hope for CHD patients who adhere to the Heart Points Programme set out in this book. (*Source:* The Cooper Clinic, Dallas.)

In women, oestrogen seems to act as a protective mechanism in ways scientists don't fully understand. But once women pass the threshold point at around age fifty, the body dramatically reduces the production of oestrogen and that immunity fades fast. Women should not be unconcerned. Overall, heart disease kills more women in western society than does any other medical problem. Women just tend to die of it later in life. If they are struck down with a heart attack, it's generally more severe and they're twice as likely as men to die soon thereafter. They fare no better when it comes to bypass surgery. Their surgical death rate is double that of men, and their bypass vessels frequently close up sooner than those of men.[6]

Family History

You may well have inherited the same defective genes that caused your father to die prematurely of a heart attack at age fifty-four, or your brother to die last year, or one aunt and three uncles to suffer for years with angina and other CHD symptoms. Simply put, your risk shoots up if any first-degree relative dies of a heart attack before age fifty-five.

Some medical conditions that are CHD risk factors can also be inherited. Examples are hypertension, diabetes, and a high LDL cholesterol level.

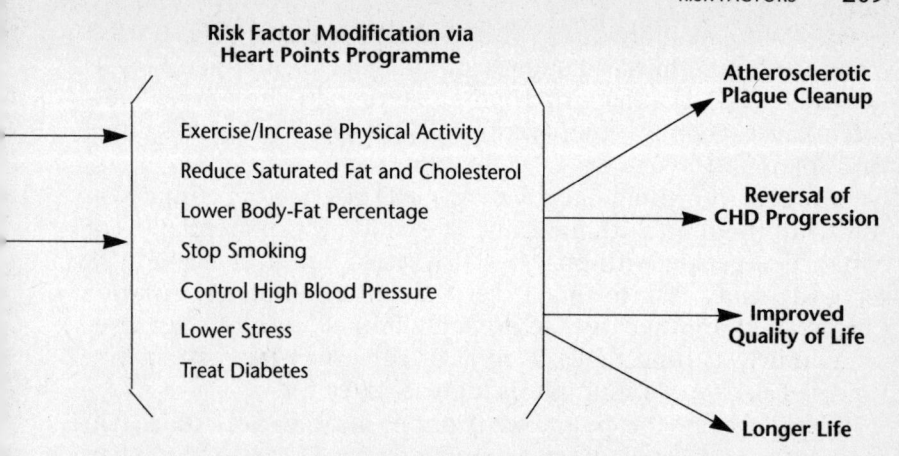

Risk Factor Modification via Heart Points Programme

- Exercise/Increase Physical Activity
- Reduce Saturated Fat and Cholesterol
- Lower Body-Fat Percentage
- Stop Smoking
- Control High Blood Pressure
- Lower Stress
- Treat Diabetes

→ Atherosclerotic Plaque Cleanup
→ Reversal of CHD Progression
→ Improved Quality of Life
→ Longer Life

Familial ties also account, at least partially, for unhealthy personal habits that some CHD patients engage in. Examples are smoking, inactivity, heavy use of salt (which exacerbates hypertension), and the consumption of rich foods (which drives up blood lipid levels and may add extra kilograms). While these habits may have been picked up by mimicking relatives and other role models in your life, they are not what we mean when we list "family history" as an uncontrollable risk factor. These are all acquired habits, even if they are a tradition in your family. They can be broken—and should be broken—not only by you, the CHD patient, but by everyone else in your family who engages in them.

Be cheered by that fact that a family history of heart disease is by no means the most important risk factor. While you can't remove a genetic predisposition to CHD, you can do a great deal to counterbalance it by getting all the other modifiable risk factors under optimal control.

SHADOW FACTORS: MANY CAUSES WITH DISASTROUS EFFECTS

As you can see, CHD is not a disease with a few simple cause-and-effect relationships. Rather, it has many causes, or risk factors, and they interact synergistically. They feed on one another, as it were. A physiological imbalance because of one risk factor often exacerbates another borderline biochemical condition, which eventually leads to the emergence of a second risk factor.

For example, individuals with diabetes mellitus (a CHD risk factor) are more likely to suffer from high LDL cholesterol levels (another CHD risk factor). High-fat and high-cholesterol diets often cause people to be overmass. Both are CHD risk factors. And so on and so on.

Another unfortunate attribute of CHD risk factors is that you can't add them up arithmetically. They add up exponentially. For instance, a person with only one risk factor has an increased risk for CHD that's two to four times that of a completely risk-free person. Add another risk factor, and the incidence of CHD rises by as much as nine times. A total of three risk factors and you may be faced with a multiple as high as sixteen.

To underscore the point, we'll put it another way: take two men without disease. One man smokes a pack of cigarettes a day and has a total cholesterol count of 6,72 and a systolic blood pressure of 140, which is at the upper end of normal. The second has an astronomical total cholesterol of 10,34, has a normal blood pressure, and doesn't smoke. Which one is at greater risk for a heart attack? This may surprise you: both have the same risk. On the basis of the numbers, the second patient might appear to be in worse shape, but you can't rely just on the numbers with this disease. The three "moderate" risk factors of the first patient add up to very high risk.

What this means is that you must know your particular mix of risk factors and mount an across-the-board campaign against all of them. Diligence concerning two, when you're saddled with six, is not much help. Indeed, this is why we developed the Heart Points System. Better than any other way we know, the system drives home the point that a little effort in one direction and none elsewhere isn't good enough. A multifront, head-on approach is the only way to combat CHD effectively (see Figure 11-1).

Risk factors are a kind of statistical destiny. Unless you interrupt the negative patterns in your life—unless you, through health education and willpower, stamp out unhealthy habits—you may get into trouble sooner than you think.

Too often, CHD patients who haven't as yet suffered a heart attack or had to undergo a major cardiac procedure (whether it be an angioplasty or bypass surgery) turn a deaf ear to talk about risk factors. But anyone reading this book has been close to death at least once, maybe several times. Those who have been cardiac patients, should take us seriously when we say that unchecked risk factors can kill you. We aren't exaggerating. By modifying your risk factors, you can stay alive for many good years to come. And that is certainly worth pursuing.

There is some speculation that certain environmental factors—such as water hardness and contamination, trace metals, chemicals used to produce food, and air pollution—increase a population's CHD risk. No one can say for sure because the evidence is still too incomplete and fragmentary. However, research is continuing in these areas and maybe some day we'll have a more focused picture of how these alleged factors affect public health.

If you've got the will to live a longer, healthier life, the chapters that follow are essential reading.

CHAPTER 12

CHOLESTEROL: A Key Factor in Restoring Your Health

WITH fat constituting such a large percentage of nutritional intake, Americans are prone to dangerously high cholesterol levels. However, South Africans have no reason at all to be complacent. Westernized South Africans in particular have similar eating habits to Americans. About 20% of westernized South Africans have cholesterol values that put them at high risk; another 60% are at moderate risk.

Accordingly, the Cholesterol Education Programme was launched by our local Heart Foundation in 1989. Its aims are to encourage the medical profession to screen high-risk patients so that an early diagnosis can be made, and to give long-term guidance to medical professionals in treating high-risk patients. The programme includes information booklets for the public and *The New Generation* cookbook. The programme has a valuable contribution to make in South Africa.

Epidemiological researchers have studied the relationship between cholesterol levels—especially LDL cholesterol levels—and CHD rates in countries around the world. Predictably, they've consistently found that national populations with high blood cholesterol levels also have a high incidence of CHD as well as high CHD death rates. They've also studied immigrants and discovered that people who migrate from a country where blood cholesterol levels are low or moderate to a country where they're high gradually acquire their new country's eating habits as well as higher blood cholesterol levels and increased risk for CHD. An example would be Japanese people emigrating to the USA.

Epidemiologists—those public health statisticians who study whole populations—have come to this conclusion, which applies worldwide: people with cholesterol values in the top 10 percent of a population have a risk of CHD death which is four times as high as the risk for people in the bottom 10 percent of the population distribution curve.

Medical researchers, too, have put together some compelling evidence which links high LDL blood cholesterol levels with CHD. In fact, they now have enough evidence to make this startling assertion: even if a person has no other risk factors for CHD, a consistently high LDL level is enough to cause CHD. They base this assertion, in part, on their knowledge of people who suffer from a rare physiological disorder called homozygous familial hypercholesterolaemia (FH). Such people are missing specific cell-surface receptors that normally remove LDL from the blood. The result can be LDL cholesterol levels as astonishingly high as 25 and severe atherosclerosis. Children with this disorder develop CHD in their teens or earlier. People with the more common heterozygous form of familial hypercholesterolaemia—a reduced number of LDL receptors, instead of none—generally develop CHD in the middle decades of life, in their thirties and early forties. About 1 in 75 or 1 in 100 people has this disorder in South Africa and they often suffer premature heart attacks.

In case you're still not convinced, consider the results of experiments with animals. Many animal species—including monkeys and baboons—develop atherosclerosis when fed diets that raise their blood cholesterol levels. The disease progresses in their bodies in much the same way scientists theorize it develops in humans. A hopeful sign is that CHD in monkeys actually regresses when their diet is changed or drugs are used to lower their blood cholesterol substantially for extended periods. Such studies and the human studies mentioned in Chapters 2 and 3 make a convincing case that CHD is reversible.

OVERCOMING THE EFFECTS OF LDL

Before we consider your blood cholesterol level—how it's measured and how to lower it if it's too high—we'd like to give you a little more background about how cholesterol affects your health. In Chapters 2 and 3 we talked about the role of cholesterol in CHD. We won't repeat the discussion there, except to say a few more words about LDL cholesterol, the most dangerous kind of cholesterol.

Receptors on the outside of cells act as a kind of gatekeeper screening LDLs. These gatekeepers latch on to circulating LDL cholesterol, pulling it inside cell walls for use in various cellular activities. However, once cells have enough cholesterol, they instruct their LDL receptors to turn away any more LDL cholesterol that attempts to enter. Fewer receptors admitting LDL cholesterol means more circulating LDLs.

Dr. Joseph L. Goldstein and Dr. Michael S. Brown, the two 1985 Nobel prize winners who discovered these receptors, suspect that people who spend a lifetime overloading on fatty foods simply don't have enough working receptors to metabolize these LDLs.[3] However, the good news is that such people *caused* their cholesterol problem and they can do something about it by radically altering their eating patterns.

The Heart Foundation recommends that everyone over twenty years of age have their total blood cholesterol measured regularly. How often will depend upon your age and your specific risk category. Provided you have normal cholesterol levels, once every five years should suffice. In all other cases you should be guided by your doctor. The Heart Foundation has age-specific action units for blood cholesterol that will put you into the normal, borderline or high risk category.

For a total serum cholesterol test, you don't need to fast ahead of time because total cholesterol concentrations don't change immediately after a high-fat meal. But be aware that certain biological conditions tend to distort test results. A heart attack is one of them. Levels may be very inaccurate until three months after a heart attack. The same advice applies to those who are acutely ill, losing mass rapidly, or pregnant.

YOUR LDL AND HDL LEVELS

By now you know that your total blood cholesterol level is by no means all that is at stake, especially if you have CHD. Other tests—which do require an overnight fast—can be done to measure concentrations of all three major classes of lipoproteins in your blood. Knowing these lipoprotein percentages is the real key to determining how cholesterol is affecting your health. For those with heart disease it's critical to know these levels. Measuring only your total cholesterol is far from adequate.

Acceptable cholesterol levels for men and women of various ages are shown in Table 12-1. Your blood cholesterol should be composed of 20–30 percent HDL, the beneficial cholesterol; 60–70 percent LDL, the deleterious cholesterol; and 10–15 percent VLDL, which isn't nearly as important.

According to Dr. William Castelli, the director of the famous Framingham Heart Study, the best index of heart attack risk is the ratio of your total cholesterol to your HDL cholesterol.[4] As an equation, it looks like this:

$$\frac{\text{Total Cholesterol}}{\text{HDL Cholesterol}}$$

For example, if your total cholesterol is 6 and your HDL cholesterol is 1,5, your ratio is 6/1,5 = 4

The lower this ratio the better, because it indicates that a higher percentage of the cholesterol in your blood is composed of the helpful HDL cholesterol and a lower percentage of the harmful LDL cholesterol. The following analogy is a useful way of visualizing the ideal balance between the HDL and LDL in your bloodstream. Think of LDL as "rubbish" floating around in your blood and HDL as the "refuse trucks". If you have a lot of LDL,

TABLE 12-1
Acceptable Blood Cholesterol Levels (mmol/ℓ)[a]

Age	Total Cholesterol	LDL Cholesterol[b]	HDL Cholesterol[c]	Serum Triglycerides	VLDL	Ratio of Total Cholesterol to HDL
Under 30	<4,78	<3,10	>1,16	<1,07	<0,52	4,1 or lower
30-39	<5,17	<3,36	>1,16	<1,30	<0,59	4,5 or lower
40-49	<5,17	<3,36	>1,16	<1,41	<0,65	4,5 or lower
50-59	<5,17	<3,36	>1,16	<1,41	<0,65	4,5 or lower
Over 60	<5,17	<3,36	>1,16	<1,41	<0,65	4,5 or lower

[a] In some countries, values are expressed in milligrams per decilitre. To convert mmol/ℓ to these units, divide by 0,02586 for cholesterol values and by 0,01129 for triglyceride values.
[b] Laboratories seldom measure LDL cholesterol directly. Instead, LDL cholesterol is calculated by subtracting the HDL cholesterol and the VLDL cholesterol from the total cholesterol level. But the VLDL cholesterol is not measured directly either; it is calculated.
[c] For women, HDL cholesterol should be above 1,42 mmol/ℓ.
Source: The Cooper Clinic, Dallas.

you need a large fleet of refuse trucks to cart it off. On the other hand, less rubbish means less need for an extensive refuse removal system.

In short, the higher your HDL level in relation to your LDL level, the cleaner your coronary arteries are likely to be and the lower your risk of another heart attack. Conversely, the higher your LDL level in relation to your HDL level, the greater your risk for a progression of your CHD in the form of dirty arteries.

Every time your cholesterol is measured, make sure you know the specific level of your LDL, HDL, and VLDL cholesterol and the ratio of total cholesterol to HDL cholesterol. Then you can compare the results from one test to the next.

The How and Where of Lipoprotein Testing. To get an accurate reading of LDL cholesterol, you must fast (except for water) for at least twelve hours before the blood sample is taken. Your doctor will arrange for the test. We do not recommend that you go directly to a lab for a blood test and try to interpret the results for yourself.

Multiple Tests. To determine what your true HDL, LDL, and VLDL cholesterol levels are, one test isn't adequate. You should have two overnight-fast blood tests, anywhere from one to eight weeks apart. The average of the two tests represents your baseline lipoprotein levels. If the results of the two tests are widely disparate, a third test may be warranted. In that case, use the average results of the three tests as your baseline or throw out the one that is most divergent.

This repeat testing is necessary for two reasons. Mostly it's because your cholesterol count varies from one day to the next. You really have a range and you're trying to find out what it is. The other reason has to do with the quality of the testing. A recent report printed in the *South African Medical Journal* indicates that different pathology laboratories may be using different techniques and reference ranges. However, they are all trying to standardise these procedures and some are referring to the Heart Foundation of Southern Africa's age-specific action limits.

Interpreting Test Results. If you follow the Heart Points Programme, you'll be reducing your CHD risk factors. The end result should be a lower LDL level and higher HDL level.

Following the advice in this chapter, you should work to lower your LDL cholesterol to below 3,36 mmol/ℓ, because levels between 3,36 and 4,1 mmol/ℓ are considered "borderline high risk" and levels of 4,14 mmol/ℓ or greater are "high risk". The ratio of total cholesterol to HDL cholesterol for men and women should be 4,5 or lower, though it would be ideal to have the ratio as low as 3,5 (see the last column of Table 12-1).

It's only fair to warn you that there are people who suffer from certain medical conditions or diseases that tend to raise their LDL levels. Or they may be taking a medication that has that effect. Among the former are thyroid disease, certain kidney diseases, diabetes mellitus, and obstructive liver disease. Among the medications are diuretics, some beta-blockers, and anabolic steroids.

If your doctor suspects the presence of such a causal link, he or she will order more laboratory tests to identify the precise cause of your elevated LDL level. In many cases, treating the medical disorder or changing medications will rectify the problem.

THE DIET SOLUTION

The purpose of a diet change is to lower your LDL cholesterol level. You may wonder why the purpose isn't the opposite—to raise your HDL level. It's because a change in the foods you eat probably won't substantially affect your HDL level. However, mass loss and exercise—both subjects we cover elsewhere in this book—can raise your HDL level, sometimes dramatically. So can giving up smoking.

At first glance, changing what you eat no doubt strikes you as a major hardship, not to mention tedious. Especially the notion of changing your diet permanently—for the rest of your life! However, when it comes to food, humans are a wonderfully adaptable species. Just think of all the widely divergent ethnic cuisines around the globe. This may be just the time for you to sample the healthier among them. Indeed, this forced diet change, due to your CHD, may lead you to discover culinary vistas you never dreamed of before. You may even find, much to your amazement, that you actually like many healthier foods better than the dubious choices you've been ingesting all these years. The Heart Foundation's recipe book contains some excellent recipes.

Our experience treating heart patients has led us to the conclusion that people only *think* they eat what they like. In actuality, they eat what they have *learned* to like. They tend to eat the foods they've been exposed to from birth. Whether from laziness, lack of curiosity, or a perceived lack of time for food preparation, they pay scant attention to healthier mealtime alternatives. For example, Mediterranean and Oriental foods, often considered gourmet cuisines, meet most of the specifications for a healthy, fat-modified diet, and these meals do not take much time to prepare.

We shall now pinpoint the three eating patterns that are most responsible for people's high LDL cholesterol levels. And in the pages that follow we shall discuss South African eating patterns from time to time. Please note that thus far, only the eating patterns of the white and "coloured" populations have been thoroughly studied. Research on the black population will be available before long.

Consumption of Too Many Saturated Fatty Acids. The ideal intake should be a maximum of 10 percent of total kilojoules, but white and "coloured" South Africans consume an estimated 13,3 and 11,6 percent respectively. Saturated fats appear to reduce the activity of LDL receptors and thereby raise the level of circulating LDL cholesterol.

Relatively High Consumption of Cholesterol. White and "coloured" South Africans consume an estimated 362 milligrams and 314 milligrams per day, when the ideal is 300 or less. And many consume a great deal more. It is true, however, that saturated fat is actually more harmful in the diet than cholesterol, for this type of fat has a greater tendency than dietary cholesterol to raise LDL cholesterol levels. This is one of the reasons why mince is a less healthy food than chicken. Both contain about the same amount of cholesterol, but mince is riddled with much more saturated fat.

Consider this: you may eat about 100 grams of saturated fat per day, but only about 600 to 800 milligrams of cholesterol, which is less than 1 gram. Just 1 gram of saturated fat does about the same damage as 20 to 30 milligrams of cholesterol. Thus, those 100 grams of saturated fat that we consume are going to raise our LDL cholesterol level far more than are the rather minimal amounts of cholesterol that we eat.

A Diet Whose Kilojoules Exceed Bodily Needs. The end result of this is obesity and elevated LDL levels. (We discuss mass loss in Chapter 13.) The aim of our programme is to get you to forswear these excesses while still eating nutritious as well as appealing foods.

Those of you who are familiar with the Heart Foundation's recommended eating plan will find our programme quite similar.

NEW EATING HABITS—IN TWO STAGES

We ask you to change, in two stages, what you eat. First, we want you to concentrate on lowering your intake of fat and cholesterol. For many of you, no further changes will be necessary. After three months, you'll find your total blood cholesterol as well as your LDL count have fallen to acceptable levels. You will then have to maintain this diet indefinitely.

Some of you won't achieve this threshold simply by following the above approach. You'll have to go further and undertake a stricter eating regimen, preferably with the help of a registered dietitian for best results. After three more months, you should once again have your blood lipids checked. At that point your LDL level should have dropped sufficiently so that you may, in some cases, be able to return to the maintenance eating programme you undertook during the first three months.

Should success still elude you after at least a year, you become a prime candidate for one of the lipid-lowering drugs now on the market. The prescription, of course, must come from your doctor. You're mistaken, though, if you think drug therapy means you can ever revert to your old pre-heart attack, high-fat eating habits. Those eating habits must be banished forever! For one thing, the diet helps minimize the drug dosage needed.

The Step 1 Eating Plan

The highlights of the Step 1 Plan are given in Tables 12-2 (see page 220) and 12-3 (see pages 221–222). Fundamental information about fats, food cholesterol, carbohydrates, and protein follow later in this chapter.

Of course, it makes no sense to begin this programme until you know your LDL and HDL cholesterol levels. Without these baseline figures, you can't judge the progress—or lack of progress— you make during the first three months of this programme.

Your goal is to lower your LDL cholesterol to below 3,36 mmol/ℓ. The Heart Foundation estimates that dietary changes can reduce blood cholesterol levels by ten to fifteen percent. The Step 1 Eating Plan aims to reduce cholesterol levels by an average of 0,78 to 1,03 mmol/ℓ, with the most dramatic reduction occurring in LDL.

TABLE 12-2
The Step 1 Eating Plan in brief

Nutrient	Percentage of Daily Kilojoule Intake
TOTAL FAT	30%
Saturated fatty acids	10%
Polyunsaturated fatty acids	10%
Monounsaturated fatty acids	10-15%
CHOLESTEROL	Less than 300 mg[a]
COMPLEX CARBOHYDRATES	50-60%
PROTEIN	10-20%

[a] 1 000 mg (milligrams) = 1 gram

Let us emphasize that this is a *lifetime* eating programme. It's not harsh or restrictive. True, it requires some creative food substitutions. But it's by no means rigidly self-denying. Rather, it's the way all health-conscious people—whether they're victims of CHD or not—should eat.

The Step 2 Eating Regimen

The Step 2 Eating Regimen is for those of you who, after three months, have not achieved your cholesterol goals on the Step 1 Plan. It's also a three-month programme. The highlights are given in Table 12-4 on page 223.

As you can see, this programme is essentially the same as the Step 1 Plan, with two notable exceptions. Now, you're required to *try harder* to lower the saturated-fat and cholesterol content of your diet. You must now lower your saturated-fat consumption from 10 percent to less than 7 percent of your daily intake; and the cholesterol in your diet must drop from 300 milligrams a day to 200. (One large egg contains 213 milligrams of cholesterol, to give you a point of comparison.)

Once again your goal is to lower your LDL cholesterol to below 3,36 mmol/ℓ. Our experience has shown that a further decline of approximately 0,39 mmol/ℓ in LDL cholesterol levels can usually be achieved on this regimen.

FOOD FACTS

Most heart patients—initially, at least—know little about nutrition. But then again, many people know very little about nutrition. Here we'd like to teach you the fundamentals of food,

TABLE 12-3
Features of the Stage 1 Eating Plan[a]

Food Type	Eat More of:	Eat Less of:
Fish, chicken, turkey, and lean meats	Fish; poultry without skin; lean cuts of beef, lamb, pork, veal	Fatty cuts of beef, lamb, pork; spareribs, processed cold meats, sausage, viennas, bacon, sardines, roe, prawns, shrimps
Skim and low-fat milk, cheese, yoghurt, and dairy substitutes	Skim or low fat (2%) milk (liquid, powdered, evaporated), buttermilk	Whole milk (plain, evaporated, condensed), cream, milk blends, non-dairy creamers, whipped toppings
	Low-fat yoghurt	Whole-milk yoghurt
	Low-fat cottage cheese (1% or 2% fat)	Whole-milk cottage cheese (4% fat)
	Low-fat cheeses	All natural cheeses (e.g., blue, Roquefort, Camembert, cheddar, Swiss)
		Cream cheeses, sour cream
Eggs	Low-fat frozen yoghurt	Ice cream and sorbet
	Egg whites (2 whites = 1 whole egg in recipes)	Egg yolks
Fruits and vegetables	Fresh, frozen, canned, or dried fruits and vegetables	Vegetables prepared in butter, cream, or other sauces

TABLE 12-3 *(continued)*
Features of the Stage 1 Eating Plan[a]

Food Type	Eat More of:	Eat Less of:
Breads and cereals	Home-made baked goods using unsaturated oils sparingly, sponge cake made with a little oil only	Commercial baked goods: pies, cakes, doughnuts, croissants, pastries, muffins, biscuits
	Rice, pasta	Egg noodles
	Whole-grain breads and cereals (oatmeal, wholewheat, rye, bran, seed, etc.)	Breads in which eggs are major ingredient
Fats and oils	Baking cocoa	Chocolate
	Unsaturated vegetable oils: corn, olive, sunflower	Butter, coconut oil, palm kernel oil, lard, bacon fat
	Polyunsaturated (soft) margarine	Hard margarine
	Mayonnaise or salad dressings made with unsaturated oils listed above	Dressings made with egg yolk
	Low-fat dressings	
	Seeds and nuts	Coconut

[a] On the Stage 1 Eating Plan, you must dramatically lower—even eliminate—certain foods in favour of other, lower-fat ones that are equally nutritious. More specifically, we are suggesting that you increase consumption of foods appearing in the middle column and lower your intake of foods in the last column.

Source: National Cholesterol Education Programme, USA

TABLE 12-4
The Step 2 Eating Regimen in brief

Nutrient	Percentage of Daily Kilojoule Intake
TOTAL FAT	25%
Saturated fatty acids	Less than 7%
Polyunsaturated fatty acids	Up to 10%
Monounsaturated fatty acids	10-15%
CHOLESTEROL	Less than 200 mg[a]
COMPLEX CARBOHYDRATES	60–65%
PROTEIN	10-20%

[a] 1 000 mg (milligrams) = 1 gram

enough for you to navigate the aisles of the supermarket with confidence and to sit down to eat knowing you're not promoting your CHD.

Before we begin, we'd like to say a few words about registered dietitians (dietitians registered with the SA Medical and Dental Council) since you may find it necessary in the course of your rehabilitation to consult one. We find that a certain percentage of our heart patients strenuously resist learning nutrition basics. Their attitude is, "If I have to change my diet, fine. Just tell me exactly what to eat. But don't fill my head with trivia about nutrition."

While we don't think that anything about nutrition is trivial—we are what we eat, after all—we also realize some people prefer regimentation. They like the meal-plan and recipe approach to eating modification. These are often people who don't derive much enjoyment from food anyway. They eat to live, not the other way around. Such patients are prime candidates for the professional services of a dietitian.

Other CHD patients who may need help from a dietitian are those who, try as they might, can't bring their LDL levels down substantially on the Step 1 Eating Plan. As they move into the Step 2 Regimen, they may justifiably feel they need more detailed guidance.

We endorse dietary counselling. You can locate a qualified professional by contacting your local branch of the Association for Dietetics in Southern Africa (ADSA) or by contacting the head office in Johannesburg: PO Box 13904, Northmead, Benoni 1511, phone 011-849-0214.

The Fat on Your Plate

For white and "coloured" South Africans, fat makes up an

estimated 35,5 and 37,2 percent respectively of total kilojoule intake. While the amount is far more than we recommend for the prevention and treatment of CHD, that's not the most shocking thing about this statistic. The worst part is the type of fat South Africans consume. Much of it is saturated, the kind of fat that elevates LDL cholesterol in your bloodstream.[5]

All fats are not alike. Just as there are harmful and helpful forms of cholesterol in your blood, there are also good and bad fats. We're going to give you some information on fats—what to avoid and what to seek out in your quest for a healthier diet.

We have nothing good to say about saturated fatty acids. They are roughly as helpful as a department store lift operator who only knows how to direct the lift upwards—they transport the LDLs, but only in the wrong direction.

There is no nutritional reason for anyone to eat saturated fat. We could all exist very well without it. Unfortunately, saturated fat comes packaged with other nutrients we do need. And therein lies the problem that saturated fats pose. Animal fats—such as fatty red meats and full cream dairy products—are high in saturated fats. So are three tropical plant oils: palm, palm kernel, and coconut. But dairy products are doubly potent. Most are high in saturated fat as well as cholesterol (see Table 12-5 on pages 225–226).

Dairy Products. In societies where people eat a lot of dairy products—the United States and Western Europe, for instance—CHD patients often find it hard to deny themselves these foods, which have been mealtime staples for so many years. Nor should they completely eliminate these nutritious foods from their diet. Rather, they must pay close attention to the low-fat substitutes or alternatives they select. Ideally, all of us should be consuming the equivalent of two glasses of milk daily.

If you're a white South African, cheese may be one of the hardest foods to trim from your diet, since people in this group eat about 8,47 kg per person every year. Other South Africans eat much less. But reduce that amount you must, for cheese is between 65 and 75 percent fat, mostly saturated. That's hardly surprising, since it takes about eight kilograms of milk to make one kilogram of cheese. Cheese also packs an amazing number of kilojoules into a tiny package, and most cheese is high in salt.

There is some good news, though: you can still eat some cheese, provided you buy the low fat variety or low fat cottage cheese.

Here's our advice about milk itself: the various kinds of milk in

TABLE 12-5
Your Dairy Product Options[a]

	Kilojoules (approximate)	Total Fat (grams)	Saturated Fat (grams)	Cholesterol (milligrams)
Milk, whole, 1 cup	642	8,25	5,20	35
Milk, low fat 2% fat, 1 cup	520	4,75	3,00	20
Milk, skim, 1 cup	365	0,50	0,30	5
Yoghurt, fruit, low fat, 225 ml	902	4,72	2,63	9
Cottage cheese, creamed, 1/2 cup	1236	25,80	15,53	31
Cottage cheese, low fat, 1/2 cup	520	5,40	3,20	18
Cottage cheese, fat free, 1/2 cup	406	0,48	0,32	8
Cheddar cheese, 30 g	505	9,93	6,33	31
Low fat hard cheese, 30 g	328	2,85	1,77	32
Processed cheese, full fat, 30 g	338	6,30	3,82	28
Processed cheese, low fat, 30 g	296	3,18	1,77	0

TABLE 12-5 (continued)
Dairy Products[a]

	Kilojoules (approximate)	Total Fat (grams)	Saturated Fat (grams)	Cholesterol (milligrams)
Cream and Coffee Creamers				
Sour cream, 1 tablespoon	25	2,5	1,6	5
Cream, 1 tablespoon	30	2,9	1,8	10
Coffee creamer with coconut or palm oil, dry powder, 1 tablespoon	10	0,7	0,6	0
Desserts				
Vanilla ice cream, 1/2 cup	135	7,2	4,4	30
Frozen yoghurt, 1/2 cup	95	1,5	1,0	6

[a] One thing about dairy products doesn't change when the butterfat content is lowered—their food value. This is important because dairy products come jam-packed with some of the most essential nutrients for a healthy diet. This table will guide you through the maze of choices on your supermarket's shelves.
Source: Food 3, American Dietetic Association-based USDA research.

the refrigerator of your supermarket all contain much the same nutrients. The difference is in the kilojoules and fat. Yes, you should be drinking skim milk, which contains about 365 kilojoules per cup, of which 13 percent are fat. Skim milk contains 1,25 grams of fat per cup, so it could be regarded as 0,5 percent milk in comparison with the so-called 2 percent milk, in which 36 percent of the energy in a cup is derived from fat. Whole milk is 3,3 percent fat, which means that 48 percent of the energy in a cup comes from fat. If you really hate skim milk, try mixing it with 2 percent milk.

Here are some other tips about dairy products:

- Experiment with low-fat evaporated milk in recipes calling for heavy cream. This should work fine in soufflés, puddings, and custards.
- Substitute low-fat yoghurt or low-fat cottage cheese for sour cream in dips and salad dressings.
- In recipes that call for milk, try substituting low-fat buttermilk. You'll actually be improving on the flavour of many dishes, especially pancakes, waffles, and baked foods.

It's useful to know how to determine the percentage of fat in a particular food. This is especially important when you're faced with foods you think are low or moderate in fat, but are really riddled with it.

Nutrient and per-serving labels are the key to a food's fat content. Most labels list both the total fat content and the saturated-fat content in grams. To determine the number of kilojoules in the food derived from fat, multiply the grams of fat or saturated fat by 38 (1 gram of fat equals 38 kJ). From this point, it's easy enough to work out the percentage of fat per serving. Here's an example:

An ice cream bar is shown to have 1 890 total kilojoules, with 25 grams of fat and 15 grams of saturated fat. The number of fat kilojoules is 38×25 = 950 kilojoules. When you calculate the percentage of fat per serving (950 kilojoules/1890 kilojoules), you can see that the ice cream bar is 50 percent fat! A similar calculation shows that the bar is 30 percent saturated fat:

$$38 \times 15 = 570 \text{ kilojoules of saturated fat}$$
$$\frac{570 \text{ saturated-fat kJ}}{1890 \text{ total kJ}} = 30 \text{ percent saturated fat}$$

Butter Basics. One tablespoon of butter contains 7 grams of saturated fat and 30 milligrams of cholesterol. That's a lot.

Maybe you've been using margarine for years. So you're already doing the right thing. Right? The answer is "Yes, in part."

There's still room for improvement. Softer margarines packaged in tubs are less hydrogenated. Hydrogenation is a process which hardens an oil and raises its saturated-fat content. It is better to seek out a soft tub margarine whose label lists sunflower oil as its first ingredient. Only 1 gram of saturated fat is in a tablespoon of the best tub spreads.

Beware of Tropical Oils. Perhaps you've wondered how commercial bakers manage to keep their products fresh and tasty when these often remain on store shelves for weeks. Homemade cakes and biscuits start going stale almost immediately. What's their secret?

Their secret is tropical oils—usually palm and coconut oil—or lard, which is rendered animal fat. These ingredients do wonders for a whole array of commercial foods. They extend the "bowl life" of many crunchy breakfast cereals; they hold cake or biscuit batter together in the oven and make the end product less crumbly; they give a distinctive, inviting taste to everything from nondairy creamers to crackers. Palm and coconut oils are so ubiquitous, in fact, that we consume them daily without knowing it, usually (in South Africa) in the form of coffee creamers.

This is unfortunate. Palm oil is 49 percent saturated fat; palm kernel oil, 81 percent; coconut oil, 86 percent. (Lard is also used in many processed foods; it is 40 percent saturated fat.)

Tropical oils are even more extensively used in America and many major American food producers have pledged to eliminate the above ingredients from their products. The substitutes will probably be soybean, cottonseed, and safflower oils, which are not available in South Africa. These are all polyunsaturates, which we'll describe later. Be aware, however, that food processors sometimes hydrogenate the polyunsaturated oils, raising their saturated fat. Read labels. As much as possible, avoid products whose labels read "hydrogenated" or "partially hydrogenated".

Avoid Fatty Red Meat. For years, we've been hearing that red meat is the prime culprit in high blood cholesterol (see Table 12-6). But more recently, medical researchers have also found something good to say about it. The mitigating factor is stearic acid, a type of saturated fat found in both beef fat and cocoa butter. In lab experiments and clinical studies, Dr. Andrea Bonanome and Dr. Scott Grundy of the University of Texas

TABLE 12-6
Red Meat: Profiles in Fat[a]

Food	Kilojoules	Protein as Percentage of Kilojoules	Fat (Mostly Saturated) as Percentage of Kilojoules
Veal, chop (60 g)	554	46%	52%
Hamburger (60 g)	680	33%	64%
Ham, baked (60 g)	672	28%	69%
Bacon (3 slices)	420	20%	78%
Lamb, chop (60 g)	966	19%	79%
Liverwurst (60 g)	714	19%	79%
Pork, loin (60 g)	861	19%	79%
Beef fillet (60 g)	1084	18%	80%
Frankfurter (60 g)	739	16%	80%
Rib roast (60 g)	1050	18%	81%
Salami (60 g)	1008	17%	83%
Sausage (60 g)	1184	7%	93%

[a] Red meat has been touted for years as being high in protein, but in the last decade the high saturated-fat content has been the cause of some concern. As a consequence, there has been a trend towards buying less red meat and more chicken and fish. Red meat can be more expensive, too. Listed here are thirteen red meats in ascending order of their fat content.
Source: USDA.

Southwestern Medical Centre at Dallas have shown that stearic acid apparently does not raise blood cholesterol levels like other saturated fats because your body immediately converts it into healthier monounsaturated fat.[6] These researchers caution that their findings don't give anyone, particularly CHD patients, permission to indulge in excess beef or chocolate. "Although they (beef and chocolate) won't raise the blood cholesterol levels as much as many people assume," they say, "people should still stick to widely accepted dietary guidelines and keep all fat intake low."

Even if your diet won't change much because of Bonanome and Grundy's discovery, it has startling implications for the food industry. It means margarines could be made that taste more like butter yet don't raise blood cholesterol levels significantly. It means we may someday be able to eat whipped cream with less guilt; that commercial bakers could substitute stearic acid shortening for lard; and that the beef industry could find ways to offer lean meat or processed meats that have less impact on LDL levels.

Meat Eating Recommendations. We're not advocating that you eliminate red meat completely. Because it's an excellent source of protein and iron, it shouldn't be banished entirely. However, do try to wean yourself from the South African habit of eating red meat at every opportunity. Cut down to three times a week maximum, and fill in with poultry (skin and excess fat removed) and fish.

When you do include red meat in a meal, limit yourself to an 85 g to 115 g extra-lean cut from which all the visible fat has been trimmed. On balance, we'd like to see you restrict your intake of lean meat, chicken, turkey, or fish to a total of 170 g per day.

Grilling meat, fish and poultry—whether in the oven or over hot coals—to the point where it's "medium done" is the best cooking method because fat has a chance to fully liquefy and drip off. Steaming, baking and stir-frying in a small amount of vegetable oil are also acceptable methods. Roasts smothered with sauces or gravy are not acceptable. And fried foods—whether meat or vegetables—should be avoided at all costs. A good tip is to chill stews after cooking and then skim off the congealed fat that forms on the surface.

While extra-lean beef is acceptable, we cannot give the same endorsement to processed meats. They contain large quantities of hidden fat and they're not particularly rich in valuable nutrients either. The fewer viennas, sausages, slices of bacon, and slices of cold meat you eat, the better off you're going to be. In fact, we advise you to avoid these completely.

Polyunsaturated Fats—the Better Alternative

White and "coloured" South Africans get an estimated 6,5 and 9,0 percent of their kilojoules from polyunsaturated fats. This means you could already be consuming fewer polyunsaturates than we allow you on our two low-fat eating plans.

You may wonder why we're being so liberal about polyunsaturated fatty acids, when we warned against consuming saturated fats. The reason is that they're safer. They don't raise LDL cholesterol levels. They also make an excellent substitute for some of the saturated fats. For example, we'd much rather see you eat more fish, which is higher in polyunsaturates than most meats.

On the other hand, polyunsaturates have some drawbacks. Like all fats, they are high in kilojoules. Overdoing it could make your mass soar. Try to limit yourself to three to eight teaspoons a day. In addition, there has been some suggestion that there may be an increase in some types of cancer if the intake of polyunsaturates is too high. So keep these down to about 10 percent of your total kilojoules.

There are two major categories of polyunsaturates—omega-6 and omega-3 fatty acids. Such vegetable oils as safflower, sunflower seed, soybean, and corn are rich in omega-6, or linoleic acid. (They also contain some saturated fat, as you can see in Table 12-7, on page 232). Oils from cold-water fish are the main sources of omega-3, or eicosapentaenoic and docosahexaenoic, acids.

The vegetable oils we've just listed should be used for cooking, and they can often be substituted for butter in baking recipes. Whether you want to use them in salad dressings instead of olive oil, which we discuss below, is more a matter of taste than health.

It's long been assumed that eating fish is a good thing, especially in light of the low CHD rates of fish-eating Eskimos. Now researchers have hard evidence. In a twenty-year study begun in 1960, Dutch scientists at the University of Leiden looked for a connection between fish consumption and mortality in 852 middle-aged men.[7] In their follow-up, they found that the subjects who had eaten at least 30 grams of fish every day were 50 percent less likely to die from CHD than those who didn't. The 78 men who died during that study period were, by and large, the ones who had eaten the least fish. The researchers concluded: "The consumption of as little as one or two fish dishes per week may be of preventive value in relation to coronary heart disease."

Today, scientific studies of this subject abound. The one we just mentioned is significant because it suggests that you don't have to eat a lot of fish to get quantifiable benefits, nor must you limit yourself to the oily varieties such as salmon, trout, and mackerel. In the Dutch study, eating even lean fish—which is not that high in omega-3—was linked to lowered risk of CHD. Apparently, the full story on fish is still unfolding.

We've all heard the claims: omega-3 fish oil, particularly in pill form, will solve your high cholesterol problems. Don't believe it. While epidemiologists have been able to find a correlation between high fish consumption and reduced LDL cholesterol levels, no reputable medical studies have convincingly been able

TABLE 12-7
Comparison of the Fats in Your Food (Saturated, Polyunsaturated, and Monounsaturated)

	Polyunsaturated Fatty Acids[a]	Monounsaturated Fatty Acids[a]	Total Unsaturated Fatty Acids[b]	Saturated Fatty Acids[a]
Vegetable Oils and Shortening				
Safflower oil	74%	12%	86%	9%
Sunflower oil	64%	18%	82%	13%
Maize oil	45%	36%	81%	15%
Soybean oil	58%	22%	80%	15%
Cottonseed oil	52%	18%	70%	26%
Olive oil	9%	73%	82%	14%
Peanut oil	34%	41%	75%	20%
Soft tub margarine[c]	33%	27%	60%	16%
Hard margarine[c]	17%	41%	58%	19%
Palm oil	9%	37%	46%	49%
Coconut oil	2%	6%	8%	87%
Palm kernel oil	2%	11%	13%	81%
Animal Fats				
Tuna fat[d]	37%	26%	63%	27%
Chicken fat	21%	45%	66%	30%
Lard	11%	45%	56%	40%
Mutton fat	8%	41%	49%	47%
Beef fat	4%	42%	46%	50%
Butter fat	2%	20%	22%	45%

[a] Values are given as percentage of total fat.

[b] Total unsaturated fatty acids = polyunsaturated fatty acids + monounsaturated fatty acids. The sum of total unsaturated fatty acids + saturated fatty acids will not be 100 percent because each item contains a small quantity of other fatty substances that are neither saturated nor unsaturated. The size of the "other" category will vary.

[c] Made with hydrogenated soybean oil and hydrogenated cottonseed oil.

[d] Fat from white tuna, canned in water, drained.

Source: U.S. Department of Health and Human Services, NIH Publication No. 88-2696, 1987.

to make the same claim for fish-oil capsules. (For more on this subject, see Chapter 19).

Monounsaturated Fats—Another Good Choice

Monounsaturated fats, mainly oleic acid, should make up 10 to 15 percent of your total kilojoule intake. That's not too far from the 13,3 (white) to 14,1 ("coloured") percent that the current average South African diet already contains.

For years, the accepted nutritional wisdom was that monounsaturates had a neutral effect on cholesterol levels, neither raising nor lowering them. Recent studies put monounsaturates in a more favourable light.[8] Indications are that they, like linoleic acid, discussed previously, may cause some decrease in LDL cholesterol levels.

It's oleic acid, primarily, that you want to add to your diet. Good sources are olive and certain types of sunflower seed oils. Peanut oil falls somewhere in between, having 17 percent saturated, 32 percent polyunsaturated, and 46 percent monounsaturated fats. (Look back at Table 12-7 for a rundown of the fat contents of various vegetable oils and animal fats.)

Shellfish as a Meat Substitute

Shellfish should be approached with caution. The Heart Foundation of Southern Africa advises that one should avoid prawns, shrimps etc. if one is watching one's cholesterol intake.

The Cholesterol in Your Food

Studies have shown that many South Africans eat far too much cholesterol every day. This is unwarranted, unnecessary, and unhealthy. Your body can manufacture all the cholesterol it needs without help from your diet.

As Table 12-9 (see pages 235–238) shows, cholesterol in food comes from animal sources and such by-products as milk and eggs. Indeed, some cholesterol is found in the flesh—muscle as well as fat—of all animals (beef, pork, lamb, chicken, and fish). Egg yolk is the worst offender, followed by liver, sweetbreads and brains.

With this type of graph your doctor can plot your cholesterol level against your age to show which cholesterol risk level you fall into.

e.g.
• | TC Level | 6 m.mol/ℓ | = A moderate TC Risk Level
  | Age | 40 |

CHOLESTEROL ACTION LIMITS

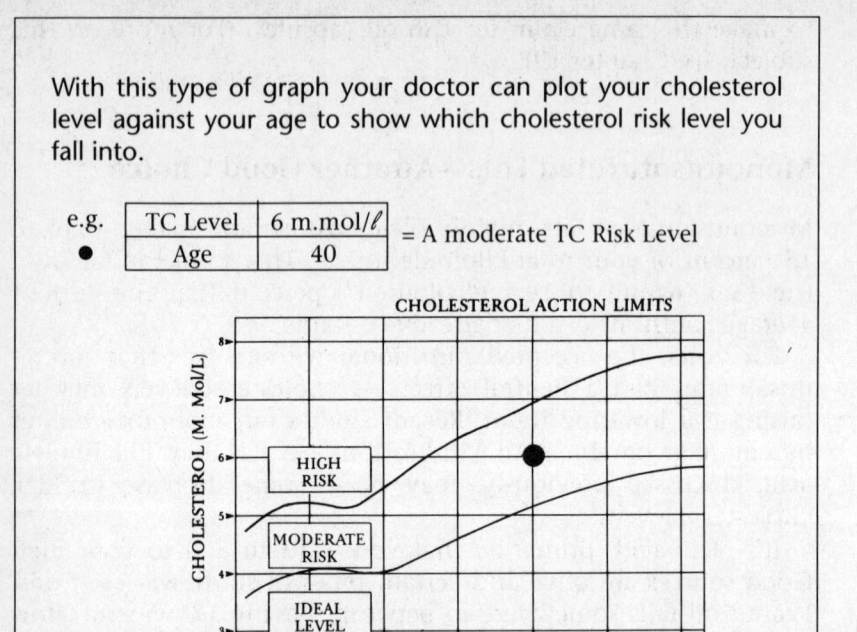

On the Step 1 Eating Plan, you should eat no more than three egg yolks per week. That's pretty restrictive when you consider the egg yolks in baked goods, various processed foods, and home cooking.

Carbohydrates

On our eating plans, we want you to eat more complex carbohydrates. White and "coloured" South Africans get an estimated 47,0 and 46,3 percent of their total kilojoules from carbohydrates. Sounds good, but often the mix is wrong. More than half of that 46 percent may be in the form of simple carbohydrates, the wrong kind for promoting health. Ideally, simple carbohydrates should be cut to 10 percent or less of total kilojoules. On the other hand, complex carbohydrates should be increased to at least 50 percent of your total kilojoules. Indeed,

Table 12-9
Cholesterol and Fat

Item	Example	Saturated Fatty Acids (grams)	Total Fat (grams)	Cholesterol (milligrams)
Beef 100 grams	Top round, lean only, grilled	2,2	6,2	84
	Ground lean, grilled medium	7,3	18,5	87
	Beef prime rib, meat, lean and fat, grilled	14,9	35,2	86
Processed Meats 100 grams	Sandwich loaf, pork and beef	6,4	17,8	47
	Sausage, smoked, beef and pork	10,6	30,3	71
	Polony, beef	11,7	28,4	56
	Frankfurter, beef	12,0	29,4	48
	Salami, dry or hard, pork, beef	12,2	34,4	79
Pork 100 grams	Ham steak, extra lean	1,4	4,2	45
	Pork, centre loin, lean only, braised	4,7	13,7	111
	Pork, spareribs, lean and fat, braised	11,8	30,3	121
Poultry 100 grams	Chicken, roasted:			
	• Light meat without skin	1,3	4,5	85
	• Light meat with skin	3,1	10,9	84
	• Dark meat without skin	2,7	9,7	93
	• Dark meat with skin	4,4	15,8	91
	• Chicken skin	11,4	40,7	83
Fish and shellfish				
60 grams	Calamari, fried in batter	0,86	6,78	16,2
70 grams	Crab, tinned	0,18	6,78	16,2
150 grams	Fatty fish, eg galjoen, snoek, steamed	1,5	5,55	120,0
40 grams	Fish cakes, commercial, fried	0,53	4,2	—
30 grams	Fish fingers, frozen	0,48	3,81	15,0

TABLE 12-9 (continued)
Cholesterol and Fat

Item	Example	Saturated Fatty Acids (grams)	Total Fat (grams)	Cholesterol (milligrams)
45 grams	Pilchards, tinned in tomato or chilli	0,71	2,43	31,5
70 grams	Prawns, boiled	0,13	1,26	140,0
125 grams	Rock lobster, cooked	0,19	1,88	130,0
35 grams	Salmon, pink, tinned in water	0,43	2,07	31,5
50 grams	Sardines, tinned in oil	2,77	14,15	40,0
80 grams	Tuna, tinned in oil	1,17	6,56	52,0
80 grams	Tuna, tinned in water	—	0,64	50,4
150 grams	White fish, eg hake or kingklip, steamed	0,21	1,2	102
Liver and Organ Meats				
100 grams	Chicken liver, cooked, simmered	1,8	5,5	631
	Beef liver, braised	1,9	4,9	389
	Pork brains, cooked	2,2	9,5	2 552
Eggs				
(1 yolk = 17 grams)	Egg yolk, chicken, raw	1,7	5,6	213
(1 white = 33 grams)	Egg white, chicken, raw	0	Trace	0
(1 whole = 50 grams)	Egg, whole, chicken, raw	1,7	5,6	213
Nuts and Seeds				
100 grams	Chestnuts, European, roasted	0,4	2,2	0
	Almonds, dry roasted	4,9	51,6	0
	Sunflower seed kernels, dry roasted	5,2	49,8	0
	Pecans, dry roasted	5,2	64,6	0
	Walnuts, English, dried	5,6	61,9	0
	Pistachio nuts, dried	6,1	48,4	0
	Peanut kernels, dried	6,8	49,2	0
	Cashew nuts, dry roasted	9,2	46,4	0
	Brazil nuts, dried	16,2	66,2	0

TABLE 12-9 (continued)
Cholesterol and Fat

Item	Example	Saturated Fatty Acids (grams)	Total Fat (grams)	Cholesterol (milligrams)
Fruits 100 grams	Peaches, raw	0,010	0,09	0
	Oranges, raw	0,015	0,12	0
	Strawberries, raw	0,020	0,37	0
	Apples, with skin, raw	0,058	0,36	0
Vegetables 100 grams	Cooked, boiled, drained:			
	• Potato, without skin	0,026	0,10	0
	• Carrots	0,034	0,18	0
	• Spinach	0,042	0,26	0
	• Broccoli	0,043	0,28	0
	• Beans, green or yellow	0,064	0,28	0
	• Squash, Hubbard or butternut	0,0604	0,31	0
	Avocado, raw, without skin or seed:			
	• Florida origin	1,74	8,86	0
	• California origin	2,60	17,34	0
Grains and Legumes 100 grams	Split peas, cooked, boiled	0,054	0,39	0
	Red kidney beans, cooked, boiled	0,07	0,5	0
	Oatmeal, cooked	0,19	1,0	0
Milk and Cream 1 cup (250 ml)	Skim milk	0,3	0,4	4
	Buttermilk (0,9% fat)	1,3	2,2	9
	Low-fat milk (1% fat)	1,6	2,6	10
	Whole milk (3,7% fat)	5,6	8,9	35

TABLE 12-9 (continued)
Cholesterol and Fat

Item	Example	Saturated Fatty Acids (grams)	Total Fat (grams)	Cholesterol (milligrams)
Yoghurt and Sour Cream 1 cup (250 ml)	Light cream	28,8	46,3	159
	Heavy whipping cream	54,8	88,1	326
	Plain yoghurt, skim milk	0,3	0,4	4
	Plain yoghurt, low fat (1,6% fat)	2,3	3,5	14
	Plain yoghurt, whole milk	4,8	7,4	29
	Sour cream	30,0	48,2	102
Soft Cheeses 1 cup (250 ml)	Cottage cheese, low fat (1% fat)	1,5	2,3	10
	Cottage cheese, creamed	6,0	9,5	31
	Ricotta, part skim	12,1	19,5	76
	Ricotta, whole milk	18,8	29,5	116
	Processed spread	30,2	48,1	125
	Cream cheese	49,9	79,2	250
Hard cheeses (250 ml)	Mozzarella, part skim	22,9	36,1	132
	Mozzarella, whole milk	29,7	49,0	177
	Swiss	40,4	62,4	209
	Blue	42,4	65,1	170
	Processed	44,7	71,1	213
	Cheddar	47,9	75,1	238

Source: U.S. Department of Health and Human Services, NIH Publication No, 88-2696, 1987.

complex carbohydrates are the main food group we want you to substitute for the fat in your diet.

We have good reason for this recommendation. Although studies have shown that replacing cholesterol-raising saturated fats with complex carbohydrates usually lowers LDL cholesterol levels about the same amount as would substituting polyunsaturated or monounsaturated vegetable oils, we prefer carbohydrates. Mass control is the major reason. No matter which fat source you eat, it will put on kilograms faster than carbohydrates will.

There are various types of carbohydrates, some much more beneficial than others:

Simple Sugars. Technically known as *monosaccharides* and *disaccharides*, these are digestible forms of carbohydrate, just as starches are.

Simple sugars are the sweet things so many of us love to eat. Table sugar and honey are two common examples. We get lots of sugar in carbonated beverages, baked goods, and, of course, desserts. Simple sugars are high in kilojoules and low in fibre, vitamins, and minerals. They should be limited to no more than 10 percent of total kilojoules.

Starches (Complex Digestible Carbohydrates). Of the two digestible forms of carbohydrate, starches are by far the more beneficial, and you should tilt your diet in their direction rather than toward simple sugars. Foods containing starches have far fewer kilojoules per unit volume than those with simple sugars, and they're much richer in vitamins and minerals. Potatoes, spaghetti and all pastas, and bread are common examples.

Fibre (Complex Indigestible Carbohydrates). Your first reaction to the notion of an indigestible food may be, "Why bother if it passes straight through my system anyway?" That's just the point. Your body's intestinal tract needs these helpmates to keep it functioning properly.

Fibre comes in two forms: insoluble and soluble. Cellulose, found in lettuce and wheat bran, is insoluble fibre. Its purpose is to add bulk to stools and to foster normal colon function. It has very little, if any, impact on your blood cholesterol. The soluble type of fibre—which comes from oats, oat bran, fruits, vegetables, and legumes such as dried beans and peas (see Table 12-10 on page 240)—has a vote of confidence from cholesterol researchers.[9] They've found that a high intake of soluble fibre (15 to 25 grams a day) tends to lower people's blood cholesterol by 5 to 15

Table 12-10
Sources of Soluble Fibre

Food	Serving	Fibre (grams)
Grains		
Oat bran	1/3 cup	2,0
All-Bran	30 g serving	5,7
Oat-bran muffin	1	1,2
Oats	3/4 cup, cooked	1,4
Rye bread	2 slices	0,6
Whole-wheat bread	2 slices	0,5
Dried Beans/Peas		
Black-eyed peas	1/2 cup, cooked	3,7
Kidney beans	1/2 cup, cooked	2,5
Lentils	1/2 cup, cooked	1,7
Split peas	1/2 cup, cooked	1,7
Vegetables		
Peas	1/2 cup, cooked	2,7
Sweetcorn	1/2 cup, cooked	1,7
Sweet potato	1 baked	1,3
Courgettes	1/2 cup, cooked	1,3
Cauliflower	1/2 cup, cooked	1,3
Broccoli	1/2 cup, cooked	0.9
Fruit		
Prunes	4	1,9
Pears	1	1,1
Apples	1	0,9
Bananas	1	0,8
Oranges	1	0,7

Source: Nutrition Action Healthletter, Centre for Science in the Public Interest.

percent. Some nutritionists even recommend more soluble fibre than 25 grams.

What's the mechanism for this phenomenon? Apparently, soluble fibre forms a gel as it moves through the intestinal tract, and in some way not fully understood, it interferes with the body's ability to absorb, or metabolize, cholesterol.

Because oats are such a good source of soluble fibre, they've been put forward as the ideal way to fight the atherosclerosis in your arteries. But caution is recommended: while two-thirds of a cup of cooked oat bran—or one cup of oats—may work these miracles, that's only if you eat it on a daily basis. Also, you have to read labels. Many food manufacturers load what could be a very healthy product with such high-fat components as coconut oil. And muffins and other baked goods may contain egg yolks. Nor should you expect oats in any form to combat the effects of an otherwise high-fat diet.

These findings about soluble fibre may be great news on the cholesterol front, but they can also be bad news for your gastrointestinal tract, at least temporarily. However, any negative side effects—such as increased intestinal gas—from upping your intake of soluble fibre usually aren't serious and will generally disappear as your body adjusts to your new way of eating. Increase your intake gradually by starting off with small quantities and building up from there.

Carbohydrate Eating Suggestions. Whole-grain breads, cereals, potatoes, pasta, rice, dried peas, and beans are all rich in carbohydrates and low in fat—provided some food producer hasn't processed them unduly, adding unhealthy ingredients, and provided you don't load them with butter or other high-fat condiments. It is untrue, by the way, that these foods are high in kilojoules, a common misconception.

For the most well-rounded meals, we'd like to see you combine larger quantities of pasta, rice, legumes, and vegetables with smaller quantities of lean meat, fish, or poultry (without skin). The result will be good nutrition with less fat and fewer kilojoules.

Protein

White and "coloured" South Africans obtain an estimated 15,4 and 14,7 percent of their total kilojoules from protein. On our eating plans, you can increase this amount to a maximum of 20 percent, although this certainly is not a necessity.

One of the best sources of protein is red meat, but fatty cuts and fatty meat products are also often high in saturated fat and cholesterol. Fortunately, you've got other choices—among them fish, poultry, cereals, dried peas and beans, and skim milk, for example.

THE DRUG PRESCRIPTION

If drugs to combat excessive LDL cholesterol are available, you may wonder why doctors don't just prescribe them immediately without insisting on painstaking diet modification. There are several reasons—the most important being that all drugs have some drawbacks. Medication will never be as safe a remedy as a good diet. Besides, if you don't change your food choices in tandem with taking a cholesterol-lowering drug, you're sabotaging yourself. Furthermore the drugs, which are sometimes used in combination therapy, may be expensive. A single drug costs between R120 and R480 per month at the highest dose.

Your doctor is the one who must decide when—or if—you're ready to follow the pharmacological route in your quest for lower blood lipids. Your physician will weigh many factors, including how hard you've really tried to cut down on fats and cholesterol-laden foods to get your LDLs down to below 3,36 mmol/ℓ.

A low HDL cholesterol level that refuses to climb to healthier levels no matter what you eat could also persuade your physician. The thinking is: "If I can't get this patient's good cholesterol up, I'll try to get the harmful type down."

Finally, your physician may hesitate because drug therapy is a prolonged regimen. It could last the rest of your life.

Before your physician places you on a drug regimen, we would expect him or her to spend considerable time explaining its implications. We don't approve of a dictatorial stance on the part of a doctor. Patients have a right to know exactly what they're getting into. Any cholesterol-lowering drug is serious business.

"When do I start taking drugs?" is a question we, and other cardiac specialists, hear frequently from patients. For a person with a history of CHD, one criterion is: "When your LDL cholesterol level is 4,14 or higher *despite dietary intervention*".

Lipid-lowering drugs come in various forms. Some are pills, some powders. They differ in their impact on the various lipoproteins in your body and in their interactions with other drugs you might be taking. Some have unpleasant side effects. When you consider all this, clearly you and your physician have plenty to chat about.

Once medication is started, expect to undergo regular blood tests, maybe as often as every three months for the first year or two. Your doctor will be checking to make sure that side effects aren't occurring, that your liver and kidneys are reacting well, that any other medications aren't interfering with your cholesterol drug or vice versa, and that target LDL levels are achieved.

LDL levels below 3,36 mmol/ℓ represent perfection. However, your physician should not try to push your LDL level below 3,36 mmol/ℓ. There is no current evidence showing that extremely depressed LDL levels produce any additional benefits.

Niacin (nicotinic acid)

You may be surprised to see mention of niacin here. The last time you noticed the word "niacin" was probably on a bottle among the B vitamins on your local pharmacy shelves. Yes, this is one LDL-lowering agent that does not require a prescription, although it is most unwise for CHD patients to institute this treatment on their own. In the doses required, it becomes a powerful drug, not an innocent vitamin.

"Niacin" and "nicotinic acid" are interchangeable terms. You may have seen "niacinamide" listed on the label of your multiple-vitamin pills. In that form, it serves nutrient purposes in your body but it does not lower blood cholesterol.

The first reports that niacin could reduce total cholesterol, LDL cholesterol, and triglycerides appeared in the 1950s and 1960s.[10] Today, there are many research studies that have come to the same conclusion.

The Coronary Drug Project, which tracked more than 8 000 people from 1969 to 1975, singled out niacin as the agent responsible for reducing non-fatal heart attacks by 29 percent.[11] It also set many doctors' minds at rest about using niacin over long periods of time. This is one drug that, with proper monitoring of blood studies and proper medical supervision, can often be taken for an extended period without major side effects. The biggest advantage of niacin, however, is the fact that it lowers LDL cholesterol at the same time that it raises HDL cholesterol. It is also inexpensive.

Another noteworthy study, conducted more recently, examined the effects of a combination of niacin and colestipol.[12] (Colestipol will be discussed further on.) Some 162 men—all non-smokers between the ages of forty and fifty-nine who had undergone bypass surgery—formed the sample. The men on the medication regimen experienced a 26 percent reduction in their total cholesterol levels, a 43 percent reduction in their LDL cholesterol levels, and a 37 percent *elevation* in their HDL cholesterol levels during the two years of the treatment. A second group, who did not take the drug, had far more atherosclerotic buildup and CHD progression than did the first group.

Many people find the primary side effect of high dosages of niacin—1 to 3 grams daily—more embarrassing than uncomfortable. Before your body becomes accustomed to it, niacin may cause a rosy, sunburn-like flush to appear not long after you take each pill. This may be accompanied by a prickly sensation in the upper body. Those who suffer a severe flush can often mitigate or even eliminate the problem by taking an aspirin an hour or so before the niacin tablet.

Occasionally, people also experience gastrointestinal upsets—everything from stomach pain to flatulence. This is why niacin should be taken with meals—but never with hot drinks. Perhaps the most troublesome side effect of all is blurred vision and an itchy rash that, unlike the flush, can last more than a day. Fortunately, not that many people have the latter reactions.

Anecdotal reports from people taking niacin in time-release capsule formulations, which may cost a lot more in some cases, indicate that there may be fewer side effects. Other users report almost no adverse effects from the regular formulations if they ease into higher doses slowly over a two-month period. We recommend that patients start at no more than 300 milligrams—100 milligrams three times a day—and work up to a maximum of 3 000 milligrams (3 grams) daily if necessary. For that matter, if your LDL cholesterol isn't unduly high, you may never require 3 grams. Researchers have reported some positive LDL-lowering effects on dosages as low as 1 gram.[13]

When long-acting, or sustained-release, niacin is used, a good starting dose is 125 milligrams taken two or three times daily with meals. Gradually, over a period of six weeks, the dose is built up to 500 milligrams two or three times daily. The higher dosages bring a greater risk of adverse reactions, however.

When Is Niacin Contraindicated? "Contraindicate" is a word you see all the time in the instructions that accompany prescription medications. It means "to give indication against the advisability of a particular remedy or treatment". In lay language, it simply means don't take this drug if you have any of the listed medical conditions or diseases.

Contraindications for these large doses of niacin are liver problems, including hepatitis and cirrhosis; severe heart arrhythmias; peptic ulcer; diabetes; and gout (high uric acid). Niacin places an extra burden on your liver, the organ that metabolizes it. This is why heavy drinkers, who may have damaged their liver, aren't good candidates for this treatment. It's also why, if you're taking niacin in these large doses, you should have liver-function as well as glucose and uric-acid tests every three to six months. As we've said, niacin, in the high doses required to lower LDL and raise HDL, is no longer an innocent vitamin. It is now a drug and must be handled with proper medical care.

Other Options

If niacin is contraindicated, if it hasn't done an effective job, or if your body simply won't tolerate it, there are other drugs.

Suppose your LDL level refuses to budge, yet your HDL level is normal and your fasting triglyceride level is not too high (less than 2,82 mmol/ℓ). Your physician will probably recommend a bile acid sequestrant, either cholestyramine (brand name Questran) or colestipol (brand name Colestid). These medications have been around for decades and there's adequate evidence of their long-term safety—which cannot be said about many other cholesterol-lowering drugs.

Sequestrants come in granular or powdered form to be mixed with water or fruit juice and drunk with meals. We recommend that patients prepare an entire daily dose each evening and refrigerate it overnight. That way, they can reach for a glass of it as they might any other liquid they drink regularly. It makes downing the concoction less onerous. One helpful hint: mix the sequestrant with a tablespoon of Metamucil. This makes the sequestrant less gritty, counteracts any constipation and bloating, and has the added benefit of helping to lower your cholesterol. Convenient cholestyramine bars are now available in America, although unfortunately not in South Africa.

Generally, slightly lower doses of cholestyramine (4 grams) deliver the same LDL-lowering effects as colestipol (5 grams). Once again, you should build up the doses of these medications gradually. The amount will vary depending on the extent of your LDL problem.

What are the drawbacks?

First of all, unlike niacin, these drugs will not raise HDL cholesterol. Some sequestrants will also cause gastric discomfort such as constipation, bloating, and flatulence. The not-so-obvious side effects take place inside your body. The sequestrants could increase your liver's production of VLDLs and thus increase your concentration of triglycerides. They may also tend to interfere with the action of some other drugs, among them beta-blockers and diuretics, as well as with the absorption of fat-soluble vitamins. To mitigate such effects, we tell patients to take other medications at least one hour before or four hours after the sequestrants.

In their favour is the fact that sequestrants are not toxic to your system, as other drugs could be, and they work very effectively to lower LDL levels. These are excellent drugs.

On the other hand, if your HDL level is too low, the fibrates (gemfibrozil, bezafibrate or fenofibrate) or simvastatin tablets may be the pharmacological agents of preference. You should know that these do not have the track record of niacin or the sequestrants. Still, the research that has been done has shown them to be very effective at lowering all your blood lipids except the good HDLs.

Gemfibrozil (brand name Lopid) is particularly good at raising HDL and lowering triglycerides. In recent research in Finland, this drug was shown to reduce the incidence of heart attack by 34 percent.[14] Lovastatin (brand name Mevacor), too, usually raises HDL, although occasionally the opposite effect occurs. It will soon be available in South Africa. Simvastatin (Zocor) is a more powerful derivative available in South Africa.

Lovastatin and simvastatin belong to a promising new class of drugs known as *HMG CoA reductase inhibitors*. (HMG CoA reductase is an enzyme involved in cholesterol biosynthesis.) These new drugs have a powerful LDL-lowering effect and they usually raise HDL. In addition, it is very easy to take—in pill form, once a day. There is some low risk of liver-function abnormalities and untoward effects on the muscles, although the latter are rare. Some animal studies suggest an increased incidence of cataracts, but there is no convincing evidence that this occurs in humans.

Because of these possible side effects, we recommend that you have an eye examination before you start the lovastatin or simvastatin therapy to look for signs of early cataract formation. Then, for the first fifteen months of therapy, we also urge that you have liver-function tests at intervals.

Another drug in the same category with lovastatin is pravastatin. Clofibrate (brand name Atromid S), like gemfibrozil, is a fibric acid derivative but may be more toxic. It's used mostly for lowering triglycerides to reduce the risk of pancreatitis in hypertriglyceridaemic patients (see the last section of this chapter). Its side effects are similar to those associated with gemfibrozil—gastrointestinal upsets, but also sometimes even flu-like symptoms.

Probucol (brand name Lurselle) is another drug of second or even third choice. In most people, it doesn't lower LDL cholesterol as effectively as niacin or the bile acid sequestrants—and certainly not as effectively as lovastatin. It is also an unwise choice for patients whose electrocardiogram readings show PVCs. In probucol's favour, though, is a general lack of annoying gastric side effects. A major disadvantage is that probucol appears to lower HDL cholesterol, but on the other hand it also appears to be an anti-oxidant and may help prevent LDL cholesterol from being incorporated in arterial plaques.

Don't be surprised if your physician—especially if he or she is a lipid specialist—prescribes more than one cholesterol-lowering agent. When all else fails, combining drugs which have synergistic actions may be the route to go.

If a drug is going to be effective, you should see results by the end of a month or two. Your doctor will schedule follow-up tests within four, six, eight, or twelve weeks after you begin your therapy, depending on the drug you are taking. Expect to undergo a blood lipid test to discover the extent of the drug's effectiveness and, perhaps, a liver-function test to make sure there are no adverse effects. Another round of tests comes later. Once assured the medication is working, your doctor will probably ask you to come back for follow-up examinations at two- to four-month intervals thereafter, at least in the early phase of your drug treatment.

When you're on drugs such as the ones we've just been discussing, do not hesitate to call your doctor between regularly scheduled visits to report any unexpected or severe side effects.

A summary of the major drugs used to lower cholesterol—their usual dosages, most common side effects, and other helpful information—is given in Table 12-11, on the next page.

Drugs, Exercise, and Your HDL Level

We've covered a lot, so let's take a moment to recapitulate. As we mentioned earlier, it's just as important for you to have a high, healthy HDL level as it is to have a low, healthy LDL level (look back at Table 12-1). As we've also said, you should try controlling these levels through diet before resorting to drugs. Exercising regularly and stopping smoking are other lifestyle changes that will improve your blood cholesterol count.

Exercise can have a positive impact on your HDL level, possibly because it lengthens the amount of time HDL stays in your body. However, about ten miles a week of running or an equivalent amount of other exercise appears to be required to significantly affect HDL levels. Recent studies have shown that both regular exercise and mass loss are approximately equally effective in raising HDL, but it may take several months to get their full effect.

Although alcohol raises HDL, it's still suspect. This is because it also raises triglycerides and blood pressure and may cause a host of other problems.

If a concerted effort to exercise, lose mass, and stop smoking doesn't raise your HDL level above 0,91, then medication should

TABLE 12-11
Most Popular Lipid-Lowering Medications

Drug	Dosages Example	Maximum	Usual Time and Frequency	LDL Cholesterol Lowering	Most Common Side Effects	Special Precautions
Nicotinic acid (niacin)	100-250 mg as single dose	3 grams/day; rarely, doses up to 6 grams are used	Three times/day with meals to minimize flushing	15-30%	Flushing; upper-gastrointestinal upset; abnormal liver-function tests	Test for high uric acid, high blood sugar, and liver-function abnormalities
Cholestyramine	4 grams twice daily	24 grams/day	Twice daily within an hour of major meals	15-30%	Dose-dependent upper- and lower-gastrointestinal disorders	Can alter absorption of other drugs; can increase triglyceride levels and should not be used in patients with hypertriglyceridaemia
Colestipol	5 grams twice daily	30 grams/day				
Gemfibrozil	600 mg twice daily	1 500 mg/day	Twice daily 30 minutes before the morning and evening meals	5-15%	Abdominal pain; diarrhoea; nausea	May increase LDL cholesterol in hypertriglyceridaemic patients; should not be used in patients with gallbladder disease, test for liver-function abnormalities; may increase prothrombin time in patients on warfarin (Coumadin)
Bezafibrate	200 mg twice daily	600 mg/day		5-15%		
Bezafibrate retard	400 mg	400 mg/day		5-15%		
Fenofibrate	100 mg twice daily	600 mg/day		5-15%		
Simvastatin	10 mg once daily with evening meal	40 mg/day	Once (evening) with meals	25-45%	Gastrointestinal and hepatic disorders; miscellaneous, including muscular effects and possible cataracts	Patients should be monitored for liver-function abnormalities and possible cataracts
Probucol	500 mg twice daily	1 000 mg/day	Twice daily with morning and evening meals	10-15%	Diarrhoea; headache; rash	May prolong Q-T interval on an ECG, must monitor ECG periodically; decreases HDL cholesterol; must monitor liver function, uric acid, and blood sugar

Source: National Cholesterol Education Programme, *Report of the Expert Panel on Detection, Evaluation, and Treatment of High Blood Cholesterol in Adults,* NIH Publication 88-2925, January 1988.

be considered. Niacin and gemfibrozil are the best choices for raising HDL, though lovastatin also works in most people.

Hypertriglyceridaemia

As you've probably worked out by now, the prefix "hyper-" indicates an excessive amount of a substance in your system ("hypo-" means just the opposite). In this case, it's too many triglycerides.

It is possible that hypertriglyceridaemia, rather than being a direct cause of CHD, simply reflects the presence of other bad atherogenic agents, a low HDL level, or diabetes or another internal problem that increases your CHD risk. There is evidence, however, that triglycerides may be an independent risk factor in women. Very high triglycerides (above 5,65 mmol/ℓ) make a person prone to abdominal pain and pancreatitis, an inflammation of the pancreas.

Technically, hypertriglyceridaemia is defined as a fasting plasma triglyceride level exceeding 2,82 mmol/ℓ. The 1,69 to 2,82 range is borderline.

The usual reason for hypertriglyceridaemia is an excess of VLDLs and chylomicrons in the blood. The causes vary all the way from obesity and heavy drinking to disease conditions and organic disorders—diabetes mellitus, hypothyroidism, chronic kidney dysfunction, and liver disease. Some drugs for high blood pressure, including thiazide diuretics and beta-blockers, as well as oestrogen hormones (for example, oral contraceptives) are also implicated in the high-triglyceride phenomenon.

A low-fat, low-alcohol, low-sugar diet and life-style changes—mass loss if you're obese, regular exercise if you're sedentary—are the best remedies for high triglycerides. For people with severe hypertriglyceridaemia, a very-low-fat diet is warranted. By that we mean a total fat intake that is no more than 10 to 20 percent of total kilojoule intake. That's two-thirds to one-third lower than what we offer on our Step 1 and Step 2 eating plans.

Drug therapy doesn't come into play with hypertriglyceridaemics unless levels are above 5 unless some other risk factors were also present. Then the preferred medications are niacin, gemfibrozil, or clofibrate. Sequestrants are not recommended.

CHAPTER 13

WHAT TO DO ABOUT EXCESS KILOGRAMS

DIETING is certainly a topic that generates a lot of heat in medical circles, not to mention among publishers, food processors, exercise-equipment manufacturers, and consumers. But, sadly, not much light seems to emerge from the debate. Quackery, misconceptions, and faddism abound, perhaps to a greater degree than in any other medical subject we can think of.

Fortunately, one message about excess mass is gradually seeping through to the lay public: sure, a fat body is unsightly and a blow to your vanity. But far more important than that, it can kill you. It can kill you because it's a risk factor for other lethal diseases, particularly CHD.

We were struck recently by a letter to the problem page of a well-known women's magazine. Unlike most correspondents, this one actually signed her name, because she was offering her husband's story in the hope it would serve as a lesson to other people who, like her husband, think it doesn't matter when the kilograms pile on, year after year:

> When I met my husband in 1977, he was 20 years old, gorgeous and weighed 73 kg. It was love at first words. We took our time and were married in 1981.
> I had a happy marriage to a wonderful man. We had love, laughter and four beautiful children. Never was a word said about the extra centimetres that crept onto his waist. Never was a word said as I altered his clothes, or bought the next size bigger because the old ones simply could no longer be buttoned.
> On March 25, 1988, I came home from the supermarket and found my husband leaning over the kitchen sink trying to breathe. His arms, shoulders and feet were numb. His skin was an awful shade of yellow. He refused to go to the hospital and would not

permit me to call an ambulance. I begged and pleaded, so he finally let me drive him to the hospital which was 20 kilometres from our home.

Five kilometres from the hospital, he turned to me and said, "I love you. Forever. Take care." Then his body stiffened, he started to turn purple and make choking sounds. Then he fell toward me and his body relaxed.

The doctors and nurses worked valiantly for what seemed like hours. I stood back, watching and praying the same words over and over, "Please, Lord, if it be your will—he's only 31." Nothing could save him. I became a widow at 29.

The children and I have memories of a beautiful, but short life of a caring man. I now have a pillow that will never again cradle the head of the man I loved. Why? Because he ate too much. I never saw him on the scale, but I'm sure he was well over 115 kilograms when he died. He was 1,7 metres tall.

On his certificate of death it reads—Cause of death: arteriosclerotic cardiovascular disease caused by excess mass.

—Katherine Kerr

THE PROBLEM OF OBESITY

According to an article by Dr. A. R. P. Walker of the University of Witwatersrand and the South African Institute for Medical Research, obesity is the commonest nutritional disorder after dental caries in both developed and developing populations. In South Africa obesity is common in all ethnic populations, females being affected much more than males. In some sectors of the white adult population (both sexes), and in urban black women, obesity rates are excessively high. They are also high in Indians and "coloureds", especially among females.

Obese people appear to be prone to hypertension-related diseases, gallstones, diabetes, cancer and other diseases.

Unfortunately, success in losing mass appears to be severely limited and many methods are both unsafe and ineffective. Benefits achieved at mass loss clinics are unclear, since few data are published. There is a great need for health authorities to make available appropriate mass reduction guidelines to the population. The limitations of ineffective or risky treatments should be clearly set out.

However, the problem of obesity is a worldwide one. And unfortunately, the cycle of gaining, losing, and regaining mass is all too common. The so-called quick-mass-loss industry is quick all right—quick to take our money but slow at coming up with any truly viable ways to keep mass off for longer than a month or two.

In this chapter, we're going to offer you a sensible approach to permanent mass control without making any claims that it's going to happen overnight or even be that easy for some of you.

For most people, excess mass is simply the result of too much of the wrong food and too little activity. However, we'll concede that there are people with a genetic propensity to obesity.

Genetic mass theories run the gamut from the idea that some people are born with too many fat cells or a low metabolic rate to the high-"set point" hypothesis. According to the latter, each individual has his or her own "set point", a mass which the body defines as ideal, neither too heavy nor too thin. The thinking is that some people have a set point above the societal norm. In arriving at a set point, their bodies don't consult the big insurance companies' ideal mass charts, after all.

While you could be a person with a genetically induced mass problem, the average person—indeed, the average patient we examine—cannot claim this excuse. At least, few can claim it's the only reason for their problem.

Research suggests that in certain overmass people, cultural and environmental factors are more responsible (perhaps by as much as threefold) than genetic factors. More likely, however, it is the compounding effect of pro-fat genetics and pro-fat cultural influences—such as a national diet built around rich, high-saturated-fat foods—that really makes our mass soar. Conclusion: there is rarely one factor that anyone can single out as the "sole cause of my mass problem".

THE PROBLEM IN THE CONTEXT OF CHD

If you're overmass, we would hope your physician has explained the rationale for getting back to your optimum level. It's important because excess mass is implicated in a number of serious physical and emotional problems.

Some of you have had personal experience with the emotional issues—the problems of lowered self-esteem, flagging stamina, and feelings of inadequacy. Beyond that is the biological damage. Health hazards related to obesity include some types of cancer and gallbladder disease, high blood pressure, impaired glucose tolerance (the precursor to diabetes), a cholesterol ratio high in the bad LDLs and low in the good HDLs, and adverse triglyceride and VLDL cholesterol levels.

Note that most of the hazards listed are risk factors for CHD. In short, the risk factor of excess mass can act as a trigger for at least three other risk factors (high blood pressure, diabetes, and high LDL cholesterol). Indeed, it would be hard to come up with one CHD culprit more villainous than obesity.

Extra mass puts a significant burden on your whole cardiovascular system. Not only does it make it harder for you to exercise, but, as someone once calculated, your body has to produce an additional 1,5 kilometres of blood vessels for each additional 450 g of fat.

What your mass should be is not the primary question. We don't care what the chart says about the ideal mass for a person of your sex, height, age, and bone structure. What you really need to know is: "How much fat am I carrying on my body?"

You may tip the scales above what the mass chart cites as perfection, but your body may be composed mostly of muscle, bone, and other active metabolic tissue—what is often referred to as "lean body mass". This does not place you at risk for CHD. Fat—that inactive metabolic tissue commonly referred to as "flab"—is what you have to seek out and shed. The technical term for it is *adipose tissue*.

To refine the question further, you might ask: "What percentage of my total mass is body fat?" Unfortunately, as people age, their percentage of body fat increases even though their mass may remain the same. This is another reason why stepping on a scale won't tell you much.

There are several methods for measuring body fat:

Self-Test Estimate. There's nothing scientific or terribly accurate about this method, but it's a good starter. Stand in front of a full-length mirror nude. Stretch your arms out at a ninety-degree angle to your torso, and turn slowly around. What do you see? Do you see rolls of fat anywhere, perhaps drooping from your upper arms, around your waist, across your lower abdomen, at the back of your thighs? If there's any doubt in your mind about where the fat on your body is lodged, jump up and down a few times and watch. What wobbles like jelly is fat. Unfortunately, there is no accurate way for you to measure the percentage of your body fat by yourself. For this, you need help.

Underwater Weighing. The most definitive technique for arriving at a body-fat value is underwater weighing. Unfortunately, this technique is not readily available to the public in South Africa. It is not used as a clinical procedure—rather, it tends to be found in research institutions.

Here is how the test is usually administered: patients are asked to remove all their clothes. First, they're weighed on a conventional doctor's scale. Then, with the assistance of a technician, they step into a 1,52 metre-deep tank filled with water. They sit on a mesh chair and they're lowered into the tepid water up to their necks. The technician asks them to expel as much air as possible as they dunk their head underwater. Then the last few bubbles of air are expelled and they hold their breath as they are weighed again while underwater. The more fat you have, the harder it is to completely submerge yourself. This submersion process is repeated several times until the technician is sure that the reading of your underwater mass is accurate.

To figure out your percentage of body fat, the technician does calculations of density. The density of bone and muscle tissue—your lean body mass—is greater than that of water. However, fat tissue is less dense than water, which is why flabby people float easily and why it's harder for them to completely submerge themselves underwater. They also weigh a lot less underwater than they do when they step on a scale. The technician uses formulas to convert density to a body-fat percentage.

Skinfold Measurements. To obtain additional data in order to estimate body-fat percentage as accurately as possible, this second technique is also used: before patients step into the underwater weighing tank, the technician analyses the thickness of their subcutaneous (under the skin) fat layer. They take patients' skinfold measurements, using calipers, at several sites. The values are then used to compute a body fat percentage. This method, which is easy to perform and available in South Africa, is acceptably accurate—provided it is performed by a well-trained health professional.

Over the years, we've determined the body-fat percentages of more than 25 000 patients at our clinic. Utilizing this extensive data base, we've devised a chart giving what we see as the acceptable body-fat percentages for men and women at various ages (see Table 13-1).

Bioelectric Impedance Method. This is one method for measuring body fat that we do not endorse at the present time—not because it's dangerous, but because it's sometimes inaccurate. It's based on the principle that lean body mass conducts electrical current more rapidly than does adipose tissue, or fat. Thus, the more body fat you have on your frame, the greater your resistance to electricity. Yes, a small amount of electricity is introduced on your skin, and the time it takes to traverse a given amount of tissue indicates body-fat percentage. This technique may be unreliable for very lean and very fat people. Perhaps in the future the procedure will be refined sufficiently to make it an accurate and valuable tool for measuring body-fat percentage. In any event, it is not readily available in South Africa.

Distribution of Body Fat

Scientific studies conducted by researchers such as Dr. Richard Donahue of the Honolulu Heart Study have narrowed down the relationship between body fat and CHD risk even further.[3] Dr. Donahue suggests that it's not just a matter of the quantity of body fat, but where it's concentrated. Fat distributed on the front

TABLE 13-1
Recommended Body-Fat Percentage Targets[a]

Age	Men	Women
Under 30	13 %	18 %
30-39	16,5%	20 %
40-49	19 %	23,5%
50-59	20,5%	26,5%
Over 59	20,5%	27,5%

[a] Here are the body-fat percentages we recommend as acceptable for men and women in each decade of life. Each percentage represents the amount of total body mass that is pure fat. You are allowed to carry more fat as you get older. Women can carry a greater percentage of body fat than men and still be healthy. Be aware that when your body-fat percentage exceeds these guidelines, you are at an increased risk for progressive heart disease.

Source: The Cooper Clinic, Dallas.

of the abdomen—"android-type" obesity—is the most dangerous because it correlates with increased CHD incidence and mortality. Such fat distribution creates an "apple" shape. Dr. Donahue measured the tendency to accumulate fat around the abdomen as opposed to elsewhere to arrive at the conclusion that people with potbellies are twice as likely to suffer heart attacks. In contrast, fat distributed on the sides of the torso or on the thighs and hips is less of a problem. This is lower-body, or "gynoid", obesity, and it creates a "pear" shape.

The fact that proportionately more men than women suffer from heart disease lends credence to this fat-deposit hypothesis. Think about it a moment. Aren't men more likely to develop potbellies—or "beer bellies"—than women are? And don't more women have an hourglass shape, even if in their later years some start looking like much of the sand has run down to the bottom?

Here's what all this means in terms of your own body conformation: the lower your waist-to-hip ratio, the more protection you're afforded from CHD. You can calculate your ratio easily enough. Measure your hips and your waist in a relaxed state. Then divide your waist size by your hip size. For example, if your waist measures 81 and your hips 104 cm, your waist-to-hip ratio is 81/104 = 0,77, well within the acceptable range. *An acceptable waist-to-hip ratio is 0,78 or less.*

SENSIBLE MASS LOSS

Your goal in reducing your body-fat percentage is sensible mass loss that's also medically and nutritionally sound. We're not going to introduce you to any new mass-loss gimmicks in this chapter. Indeed, we feel that mass control is essentially a matter of simple arithmetic. What you must learn to do—all the time, not just during the short span of a diet—is to balance the number of kilojoules you take in on an average day with the number you expend. When you want to lose mass, that means creating a kilojoule deficit for a time. To do this, you must either decrease your intake of kilojoules or increase your utilization through more activity. Or do both at once. The latter is what we recommend.

Consider this statement: *it's not really that easy either to gain a kilogram or to lose it.* It takes an accumulation of about 14 700 food kilojoules to create 450 grams of body fat. That's a lot of food. If you frequent hamburger outlets, it would mean consuming—in one sitting, mind you—six big hamburgers and a large Coke. Or you might try wolfing down, all at once, three small pizzas. How about fifteen slices of cake? Or drinking a case of beer? Not easy even for people with gigantic appetites.

What does it take to burn off that many food kilojoules? You'd have to run for a straight three or four hours, or walk ten hours without a break. In the first case, we're talking about running a marathon, and walking ten hours a day is no small challenge either.[4]

Our point in telling you this is to emphasize that the best way to drop kilograms is to combine a kilojoule-restricted diet with moderate exercise.

- Generally, for men who want to lose mass, we recommend a drop in kilojoules to about 6 300 a day.
- Women who want to shed kilograms should aim for about 5 040 kilojoules a day.

The above kilojoules-per-day targets apply unless unusual circumstances are present. That's why you should consult your doctor about your plans to lose mass. Combined with exercise, these targets should enable you to lose about 0,5 to 1 kilogram a week without feeling either starved or weak.

While we're not going to offer instant miracle "solutions" in this chapter, we do expect to impart some valuable information that should give you a new slant on mass loss. Perhaps the most valuable is a concept called *kilojoule packaging*.

As Gertrude Stein might say, a kilojoule is not a kilojoule is not a kilojoule. The kilojoule chart tells you that a small potato and a third of a typical chocolate bar both contain about the same number of kilojoules. But consider what the potato kilojoules represent: a potato is rich in starch and vitamin C and contains small amounts of protein, many B vitamins, a half dozen minerals, and fibre. And the chocolate bar? It's composed of the simple sugar sucrose, several times the fat, and little or no fibre. In terms of kilojoules, the potato and chocolate bar are similar. Nutritionally, they have little in common.

The same point can be made about all manner of foods that, on the surface, appear to be equal. In terms of kilojoule *quantity—the amount of energy they pack—*they're equal. But nutritionally—in terms of kilojoule *quality*—they're not even in the same league at all.

Clearly, a wise dieter is someone who knows enough about food chemistry to make wise choices. Your reaction right now is probably, "I'm no nutritionist, nor do I want to become one, thank you." We're not asking you to. To become a more knowledgeable dieter, all you need is an understanding of a few elementary food and exercise concepts.

The concepts are as follows:

Concept 1: Eat Fewer Kilojoules While Exercising More

Studies have been done to ascertain the relationship between dieting and moderate exercise. Are they, indeed, a synergistic duo? The answer from all quarters is an unqualified yes.

We've already mentioned that exercise helps you create that important daily kilojoule deficit—fewer kilojoules taken in coupled with more kilojoules expended. But there are other reasons why exercise is critical to the success of a slimming programme: during a period of kilojoule restriction, moderate exercise helps people keep their metabolism (specifically, their *resting metabolic rate,* or "RMR") operating at a lively clip. In contrast, severe kilojoule restriction without any exercise—the crash diets you hear so much about—is self-defeating because people's RMRs slow down in the face of what their bodies interpret as starvation conditions. This slower RMR accounts for the plateau effect these dieters experience. Their bodies have adjusted to the new meagre food rations in order to conserve their fuel stores of body fat as long as possible. If your object is mass loss, this is precisely what you do not want your body to do.

Exercise imparts another benefit: it ensures that you retain good, solid lean body mass. It appears that as much as 25 percent of mass loss through dieting alone is from lean body mass. That means a loss of vital muscle, bone, and other metabolically active tissue. This is bad. It's deadmass body fat you want to shed, not protein tissue. Exercise helps build up active bone and muscle protein tissue while working off passive flab.

Concept 2: Get Your Daily Kilojoule Allowance from Nutritionally Dense Rather than "Empty-Kilojoule" Foods

We've touched on this topic already. You're probably groaning because you think we want you to analyse every food on your plate before you allow it past your lips.

Relax. We realize many of you have neither the time nor the inclination to delve deeply into food science. For you, we offer the following guidelines, which dovetail nicely with our previous dietary advice on cholesterol. Provided you are capable of spotting whether a food is composed predominantly of fat, protein, simple carbohydrates, or complex carbohydrates, these dieting principles should suffice:

Get Fewer Kilojoules from Fat. Compared with protein and complex carbohydrates, fats are high in kilojoules, often "empty kilojoules". Fat has 38 kilojoules per gram, while protein and complex carbohydrates each have 17 kilojoules per gram. That's not all. Saturated fats, as you know, raise your blood cholesterol level. They also encourage your body to make that unwanted adipose tissue. The long and the short of it: fat kilojoules are treacherous for cardiac patients.

Animal studies have shown that mammalian bodies do not process all kilojoules in the same way. The body discriminates. It reacts to fat kilojoules differently to the way it reacts to protein and carbohydrate kilojoules. For reasons that are not fully understood, our bodies tend to turn fat kilojoules into flab faster than they do either protein or carbohydrate kilojoules.

A recent study bears this out. Researchers from the Harvard School of Public Health studied the food and exercise habits of 141 nurses over a year's period.[5] The women were between the ages of thirty-four and fifty-nine. The researchers found no significant correlation between quantity of kilojoules consumed and obesity. There was a strong correlation, however, between fat intake and obesity. The overmass nurses tended to eat foods high in saturated fats, even though their overall kilojoule intake was about the same as that of the slimmer nurses.

As you learned in the previous chapter on cholesterol, one of the best ways to cut back on your fat intake is to limit your consumption of dairy products and meat. In fact, by following the low-saturated-fat Step 1 Eating Plan we outlined in Chapter 12, you should find yourself losing mass as well as getting your cholesterol level down.

Get Fewer Kilojoules from Sugar. Sugar is a carbohydrate, but a simple carbohydrate, not the complex kind we recommend.

There aren't a lot of good things to say about sugar. Except to satisfy an occasional craving for sweets, most of us simply don't need it in our daily diet.

While we may not need it, South Africans certainly get plenty of it—and in the most unlikely places. In case you haven't noticed, all manner of processed foods from canned spaghetti sauces to fruit yoghurt to salad dressings contain sugar. Reach into your cupboard right now and read a few of the ingredient labels. You'll be shocked at the sugar you're consuming in foods that don't even taste sweet.

The white, refined sugar in your sugar bowl and the other forms of sugar incorporated in processed foods mostly come from sugarcane. Sugar is produced in vast quantities in South Africa, which may partly explain local food manufacturers' tendency to use sugar in food preparation.

Today, white and "coloured" South Africans get 13,5 and 15,9 percent of their kilojoules from *added* sugars. This does not include natural sugars such as those in milk and fruit. You should cut sugar consumption way down to less than 10 percent of your daily kilojoule intake.

Get More Kilojoules from Complex Carbohydrates. Complex carbohydrates are found in vegetables, grains, and fruits. Such foods are a rich source of vitamins and minerals, yet aren't dense in kilojoules like fats. We urge you to make them the centrepiece of your eating plan. They should account for as much as 60 percent of your total kilojoules.

Complex carbohydrates have a lot going for them. They have more water and bulk per unit volume of food, which is why their kilojoule content is relatively low. Starches in particular satisfy hunger, which is important when you're trying to restrict kilojoules and lose mass. Starches also make your digestive system work harder than fats do. The result is that more carbohydrate kilojoules are expended immediately during the process of carbohydrate metabolism, so there are fewer left over to turn to body fat.

Good sources of complex carbohydrates are whole-grain breads, pasta, and hot cereals. Porridge tends to be better than cold cereals. Nor do we set much store by the health food faddists' favourite breakfast, granola. Compared with many other cereal choices, it has more kilojoules and fat, and it costs more.

Changing Your Eating Habits

There are lengthy treatises devoted to the issue of how to alter people's relationship with food. We don't pretend to be psychologists, but we do think a few nuggets of wisdom about constructive mealtime behaviour bear repeating:

Make Eating an Isolated Activity. In other words, enjoy the act of eating, even if it's just a snack. Concentrate on the taste of your food, not on a television programme across the room or the book you've got propped up next to your plate. If you eat while you're distracted, you'll tend to shovel it in and eat more than you should.

Don't Eat on the Run. You should strive to make each meal last at least twenty minutes because that's about how long it takes for your body to register a feeling of satiety. Gobbling up food faster means you won't feel full until you've eaten too much.

Chew Slowly and Put Your Fork Down Between Mouthfuls. This is a corollary to the above. Try to make meals a social event focused on good conversation and good food, not an eating frenzy.

Remove Temptation. If food is your passion, why suffer? Do yourself a favour and keep temptation well out of sight and mind. Don't leave food, particularly items you crave, on the kitchen counter or in see-through containers. Do a little re-arranging in the refrigerator. Keep the carrot sticks and bread in front and push the sweets and rich foods to the back.

Understand the Psychology of Cravings. Most food urges pass within minutes. The trick is to keep food far enough away so that you cannot respond immediately to every food whim that crosses your mind. Ride out the feeling. Distract yourself. We've even heard patients say they drink a large glass of water at such times. Minutes later, they realize that what they thought was appetite was nothing more than a passing food fantasy.

Find Replacements for Food Rewards. If a chocolate sundae is how you reward yourself for a job well done or for living through a stressful event, or how you compensate for the fact that your father doesn't love you, you've got some soul-searching to do on the whole subject of emotional rewards. List five things that you enjoy more than eating. Then, whenever you're tempted to gorge, substitute one of them. Psychological rewards are fine, just not empty-kilojoule ones.

Go Food Shopping on a Full Stomach. Picture what will happen if you do the opposite and go food shopping when you're hungry. All your worst food impulses will run amok. You'll come home with bags full of foods that should be anathema to a person on a controlled diet.

Be Realistic. Decide which off-limits foods are most important to you. Then occasionally work one into your meal plan. We're not asking you to be superhuman. We're asking you to be sensible and make logical trade-offs. Eating a piece of chocolate cake one night simply means you must counterbalance it with particularly low-kilojoule foods the next day.

Having stated all this, we know some of the experienced dieters among you are saying, "Yes, but ..." You can't accept our eating advice because you continue to harbour mistaken notions about mass loss. You're not alone. A large portion of the general population subscribes to these myths, too. In the next sections, we'd like to lay a few of the most common ones to rest, once and for all.

Myth: High-Protein/Low-Carbohydrate Diets Are the Most Effective

These diets have been riding a wave of popularity for half a century. The infamous Scarsdale diet is in this tradition. They're the reason why so many people still believe that bread, pasta, rice, and potatoes are fattening. In fact, as we've just shown, these are excellent complex-carbohydrate foods. They aren't fattening, but the butter on the bread, the sour cream on that baked potato, and the creamy sauce on the pasta are. Why? Because they're high in fat. And fat is fattening!

The main problem with high-protein diets is that they turn out to be high-fat diets in disguise. On such diets, lean meats, poultry, and fish are staples. But no matter how lean the cut, these foods contain some fat. And it's fat that does the damage.

True, these low-carbohydrate diets give the illusion of quick mass loss. But it's only an illusion. Carbohydrates absorb water, so having fewer of them in your system induces your body to shed "water mass", a physiological effect that ends after a few days. After a week or two on a high-protein diet, you're left with fewer kilograms, perhaps, but essentially the same amount of body fat.

Myth: Certain Special Foods, Such as Boiled Eggs and Grapefruit, Promote the Burning of Kilojoules

Sorry. This is wishful thinking. There are no magic foods. As we've already said, complex carbohydrates do seem to cause your body to expend more energy during digestion, but nowhere near enough so that body-fat stores have to be mobilized to help out.

Myth: The Timing of Your Daily Food Intake Is a Key Factor in Mass Loss

The old saying goes that you should eat like a king at breakfast, a queen at lunch, and a pauper at dinner. The old saying may be misleading. In truth, the most important thing you need to do is create a kilojoule deficit at any time over a twenty-four-hour period. We've seen no evidence proving that the time at which you take in and expend the kilojoules is critical, although a few studies have suggested it is best to eat most of your kilojoules before lunch. The final answer is not yet in. But it is certainly true that the timing of kilojoule intake is not among the most important factors in mass control.[6]

Myth: Doing Sit-ups Will Remedy the Risk of Having a Potbelly

This is the myth of spot-reducing adapted to cardiac rehabilitation. It doesn't work when people try to spot-reduce for vanity's sake. And it won't work when you try to do it for CHD reasons.

No matter what the exercise tape or the lavishly illustrated exercise book says, you cannot rid your body of fat in specific places. Some of these very targeted exercises may improve your muscle tone in specific places, but your body has its own timetable and flab map. It decides when and where. Look at it this way: all the fat in your body is connected, so it's not simply a matter of turning on a valve here or turning one off there. You must accept the fact that your only option is to fuel your body's fat-burning process by providing a steady daily kilojoule deficit.

Myth: Fast Mass Loss on a Crash Diet Is Preferable

Yes, it's preferable to the purveyor of the crash diet. But it could be dangerous for you. Earlier, when we talked about your resting metabolic rate, we explained why starvation diets don't work. When undertaken by themselves without exercise, such diets slow down your metabolism (RMR), thus making it harder to burn off body fat.

Crash dieting accounts for the "dieter's dilemma" or "yo-yo syndrome" we hear so much about. Take a person who normally eats 10 080 kilojoules a day. He cuts back to 6 720 on a diet and has initial success at mass loss. But within a week or so, his RMR adjusts to the new eating regimen and kilograms are shed more slowly. To get any more mass off, our man has to reduce daily kilojoules even more. And the same thing eventually happens—he reaches another plateau. The worst part is the fast mass gain when he finally falls off the diet wagon and goes back up to, say, 8 400 kilojoules a day.

Dr. Kelly Brownell and associates at the University of Pennsylvania duplicated the yo-yo syndrome with laboratory rats, adding to its credibility.[7] The researchers separated twenty-eight genetically similar rats into three groups. Control Group A was fed Purina Rat Chow in amounts that kept them at a healthy lean mass. Control Group B ate high-fat food and got obese. Group C—the experimental group—went through two cycles of fast mass gain and loss.

During Cycle 1, Group C was fed a high-fat diet duplicating that of Control Group B and they, too, got fat. Later, their kilojoules were cut in half, forcing them to lose mass until they reached the leanness of Control Group A. Once they achieved the lower mass, Cycle 2 was set in motion. The Group C rats were again given high-fat foods to make them regain mass to match that of Control Group B. Then, for the second time, they were starved until their mass plummeted to match that of Control Group A.

The results were revealing: During Cycle 1, it took twenty-one days for the Group C rats to lose the mass. During Cycle 2, it took forty-six days for them to lose the same amount of mass. Furthermore, the rats regained the mass the first time over a period of forty-six days. The second time, it took them only fourteen days to regain the same amount of mass. With repeated cycles, the researchers postulate that the rats—or humans—would lose mass more and more slowly and regain mass faster and faster.

Here are our conclusions:

1. Repeated dieting jeopardizes a person's ability to lose mass and keep it off.
2. In particular, starvation diets, in which kilojoule intake is very low, are a very bad idea. They alter your metabolism, making mass loss increasingly difficult over time.
3. A person who diets should take it seriously, follow through, and keep the mass off through a combination of careful food choices and exercise. A frivolous attitude—"Oh well, it doesn't matter; there's always another diet to try if this one stops working for me"—is counterproductive and it borders on being dangerous.

The quick mass loss attempted on crash diets isn't safe mass loss. Of course, how fast you can—or should—shed bodyfat mass is, to a great extent, an individual matter. It depends on such factors as your motivation; the severity of your associated medical disorders; your family history, in terms of both heredity and health habits; the fat distribution on your body (your body conformation); and the effect that exercise may have on your joints. It's also influenced by your height, mass, age, and the extent of your obesity.

For some people who are massively overmass and for whom the methods we just outlined have not been successful, a medically supervised modified fasting diet may be required.

For most people, though, a rate of 1 percent of body mass per week is an appropriate and manageable mass-loss target.[8] That means if you tip the scales at 100 kilograms, your weekly mass-loss goal is a mere 1 kilogram until you reach your ideal mass. If you've got a lot of mass to lose, granted, that could mean you'll be on a diet for several months.

In truth, the "secret" to controlling mass isn't a secret at all. It involves changing your basic eating patterns permanently, not just for that short period of time when you proclaim, "I'm on a diet." It involves making the right food choices day in and day out. It's the small choices that gradually add up to a big difference in your body-fat percentage and total mass, not the crash diet you undergo several times a year that doesn't work over the long term anyway.

Do I Go It Alone or Sign Up for a Mass-Loss Programme?

Like heavy drinkers who join Alcoholics Anonymous to kick their habit, many overmass people, too, need a structured programme and the moral support of peers in order to shape up and eat right. If you fall into this category, you've got a lot of options, some rather expensive. From our point of view, some commercial programmes tend to have one important drawback: they encourage you to follow orders instead of teaching you about nutrition so that you can begin making wise food choices for yourself.

To help you be a wise consumer, here are some questions we urge you to get answered before you sign up for any programme:

- What is the food plan? Is it balanced, nutritious, and reasonably easy to follow?
- What are the programme's claims? Does it stress losing mass fast? Slowly and steadily? Safely? Keeping mass off over the long term?
- Is exercise a component of the programme? Does the programme provide exercise facilities?
- Is modification of eating behaviour covered? How about stress management?
- What are the credentials of the professional staff?
- What verifiable evidence is there that the programme works? (Are the salespeople willing to give you references so you can actually talk to some people who have completed the programme? Ask for the names of people who finished the course at least a year ago. Losing mass initially is not as great a challenge as keeping mass off in the long term.)

Finally, it would make good sense to ask your physician which programme he or she recommends. One very reputable diet organization is Weigh Less: you may like to get in touch with your local branch. You could also contact your local branch of the SA Heart Foundation for information.

The Heart Mark

Changing your eating habits to reach or maintain a desirable cholesterol level begins with making changes in the food you buy at the supermarket. Shopping for the right food doesn't have to be confusing or overwhelming. With a little practice, you can develop skills for choosing the right fats, reading labels, and making sensible selections at the supermarket.

Many foods have been given the Heart Foundation's mark of approval — as an aid to shopping for healthier food. Look for this mark in your supermarket.

Approved as part of the Heart Foundation Eating Plan

The Heart Foundation's Heart Mark helps the consumer to identify foods that are not only low in fat (especially saturated fat), cholesterol and salt, but also high in fibre. These products are approved as part of the Heart Foundation Eating Plan.

Include food from the following food groups as part of your daily eating plan:

- Lean meat, fish, poultry, dried beans and lentils
- Low fat dairy products (milk, cheese, yoghurt)
- Bread and cereal products — rich in fibre (wholewheat bread, brown rice, oats)
- Fruit and vegetables
- Polyunsaturated oils and margarines (in small amounts)

Once you get to know the foods to avoid, you'll get used to leaving them out of the shopping basket and before long your cupboards will be stocked with a whole range of alternative, but not more expensive, foods.

Recipe modification for low-fat, low-sodium eating

Special recipes are an important part of family tradition. But many of those treasured favourites are too heavy and rich for today's generation of health-conscious cooks. You don't have to give up those old favourites — just convert them. These basic guidelines for substituting ingredients will help you modify your recipes to make them lower in fat and sodium.

When you recipe calls for	Use
1 cup butter	1 cup polyunsaturated margarine OR $7/8$ cup oil
1 cup hard margarine	1 cup oil OR 1 cup oil plus 3 tsp margarine
1 cup whole milk	1 cup skim milk OR 2% milk
1 cup light cream	3 tsp oil and skim milk = 1 cup OR 1 cup low fat evaporated milk
1 cup whipping cream	$2/3$ cup skim milk and $1/3$ cup oil
1 cup sour cream	1 cup plain yoghurt OR 1 cup smooth cottage cheese OR $3/4$ cup buttermilk and $1/4$ cup oil
1 whole egg	1 egg white and 2 tsp oil OR 2 egg whites
30 g cheddar cheese	30 g mozzarella, edam, ricotta, parmesan OR 2 tsp cottage cheese

Suggestions for Low Salt Cooking

Instead of salt:

- Use garlic, dry mustard and chopped vegetables such as pepper, onions, mushrooms and tomatoes to add flavour to meat and vegetables.
- Add a little wine or fruit fuice to casseroles and stews. The alcohol will evaporate during cooking, but the flavour remains.
- Add sliced lemon or lemon juice to white meats and fish.
- Use herbs such as basil, marjoram, oregano, sage and thyme.
- Use spices such as cardamom, cinnamon, cummin and nutmeg.

CHAPTER 14

THE INSIDIOUS EFFECTS OF STRESS ON YOUR BODY

A PERIOD of intense stress is often the final straw that precipitates a heart attack or the compelling need for immediate bypass surgery. Usually, there are several risk factors present. Stress simply exacerbates them. Undue stress makes the person overindulge in food or alcohol or smoke excessively—or stop exercising just when the workouts would be most beneficial.

With all the individuals we've seen over the years, we're no longer surprised when such a confluence of risk factors, topped off by stress, pushes a patient over the line. What still amazes us, though, are the rare cases where stress alone seems to cause the event. Michael Travelstead falls into this category.

Mike is a young, successful entrepreneurial investor. Buying businesses, improving their management, and eventually selling them for tidy profits is his forte. Most of us couldn't do what Mike does and still sleep at night, because of the enormous financial risks involved. But he seems to accept his occasional losses as part of the game.

While a picture of Mike as a typical Type A personality—hard driving, relentless, combative, impatient, achievement obsessed—may be crystallizing in your mind, it's not quite accurate. Mike does want to succeed in all his endeavours, but he still maintains a healthy balance between work and play. He has young children, and his family is very important to him. Likewise, he's very athletic, and never lets business interfere with a good squash game. In fact, when he had his heart attack, his aerobic fitness was at a peak. Only a month before, he'd competed in the provincial squash championships and had trained for two hours a day for the previous six months. When the following happened to him, he was only thirty-eight years old:

I spent the day driving many kilometres to several board meetings. The morning meeting was at a newly acquired bank where my partners and I had the unpleasant task of removing current management against their will. Lawsuits were also on the agenda. At noon, while I was driving to a second meeting, I noticed I had heartburn, something I never get. I bought an over-the-counter remedy to relieve the discomfort and attended two more meetings.

I got home just in time for an evening squash match. That's where the real symptoms started—the pain in the right arm, chest tightness, dryness of the mouth that turned into nausea. I rationalized it away as a hiatal hernia attack and drove home. But the pain wouldn't let up. Finally, I asked my wife to drive me the 30 kilometres to the nearest hospital.

About halfway there, I had the major infarction. The pain was excruciating. We'd just had a child by natural childbirth, so I tried Lamaze breathing techniques. Nonetheless, the world started slipping away. Just like all the books say, I was looking down this long tunnel surrounded by bright lights. I didn't hear the angels sing but I knew I was near the brink—and I didn't want to go. I concentrated very, very hard on our two small babies, and in about five minutes I began to feel myself come back to consciousness.

No doubt you think the business meeting where Mike had to fire employees was the stress he couldn't handle. Not at all. Mike says he makes these kinds of decisions all the time. No, the stressful situation that did the damage was a long, drawn-out tangle of events involving a private airline in which Mike was a major investor. A plane had crashed and thirteen people were killed. It was a situation that, for the first time in his career, was beyond his control.

That tragedy kicked off a series of the most frustrating situations I've ever encountered—everything from officials who wouldn't issue death certificates to bureaucrats who kept changing the rules. My partners, who were also friends, finally insisted that we declare bankruptcy to extricate ourselves. Bankruptcy is anathema to me. I violently disagreed and actually resigned from the board and stormed out of the meeting in a fury. That was a day before my heart attack.

This was unlike my normal business dealings—for the first time in my life I'd been faced with problems I couldn't resolve in some reasonable fashion. It didn't matter what I did, how hard I worked, how clever I was, or how much money I poured in. I couldn't put a dent in the problem. It drove me mad.

Mike is describing one of the classic stressors—a feeling that you're helpless. You're no longer in charge, either of an event or of yourself. Mike also let his values—his strongly held beliefs about bankruptcy—cloud his ability to assess the problem objectively. In actuality, it was a no-win situation and his partners recognized it. Like them, he should have distanced himself from the whole matter and tried to view it in a more objective way.

Mike isn't alone. The world is filled with people who seem to manage stress reasonably well—until that one special event occurs that sets off all sorts of psychological and emotional alarms. Suddenly, a survivor turns into a person struggling, perhaps like Mike, just to stay alive.

People vary enormously in their ability to withstand stress. We've all known people who've suddenly experienced "the full catastrophe". A number of the major stressful life events rated on the ever-popular Holmes-Rahe scale hit these people simultaneously, yet they somehow managed to pull through it all relatively unscathed. Other people have one disaster—a divorce or a new boss they hate—and they crumble. What separates the survivors from the crumblers is the ability to cope.

For a heart patient, this coping ability is an absolute necessity. You must acquire stress-management skills if you haven't done so already. These skills will pay off again and again and again.

STRESS: YOU CAN'T AVOID IT

The issue we're discussing here is not how to avoid stress. Hardly, for a certain amount of stress and tension is inevitable. Sources of stress—or stressors—can be almost anything: an event, a confluence of unfortunate circumstances, your environment, certain people, even your own feelings and attitudes.

Try as you might, you'll never be able to duck many of our society's prime stressors: you work for a company for twenty years and suddenly it's taken over. Will you have a job tomorrow? Will you still get the generous retirement package you've counted on? Will the new management allow you the same level of autonomy you've grown used to as manager of your department? Or you've spent most of your career building up a business and the bottom falls out of the local economy. You and everyone else in your region suffer the consequences. Or you raise a family with your spouse, thinking your relationship is a solid one. In a flash, your mate dies or walks out on you.

Such, unfortunately, is life—unless you're a hermit. Believe it or not, even that life-style is now considered stressful. Why?

Because it's so unnatural. Psychologists have evidence that boredom, loneliness, and too little social interaction can be just as stressful as too much stimulation and pressure.

Suffice it to say that your body and health, not to mention your mind, require a certain level of activity and aspiration. The question is: how much is too much? The answer is different for everyone. After all, one person's challenge is someone else's stress.

You might say that handling stress is like tuning a violin. If the strings are too loose, the sound is out of tune. If the strings are too tight, they may snap. Only when the strings are adjusted somewhere in between can beautiful music be made.

Stress experts tell us that the individuals who get into the most trouble with stress are those who react to it with either open or suppressed hostility. Indeed, the experts emphasize that stress in and of itself is not the problem. The problem comes from how people react to it.

How well do you cope with stress? Tables 14-1 and 14-2 (see pages 273 and 274) are quizzes designed to assess how you typically react to stress. The first is a self-test. The second is one that people who know you well should take. By comparing the results of these tests, you'll have an objective stress reading on yourself—which is absolutely essential for the cardiac patient.

THE MYTH OF THE TYPE A PERSONALITY

No doubt, you expected to see this topic addressed early on in this chapter, for the term is invariably associated with heart attacks in middle-aged people. By now, doesn't everyone know that Type A people are flirting with heart problems, if not premature death?

Like many other popular hypotheses in medicine, this one has been clinically tested and retested dozens of times, ever since San Francisco cardiologists Dr. Meyer Friedman and Dr. Ray Rosenman first introduced it in the 1950s. (They explained the concept more fully in their best-selling book, *Type A Behaviour and Your Heart,* in 1974[1]). It may surprise you to learn that this is one scientific concept that hasn't withstood investigators' scrutiny all that well.

Granted, the notion of personality types is useful because it helps characterize the different ways people deal with stress.

TABLE 14-1
Stress: How Much Does It Affect Me?[a]

Circle the number that describes you most accurately:

I Experience This Behaviour or Emotion...	Often	A Few Times a Week	Rarely
1. I feel tense, anxious, or have nervous indigestion.	2	1	0
2. People at work/home make me feel tense.	2	1	0
3. I eat/drink/smoke in response to tension.	2	1	0
4. I have tension or migraine headaches, or pain in the neck or shoulders, or insomnia.	2	1	0
5. I can't turn off my thoughts at night or on weekends long enough to feel relaxed and refreshed the next day.	2	1	0
6. I find it difficult to concentrate on what I'm doing because of worrying about other things.	2	1	0
7. I take tranquillizers (or other drugs) to relax.	2	1	0
8. I have difficulty finding enough time to relax.	2	1	0
9. Once I find the time, it is hard for me to relax.		Yes—1	No—0
10. My workday is made up of many deadlines.		Yes—1	No—0

IDENTIFYING YOUR TENSION LEVEL

Maximum total score=18   My total score is_____

___My tension level is extremely high as shown by my score of 14–18
___My tension level is above average as shown by my score of 9–13
___My tension level is average as shown by my score of......................5–8
___My tension level is below average as shown by my score of 3–4
___My tension level is extremely low as shown by my score of.............0–2

[a] This is your view of how you react to stress. Other people may see it differently. Ask several people close to you to do the short test given in Table 14-2. Then compare the two test scores.

Source: Adapted from John Farquhar, *The American Way of Life Need Not Be Hazardous to Your Health,* pp. 57-58, "Simplified Self-Scoring Test for Gauging Stress and Tension Levels." Reading, MA: Addison Wesley Publishing Co., 1987.

According to Dr. Friedman and Dr. Rosenman, the classic Type A is a middle-aged superachiever, usually male, who has a hard time delegating responsibility or relaxing, feels under constant

Table 14-2
Stress: How Observers Say It Affects Me

Circle the number that most accurately describes the subject:

Subject Behaves in the Following Manner:	Never	Seldom (once or twice a week)	Often (practically every day)	Very Frequently (at least once a day)
1. HARRIED: Eats and/or moves fast, as if time is of the essence.	0	1	2	3
2. SPEECH PATTERN: Speaks fast, in an explosive manner. Repeats self unnecessarily and/or interrupts others.	0	1	2	3
3. LISTENING: Has to have things repeated, apparently because of inattentiveness.	0	1	2	3
4. WORRIES: Expresses worries about trivia and/or things he/she can do nothing about.	0	1	2	3
5. ANGER/HOSTILITY: Becomes angry at self and/or others.	0	1	2	3
6. IMPATIENCE: Tries to hurry others and/or becomes frustrated with own pace.	0	1	2	3
Maximum total score = 18	The total score is _____			

Source: Adapted from John Farquhar, *The American Way of Life Need Not Be Hazardous Your Health*, p. 59, "Observer Behavior Rating Inventory." Reading, MA: Addison Wesley Publishing Co., 1987.

time pressure, and is distrustful, bossy, competitive, impatient, and combative. You might say that a Type A's every waking moment is a relentless struggle to achieve more and more in less and less time despite the constant opposition of saboteurs in the form of interfering people or things.

More recent studies show that Type A behaviour applies to women to the same degree as to men—and with similar deleterious health consequences. Indeed, as more and more women enter the work force, rise to levels of high responsibility, and juggle a career and family, they too are at great risk of experiencing the physical consequences traditionally bequeathed to men.

Nor are those who care for families immune. A study by University of Kansas psychologist B. Kent Houston reveals that many homemakers, striving to do it all themselves, create a situation that's just as stressful as many work environments, especially if their obsessive-compulsive behaviour is coupled with marital dissatisfaction.[2]

An apt symbol of the Type A, male or female, is a clenched fist whose wrist is adorned with a stopwatch.

Popularized in countless magazine articles and on radio and TV talk shows over the years, the Type A concept has become one of commendation in some people's minds. Often, the term is used to single out society's heroes and leaders, the people who, against all odds, get things accomplished, even if it's at the expense of their cardiovascular health.

However, the people using the term in this way haven't kept up with the latest research. Recent analyses of people on top of the corporate pyramid, for example, tend to show that just as many are Type B personalities. These are people who are less impulsive, calmer, less hostile, and far more flexible than Type A individuals. They're better able to adjust to change and make reasoned decisions. In short, the linking of Type A behaviour with success is, to a great extent, a myth.

The other discovery about Type A behaviour is even more myth-shattering. If recent research is accurate,[3] only two components of Type A behaviour take a significant cardiovascular toll: hostility and anger, either overtly expressed or suppressed. This is why we said in Chapter 11 that it's an aggressive reaction to stress that's a risk factor for CHD, not simply pressure per se.

Among the definitive research in this regard is a long-term study of men who, in law school, took a standardized personality test which identified some as hostile. Twenty-five years later, it was found that the death rate of the men with the higher hostility scores was 4,2 times greater than that of the men who had low scores.[4]

Dr. Redford B. Williams, the Duke University psychiatrist who spearheaded the above study, has also conducted inquiries into the hostile, distrustful Type A person's biochemical reaction to pressure. In one experiment, his researchers measured the blood pressure of men grappling with a difficult mental puzzle while being harassed. True to form, the angry men showed a markedly sharper leap in blood pressure than did the calmer Type B subjects. The Type B subjects also recovered physiologically much more quickly than their antagonistic Type A counterparts.[5]

Based on his own research as well as a comprehensive review of the extensive Type A literature, Dr. Williams now concludes: "Of the three characteristics—time urgency, competitive achievement striving, and hostility—making up the global Type A pattern, only measures of the latter are independently related to a wide variety of CHD endpoints. The research also suggests that the hostility complex may play a role in increasing the risk of dying from *any cause.*"[6] (italics added)

In short, hostility and anger can be toxic. They're clearly the most dangerous components of the whole Type A construct.

YOUR BODY'S REACTION TO STRESS

It's difficult to give a succinct definition of stress. Dr. Hans Selye, the Montreal-based author of the book *Stress Without Distress*, perhaps comes closest. He says it's "the non-specific response of the body to any demand made upon it".[7] In other words, stress is the body's natural and necessary reaction to a challenge.

In terms of body chemistry, though, stress is easy to pinpoint. It's a collection of predictable responses evoked largely by the release of adrenaline-like substances that speed up your heart rate and blood pressure. Scientists today know so much about the body's physiological response to stress and tension, in fact, that they could inject you with the aforementioned substances and be assured that you'd immediately feel the physical and emotional sensations associated with stress.

Back in 1914, a Harvard University physiologist, Dr. Walter B. Cannon, labelled this state of arousal the "fight or flight" response.[8] The phrase stuck because it aptly describes a living organism's exquisite ability to respond, appropriately and instantaneously, to physical threats.

Dr. Selye has a different label. He calls it the general adaptation syndrome, or "GAS". He points out, however, that in the human animal the response may no longer be all that appropriate. In most contemporary societies, it's seldom a physical threat that triggers GAS. Rather, it's a whole panoply of social and psychological stimuli. But because of the responses we have inherited, we continue to experience this strong bodily reaction nonetheless. Some researchers now feel that in Type A people,

GAS may be exaggerated far beyond what is an adequate response in the less excitable Type B people.

Of course, for people who are young and healthy, this state of optimal readiness can be enormously productive. But there's danger, too. Should they try to sustain this level of peak arousal over an extended period, even those in the best of health will eventually experience chronic exhaustion. Taxed to the limit in this way, their bodies' immune systems may no longer be able to ward off sickness and disease. The early warning signs are bouts of insomnia, heart palpitations, gastrointestinal distress, headaches, and/or back pain, to mention just a few.

In a cardiac patient, such a scenario can be suicidal. The first warning sign may be a fatal heart attack. Thus, it's absolutely imperative for you to learn to recognize when you're under excessive stress. This may sound ridiculous. Doesn't everyone know when they are stressed? The answer is no, especially those deniers among you who have spent a good deal of your adult life under stress, thinking that's just the way things are.

The various manifestations of stress are listed in Table 14-3 on the next page. How many of them are characteristic of you?

In our experience, stress is the one CHD risk factor that many recovering heart patients single out as "the culprit". While this version of what caused a heart problem is invariably too simplistic, it cannot be dismissed out of hand, for there is a growing body of clinical evidence that mental stress can indeed have a pronounced impact on the heart. In controlled experiments, the responses that have been detected range from ischaemia and arrhythmias to the more indirect threats of chronic elevated blood pressure and blood cholesterol.

Take the recent study by doctors at Charing Cross Hospital in London.[9] They outfitted thirty CHD patients with Holter monitors in order to study what triggered their episodes of ischaemia. They also asked subjects to keep diaries. All told, the patients suffered 515 ischaemic attacks, but in only 174 cases did accompanying pain make the sufferers aware of their condition. Of the 341 "silent" episodes, many were associated with specific instances of tension and worry. Interestingly, these episodes tended to last longer than the painful ones. The team concluded that "psychological stress may exacerbate myocardial ischaemia which is frequently painless".

This isn't the first study to link heart events in CHD patients with mental or emotional exertion. Researchers at Cedars-Sinai Medical Centre in Los Angeles conducted a study that compared

Table 14-3
A Checklist: Signs of Stress

Physical Symptoms

____ Rapid heart rate	____ Sweaty palms
____ Dry mouth	____ Muscle tightness
____ Clenched jaw	____ Headaches
____ Cold hands and feet	____ Knot in stomach
____ Fatigue that's persistent	____ Indigestion
____ Sighing	

Behaviour

____ Agitation	____ Biting your nails
____ Frequent urination	____ Twirling strands of your hair
____ Indecisiveness	____ Accident proneness
____ Forgetfulness	____ Daydreaming
____ Disorganization	____ Overeating
____ Difficulty coping with job	____ Excessive/compulsive smoking
____ Problem concentrating	____ Abuse of alcohol and/or drugs
____ Inability to prioritize effectively	

Emotions

____ Feeling of loss of control	____ Lack of self-esteem
____ Depression, sadness	____ Nervous or inappropriate laughter
____ Anxiety	____ Crying easily
____ Moodiness	____ Bad dreams
____ Hostility	____ Impulsiveness
____ Irritability, argumentativeness	____ Desire to escape from it all
____ Suspicion verging on paranoia	

Source: The Cooper Clinic, Dallas.

ischaemia induced by two types of mental stress with that induced by physical exertion.[10] They found that psychologically triggered silent ischaemia occurs at heart rates well below the threshold for ischaemia from exercise. Furthermore, after establishing this strong link between mental stress and ischaemia, they were even able to discuss the type of mental stress that causes the strongest reaction. It's a personally relevant mental task tinged with emotion, as opposed to an impersonal mental test of ability.

On the latter score, other studies have shown that people with CHD grappling with a challenging mental arithmetic task often suffer transient ischaemia as well as mild to severe arrhythmias.

But the study of the most interest to you may be one that used 125 post-heart attack patients as subjects.[11] It showed that psychological distress does indeed touch off arrhythmias, the beginning of a chain reaction which can culminate in sudden death. In this study, patients who experienced a lot of life stress as well as social isolation had nearly four times the incidence of mortality over a three-year follow-up period as those who didn't.

POSITIVE VERSUS NEGATIVE STRESS

We don't want you to misunderstand our position. Although we have expressed a number of cautions, we do not want, nor do we expect, cardiac patients to retire from life, especially since stress experts tell us that social isolation is itself a stressor. In every respect, we encourage our cardiac patients to resume their lives, to enjoy themselves to the fullest, and to continue to meet life's various challenges with optimism and confidence.

Indeed, we're well aware of the psychological and emotional problems engendered in recuperating heart patients whose doctors are too conservative. Instead of helping their patients get well, they help them get sicker by saying no to a reasonable level of exercise and activity.

Certainly, positive stress—or the mastery of challenge—is a prerequisite for achieving a sense of fulfillment and excitement in life. To be sure, if you think back over your life for a moment, you'll find that many of the most rewarding experiences represent examples of stress channelled to highly productive ends.

Our point is simply this: it's a question of striking the right balance between stress and relaxation. As we said earlier, it's all a matter of learning how to manage stress constructively.

STRESS-CONTROL TECHNIQUES

The techniques that follow will help you achieve a sense of harmony in your life. They're geared toward restoring equilibrium and control as well as giving you a better perspective on your emotions.

Incidentally, just in case you still think control isn't a key stress-management concept, picture this: two people are hurtling down a hill on a toboggan. Who has the most stress—the person in the front who is steering, or the one in the back who's simply a passenger? The person in the back, of course, because that individual has no control.

For reducing the stress in your life, here are our recommendations:

Educate Yourself

In heart patients, there are few things more stressful than an imagination run rampant. In our experience, poorly informed patients are often depressed patients. Left to their own devices, they can conjure up the most dire scenarios, usually far removed from reality.

To allay your fears, get answers to your nagging cardiac questions. Be assertive about it. Don't let health professionals brush you off with explanations so glib, technical, or obtuse that they leave you scratching your head. The day of the dictatorial, uncommunicative physician is over. A large part of our job as doctors is to teach patients about preventive medicine. By explaining the importance of life-style changes, we seek to keep disease in check, stave off pain and suffering, and give patients as accurate a picture as possible of their prognosis. Our job is not simply to examine bodies and dispense pills.

Enlist the Aid and Support of your Family and Friends

Everything you learn about your health status must be shared with those closest to you. Otherwise, you and your family could be operating at cross-purposes, a confusing and stressful situation for a recuperating patient.

We encourage our patients to include their spouse or a family member in post-infarct or postoperative counselling sessions. We've found it especially useful to allow mates to observe treadmill stress tests. Doing so proves, better than anything we know, that the patient is not a fragile egg, ready to break at the slightest touch. That, in fact, is what many concerned spouses think. Rather than supporting our efforts to get heart patients out of bed and active as soon as possible, many spouses are overprotective. They coddle their husband or wife. This approach is exactly the opposite of what we recommend.

In short, the more contact there is between you and your doctor and those who are close to you, the more goal-oriented and consistent a recovery you're likely to have.

Acknowledge Your Feelings

Many heart patients are classic deniers. They've got rationales and excuses for everything—including the intense pain of a heart attack. Right up to the time the casualty doctor leans over them and announces, "You're having a heart attack," they refuse to accept it. Likewise, they lead lives filled with intense pressure and tension, yet they stoically endure it, refusing to admit any of it bothers them.

We ask you, is this any way to operate a human body? You are your body's maintenance engineer, after all. It's your responsibility to keep your "machine" in good working order.

Granted, the phrase "get in touch with your feelings" sounds like psycho-babble, but there's value in the concept, especially for coronary patients. Bottling up feelings is unhealthy, especially at a time when your physical condition is tenuous, to say the least.

Release Your Feelings in Constructive Ways

Discussing feelings with your loved ones is probably the best form of release. A University of New Mexico School of Medicine study underscores this point.[12] Investigators from the departments of medicine and psychiatry examined 256 healthy elderly adults who had good, solid relationships with trusted people in whom they could confide. These senior citizens, at an age when many are frail and ailing, had good cholesterol levels and well-functioning immune systems. In other studies, too, it's been found that strong family, community, church, and other group associations go hand in hand with an ability to handle stress well.

This brings up another reason to open up and start talking. Being uncommunicative about feelings is hard on those around you. If you want to retain satisfying relationships well into your old age, you'd better learn how to behave so that people continue to want you around.

What we don't want you to do is release your feelings in destructive ways, such as smoking and overeating. We recently counselled a woman who weighed 107 kilograms. She was excessively obese. When we asked her to go on a strict diet, she agreed cheerfully. She explained that she didn't like food much anyway and ate to excess only to distract herself from the unhappiness in her life.

While this woman is no role model for anyone, we do give her credit for knowing herself. She understood the link between her overeating and her negative feelings. Her diet has been successful only because she's found new forms of distraction and release, namely, exercise and psychiatric counselling.

Exercise—for Your Health and to Vent Steam

We've asked you to make exercise the keystone of your rehabilitation effort for many reasons we've already outlined. Here we ask you to do it for purely psychological reasons. Steady workouts will help you alleviate tension and ward off depression.

You could say that exercise is nature's tranquillizer. Many experts believe that this tranquillizing effect occurs in part because exercise triggers the release of endorphins, a hormone produced by the pituitary gland. Once endorphins enter the bloodstream, their beneficial effects are thought to last two or three hours. Those effects are relief from pain and a sense of euphoria—a feeling that all is right with the world.

Many people who make time for exercise, including cardiac patients, report a sense of relaxation and well-being after their workouts. Robert Swart, in particular, says that since his heart attack in 1984, he's learned to use exercise for tension control.

Robert is the owner of nine restaurants, with 400 employees to pay and thousands of customers to please. Admittedly, he's under a lot of pressure—something he's learned to understand and counterbalance with exercise.

Robert's mother died of a heart attack in 1982 and he had an angioplasty that same year. Still, that wasn't enough to get him to change his poor health habits. He says back then he was "a short, pudgy cigarette smoker with a high cholesterol count who seldom exercised". It took his heart attack at age forty-eight to bring him to his senses. He says, "It killed 20 percent of my heart muscle. The last thing I wanted was for any more of it to be put out of commission through my own inattentiveness."

Here's what Robert did:

> After my attack—by far the most painful thing that's ever happened to me—I started going to the physician for regular annual checkups and took stock of my whole life. Now, at the least sign of stress, I hop on my stationary bike and pedal away, or I run. I no longer eat red meat or other taboo foods. My mass is down to 68 kg or so and I watch it very closely. My cholesterol count has plummeted from a high of 7,76 to 4,14, with a ratio of about 3,3 to 3,5. Today, I feel fine.

Robert exemplifies another important benefit that heart patients can derive from exercise. As we pointed out earlier, people invariably feel stress when they lose control, even if it's control of their health via a heart attack. A regular exercise programme puts cardiac patients back in the driver's seat. It gives them a sense of self-reliance and self-esteem about their body. The patient feels, "Here is one area where I am confident that I can direct my destiny and improve my condition. No matter what else goes wrong, at least I know I remain in charge of this important segment of my life."

We encourage you to go for that sense of self-control and self-discipline that a regular exercise programme imparts. Then, once you've proved you have the willpower to stick to your weekly workout schedule, you'll find it easier to extend that sense of self-mastery into other parts of your life, as Robert Swart did. You'll find it much easier to stop smoking or radically alter your diet, for example.

Prioritize—with Your Health at the Top of the List

As Robert points out, there's nothing more motivating than a glimpse into eternity to get even the worst workaholic to see matters in a new light. Legion are the stories of people who have totally reordered their lives after a close brush with death. Mike Travelstead, our patient whom you met earlier, is a case in point.

Although Mike was in peak aerobic condition prior to his attack, he was by no means a paragon of virtue in terms of his eating habits. Or his hectic business schedule. But one thing about Mike—he's very enthusiastic. He probably learned as much about cardiology in the first few months after his attack as some medical students learn in a year. He read everything he could on the subject and consulted three different physicians, just to be sure. He had a baseline angiogram done just after his MI and then designed his own recuperation programme. It lasted one year.

During that time, Mike drastically altered his priorities. He went into his office around four hours a day to answer mail, supervise his employees, and attend to his best customers. The rest of the time he played with his children, exercised frequently, often with his wife, and made sure he did all the things that progressive rehabilitation cardiologists recommend.

Mike admits he had a grand plan:

Even though I was pretty certain I was going to recover 100 percent, I also realized nobody elected me God. I could drop dead tomorrow. But I wasn't bowing out without knowing everything there was to know about my babies. So I made a choice. Because I could afford to financially, I let my work go to hell. I hired other people to do the job. And I concentrated on my family and my health.

At the end of a year, I had a second angiogram. The results convinced me that my heart's condition hadn't deteriorated any further, and, if I was intelligent about it, I could resume a full schedule without backsliding.

Now I'm back in high gear. But, believe me, once something like this happens to you, you never forget it. I'll never take my life or good health for granted again.

The eminent cardiologist Dr. Robert Eliot, an authority on the link between stress and CHD, developed the Six-Months-to-Live Test.[13] He touts it as an excellent way to get harried people, especially Type A coronary patients, to focus on what's really important in their lives.

Dr. Eliot has patients make three lists. The first should identify the things you must do; the second, those you want to do; and the third, things you neither have to do nor want to do. After you're done, throw away List 3, attend to List 1, but concentrate on List 2, for these are the things that give your life meaning, because they reflect your individual values, interests, and talents.

Modify Those Negative Type A Traits

While hostility may be the Type A component that causes the most myocardial damage, the other elements of this particular personality constellation aren't all that healthy either.

There have been several studies aimed at modifying the Type A behaviour of post-MI patients. The most important was conducted by Dr. Carl E. Thoresen and Dr. Meyer Friedman at Mt. Zion Medical Centre in San Francisco and at Stanford.[14] Initiated in 1977, it involved a five-year clinical trial—the Recurrent Coronary Prevention Project. The subjects were 1 012 post-infarct patients whom the researchers studied to answer the questions: (1) Can Type A behaviour be changed? (2) If so, will patients' toned-down reactions to stress lessen the recurrence rate for another coronary event?

More than half of the subjects received diet and exercise instruction as well as group behaviour counselling, weekly for two months, then monthly thereafter. They were taught how to speak and eat more slowly, interrupt others less often, and deal better with situations that previously made them furious or impatient. They were encouraged to practice relaxation at least twenty minutes daily, set more reasonable deadlines, and drive as much as possible in the right or slower traffic lanes. They also kept records of their thoughts and emotional reactions to events. Counsellors used these diaries to point out how patients' negative outlooks and self-accusations fuelled a lot of the stress in their lives.

The result: the recurrence rate for those receiving the Type A behaviour modification therapy was almost 50 percent less than for those who received just diet and exercise counselling or no special treatment. Moreover, those patients whose Type A behaviour was lessened the most had the lowest recurrence rate of all.

Fortunately, psychologists tell us that Type A people make excellent students. Once they're convinced of the efficacy of Type B behaviour—and recognize that their counterproductive behaviour is acquired, not inherited—they generally approach the change process with characteristic Type A verve and energy. In short, Type A achievement values can be marshalled to motivate Type A people to convert to Type B behaviour.

Here are a few tips to get you started down that path: the next time you feel yourself exploding over something, stop and ask yourself: how important is this going to be a year from now? Five years from now? Probably your answer will be: "I won't even remember it two days from now."

Along the same lines, Dr. Robert Eliot, to whom we referred earlier, says there are two rules to bear in mind: (1) Don't sweat about the minor issues. (2) They're *all* minor issues.

Dr. Eliot suggests that people try to "flow" with events instead of fighting or fleeing. He says:

Why pay the price of hatred if a little dislike will do?

Why go into a panic if a little nervousness will do?

Why get depressed if a little sadness will do?

Why get ruffled when a good quip works better anyway? Winston Churchill knew the value of the well-aimed one-liner. Once, a woman opponent, in utter exasperation, spluttered, "If you were my husband, Winston, I'd put cyanide in your drink." Unperturbed, Churchill replied, "My dear lady, if you were my wife, I'd drink it!"

Laugh a Little

Adopting a grim outlook on life is about the worst thing a recuperating cardiac patient—or any other kind of patient—can do.

The therapeutic value of humour is a subject that's appeared in the medical literature for years. It was viewed with skepticism until Norman Cousins, a respected magazine editor, wrote the best-selling *Anatomy of an Illness*.[15] There he described how he used humour to help cure himself of a mystery illness that resisted conventional medical treatment. In desperation one day, he stopped taking all medication and sequestered himself with a videotape machine and old Marx brothers films and "Candid Camera" tapes. He maintains that his sustained laughter over a period of time was the key to his recovery.

While many in the medical community may discount humour's effectiveness, we feel it is useful. After all, a good belly laugh makes the world seem a brighter place for a moment.

Practice Relaxation Therapy

We find that some of our excessively tense patients respond well to formal relaxation therapies such as deep-breathing exercises, transcendental meditation, yoga, massage, biofeedback, progressive muscle relaxation, and relaxation training involving the use of repetitious sounds along with mental imagery. If you scored very high on the twin stress tests earlier in this chapter, we recommend you give one or several of these approaches a try.

To get you started, we describe two well-known methods of muscle and mental relaxation in the boxes on pages 287 to 288. Once you've mastered them under ideal environmental conditions, you'll be ready to put your newfound powers of mental concentration to the test in less ideal conditions—when you're stranded in a long, slow-moving line of traffic during rush hour, for instance (see the box on page 289).

Two good books on the subject, both by Harvard Medical School physician Dr. Herbert Benson, are *The Relaxation Response* and its sequel, *Beyond the Relaxation Response*.[16] If a class or individual instruction in one of these techniques is more to your liking, your local branch of Lifeline should be a good source of information.

Take Medication as the Very Last Resort

By now, you've probably noticed that this is always our approach. Drugs, to our way of thinking, are always a last resort after more

TO REDUCE THE PHYSICAL SYMPTOMS OF STRESS: DEEP MUSCLE RELAXATION

The idea of autogenic—or self-generated—relaxation originated with Dr. W. Luthe and Dr. V. H. Schultz in Germany. It has gained wide currency in Europe, although it is by no means the only way to reach the nirvana of complete bodily relaxation. However, as adapted by the Stanford Centre for Research in Disease Prevention in the United States, the method is easy to learn and practise.

During periods of high stress, practise this deep muscle relaxation at least twice daily for 15 or 20 minutes each session. However, do not exceed four times a day, because the exercise will become less effective. Either do it before meals or wait at least one hour afterward. This technique is especially useful before an anticipated stressful experience.

Your goal in pursuing this route to relaxation is to diminish or eliminate many of the manifestations of stress that are listed in Table 14-3.

Step 1. Seek out a place that's quiet and where you won't be interrupted.

Step 2. Lie on your back in a comfortable position, or sink into a comfortable chair. Relax and close your eyes.

Step 3. If you're right-handed, begin by physically tensing your right hand (if left-handed, your left hand). Keep it tensed to the count of five, then relax it. In your mind, talk to your hand. Tell it to feel heavy and warm.

Step 4. Continue the same procedure with the rest of that side of your body. Move up to your forearm, your upper arm, and shoulder. Next, start at your feet, and move up to the lower leg and then the thigh.

Step 5. Follow the same procedure on the opposite side of your body. When you're finished, your hands, arms, feet, and legs should feel relaxed, heavy, and warm.

Step 6. Repeat the process with the muscles of your hips and abdomen. When you relax them, you should feel a wave of relaxation move up through your chest.

Step 7. Do not tense your chest or upper body. Instead, relax them by telling them to feel heavy and warm. Monitor your body's responses. You'll notice your breathing becomes slower and deeper, emanating from the diaphragm, just below the rib cage.

Step 8. By this time, you should have mastered the feeling of relaxation, so you won't need to tense your muscles first before relaxing them. Now let the wave of relaxation continue up through your shoulders, neck, jaw, and the muscles of your face. Pay special attention to the muscles controlling your eyes and forehead.

Step 9. Finish up by telling your forehead to feel cool, as if a breeze is wafting over it.

Source: Adapted from John Farquhar, *The American Way of Life Need Not Be Hazardous to Your Health,* p. 64, "Deep Muscle Relaxation Drill". Reading, MA: Addison Wesley Publishing Co., 1987.

WIPING THE MENTAL SLATE CLEAN: ROUTINE FOR EXPUNGING STRESSFUL THOUGHTS FROM YOUR MIND

Once you know how to wring the tension from your body through muscular relaxation, you'll want to wring the disturbing thoughts from your mind in a similar fashion. This is accomplished through an exercise that you undertake as a continuation of the deep muscle relaxation explained in the box above. That's why the first step below is labelled 10 instead of 1.

Step 10. Enjoy the deep sense of relaxation all over your body. Your eyes are closed and your forehead is cool.

Step 11. Move into a passive state in which you stop trying to control your thoughts. They begin to flow through your mind at random.

Step 12. If thoughts recur, respond by murmuring no under your breath.

Step 13. Summon all your powers of imagination. Visualize a cloudless blue sky ... or a calm body of clear blue water ... or any solid stretch of light- to medium-blue colour. Envelop yourself in the colour. (There is physiological evidence that this colour exerts a relaxing influence.)

Step 14. Turn your attention to your breathing—which by now is slow and natural. Concentrate on each breath as you inhale and exhale.

Step 15. If a placid, restful state still eludes you, try the mental exercise of silently repeating a word you find soothing, either because of its meaning ("God," "love," a special person's name, etc.) or because of its inherent sound ("moooooonnnn," "aaaaaahhhh," etc.). In your head, say the word over and over, especially during exhalation, which should be longer than your inhalation. Occasionally, remind yourself to keep your facial muscles flaccid and your forehead cool.

Source: Adapted from John Farquhar, *The American Way of Life Need Not Be Hazardous to Your Health,* pp. 66-67, "Mental Relaxation Drill." Reading, MA: Addison Wesley Publishing Co., 1987.

> **ANYWHERE, ANYTIME: HOW TO ACHIEVE INSTANT RELAXATION**
>
> You've mastered the art of muscular and mental relaxation through several weeks of disciplined practice (see the boxes on pages 287 to 288). With your newfound knowledge, you're now ready to move on and learn how to harness your powers of concentration and relaxation in less ideal environments—while you're waiting in a long queue, standing in the wings before a stage appearance, sitting on a dais before rising to give a speech, etc. Despite the hustle-bustle around you, you can achieve at least partial relaxation via the following method:
>
> *Step 1.* Sit down if you can. Otherwise, remain standing.
>
> *Step 2.* Inhale deeply. Hold your breath to a slow count of five. Exhale gradually while concentrating on the sensations in your body and telling your muscles to relax.
>
> *Step 3.* Do this several times, becoming more relaxed with each repetition.
>
> *Step 4.* If circumstances permit, close your eyes and think a pleasant or positive thought ("I'm beginning to feel at ease," "I really want to be here in the midst of this _____," etc.). Or paint a mental picture of an inviting indoor or outdoor scene (e.g., sitting with someone you love in front of a blazing fireplace, taking a leisurely wade through a mountain stream, floating across a calm lake, etc.).
>
> Source: Adapted from John Farquhar, *The American Way of Life Need Not Be Hazardous to Your Health,* p. 69, "Instant Relaxation Drill." Reading, MA: Addison Wesley Publishing Co., 1987.

natural methods have failed. This is equally true of antistress, anti-anxiety, and antidepressant medications.

Our guidelines for writing out a prescription are these: the patient must be suffering from moderate to severe depression, or anxiety and stress significant enough to interfere with their ability to function at home or work. We also give psychotherapeutic drugs serious consideration if the patient's mental distress is producing physical symptoms, such as loss of appetite, insomnia, palpitations, uncontrollable crying, stomach pain, chest tightness, etc. However, before putting pen to prescription pad, we always check out a patient thoroughly to make absolutely sure it's mental anguish, rather than an organic malady, that's causing the problem. For readers who wish to explore the psychological aspects of heart disease and its psychological management, the book *Clinical Health Psychology: A Behavioural Medicine Perspective* by Prof. L. Schlebusch is recommended,[17] especially Chapters 5, 7, 8 and 23.

CHAPTER 15

REDUCING YOUR OTHER RISK FACTORS

WE CAN'T repeat it often enough: there are seven modifiable risk factors for coronary artery disease. You can alter every one of them, for these are factors within your control. They involve little choices and behaviours you engage in every day.

SMOKING

Smoking is a prime example. Most people who smoke realize they're flirting with lung cancer. Yet despite the government health warning that appears on every cigarette pack, thousands of South Africans still smoke.

But lung cancer is only part of the story. People die from heart disease caused directly by their smoking as well as from lung cancer caused by smoking.

According to a 1984 Medical Research Council study, the percentages of all deaths that are smoking-related are as follows for the South African population: whites 34,5%, "coloureds" 14,5%, Asians 24,5% and blacks 3,9%. In addition, smokers who suffer a heart attack stand a greater chance of dying from it. And those who survive either a heart attack or bypass surgery and continue to smoke increase their chances appreciably of dying soon thereafter.

In your situation, having just survived a heart attack or come through bypass surgery or angioplasty, you can't afford to take a drag on one more cigarette—or cigar or pipeful of tobacco. In fact, stopping smoking may be the single most important thing any heart patient can do to stack the odds in favour of staying alive.

Each cigarette you smoke raises the circulating levels of fibrinogen and adrenaline-like hormones in your blood, makes blood platelets more sticky, decreases the blood's oxygen-carrying capacity, interferes with tissue utilization of oxygen, lowers HDL, constricts blood vessels, and makes your heart more irritable. No wonder lighting up a cigarette twenty or thirty times a day can cause a heart attack.

Let's consider, for a moment, the damage your smoking habit has already inflicted. The degree of damage has a lot to do with how much you smoked. One-pack-a-day smokers have double the risk of heart attack of people who have never smoked. Two-pack-a-day smokers have a risk that's three times greater.

Put another way, if you've been smoking two packs a day, you have only half the chance of reaching age sixty-five that a non-smoker has. A statistician and an actuary got together and worked out that people who smoke this much are reducing their life span by one minute for each minute they smoke. It's a direct trade-off.

But these are just numbers. See if the following images don't bring the message home more graphically: pack-a-day smokers pour one full cup of tar into their lungs over the course of a year. One cigarette contains 640 times more carbon monoxide—which provides a painless method of suicide for people with a car and a well-insulated garage—than the federal Occupational Safety and Health Administration in the USA allows in the workplace. It's ironic. This organisation protects Americans from poisoning at the hand of employers. And what do many of them do, after hours, of their own volition? Poison themselves—with cigarettes.

Inside a Smoker's Blood Vessels

One recent study gives a particularly revealing picture of what goes on inside the cardiovascular system of a smoker.[1] The subjects were sixty-five people (fifty-two men and thirteen women) between the ages of thirty-six and seventy-five. All were CHD patients who suffered from myocardial ischaemia. Over a twenty-four-hour period, the patients were subjected to Holter monitoring. The researchers found that the twenty-four smokers in the group, on average, had ischaemic episodes three times more often than the non-smokers. The duration of their attacks was also much longer. The non-smokers' episodes were about two minutes long; the smokers' episodes were, on average, twenty-four minutes long. Another significant finding was that the actual smoking of a cigarette didn't trigger the subjects' ischaemic episodes. This suggests that smoking has residual negative effects on the cardiovascular system. It creates a continual, or chronic, severe ischaemic condition.

Indeed, one of the worst effects of smoking is not sudden death. It's the fact that it creates a lingering disability of the kind that reduces many lifelong smokers to a frail, decrepit, invalid state in their later years. Fortunately, it's not too late for you to reverse some of the damage that smoking has wrought.

At least five long-term epidemiological studies have considered the question dearest to your heart: "Will giving up at this stage, after I've already had my heart attack, really make any difference?" Table 15-1 shows the answer. In these major cardiac studies, researchers compared patients of all ages who stopped smoking after their heart attacks with those who stubbornly persisted in their habit. The end result was that the abstainers reduced their chances of an MI recurrence—and death—by anywhere from 38 to 60 percent. So the answer is a resounding YES! It pays to stop smoking at any time, no matter how old you are.

Elderly smokers have been the subject of several recent smoking-cessation studies. The consistent conclusion is that to stop smoking at any age is to add years to your life. The beneficial effect one gets from abstinence does not decline with advancing age.[2,3]

As doctors, we find that giving patients a detailed picture of how smoking pollutes the cardiovascular system often helps

TABLE 15-1
After a Heart Attack: Stop Smoking Now to Increase Your Chances of Living Longer[a]

Study	Number in Study	Follow-up Period	Percentage Reduction in Mortality
Göteborg	938	10 years	38%
Dublin	374	13 years	55%
Framingham	202	6 years	60%
Helsinki	648	5 years	60%
North Karelia (Finland)	523	3 years	40%

[a] In the five major longitudinal heart studies cited here, myocardial infarction patients who stopped smoking were compared with those who continued their habit. As the last column shows, the abstainers experienced a marked reduction in M.I. recurrence and death.

Source: "Coronary Heart Disease: Epidemiology of Smoking and Intervention Studies," *American Heart Journal,* 115, No. 1, Part 2 (January 1988): 242–249.

dissuade them from the habit. So here's what smoking does: it reduces your body's good HDL cholesterol concentration. It elevates your white blood cell count, which by itself may also be a predictor of heart attack independent of smoking. It changes the composition of your blood, giving it the tendency to form clots, which, of course, may result in a heart attack or stroke. A thrombosis in the brain is a stroke. A thrombosis in your heart arteries results in a heart attack. Either one can kill you.

For the heart, the biggest villains as far as smoking is concerned seem to be nicotine and carbon monoxide. They're like two independent death squads, operating at cross-purposes to kill you.

Nicotine is a stimulant. It's responsible for that "lift" you feel just seconds after your first puff. The lift comes from a sudden increase in your heart rate of 15 to 25 beats a minute, and a rise in blood pressure of 10 to 20 points. The nicotine, in effect, causes your body to require more oxygen by stimulating the release of adrenaline-like substances. These substances also constrict your blood vessels, which causes the increase in blood pressure. And they make the heart more susceptible to ventricular tachycardia or fibrillation—life-threatening rhythm disturbances, especially in cardiac patients.

In addition, the carbon monoxide in tobacco has terrible effects. It binds to the oxygen-carrying haemoglobin in your blood, thus reducing the oxygen transport in your body. In the presence of carbon monoxide, your oxygen supply decreases by about 20 percent. Smokers have up to ten times more carbon monoxide in their blood than non-smokers.

Here you have the biological explanation for the prolonged episodes of myocardial ischaemia experienced by smokers in the study we just reported on. It's a Catch-22 situation. Just when your body is crying out for more oxygen delivery, many of your blood transporters are unavailable because they're already carrying carbon monoxide.

The vehicle metaphor is an apt one, for traffic exhaust is largely composed of carbon monoxide. A recent study, in fact, links the high heart attack rates of people who collect toll fees in American traffic tunnels with the traffic exhaust they inhale on a daily basis.[4] The study followed workers in New York City. These employees are rotated daily, from the tollbooths outside the tunnels to glass-enclosed surveillance booths inside the tunnels. They're also given a half-hour "air break" every four hours. Still, the researchers found that the workers had extremely high death rates, mostly due to CHD. Deaths among employees who had been on the job for more than ten years were 88 percent higher than normal.

It's no wonder, when you learn that the carbon monoxide levels at those tunnels reach more than 400 parts per million during traffic snarls and peak commuter hours. The current USA workplace safety standard for carbon monoxide is a level not to exceed 50 parts per million. Frank Stern, the epidemiologist who headed up the study for the National Institute for Occupational Safety and Health, says the report is especially significant because "up to now no one has determined for certain what in cigarette smoke causes increased heart disease in smokers". This study clearly points to carbon monoxide as a prime suspect.

This is not to diminish nicotine's role in the dirty work of CHD progression—or that of any of the 4 000 other substances that lab researchers have identified in cigarette smoke. While we still may not know which substances are the most lethal, we do know what their combined effects are.

Cigarette smoke appears to injure the walls of blood vessels, which allows more blood cholesterol to seep through and be deposited in plaques. It also changes the viscosity of blood. It thickens blood, causing it to become stickier and clot faster.

Fibrinogen

Fibrinogen is a protein in the blood that fosters clotting. Smokers often have fibrinogen levels above the normal range of 2 to 4 grams per litre. Overmass people, those with diets high in fat, and the sedentary may also find their fibrinogen levels above normal.

Studies of the effects of elevated fibrinogen have been relatively consistent in their findings. People with this health problem are at increased risk of stroke and heart attack.[5] The precise manner in which smoking and high fibrinogen levels interact to aid CHD progression is not known, but presumably the enhanced risk of thrombosis plays a part. Some cardiac researchers, including those involved in the famous Framingham Study, feel that elevated fibrinogen is such a good predictor of thrombosis that it should be added to the list of major CHD risk factors.

Along with giving up smoking, it appears that losing mass, exercising regularly, and lowering both blood pressure and blood sugar levels may help people reduce their fibrinogen levels. Taking an aspirin a day can also help counteract the negative effects of an elevated fibrinogen level, which is easily measured with a blood test.

The Willpower to Stop

Studies have shown that up to half of all people who live through an acute heart attack stop smoking—some forever, others for extended periods of time. Oddly enough, the average female heart patient seems to find it harder to stop than her male counterpart, a fact borne out both by scientific studies and by testimonials in the medical literature.

One particularly poignant account comes from a forty-seven-year-old nurse who had severe angina and bypass surgery and lived to share the experience with her professional peers in a first-person article published in a medical journal. She writes:

> One of the most compelling forces that keeps me on the diet and regular exercise programme is guilt over my failure to stop smoking.
> I stopped smoking for three months after the surgery, but I never lost the desire for a cigarette, and made the mistake of smoking "just one." Over the next three weeks I gradually increased to nearly a pack a day. I switched to low-nicotine, low-tar cigarettes and have since stopped and started six times, with a week being the longest time I was cigarette-free.
> I realize how harmful smoking is, and I continue to experience severe guilt. I firmly believe that these two facts alone will motivate me to keep trying to stop smoking until I am successful.[6]

You'll notice that our nurse cardiac patient tried switching to low-nicotine, low-tar cigarettes. This is common. Psychologically, it indicates the person is concerned about his or her unhealthy habit. But physiologically and in terms of CHD risk, it has little significance.

Why?

The answer involves addiction. A smoker is really a drug addict. Nicotine is one of the most addictive substances in our society and cigarettes are one of the most effective drug delivery systems we have ever invented. The average smoker probably self-administers 70 000 nicotine "hits," or doses, a year. Smokers do this because it makes them feel better, both physically and emotionally. It makes many people feel more alert, it quiets their nerves, and it helps them control their appetites.

Experienced smokers can fine-tune the physiological and emotional responses they get from tobacco. They do this merely by varying the rate and depth of their puffs, which regulates the amount of nicotine that enters the body. Most smokers do this unconsciously.

What happens when smokers switch to "healthier" cigarettes or try to smoke less of their usual brand is fairly predictable. Their bodies, which are hooked on nicotine, feel the deprivation, and the brain sends signals to inhale more deeply to stop the feelings of discomfort that are starting to develop. Smokers oblige. The end result is that their altered smoking pattern gets as much nicotine into the body as before. Ironically, their new habit of inhaling more deeply may even increase CHD risk because now they're also exposing themselves to more of the other harmful substances in cigarettes.

Smokers often ask us about pipes and cigars. Aren't they safer than cigarettes?

If pipe and cigar smokers didn't inhale, they would suffer fewer negative effects. But this is seldom the case, especially if the smoker has switched from cigarettes. Also, research indicates that pipe and cigar smokers—and the people in the room with them—may actually have a significant CHD risk because of "sidestream exposure" to smoke. Non-smokers in smoke-filled rooms all day long might as well have smoked five or more cigarettes.

Excuses, Excuses

As cardiac physicians, we've probably heard every excuse in the book for continuing to smoke. Our favourite came from a woman who smoked three packs a day. She had early bronchitis and emphysema, and her risk of CHD was extremely high. When told that she had to stop smoking, she listened, then smiled devilishly. "Doctor, I can't stop smoking," she protested. "Coughing is the only exercise I get."

The most horrifying response also came from a woman. She was young and attractive and was obsessed with her appearance. After our brief antismoking lecture, she noted that one of her friends had stopped and immediately gained 5 kilograms. (On average, ex-smokers gain 1,5 to 3,5 kilograms.) We countered that that would be a small price to pay for eliminating the tremendous health risk that smoking represents. She retorted coldly, "I'd rather be dead than fat."

If vanity is really her main reason for smoking, she and others like her should know about a newly identified medical syndrome called "smoker's face." If you're not willing to quit to save your heart, you may want to stop to save your complexion. There is now clear evidence that smokers are at high risk for developing premature wrinkles, a pasty, grey-yellow complexion, and cyanosis of the lips (cyanosis is a bluish skin or tissue colour, indicating a lack of oxygenated blood).

Stopping at Last

It would be a mistake to think that stopping is easy. On the other hand, millions of people do it every year, and only a relatively small percentage of them have the inducement of a heart condition. So, clearly, it can be done.

Withdrawal symptoms represent the biggest hurdle. Their severity and duration depend on the extent of your addiction, which you can measure by doing the quiz in Table 15-2, on pages 298–299. Notice that how much you smoke is the key indicator of your nicotine addiction—not your age, your sex, or the number of times you have already attempted to stop.

Should you stop smoking abruptly, expect to experience one or more of the following symptoms within twenty-four hours:

- A craving for tobacco
- Irritability
- Bouts of anxiety
- Difficulty in concentrating
- Restlessness
- Headaches
- Drowsiness
- Gastrointestinal disturbances

Fortunately, these withdrawal discomforts are temporary. They are the most intense during the first two or three days, decrease for the remainder of the first week, increase somewhat in the second week, then decrease gradually thereafter. The acute phase of smoking withdrawal is generally over within three weeks. However, even after your body is free of nicotine, you may still experience cravings for several months, but they will be psychological rather than physical in origin. The danger period is the first six months. That's when most relapses occur.

It's up to you whether you opt to go it alone or join a smoking-cessation group. However, even if solo cold turkey is the route

TABLE 15-2
You Smoke, but How Addicted Are You?

Smoking is an addictive act. When you try to stop, your withdrawal symptoms will vary according to the degree of your nicotine addiction. Here is a multiple choice quiz to help you ascertain your dependency:

1. How soon after you wake up do you smoke your first cigarette?
   - (a) after 30 minutes
   - (b) within 30 minutes
2. Do you find it difficult to refrain from smoking in places where it is forbidden, such as the library, theater, or doctor's office?
   - (a) yes
   - (b) no
3. Which of all the cigarettes you smoke in a day is the most satisfying?
   - (a) any other than the first one in the morning
   - (b) the first one in the morning
4. How many cigarettes a day do you smoke?
   - (a) 1-15
   - (b) 16-25
   - (c) 26 or more
5. Do you smoke more during the morning than during the rest of the day?
   - (a) yes
   - (b) no
6. Do you smoke when you are so ill that you are in bed most of the day?
   - (a) yes
   - (b) no
7. Does the brand you smoke have a low, medium, or high nicotine content?
   - (a) low (0,9 mg or less)
   - (b) medium (1-1,2 mg)
   - (c) high (1,3 mg or more)
8. How often do you inhale the smoke from your cigarette?
   - (a) never
   - (b) sometimes
   - (c) always

SCORING YOUR ANSWERS

1. (a) 0	(b) 1	
2. (a) 1	(b) 0	
3. (a) 0	(b) 1	
4. (a) 0	(b) 1	(c) 2
5. (a) 1	(b) 0	
6. (a) 1	(b) 0	

TABLE 15-2 *(continued)*
You Smoke, but How Addicted Are You?

7. (a) 0	(b) 1	(c) 2
8. (a) 0	(b) 1	(c) 2

INTERPRETATION: If your score is 6 or greater, there's a high probability that your body is addicted to nicotine. In the first week or so of your stop-smoking programme, you may experience some uncomfortable withdrawal symptoms.

Source: Clinical Opportunities for Smoking Intervention, U.S. Department of Health and Human Services, NIH Publication No. 86-2178, August 1986.

you choose, we encourage you to enlist the support of your family and closest friends. If you and your spouse both smoke, we recommend you stop together. The odds of one-half of a marital duo stopping successfully while the other continues are not good.

Perhaps you should gain the social support of an ex-smoker who can identify with your struggle. In America the Cancer Society maintains lists of ex-smokers who have volunteered to help those in the throes of giving up. This buddy-system approach is similar to that of Alcoholics Anonymous, where the new recruit links up with a "sponsor" who is only a phone call away when a craving hits. There is no such organised system in South Africa at present, but there is no reason why you can't get a friend who's given up smoking to be your sponsor.

The National Cancer Association of South Africa has a wealth of information available to the public. This information covers everything from the health effects of smoking to smoking prevention to how to give up smoking. In the future they will be devoting more and more attention to preventing smoking among children—a serious problem worldwide and one that is on the increase in South Africa. To obtain information from them, write to the Information Service, National Cancer Association of South Africa, PO Box 186, Rondebosch 7700, or phone them at Cape Town (021) 689-5347.

What Works, What Doesn't?

To be sure, there are a lot of stop-smoking programmes available. They range from the medically oriented, such as hypnosis and acupuncture, to the psychosocial, which stress motivation and social interaction.

To date, controlled studies of acupuncture and hypnosis are lacking, so it's hard to say how successful they are. However, behavioural methods have been analysed in order to determine what ingredients are most likely to make a programme effective.

In one study, researchers examined thirty-nine different smoking-cessation programmes.[7] They found that repeated face-to-face advice from physicians and/or lay counsellors, whether on a one-to-one basis or in a group, seemed to do the most good; another successful technique was the use of nicotine chewing gum. In conclusion, the researchers said that reinforcement, rather than gimmicks, works best: "Success was not associated with novel or unusual interventions. It was the product of personalized smoking cessation advice and assistance, repeated in different forms by several sources over the longest feasible period."

Nicotine gum can be a helpmate in the quitting process. We've found it especially useful for people who are heavily addicted or who experience rapid mass gain upon cessation. We do not prescribe it for first-timers, though. We resort to the gum only after a patient has tried other stop-smoking methods with little success.

The gum is sold under the trade name Nicorette and requires a doctor's prescription. It contains either 2 or 4 milligrams of nicotine, although a more potent gum, already available in Europe, is currently undergoing safety trials.

Chewing the gum—and there is a knack to it—releases enough nicotine into the blood to relieve the worst nicotine cravings. It can be chewed for a maximum of six months after the patient smokes his or her last cigarette. The idea is to provide the patient with a partial substitute for the nicotine in cigarettes so that the initial phase of tobacco withdrawal is less unpleasant. We must emphasize that the gum is not a panacea in and of itself. It must always be used in conjunction with behavioural treatment, whether it be self-administered therapy or within a group context.[8]

The gum becomes counterproductive, of course, if the patient gets hooked on it. This can happen. That's why its use must taper off steadily over the course of the treatment. However, during the early weeks of cigarette withdrawal, it's the patient who must decide the optimum dosage. There is simply no way a physician can equate a former cigarette habit with the number of sticks of gum it will take to relieve the craving. Over the remaining course of the treatment, the doctor must make sure usage diminishes—twelve pieces a day should go down to ten after two weeks, for example. Nicotine gum is most definitely a drug, one that doctors must prescribe with discretion and monitor judiciously.

Nicotine gum affords a slow letdown from the euphoric effects of smoking. At the opposite extreme is a stop-smoking method that is so radical it makes you feel sick. It involves rapid smoking, an aversion technique designed to make you forever after associate smoking with highly uncomfortable sensations.

For some people, rapid smoking is the preferred way out because it works; certainly no one chooses it because it's pleasant. Long-term abstinence rates are high. However, before going this route, you must get your doctor's permission. For cardiac patients, especially older people, this method can have some drawbacks.

If smoking were merely a physical addiction, it might be easier to "cure." But it has a strong psychological component that smokers must be aware of if they're going to conquer their habit successfully.

In order to stop, smokers must know the cues, or triggers, that stimulate them to light up. Many triggers are situational, such as eating, driving, or partying. Others involve emotions, good or bad, such as anger and frustration or elation and pleasure.

Almost all behaviourally oriented smoking-cessation programmes ask you to keep a diary in which you record your cigarette cravings and what triggered them. The American Heart Association, in its booklet *The Good Life: A Guide to Becoming a Non-smoker,* lists these as the most common triggers: drinking coffee; working under pressure; watching television; observing someone else smoke; playing cards; having a drink; feeling lonely; talking on the telephone; taking a work break; finishing a good meal; waiting for public transportation; having a family argument; reading a newspaper; meeting with your boss; driving a car; waiting for food to be served in a restaurant.

Your diary is meant to help you learn what your triggers are so you can break the association. Instead of sitting down for a cocktail and cigarette the moment you get home from work, you might walk around the block. Instead of drinking coffee and smoking at your desk, you might substitute fruit juice and fiddle with a pipe cleaner. And so forth.

Diaries can also contain all the coping methods you devise to keep yourself on the straight and narrow. For some people, that means a hefty list of rational reasons for quitting; for others, a set of relaxation methods that help them deal with the newfound bodily tensions that nicotine used to suppress. Still others engage in very personal self-talk, coming up with slogans and admonitions only they can respond to. And other people may keep going with a series of rewards—one at the end of each week they're cigarette-free.

We've even known people who have thrived on visual images. We had a patient who liked to imagine how pink and clean her honeycomb lungs would look after the cigarette soot disappeared. Another viewed his addiction as a horrible hydra-headed monster inside his body. Without its usual nicotine meals, the monster was starving to death, resulting in the unpleasant withdrawal symptoms he was experiencing. He said the monster became so real to him, and he hated it so much, that he almost began to enjoy the pain of it all.

We want to emphasize that a relapse is not a failure. It's a fact of life. Most smokers need more than one attempt before they stop forever.

Most relapses occur in the first three months after stopping. They occur for social reasons—you just can't resist in situations where all the triggers scream SMOKE. Or your reasons are psychological—you're depressed or going through a stressful time. Or you can't overcome your physiological needs—your urge for a cigarette is just too great; you can't abide your withdrawal symptoms and mass gain.

Whatever the reason, just view your previous unsuccessful attempts as rehearsals for the attempt that finally works.

HYPERTENSION: THE SILENT CHD MENACE

We're steadily winning the fight against smoking. And, fortunately, the same can be said about high blood pressure, technically known as *hypertension*. Back in 1945, when U.S. President Franklin D. Roosevelt died of a stroke caused in great part by high blood pressure, there was no recognized treatment for this symptomless malady. Today, the picture is very different. We have ways of detecting what's causing hypertension as well as effective means for treating it.

The proof is in the numbers. People with uncontrolled, persistent high blood pressure may get CHD and have an eventual stroke or heart attack in the future—hardly a pleasant prospect. However, since 1972, when the U.S. government first mounted a campaign to rid its population of this menace, there has been a 50 percent decline in the age-adjusted stroke mortality rate and a nearly 40 percent decline in CHD in that country.[9]

The nearly 40 percent decline in CHD is, of course, only in part related to better control of high blood pressure.

In this country we have much to be concerned about. Hypertension is a significant problem in South Africa and black people in particular seem to be predisposed towards it. Unfortunately the local situation is not as well researched as the American one is and we have not had the same kind of public awareness campaigns as the Americans. It will not be easy to get people focused on high blood pressure when it usually causes them no discomfort and some of the medication to treat it does.

What Is Hypertension?

The medical definition is systolic blood pressure equal to or greater than 140 mm Hg and/or diastolic blood pressure equal to or greater than 90 mm Hg. Back in Chapter 3, we explained that the systolic figure—always shown first in a blood pressure reading—represents the pressure that is exerted on the walls of your arteries when your heart contracts, forcing blood out to all parts of the body. A reading of 140 means that your heart is pumping hard enough to drive a column of mercury (Hg) up a tube to a height of 140 millimetres (mm).

The second number represents the diastolic pressure being exerted between heartbeats, when your cardiovascular system is taking a tiny rest break. If the diastolic pressure is elevated, your arteries remain unduly stressed even when your heart is relaxed and simply filling with blood in preparation for its next beat.

Below is a fuller categorization of the accepted systolic and diastolic readings for people eighteen years of age and older:

Systolic (when diastolic is less than 90):

Less than 140	Normal blood pressure
140–159	Borderline isolated systolic hypertension
160 or greater	Isolated systolic hypertension

Diastolic:

Less than 85	Normal blood pressure
85-89	High normal
90-104	Mild hypertension
105–114	Moderate hypertension
115 or greater	Severe hypertension

Let us caution you that a single elevated reading is not necessarily a sign of hypertension. Your blood pressure could be high at that moment for a very understandable reason—you rushed to the doctor's office in the middle of an unusually hectic day, for example. Or it could be uncharacteristically low because you were lying down asleep just before the reading.

You must have at least two or three readings on more than one occasion, which are then averaged out. Only after this averaging can your physician decide if you have a problem. Moreover, each reading must be done correctly. Before having your blood pressure taken, you should rest quietly for five minutes in a seated position. The cuff should be put on a bare and extended arm, which the technician should support at your heart level. The reading may be inaccurate if you've smoked or had any beverage with caffeine within the last half hour. People with widely disparate readings may need to undergo, under controlled conditions, a twenty-four-hour blood pressure test with a portable monitor.

Causes and Treatment of High Blood Pressure

A number of factors predispose a person to high blood pressure. Obesity, alcohol excess, and high salt intake are just three. Age is another. The older you are, the more likely you are to have elevated readings.

Hypertension seems to be more prevalent in black people of any age. Based on 1980 statistics from the USA, 38 percent of all adult black males and 39 percent of adult black females had high blood pressure. That compares with 33 percent of all adult white men and 25 percent of adult white women.[10] Indications are that South African blacks, especially in urban areas, have the same problem. Women who are pregnant or taking oral contraceptives are at special risk. People can also develop the problem as a result of kidney disease or some hormonal abnormality.

In chronic cases of hypertension, it's seldom easy to identify the precise underlying cause. In fact, the most important and common cause is genetic predisposition, which for some unknown reason increases the resistance to blood flow in the small arteries in the body. Nevertheless, the factors mentioned above can have a dramatic effect on blood pressure levels, even when the major cause is genetic. So if you've got a genetic predisposition and are overmass, drink too much alcohol, and don't exercise, be aware that you're radically increasing your chances of developing hypertension.

The good thing about hypertension is that it can often be reduced to normal levels without drugs. Medication, which we'll cover in a minute, usually should be used only if the non-drug methods we're about to recommend don't work or aren't enough to bring the pressure to normal.

You'll be gratified to learn that our prescription for controlling hypertension includes many of the life-style changes we've already suggested elsewhere in this book. You may be instituting many of them, so your blood pressure could have dropped significantly already.

Here is what you can do on your own to alleviate your problem:

Lose Mass. When it comes to hypertension, obesity is public enemy no. 1. This is borne out in worldwide epidemiological studies in which obesity and blood pressure are always found to be closely coupled. Indeed, in most people, mass is such an important factor that their blood pressure seems to move up and down in tandem with it. Needless to say, if this is the case for you, we urge you to heed the advice in Chapter 13. Take mass loss to heart and do something about it today!

Control Your Drinking. By drinking, we mean alcohol intake. When people think of alcoholism, they usually think of liver problems. But hypertension is right up there too as a complication of drinking. If you must drink, hold the line at one serving a day as an absolute maximum. This quantity is not that restrictive. It amounts to two 25 ml tots of 100-proof whisky, approximately 150 ml of wine, or 250 ml of beer a day.

Stop Smoking. We've said our piece on this subject earlier in this chapter. Lowering your blood pressure is just one more reason to do it.

Exercise Regularly. This is another topic we've covered exhaustively elsewhere in this book. On the specific issue of high blood pressure and exercise, we'd like to add one final note: all the data from our own patients are used in our research. These data afford an excellent opportunity to study the links between fitness and various medical problems, among them hypertension. In one study, which lasted for four years, we followed 6 039 adults who at the outset had normal blood pressure. We found that those who were most fit had a 34 percent lower risk of developing hypertension. We concluded that exercise not only affords immediate benefits for high blood pressure, it also helps guard against it in the future.[11]

Relax. By this we mean find effective ways to deal with the rat race of life. As we discussed in the previous chapter, to save wear and tear on your body you must learn to temper your responses to stressful situations.

According to clinical researchers, there are various behavioural approaches that seem to have a moderating effect on blood pressure. Dr. Stephen Weiss, in a recent article in the *American Heart Journal,* reviewed thirty-nine separate studies covering eighteen different biofeedback and twenty-one different relaxation therapies.[12] The methods ranged from yoga-type meditation to progressive muscle relaxation. Dr. Weiss added up the collective results and found that biofeedback techniques reduced subjects' blood pressure readings by an average of 7,8 mm Hg (systolic) and 5,6 mm Hg (diastolic). Relaxation methods lowered them by 11 mm Hg (systolic) and 7,1 mm Hg (diastolic).

Dr. Weiss also reported on the findings of one researcher who had experimented with combinations of biofeedback and bodily relaxation. The researcher discovered that biofeedback followed by relaxation training appeared to be the most successful.

Reduce the Salt in Your Diet. No doubt you expected to see this admonishment here. It's well known that heart patients shouldn't consume salt. But do you know why? Normal people have the ability to flush out excess sodium in their urine, but some people are "salt-sensitive" and can't. The sodium induces their bodies to retain fluid, which increases blood volume and drives up blood pressure. The more salt they take in, the higher it gets.

We've used the terms "salt" and "sodium" interchangeably, but this isn't really accurate. Common table salt is 40 percent sodium and 60 percent chloride. It's sodium that heart patients need to avoid.

A typical American takes in as much as 7 000 milligrams of sodium a day. That's an amazing thirty-five times more than is needed for proper functioning of the body. Amounts for South Africans with westernized lifestyles could be similar. Your body requires only about 200 milligrams of sodium each day, although the National Academy of Sciences in the USA recommends that healthy adults—not those with CHD—consume 1 100 to 3 300 milligrams daily.

Where does the 7 000 milligrams come from? About a third comes straight out of a salt cellar at the table. Another quarter comes from sodium that is naturally present in food. The remainder comes from processed foods—the largest single source. Just like sugar, salt (in the form of sodium chloride, sodium nitrate, etc) is one of those ingredients that seems to be in everything, even things that don't taste salty. We think you'll find Table 15-3, on pages 308–311, a real eye-opener.

Considering all the sodium in processed foods, those of us with high blood pressure clearly have to do more than just remove the salt cellar from our table or use one of the salt substitutes listed in the box on page 312. If the cholesterol chapter earlier on didn't get you reading ingredient labels on food items, we urge you to do so now. When a product says "low sodium" in big letters, reach for it.

Guidelines for cutting back on sodium without spoiling the pleasure of eating are contained in the box on page 313. Reading through that list, you'll see you've got plenty of options. We predict, in fact, that a salty flavour is something you won't miss for long. Some people seem to be born with a craving for sugar. The same cannot be said about salt. Use of excess salt is a bad habit you acquire as you go through life. Like any bad habit, it can be broken. After two or three months of relative abstinence, your taste buds will become ultrasensitive to salt and recoil at your former high doses.

Increase Your Potassium Intake—Cautiously. Potassium, like sodium, is an electrolyte (a small, electrically charged particle that moves back and forth across cell membranes). Unlike sodium, however, it appears to have a beneficial rather than a harmful effect on blood pressure. Because it tastes somewhat salty and has no negative impact on blood pressure, potassium is usually a major

Table 15-3
Sodium (Na) Content of Various Foods

Protein Foods	Amount	Na (mg)
Fresh beef, veal, pork, lamb, chicken, turkey, fish	85 g	60
Fresh lobster, shrimp (6)	85 g	200
Fresh crabmeat	85 g	775
Processed meats: polony, salami, bacon (2 slices); 2 pork sausages; dried chipped beef, cured ham, or salt pork (2 slices)	85 g	1 200
Bacon	2 slices	200
Low-cholesterol hamburger patties	2	900
Processed fish: Tuna, salmon, crab—canned (in oil); or frozen oysters	85 g	200
Tuna, salmon, crab—canned (in water)	85 g	130
Tuna, salmon, crab—canned (low-sodium)	85 g	40
Sardines—canned in oil, drained	85 g	700
Smoked herring	85 g	5 234
Beans, dried		
homemade	1 cup	10
canned	1 cup	600–900
Peanut butter		
ordinary	1 Tbs.	50–80
unsalted	1 Tbs.	0
Egg		
fresh	1	60
substitute (low-cholesterol)	¼ cup	120

Condiments, Dressings	Amount	Na (mg)
Salt	1 tsp.	2 300
"Light" salt	1 tsp.	1 100
Salt substitutes	1 tsp.	0
Bouillon cubes	1	900
Hot sauce	1 Tbs.	30
Tabasco sauce, mayonnaise	1 Tbs.	80
Barbecue sauce, tartare sauce	1 Tbs.	120–140
Mustard, tomato sauce, Worcestershire sauce	1 Tbs.	200
Soy sauce		
regular	1 Tbs.	1 000
mild or "light"	1 Tbs.	50
Teriyaki sauce	1 Tbs.	700

TABLE 15-3 *(continued)*
Sodium (Na) Content of Various Foods

Condiments, Dressings	Amount	Na (mg)
Salad dressing, bottled		
ordinary	1 Tbs.	100–300
unsalted	1 Tbs.	5
Margarine		
ordinary	1 tsp.	50
unsalted	1 tsp.	1
Pickles		
dill	1 large	1 400
sweet	1 large	575
Olives, green	4	600

Miscellaneous	Amount	Na (mg)
Frozen dinners	1	1 100–2 000
Frozen pizza	2 slices	1 100
Soup	$1/2$ can	1 100
Chilli	1 cup	1 350
Nuts, salted	$1/2$ cup	530
Potato chips	10 chips	200
Popcorn		
unsalted homemade	2 cups	2
salted homemade	2 cups	350
microwave, commercial brand	2 cups	260
microwave, unsalted, commercial brand	2 cups	2
Pretzels		
salted	30 g	200
unsalted	30 g	10
Cookies (2), biscuits (2), cake ($1/12$ cake), pie ($1/8$ pie)	1	200–500
Sweets, hard (30 g), jelly ($1/2$ cup)	1	50

Milk and Milk Products	Amount	Na (mg)
Milk		
skim, 2%, whole, chocolate	1 cup	120
buttermilk	1 cup	240
from dry powder ($1/3$ cup powder makes 1 cup)	1 cup	125
yoghurt, ice milk, ice cream	1 cup	120
Pudding		
homemade	$1/2$ cup	80
instant	$1/2$ cup	450

TABLE 15-3 *(continued)*
Sodium (Na) Content of Various Foods

Milk and Milk Products	Amount	Na (mg)
Cheese, natural		
blue, Edam, feta, Parmesan	30 g	400
cheddar, Brie, Camembert,		
Limburger, Gouda	30 g	200
Swiss, ricotta, Gruyère, mozzarella	30 g	100
Cheese, processed		
Cottage cheese (regular or low-fat)	1/2 cup	450
Swiss, cheese spread, Parmesan	30 g	400
Cheese, low-sodium, all types	30 g	5

Fruit Juice	Amount	Na (mg)
Fresh, frozen, canned	1 or 1/2 cup	2

Vegetables	Amount	Na (mg)
Fresh or frozen	1/2 cup	3–30
Tomato juice	1/2 cup	500
Green peas or beans		
frozen	1/2 cup	100
canned	1/2 cup	200–450

Sauces, Gravies	Amount	Na (mg)
Tomato paste	1/2 cup	30–300
Tomato sauce		
unsalted	1/2 cup	25
other	1/2 cup	600–850
Spaghetti or barbecue sauce	1/2 cup	1 000
Brown gravy mix, prepared	1/2 cup	600

Bread/Grain Products	Amount	Na (mg)
Bread (whole-grain, white, rye, etc.)		
regular	1 slice	120-170
low-sodium	1 slice	5

TABLE 15-3 *(continued)*
Sodium (Na) Content of Various Foods

Bread/Grain Products	Amount	Na (mg)
Biscuit, corn bread, English muffin, bagel	1	300
Roll	1	150
Crackers		
ordinary	6	240
low-sodium	6	6
Cereals, cooked (oatmeal, Cream of Wheat)		
ordinary (5 min.)	3/4 cup	5
instant (1 min.)	3/4 cup	100–700
Cereals, dry		
shredded wheat, puffed wheat or rice	3/4 cup	2
low-sodium cornflakes or Rice Krispies	3/4 cup	2
cornflakes, granola, bran flakes	3/4 cup	350–450
Grapenuts	3/4 cup	600
Pancakes, waffles, pastries		
frozen French toast, pancakes, waffles	1	300–700
pancake mix	1 pancake	500
pancakes, homemade	1 pancake	300
Pasta (noodles, macaroni, etc.) or rice	3/4 cup	5
Stuffing mix, packaged	1/2 cup	850

Fast Foods	Amount	Na (mg)
Hamburger	1 med.	500–900
French fries	1 reg.	200
Coleslaw	1/2 cup	250
Chicken, fried	1 breast	500
Pizza	2 slices	1 100

Source: The Cooper Clinic, Dallas.

ingredient in the various salt substitutes on the market (see the box on page 312).

The evidence linking higher potassium consumption with lowered blood pressure is incomplete and largely anecdotal. Perhaps the most interesting corroboration came from a close analysis of the eating patterns of residents of two Japanese villages.[13] In one village, the incidence of hypertension was much lower than in the other. The only major difference between their diets was that, in the village with less hypertension, the people often ate apples—which are high in potassium.

The precise role that potassium plays in blood pressure regulation is unknown. One hypothesis holds that potassium, by itself, exerts no positive influence; rather, it's the interplay, or ratio, between sodium and potassium that holds the key to moderate blood pressure levels. It's worth pointing out that when youcut back on processed foods, replacing them with fresh foods, you're automatically reducing sodium and increasing potassium in your diet. Especially good sources of this electrolyte are bananas, potatoes, tomatoes, and dried peas and beans.

With the evidence still so fragmentary, though, we caution you against consuming too much potassium. An excess can lead to a condition called *hyperkalaemia*. You'll notice that hyperkalaemia may be a side effect of some of the blood pressure-lowering drugs we discuss next. This is why heavy use of salt substitutes, high in potassium, while you're taking certain anti-hypertensive medications is not wise.

Consume More Calcium. This is another contentious area. Some studies do seem to indicate an inverse relationship between dietary calcium levels and blood pressure. The most dramatic concerned a group of hypertensive blacks participating in clinical trials at Wayne State University in Detroit.[14] Despite their high-salt diets, those who were given calcium supplements had a drop in blood pressure—in some cases even to normal levels.

On the other hand, if you lined up all the calcium-blood pressure studies, you'd find that only about half of the hypertensive study subjects responded favourably to calcium supplementation. Once again, there's a danger in going overboard. Too much calcium can lead to kidney problems.

Drugs to Combat Hypertension

As we emphasized when we discussed cholesterol-lowering medications, drugs should never be the first line of attack unless a medical problem is so severe that immediate intervention is necessary. This is definitely true of anti-hypertensive medications.

While there's a large assortment of blood pressure-lowering drugs, none are perfect. For example, some do not interact well with other drugs, such as antidepressants, adrenal steroids, non-

10 DIETARY TIPS FOR REDUCING SALT

Tip 1. Choose fresh or frozen unprocessed foods over those that are canned, cured, smoked, or processed. The latter all have sodium added as a preservative as well as for flavour. By starting with fresh foods, you're able to control what seasoning is added during cooking.

Tip 2. Eat food freshly prepared at home as often as possible—and avoid shop-bought baked goods, spaghetti sauces, pizzas, etc. Foods that are processed and prepackaged are generally preserved in sodium. Fast and prepackaged foods are notorious for their high salt content.

Tip 3. Reduce salt in cooking and in recipes to $1/2$ the amount—or omit salt completely and substitute your own seasoning blend (see Tip 5 below.)

Tip 4. Use pure herbs and spices instead of seasoned salts. For example, buy garlic powder instead of garlic salt, onion powder instead of onion salt, etc.

Tip 5. Create your own herb and spice blend, and put that in your salt cellar instead of salt.

Tip 6. Use a salt cellar with small holes—or cover all but one hole with tape.

Tip 7. See how you like the taste of toasted sesame seeds in salads and rice and in chicken and fish dishes.

Tip 8. Avoid canned or bottled sauces such as barbecue, soy, steak, chilli, Worcestershire, tomato, salad dressings, etc. Make your own sauces using your favourite salt substitute or herb/spice blend.

Tip 9. At the table, taste food before you sprinkle salt on it. After all, how do you know it needs salt—or a salt substitute—until you taste it?

Tip 10. When eating out in good restaurants, ask your waiter to have your food prepared without adding salt. Making this request in fastfood outlets won't do you any good, of course, since such food is either precooked or preprocessed by commercial suppliers.

Source: The Cooper Clinic, Dallas.

steroidal anti-inflammatory drugs, nasal decongestants, and oral contraceptives.

Some anti-hypertensive drugs also have the unfortunate tendency to raise LDL and lower HDL cholesterol levels. So if you have the double problem of high cholesterol and high blood pressure, your doctor will have to proceed cautiously in mapping out a drug regimen for you. Usually both can be controlled effectively by making the right drug choices.

Finally, there's the unpleasant issue of anti-hypertensive drug side effects, which range from rashes to more serious maladies. To mitigate side effects—one of the most common of which is dizziness or light-headedness when people rise to a standing position—most doctors today are using lower doses, which are often just as effective.

We can understand why some patients find it hard to stay on these drugs. It's as if we're asking them to take a pill that often makes them feel less well than they felt to start with, since the "disease" of hypertension usually has no physical symptoms whatsoever. We must emphasize, however, that taking medication, if it is necessary to keep the blood pressure normal, is far better than letting it go, even if minor side effects do develop. And in many cases a regimen can be found where no side effects occur.

Of course, the ideal is to control your blood pressure via the do-it-yourself methods we described earlier. Should these fail, though, your doctor will surely recommend drug treatment as the only viable route left open to you. In that event, you'll want full knowledge of your medication choices, which we outline in Appendix E at the back of the book.

When it comes to medication, a certain amount of trial and error is always involved until you and your doctor hit on the right drug and dosage—or combination of drugs and self-treatment.

Your goal is hypertension control with minimal or no side effects. This means you'll have to monitor your body's reactions to each drug carefully so your doctor can decide if and when a new treatment regimen is warranted. The long-term objective of drug therapy, of course, is to prevent any damage to your heart and arteries.

Here are some important points about the various types of anti-hypertensive drugs:

Diuretics. These drugs, which should be taken in low doses, flush excess fluids and sodium from the body. In the process, they can also deplete the body of potassium, cause diabetes, and drive up cholesterol levels, as well as inducing a sense of general malaise and sometimes leading to impotence in men. Black hypertensives in particular tend to respond favourably to diuretics; in contrast, black South Africans generally do not respond well to beta-blockers (see below).

Adrenergic Inhibitors. These include beta-blockers, which are often the drugs of choice for CHD patients since they can decrease angina and reduce the risk of a repeat heart attack. Beta-blockers lower blood pressure by blocking the action of catecholamines, the natural stimulant hormones discussed in earlier chapters. However, as the information in Appendix E indicates, beta-blockers can raise triglycerides and lower the good HDL in your blood. Some people experience fatigue or weakness, and sexual function may decrease.

Also, by themselves, beta-blockers often don't work especially well on black people who are hypertensive, although they can be quite effective in young white patients.

Incidentally, studies have shown that you may be negating most beneficial CHD effects you might realize from beta-blocker therapy if you continue to smoke, which to some extent is true with all these drugs.

Vasodilators. As their name implies, these cause the muscles in blood vessel walls to relax and widen (dilate). Dilated arteries lower blood pressure by reducing the resistance to blood flow.

ACE Inhibitors. This relatively new category of drugs may be one of the best choices for people with hypertension. The drugs neutralize the activity of the enzyme ACE, which acts in your lungs. This, in turn, interferes with the production of the hormone angiotensin II, whose primary purpose is to tell your body to increase blood pressure. Unlike many other classes of antihypertensive drugs, ACE inhibitors may produce no side effects, or only minor ones. They seldom cause weakness, fatigue, or impotence.

Calcium Antagonists. Also called calcium channel blockers, these interfere with your blood-vessel muscles' ability to contract by blocking the entry of calcium. They have relatively few side effects compared with other anti-hypertensive medications, because they are very targeted and don't affect the rest of your body. Studies have shown these to be particularly good drugs for controlling hypertension in the elderly. Many of you with hypertension will already be taking beta-blockers or calcium antagonists to help your heart—and thus you get the anti-hypertensive benefit at no extra charge, so to speak.

DIABETES

Diabetes—technically known as diabetes mellitus—is a chronic disorder affecting your body's sugar metabolism. It occurs when the pancreas produces little or no insulin, a hormone that keeps blood glucose in check, or when other conditions, such as obesity, make the body's insulin less than effective. Diabetics are two times more likely to become heart attack victims than are non-diabetics. And women seem to be more vulnerable to the cardiovascular effects of diabetes than men.

Type I diabetics usually develop the deficiency early in life and require insulin injections throughout their life to maintain proper blood glucose levels. Type II diabetics develop it later in life. Symptoms are increased thirst and hunger, frequent urination, a mysterious mass change, dizziness, and chronic fatigue.

Adult-onset diabetes (Type II) is usually milder. But it, too, increases CHD risk and often goes undetected and untreated for years. In this instance, the pancreas does produce insulin, but it's either insufficient or ineffective. With Type II diabetes, insulin injections may not be necessary because oral medications are available. Frequently, though, nutrition and life-style changes are enough to solve the problem completely.

For obese diabetics, mass loss is absolutely crucial since it could be the primary cause of the elevated blood sugar. In cases of mild diabetes, lowering your mass to a normal range will often clear up all traces of the abnormality.

Diabetes and cholesterol abnormalities are closely intertwined. In fact, even mild diabetes that goes untreated is a CHD risk factor because of its negative influence on blood lipid levels. Thus, from a heart standpoint, the first thing diabetics must do is get their blood sugar levels regulated. That alone could help their cholesterol problems. If it doesn't, patients should adhere to the low-fat diets we outlined in Chapter 12.

Studies have also shown that exercise can help by increasing the body's insulin sensitivity—which is why new exercisers on insulin therapy need especially close monitoring. Over time, the insulin dosage should decrease.

A high blood sugar level can be detected with a simple urine test, but a blood test is more accurate. The presence of any sugar in the urine—or a fasting blood sugar level of over 7,7 mmol/ℓ on two occasions—makes it likely that the patient has diabetes.

PART FIVE

POINTING THE WAY TO BETTER HEALTH

CHAPTER 16

INTRODUCING THE HEART POINTS SYSTEM

MOTIVATING patients to follow our medical instructions is always a concern. It can spell the difference between life and death, after all.

In laying out a medical regimen for our heart patients we always feel we're straddling several fine lines. First, as physicians, we have to educate our patients adequately so that their excuse can never be "I didn't understand." Then we have to alert patients to the seriousness of their condition without leaving them with the feeling that it's hopeless. And, most important, we have to impress on patients the fact that drugs and medical care can only go so far in making them well. They must do the rest.

Our Heart Points System developed out of these various needs, especially the necessity of making you responsible for your own health. With our Heart Points System, you have a way to chart the progress of your recovery. You gain Heart Points for the factors that are directly related to your heart's health. They're all factors *within your control*.

In all aspects of life, we humans like to know where we stand in our endeavours. We like to get report cards. Our Heart Points System is a kind of report card on your health—but you fill it out.

Our Heart Points System enables you to quantify the constructive life-style changes you can easily undertake to improve— even reverse—your CHD. It gives you a way to chart your progress mathematically so that you can see, in black and white, what you are accomplishing and where you stand.

Our Heart Points System targets six of the seven key risk factors—exercise, LDL cholesterol, blood pressure, mass control, stress, and smoking. These are the modifiable factors, not counting diabetes, that you learned about in the preceding chapters. In this chapter, we give you specific Heart Points guidelines for controlling them and a way to track your efforts numerically.

You may be asking yourself, "Why aren't HDL cholesterol and diabetes included as risks in this Heart Points System?"

Good question. After all, HDL cholesterol is just as important a risk factor for the progression of coronary heart disease as LDL cholesterol. In truth, HDL cholesterol has been left out of our Heart Points calculations only to help simplify the system. The most important behavioural steps you can take to raise HDL cholesterol are to (1) exercise regularly, which is highlighted in our Heart Points System; (2) lose mass if you're overmass, another factor that's covered; and (3) stop smoking if you smoke—also included. Thus, if you follow the recommendations for exercise, mass loss, and smoking included in the Heart Points System, you'll automatically be doing everything possible for your HDL cholesterol. Therefore, we elected not to add another calculation to the system even though HDL cholesterol is very important. The reasons for leaving out diabetes are similar.

Here's how the Heart Points System works: your initial eight-week introductory phase of exercise (see Appendix C) doesn't count because, during that time, you're still working up to an appropriate level of exertion. It's after this preparatory phase that you start earning points for your workouts. Charts to help you convert your exercise efforts into Heart Points are given in Appendix B.

We're aware that some of our readers in the high-risk category —or those of you who suffer from musculoskeletal disorders— may not be able to attain the desired weekly number of Heart Points for exercise. Or the problem may be that you decide to do an exercise that we don't provide point charts or equations for in Appendix B. Don't become discouraged. Provided you perform some type of aerobic exercise for a minimum of twenty to thirty minutes at least three days a week, you'll get some health-related benefits, to be sure. Although these benefits may not be optimal, they're still definitely well worth the effort!

In our Heart Points System, you'll find that the points you earn for the other five modifiable risk factors are scored a little differently from those for exercise. For these, *points are subtracted if you don't follow our guidelines for lowering the stress in your life, controlling your mass and blood pressure, reducing your LDL cholesterol level, and giving up smoking.*

We've set up our scoring system this way by design. Theoretically, you can gain 100 points a week for exercise and, during that same week, lose all those points and more by ignoring our advice about the other risk factors. Yes, you could end up with a minus point total at the end of a week. This is realistic. Even if you exercise conscientiously, atherosclerosis can progress because of laxity about the other risk factors.

We think you'll find Heart Points a simple, practical system to help you regain your health. Nor should you discard it even after you've recovered. Our Heart Points System can be followed for the rest of your life to ensure that you remain in an optimal state of health.

Weekly Exercise Tally

YOUR WEEKLY GOAL: To expend between 60 and 85 kilojoules per kilogram (or 2,2 pounds) of body mass per week. Doing this earns you a maximum of 100 points. (Consult Appendix B's point charts for your category of exercise. For more precision, bypass the charts and use the formulas in Appendix B; to convert your kJ into Heart Points, use the formula that follows.)

It is not necessary to exceed 85 kilojoules per kilogram of body mass per week (or 100 points). A greater level of exercise increases the chances of injury. Moreover, it's a fallacy to think that excessive exercise can offset bad habits concerning other risk factors.

Exercise Heart Points Scoring Formula:

Body mass in pounds:

kJ earned from each exercise session $\times \dfrac{2{,}62}{\text{body mass in pounds}} = $ _____ EXERCISE HEART POINTS
(See formula for your exercise in Appendix B)

Body mass in kilograms:

kJ earned from each exercise session $\times \dfrac{1{,}19}{\text{body mass in kilograms}} = $ _____ EXERCISE HEART POINTS
(See formula for your exercise in Appendix B)

MONDAY	TUESDAY	WEDNESDAY	THURSDAY	FRIDAY	SATURDAY	SUNDAY	TOTAL WEEKLY EXERCISE POINTS
+ ____ pts.	+ ____ pts.	+ ____ pts.	+ ____ pts.	+ ____ pts.	+ ____ pts.	+ ____ pts.	= ____

(100 pts. maximum) Transfer this amount to the weekly scorecard in Chapter 17.

Interpreting the Effectiveness of Your Weekly Exercise Effort

100 Heart Points from exercise — Ideal. *You couldn't do better!*
70–99 Heart Points from exercise — Very good. *Be proud of yourself.*
40–69 Heart Points from exercise — Good. *But you could do better.*
20–39 Heart Points from exercise — Fair. *Try a bit harder.*
10–19 Heart Points from exercise — Poor. *Come on now.*
Less than 10 Heart Points from exercise — Very poor. *Need we say more?*

Weekly Cholesterol Tally

YOUR GOAL: To lower your LDL cholesterol level.

WHAT YOU MUST KNOW: My LDL cholesterol level is _____. (See Chapter 12 for information about cholesterol testing.)

Cholesterol Heart Points Scoring System:

The number of points you lose for not following our cholesterol guidelines outlined below depends on your LDL cholesterol level (see following chart). Any day that you ignore Guidelines 1 and 2, record the loss of Heart Points in the column for that day of the week. Guidelines 3-6, on the other hand, involve weekly behavior. Record any loss of Heart Points in the weekly column to the far right.

If My LDL Level Is:	Heart Points Lost Per Day or Ignoring Guidelines 1 & 2	Heart Points Lost Per Week for Ignoring Guidelines 3–6
Below 3,36	–1	–4
3,36–4,13	–2	–8
4,14–4,90	–3	–12
4,91+	–4	–16

We hope the reason for this scoring system is obvious. More points are lost if your LDL cholesterol is high because a person with high LDL to begin with is exacerbating an already bad situation by continuing to eat high-saturated-fat and high-cholesterol foods.

TOTAL WEEKLY CHOLESTEROL POINTS

MONDAY	TUESDAY	WEDNESDAY	THURSDAY	FRIDAY	SATURDAY	SUNDAY
– ____ pts.	– ____ pts.	– ____ pts.	– ____ pts.	– ____ pts.	– ____ pts.	– ____ pts.

= – ____

GUIDELINE 1 (Daily): Men should eat no more than 225 grams of meat per day. Women should eat no more than 170 grams per day.

GUIDELINE 2 (Daily): Men should eat no more than 3 tablespoons of fat per day. Women should eat no more than 2 tablespoons per day. We refer here to the fat you can see in gravy, cooking oil, salad dressing, and creamy sauces.

MONDAY	TUESDAY	WEDNESDAY	THURSDAY	FRIDAY	SATURDAY	SUNDAY	TOTAL WEEKLY CHOLESTEROL POINTS

We are not referring to fat hidden in such foods as meat, cereal, dairy products, etc.

Besides this visible fat in salad dressings, cooking oil, etc., you must account for additional disguised fat that you eat in restaurant-prepared food or food obtained in other public places as follows:

Count every 1/2 cup of commercially prepared or restaurant-prepared vegetables, starches, or other side dishes as 1/2 teaspoon of fat. Count every commercially prepared or restaurant-prepared entree as 1 tablespoon of fat.

_____ pts. _____ pts. _____ pts. _____ pts. _____ pts. _____ pts. _____ pts. = _____

GUIDELINE 3 (Weekly): Eat no more than three servings of red meat per week. _____

GUIDELINE 4 (Weekly): Eat no more than three servings of cheese, ice cream, or whole milk per week. _____

GUIDELINE 5 (Weekly): Eat no more than one egg per week. _____

GUIDELINE 6 (Weekly): Eat no more than one fried food per week. (Remember, potato chips and all fast foods other than salad are fried.) _____

WEEKLY TOTAL _____

(−126 pts. maximum) Transfer this amount to the weekly scorecard in Chapter 17.

326

Weekly Blood Pressure Tally

<u>YOUR GOAL:</u> To reduce salt and alcohol intake.

<u>WHAT YOU MUST KNOW:</u> My systolic blood pressure is _____. My diastolic blood pressure is _____.

Blood Pressure Heart Points Scoring System:

The number of points you lose for not following our hypertension guidelines outlined below depends on your systolic and diastolic blood pressure (see following chart). Points are lost for either an elevated systolic or diastolic blood pressure—not both. Calculate your points using the most abnormal of the two.

If My Systolic Pressure Is:
Below 140
140–144
145–154
155 +

Heart Points Lost Per Day for Ignoring Guidelines 1–3
0
–1
–2
–3

If My Diastolic Pressure Is:
Below 9
90–94
95–99
100 +

Heart Points Lost Per Day for Ignoring Guidelines 1–3
0
–1
–2
–3

MONDAY	TUESDAY	WEDNESDAY	THURSDAY	FRIDAY	SATURDAY	SUNDAY	TOTAL WEEKLY BLOOD PRESSURE POINTS

GUIDELINE 1 (Daily): Do not use the salt cellar either during the cooking process or at the table.

____ pts. ____ pts. ____ pts. ____ pts. ____ pts. ____ pts. ____ pts. = ____

GUIDELINE 2 (Daily): Do not eat any of these high-salt foods (subtract points if you use any, but no additional points if you use more than one):

    processed meats   fast-food sandwich
    spaghetti sauce   ordinary cheese
    (other than home-
    made)   sausage or ham
    pizza   soup (other than home-
         made)
    frozen dinner   pickles

____ pts. ____ pts. ____ pts. ____ pts. ____ pts. ____ pts. ____ pts. = ____

GUIDELINE 3 (Daily): Drink no more than one serving of alcohol a day. (One serving is equal to 300 ml of beer, 150 ml of wine or 50 ml of hard liquor.)

____ pts. ____ pts. ____ pts. ____ pts. ____ pts. ____ pts. ____ pts. = ____

WEEKLY TOTAL = ____

(−126 pts. *maximum*)
Transfer this amount to the weekly scorecard in Chapter 17.

Weekly Mass-Control Tally

YOUR WEEKLY GOAL: To control your mass according to your body-fat percentage.
WHAT YOU MUST KNOW: My baseline body-fat percentage before I begin a mass-monitoring and/or mass-reduction programme is _____

Mass-Control Heart Points Scoring System:

The number of points you lose depends on where you fall in the body-fat percentage chart below and how much mass you've lost in a week's time.

Men

Age 30–39	Age 40–49	Age 50–59	Age 60–69	Age 70+
7,0	9,1	10,9	10,8	13,6
8,9	11,4	13,3	13,0	14,2
10,0	12,8	14,3	14,2	15,9
12,0	14,8	16,4	17,3	18,0
13,3	16,1	17,7	18,4	19,1
14,4	17,2	19,0	19,4	19,9
15,5	18,2	19,8	20,3	21,2
16,4	19,0	20,6	21,0	22,2
17,2	19,7	21,3	21,7	22,6
①	①	①	①	①
18,0	20,4	22,1	22,4	23,6
18,8	21,1	22,7	23,0	24,2
19,5	21,8	23,3	23,5	24,7
②	②	②	②	②
20,2	22,4	23,9	24,2	24,9
20,9	23,1	24,6	24,9	25,5
21,8	23,9	25,3	25,8	26,5
③	③	③	③	③
22,7	24,6	26,0	26,5	27,4
23,6	25,5	26,8	27,3	28,3
24,6	26,4	27,6	28,3	28,9
25,9	27,4	28,7	29,1	29,5
27,3	28,9	30,1	30,4	31,2
29,5	31,0	32,0	32,5	32,4
33,9	34,5	36,4	35,4	36,6

Women

Age 30–39	Age 40–49	Age 50–59	Age 60+
12,4	13,5	14,1	12,8
14,1	14,7	15,5	15,2
15,0	15,5	16,4	16,5
16,0	16,8	18,3	18,4
16,8	18,1	19,4	20,3
17,5	19,1	20,9	21,6
18,1	20,2	22,5	23,7
18,9	21,2	23,9	25,3
19,7	22,3	25,4	27,0
①	①	①	①
20,5	23,3	26,3	28,2
21,3	24,2	27,2	28,9
22,2	25,1	28,2	29,9
②	②	②	②
23,1	25,9	29,3	30,9
24,0	26,7	30,3	31,9
25,2	27,7	31,1	32,6
③	③	③	
26,2	28,8	32,2	33,4
27,4	30,1	33,3	34,6
28,6	31,1	34,6	35,7
30,0	32,5	35,6	36,6
32,3	34,4	36,8	38,2
34,6	37,0	38,3	39,8
39,3	39,5	40,4	40,9

330

	TOTAL WEEKLY WEIGHT-CONTROL POINTS

If your body-fat percentage is lower on the scale than the circled number one, then 0 Heart Points are subtracted. (Note that these body-fat percentages are in ascending order, moving from low to high.) Continue to subtract 0 points if your body-fat percentage remains about the same from one week to the next. **If you gain or lose more than 4,5 kg, your percentage should be measured again.** = – _____

If your body-fat percentage falls between the circled numbers one and two, then subtract 8 points if you do not lose . . . .
0,45 kg a week if you're a man   0,225 kg a week if you're a woman = – _____

If your body-fat percentage falls between the circled numbers two and three, then subtract 16 points if you do not lose . . . .
0,45 kg a week if you're a man   0,225 kg a week if you're a woman = – _____

If your body-fat percentage is higher than the circled number three (i.e., closer to the bottom of the chart), then subtract 24 points if you do not lose . . . .
0,45 kg a week if you're a man   0,225 kg a week if you're a woman = – _____

If your body-fat percentage falls between the circled numbers one and two and you gain any mass this week, then subtract 16 points. = – _____

If your body-fat percentage falls between the circled numbers two and three and you gain any mass this week, then subtract 32 points. = – _____

If your body-fat percentage is higher than the circled number three and you gain any mass this week, then subtract 48 points. = – _____

WEEKLY TOTAL = – _____

(–48 pts. maximum)
Transfer this amount to the weekly scorecard in Chapter 17.

Weekly Stress-Reduction Tally*

YOUR WEEKLY GOAL: To reduce the amount of stress—external or self-induced—that you have in your life.

Stress-Reduction Heart Points Scoring System:

Each week, evaluate whether your behaviour is consistent with the 10 guidelines listed below and subtract points as shown. You're grading yourself, so try to be as objective as possible.

	All the Time (0 points)	Frequently (–1 point)	Occasionally (–2 points)	Seldom (–3 points)	Total Weekly Stress Points
1. **I prioritize.** Each time I am faced with a stressful situation, I am careful to ask myself: How important is this going to be a year from now? Five years from now?	___ pts.	___ pts.	___ pts.	___ pts.	___ = ___
2. **I spread out major life events** to allow time between such events to recuperate. For instance, I don't allow a wedding, a job change, and a move to take place close together.	___ pts.	___ pts.	___ pts.	___ pts.	___ = ___
3. **I say no** when someone asks me to shoulder an additional work load that is too great.	___ pts.	___ pts.	___ pts.	___ pts.	___ = ___
4. **I withdraw in order to relax.** I am not accessible 24 hours a day, 7 days a week. I take midday relaxation breaks. I take at least 2 days off each 7-day week. I don't plan any activity at least 2 evenings a week. I take holidays that are stress-relieving, not stress-producing.	___ pts.	___ pts.	___ pts.	___ pts.	___ = ___
5. **I acquiesce to things beyond my control.** I accept events that I cannot change, such as getting caught in a traffic jam when I'm late for an appointment.	___ pts.	___ pts.	___ pts.	___ pts.	___ = ___
6. **I am agreeable and willing to compromise** in situations that previously made me angry or hostile.	___ pts.	___ pts.	___ pts.	___ pts.	___ = ___
7. **I am able to distinguish between worries that are realistic and those that aren't.** (Mark Twain once said, "I have known a great many troubles, but most of them never happened.")	___ pts. ___ pts.	___ pts. ___ pts.	___ pts. ___ pts.	___ pts. ___ pts.	___ = ___ ___ = ___
8. **I get adequate exercise.** Exercise is nature's tranquilliser.	___ pts.	___ pts.	___ pts.	___ pts.	___ = ___
9. **I express my feelings** to my family and friends and do not hold my emotions in check. When my emotions are negative, I analyse them to find out if they are truly warranted.	___ pts.	___ pts.	___ pts.	___ pts.	___ = ___
10. **I practice relaxation techniques** on any day when I feel my stress level is high.	___ pts.	___ pts.	___ pts.	___ pts.	___ = ___

WEEKLY TOTAL (–30 pts. *maximum*) Transfer this amount to the weekly scorecard in Chapter 17.

*Adapted from Dr. Roy Vartabedian's In-Residence Program, the Cooper Clinic.

Weekly Smoking Tally

YOUR GOAL: To stop smoking completely.

MONDAY	TUESDAY	WEDNESDAY	THURSDAY	FRIDAY	SATURDAY	SUNDAY	TOTAL WEEKLY SMOKING POINTS
-___ pts.	-___ pts.	-___ pts.	-___ pts.	-___ pts.	-___ pts.	-___ pts.	= -___

If you smoke one or more cigarettes, subtract 10 points for the day.

If you smoke a cigar or pipe even once, subtract 5 points for the day.

MONDAY	TUESDAY	WEDNESDAY	THURSDAY	FRIDAY	SATURDAY	SUNDAY	
-___ pts.	-___ pts.	-___ pts.	-___ pts.	-___ pts.	-___ pts.	-___ pts.	= -___

WEEKLY TOTAL

(-105 pts. maximum) Transfer this amount to the weekly scorecard in Chapter 17.

CHAPTER 17

YOUR WEEKLY HEART POINTS SCORECARD: What It Says about Your Recovery

CHAPTER 16 contains six charts, each covering the span of a week. This chapter contains one chart covering a month's time.

This Heart Points Scorecard is where you will tally up your individual scores for each of the risk factors. At the bottom of the chart, you'll find our interpretation of your score.

The charts in this and the previous chapter are intended to be photocopied and placed in a loose-leaf notebook. We suggest this because we want you to be very businesslike and systematic about your recovery programme. To be sure, your heart and health are serious business. We urge you to put as much effort and brainpower into following our Heart Points System as you'd direct toward any other important task in your life, such as succeeding at your job or buying a house.

One final piece of advice: ideally, CHD prevention should be a family affair. After all, your spouse and children share many of your risk factors. Just because you're the one that had the heart attack or major cardiac procedure doesn't mean they won't follow in your footsteps. Try to get as many family members as possible involved in this Heart Points System. Encourage everyone to have their cholesterol and blood pressure levels checked. In more ways than one, you're all in this together.

(Month) _____

Heart Points Scorecard

Total Points Earned for Exercise—or Subtracted for Not Following Other Risk Factor Guidelines

Controllable Risk Factors	Week 1	Week 2	Week 3	Week 4
Exercise	(+100 pts. max.)	(+100 pts. max.)	(+100 pts. max.)	(+100 pts. max.)
Cholesterol	(−120 pts. max.)	(−120 pts. max.)	(−120 pts. max.)	(−120 pts. max.)
Blood Pressure	(−126 pts. max.)	(−126 pts. max.)	(−126 pts. max.)	(−126 pts. max.)
Mass Control	(−48 pts. max.)	(−48 pts. max.)	(−48 pts. max.)	(−48 pts. max.)
Stress Reduction	(−30 pts. max.)	(−30 pts. max.)	(−30 pts. max.)	(−30 pts. max.)
Smoking	(−105 pts. max.)	(−105 pts. max.)	(−105 pts. max.)	(−105 pts. max.)
WEEKLY TOTAL	(100 pts. max.)	(100 pts. max.)	(100 pts. max.)	(100 pts. max.)

Interpretation

100 total Heart Points	Ideal. You couldn't do better!
70–99 total Heart Points	Very good. Be proud of yourself.
40–69 total Heart Points	Good. But you could do better.
20–39 total Heart Points	Fair. Try a bit harder.
10–19 total Heart Points	Poor. Come on, now.
0–9 total Heart Points.	Very poor. Need we say more?
Below 0	Extremely poor.

PART SIX

MEDICAL TREATMENT OPTIONS

CHAPTER 18

WHEN ANGIOPLASTY OR BYPASS SURGERY BECOMES NECESSARY

As you learned in Chapter 5, severe residual myocardial ischaemia after a heart attack is dangerous and places sufferers in a higher risk category. It not only worsens patients' prognoses, but it can also impair their quality of life. This is particularly true if the residual myocardial ischaemia causes angina that doesn't respond to the usual medical therapy.

There are various treatments for residual myocardial ischaemia. They range from drug therapy—such as beta-blockers, long-acting nitrates, and calcium antagonists—to bypass surgery and angioplasty.

It wasn't that long ago that physicians were extremely pessimistic about the feasibility of open-heart surgery. Then, in the mid-1960s, the first successful bypass operation was performed and medical thinking started to change. Today it's an accepted mode of treatment, with an estimated 200 000 such operations performed in the United States alone each year. (Figures for South Africa are not available.)

The first angioplasty was performed in 1977 by Dr. Andreas R. Gruntzig, a Swiss cardiologist. Because of the limited number of hospital beds in Zurich for patients wanting an angioplasty, Dr. Gruntzig moved to the United States in 1980 and joined the Emory University faculty in Atlanta. Over the next five years, he refined further coronary angioplasty procedures. Unfortunately, in 1985, at the very prime of his life and the peak of his medical career, Dr. Gruntzig was killed in an air crash. Nonetheless, thanks to his pioneering work, about 200 000 angioplasties are currently performed each year in America.

In this chapter we'll answer some of the more common questions that patients ask us about angioplasty, bypass surgery, and angiography, the specialized X-ray technique that precedes both procedures.

> **"Why is coronary angiography needed before I can undergo an angioplasty or bypass surgery?"**

The basic goal of an angioplasty or bypass surgery is the same: to promote myocardial revascularization, which means to re-establish an adequate blood supply to areas of the heart muscle that became deprived over the years due to the buildup of atherosclerotic plaque in the coronary arteries.

An angioplasty achieves the goal of myocardial revascularization by dilating the coronary arteries at the sites where they've become narrowed by plaque. Bypass surgery can do this too, in this case by detouring blood around the narrowed parts of the coronary arteries.

Obviously, before either procedure can be performed it's essential to pinpoint the actual sites of narrowing in your heart arteries. Currently, coronary angiography is the only practical way to do this accurately.

As Dr. F. Mason Sones, one of the pioneers in this field, has pointed out: "Clinical acumen and indirect information are not as helpful as a good length of motion picture film. For the surgeon, the obstruction is pinpointed, and he is handed a road map to work by."

> **"What can I expect to happen while I'm in the hospital for an angiogram?"**

Each hospital has its own special procedures which doctors follow when performing coronary angiography there. So what we'll describe are the broad outlines of what you can expect.

At many hospitals, you're admitted the day before your scheduled angiogram to undergo some tests including an ECG, a chest X-ray, and routine blood tests.

The next day, about an hour before the angiogram, you'll be given a sedative to help you relax. The actual angiogram is performed in the catheterization lab, to which you're wheeled on a movable bed or wheelchair. In the lab, you're transferred onto an examining table, directly under the X-ray camera, and you're hooked up to an ECG monitor. The lab assistants will drape you with sterile towels, leaving either your groin or your arm exposed, depending on where the doctor intends to insert the catheter. The area is shaved and cleansed.

Although you'll be awake during the entire procedure, you should feel only slight discomfort or pressure because the place where the catheter is inserted is numbed via a local anaesthetic.

Your doctor inserts the catheter into either your groin or arm artery. (The groin is a far more popular site.) While your doctor watches the X-ray monitor, he or she is threading the catheter up to the portion of your aorta from which the coronary arteries originate (see Figure 18-1). Next, your doctor inserts the catheter tip into your right and then left coronary arteries and shoots radiopaque dye or contrast medium through the catheter and into these arteries while a series of X-ray pictures is taken.

The catheter is also placed inside your left ventricle and dye is injected there as well. This procedure is called *left ventriculography,* and is routinely performed during coronary angiography. It enables your cardiologist to assess accurately the functional

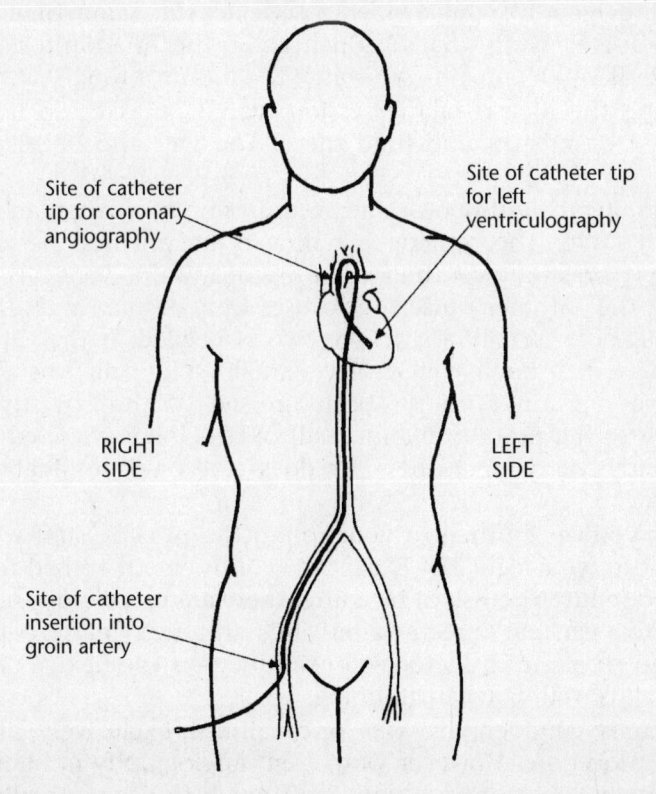

Figure 18-1. Sites ot insertion of catheter and catheter tip during coronary angiography. The catheter is usually inserted into a large artery in the groin and advanced, under X-ray monitoring, to the heart.

capacity of your left ventricle, a critical heart function, as you learned in Chapters 3 and 5.

Although you won't be able to feel the catheter's movement up through your body, you may experience a sensation of warmth or tingling when the dye is flushed through the catheter. This is greatest during left ventriculography because a relatively large amount of dye is infused then. However, the sensation, at its worst, seldom lasts more than thirty seconds and it's not painful.

Some patients do experience angina during the procedure. If this happens to you, be sure to let your physician know. But don't worry too much about it. It should subside within a short time and is not cause for alarm.

Throughout the whole angiography procedure, the X-ray camera is being moved into various positions so the doctor can view your heart and arteries from different angles. These X-rays are being recorded on a videocassette at the same time your physician is viewing what's happening on the TV monitor in the cath lab. If you want, you can watch the monitor too.

During the picture-taking session, you'll be asked to take in several deep breaths and hold them. You will also be asked to cough.

Generally, the entire procedure requires no more than an hour. When it's over, the catheter is removed and medical personnel will apply pressure over the area of insertion to prevent bleeding. Usually the catheter's insertion causes only a small nick in the skin, but occasionally a stitch or two is needed. If the catheter was inserted through your groin, a small weight may be placed over the incision once it's been dressed. Within twenty-four hours after the procedure almost all of the dye is excreted from your body via your kidneys; it does not have residual toxic effects.

After you've returned to your room, the nursing staff will be monitoring you regularly. Except for confinement to bed for six hours to reduce the risk of bleeding, there are no onerous restrictions. You can eat directly afterward, although many patients prefer to sleep. Your doctor will examine you the next morning and, if all is well, you can go home.

Coronary angiography was once almost exclusively an inpatient procedure. However, outpatient angiography has become increasingly common in America, although this is not really the case in South Africa.[2] The procedure doesn't vary much from that performed on an inpatient—except that the arm rather than the groin may be the site for catheter insertion. Outpatients are admitted in the morning, and four or five hours after the angiography they are encouraged to walk about. If their condition is stable, they are discharged an hour or two later. Those patients who do not live nearby are advised to stay overnight in a nearby hotel. Full activities are allowed the next day.

"Is coronary angiography a risky procedure?"

Although the injection of contrast medium through a catheter into the chambers of the heart was already a proven technique in the 1950s, cardiologists feared that direct injection into the coronary arteries themselves could trigger fatal ventricular fibrillation. Fears eased, though, in 1958 when a large amount of contrast medium was accidentally injected into one patient's coronary arteries. To everyone's surprise, ventricular fibrillation did not in fact occur. Subsequently, the coronary angiography procedure was refined by Dr. F. Mason Sones at the Cleveland Clinic Hospital.

Today, coronary angiography is a very safe procedure. Overall, the risk to life is less than 0,2 percent and the risk of major adverse health consequences—such as heart attack, stroke, or severe haemorrhaging—is less than 0,5 percent when the procedure is performed correctly.

"How will my physician decide whether I need an angioplasty or bypass surgery?"

Your physician plays back the videocassette that was made during your angiogram in order to pinpoint the exact spots where your coronary arteries are narrowed by plaque. Your doctor uses this information and the results of your left ventriculography—as well as everything else he or she knows about your case—to decide whether you're a suitable candidate for either angioplasty or bypass surgery. Important considerations during this decision-making process are your symptoms, how well you're responding to drug therapy, your age, the results of your exercise ECG, and your left ventricular function. Finally, your doctor notes the number of narrowed coronary arteries, and the sites and severity of the plaque buildup.

Over the years, angioplasty's popularity has grown. During the early years, angioplasty's use was restricted to patients with partial blockage of the initial portion of a single coronary artery. Of all CHD patients, only 5 to 10 percent were considered for angioplasty. When it was performed, angioplasty was successful in only 60 percent of cases.

Today, all this has changed. Angioplasty is routinely used in patients with more complex CHD, including those with narrowings farther down a coronary artery or in multiple arteries, with a totally blocked artery, or with bypassed vessels that have become obstructed. The success rate of angioplasty exceeds 90 percent despite its use in progressively more challenging situations. This is due to cardiologists' greater experience with the technique and the availability of more sophisticated equipment.

When the pros and cons of angioplasty versus bypass surgery are considered, a number of factors speak in favour of angioplasty. It requires a shorter hospital stay, there are fewer complications, and it's cheaper, not to mention the fact that it's a less radical procedure. Today, angioplasty closely rivals bypass surgery as a revascularization technique. Indeed, one recent survey of cardiologists reveals that 39 percent of patients who underwent coronary angiography were referred for angioplasty, compared with only 28 percent for bypass surgery.[3]

Still, it's important to understand that not all patients with CHD are candidates for angioplasty. In fact, bypass surgery is the only revascularization procedure that should be used in patients who have atherosclerotic obstructions in their left main coronary artery. This is because the left main coronary artery is the most dangerous spot at which to have a blockage, and angioplasty is unacceptably risky there. Patients with long-standing total occlusions are also more appropriately treated with bypass surgery, as are those with very long, tortuous atherosclerotic narrowings in their coronary arteries.

In short, as a rule of thumb, angioplasty is not—or should not be—performed in any situation where the result is likely to be inferior to that obtained via bypass surgery.

In general, single-vessel obstructions respond well to angioplasty—with the exception of blockages in the left main coronary artery. When it comes to obstructions in multiple coronary arteries, a more definitive answer about which technique is preferable will have to await the completion of several current studies.[4]

"What are the risks associated with angioplasty?"

Overall, angioplasty is a relatively safe procedure. However, like most other invasive procedures, angioplasty has some drawbacks. Although the initial success rate is now greater than 90 percent, the dilated coronary arteries become obstructed again within about six months in about 25 to 30 percent of patients who undergo successful angioplasty. The procedure sometimes has to be repeated on more than one occasion in such patients.

According to the USA's National Heart, Lung and Blood Institute's registry of coronary angioplasties, complications result in death, heart attack, or the immediate need for bypass surgery in some 7 percent of patients undergoing angioplasty. (It's because of this remote possibility that angioplasty should always be performed with an emergency heart surgery team on standby.) The precise risks involved are related to a variety of factors such as the reasons for performing the angioplasty, the patient's status just prior to the angioplasty, and the number of coronary arteries that are dilated.

Regarding the latter, the in-hospital death rate for patients having an angioplasty on a single coronary artery is only about 0,2 percent, or 1 in 500. It's 0,9 percent—or 1 in 111—for those having an angioplasty performed on two coronary arteries.

Researchers in this rapidly growing area of cardiology are currently focusing much attention on developing more sophisticated techniques for performing angioplasties and on identifying those few patients who are at increased risk for complications. Their research should culminate in an even greater success rate and fewer complications in the near future.

"How will my hospital stay for angioplasty differ from what you described for angiography?"

The procedure for angioplasty is, in fact, very similar to that for coronary angiography. Patients are often admitted the day before an angioplasty and they undergo laboratory tests the same as or similar to those for angiography.

Angioplasty is also performed in the cath lab, and the patient is awake and prepared in much the same way as for an angiogram. A local anaesthetic is used, and the catheter once again is inserted into an artery in the patient's groin or arm and guided into the coronary artery under constant X-ray monitoring (see Figure 18-2).

Here's where the procedures differ: at this point, a second, smaller catheter is passed through the first catheter into the coronary artery. This second catheter has a deflated balloon on its tip. Small amounts of contrast medium are flushed through the coronary artery, causing it to become visible on the X-ray monitor. This enables the physician to guide the balloon-tipped catheter into the narrowed area of the coronary artery. Next, the doctor inflates the balloon in order to compress the atherosclerotic plaque and open up the coronary artery (see Figure 18-3).

As you can well imagine, the lumen (inside) of the coronary artery is totally occluded during balloon inflation and angina may result. However, the angina subsides after the balloon is deflated. Because the balloon is inflated for only a short period of time, the angina should not be of much concern to you. It can

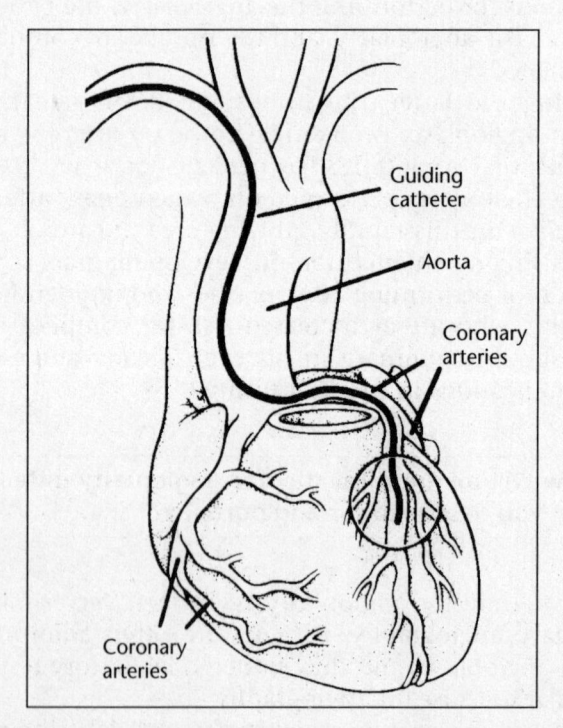

Figure 18-2. Insertion of guiding catheter into the blocked coronary artery during an angioplasty. The catheter is advanced to the site of the obstruction in the coronary artery. (Reproduced with permission. © Illustration and Symbols Kit, 1987. Copyright American Heart Association.)

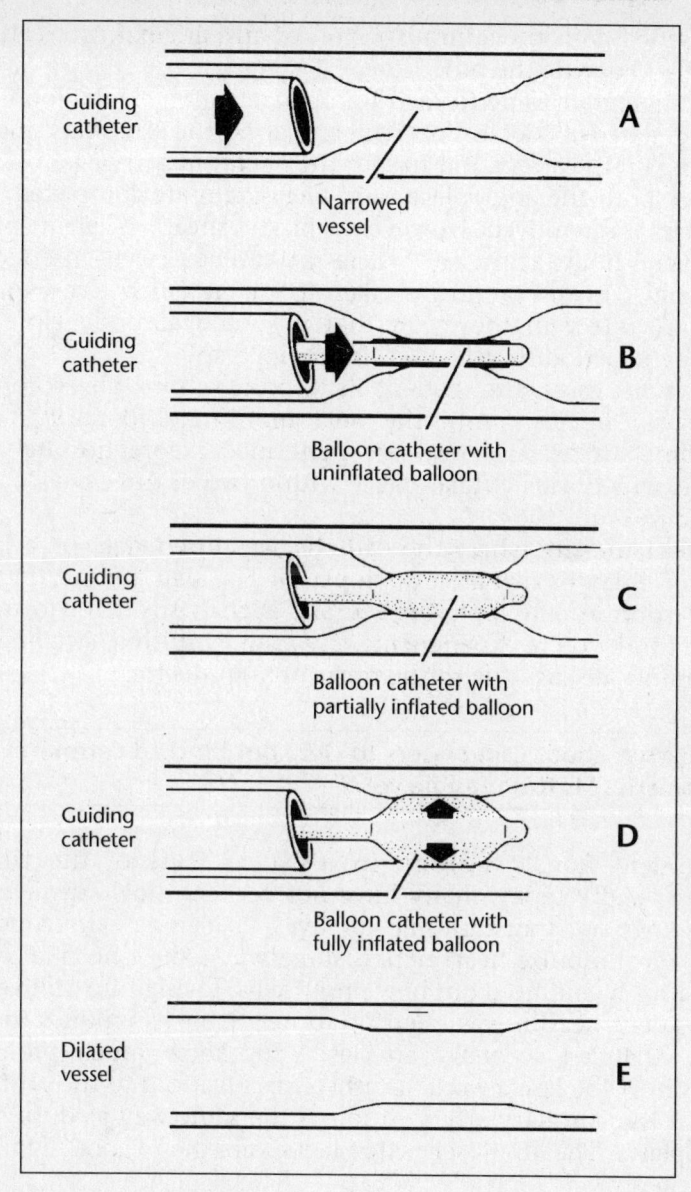

Figure 18-3. The five steps involved in re-establishing an adequate blood flow through angioplasty. (Reproduced with permission. © Illustration and Symbols Kit, 1987. Copyright American Heart Association.)

be lessened with the administration of anti-anginal medications before and during the procedure.

An angiogram is performed immediately after the balloon has been deflated to determine if it has done the necessary job of opening up the artery. If it hasn't, the doctor may try again.

Once both the angioplasty and angiogram are completed, the catheters are removed. However, a plastic sheath is left in place for several hours at the site where the catheters were inserted in the groin. This precaution is taken to enable quick access to the coronary artery in the event that it should abruptly close off during the period shortly after the angioplasty.

In most cases the patient is monitored in the coronary intensive care unit until the next morning. Laboratory tests, including an exercise test, are performed before hospital discharge, which usually takes place within two or three days of the procedure.

Expect the site where the catheter was inserted to be a little sore for a day or two after angioplasty. The skin around the site of insertion usually looks bruised and slightly swollen. However, if you think you're experiencing any undue bruising, swelling, or discomfort, discuss it with the nurse or your doctor.

"What about using lasers to clear out blocked coronary arteries? Is this feasible yet?"

President Ronald Reagan, in his 1985 State of the Union address, said: "Today, many have not yet seen how advances in technology are transforming our lives ... New laser techniques could revolutionize heart bypass surgery ... reduce hospital costs dramatically and hold out new promise for saving human lives."

President Reagan was referring to new laser techniques to unblock occluded coronary arteries. They show much promise. Here's how the lasers work: a catheter is advanced to the obstruction in the coronary artery in much the same way as during an angioplasty. The atherosclerotic plaques are then vaporized using laser energy.

Lasers are currently being investigated on an experimental basis at several medical centres in the United States. These investigations will determine whether lasers can improve on the two major limitations of angioplasty: (1) its inability to unblock longstanding total occlusions, especially if the occlusion is older than three months (in these mature occlusions, dilation is successful in less than 50 percent of patients), and (2) the tendency for re-occlusion of unblocked coronary arteries only months after the angioplasty.

> **"Bypass surgery is such a radical approach. What evidence is there that it prolongs life?"**

Few topics in contemporary medicine have been more hotly debated. The reasons are obvious: although bypass surgery is a relatively safe procedure, the operation is not without risk to life, it is expensive, and, most important, there is still uncertainty concerning the effects of this surgery on long-term survival in some types of patients.

When patients have angina that does not respond to medical therapy, bypass surgery can be effective in alleviating these symptoms and thus improving their quality of life. Several major clinical trials comparing bypass surgery and drug therapy have documented better long-term survival after surgery for patients with either of these two conditions: (1) obstructions in the left main coronary artery or (2) in the case of patients with left ventricular dysfunction, obstructions in all three of the other major coronary arteries (often referred to as triple-vessel disease).

Although bypass surgery's role in improving survival in other CHD patient categories is less clear, recent studies have shown that there's a significant improvement in the survival of CHD patients even when you exclude people in the two categories mentioned above. Indeed, according to a study of some 5 809 patients performed by Dr. Robert M. Califf and his colleagues from the Duke University Medical Centre, contemporary surgical techniques result in improved longevity in the majority of patients with ischaemic heart disease, especially those with extensive narrowings of their coronary arteries and a high risk for future complications.[5]

Obviously, your physician will evaluate your particular risks and expected benefits carefully before recommending bypass surgery. He or she won't recommend it unless the benefits far outweigh the risks—and the benefits from surgery can be expected to be superior to those emanating from drug therapy or angioplasty.

Take two examples: a cardiologist would probably not recommend bypass surgery to a person with good left ventricular function (ejection fraction = 60 percent; see Table 18-1 on page 348) and an obstruction in a single coronary artery which is not the left

TABLE 18-1
Expected Percentage Risk of Death during Bypass Surgery and Five-Year Survival According to the Number of Occluded Coronary Arteries and Left Ventricular Function: Data from the Duke University Medical Centre, Durham, North Carolina[a]

Ejection Fraction (%)	Number of Significantly Occluded Coronary Arteries	Estimated Risk of Death during Surgery (%)	Estimated 5-Year Survival (%) Patients Receiving Medical Therapy	Estimated 5-Year Survival (%) Patients Undergoing Bypass Surgery
40	1	2,6	89,0	94,5
	2	2,6	83,0	93,2
	3	5,1	74,2	91,7
60	1	0,9	95,2	97,7
	2	0,9	91,0	96,5
	3	1,7	83,6	94,9

[a] These estimates are based on their 1984 experience. It is evident from these estimates that patients who have the most severe CHD (those with ejection fractions lower than 40 percent and three occluded coronary arteries) derive the greatest relative benefit from bypass surgery as opposed to medical therapy. Your physician will carefully evaluate your particular risks and benefits before recommending bypass surgery for you.

Source: Adapted from Robert M. Califf et al., "Changing Efficacy of Coronary Revascularization: Implications for Patient Selection." *Circulation* 78 (1988): I-185–I-191.

main coronary artery. In contrast, a cardiologist would probably recommend the operation for a patient with impaired left ventricular function (ejection fraction = 40 percent; see Table 18-1) and triple-vessel disease. (Remember that ejection fractions were discussed in Chapter 5: 60 percent is normal and anything under 45 percent indicates severe left ventricular dysfunction.)

Dr. J. Willis Hurst succinctly summed up today's therapeutic dilemma concerning bypass surgery. He says the issue is no longer whether or not bypass surgery prolongs life, because we know it does; rather, it's "to determine which patients who were formerly subjected to bypass surgery are candidates for coronary angioplasty."[6]

"How is blood detoured around a blocked coronary artery during bypass surgery?"

There are two major ways in which blood can be detoured around a blocked coronary artery.

In the first, the detour is accomplished by sewing a section of the saphenous vein, a superficial vein that runs down the inside of your legs, to both the aorta and a portion of the blocked coronary artery just beyond the site of the atherosclerotic plaque (see Figure 18-4). Because the saphenous vein is not a major vein, it does not need to be replaced and you won't miss it.

The second type of detour is created using an internal mammary artery (see Figure 18-4). There are two internal mammary arteries—the left and right—located just below the ribs and running down the chest about half an inch from the margins of the sternum. In most instances, the upper end of the internal mammary artery, which attaches to the subclavian artery, is not removed and the lower end is sewn onto the occluded coronary

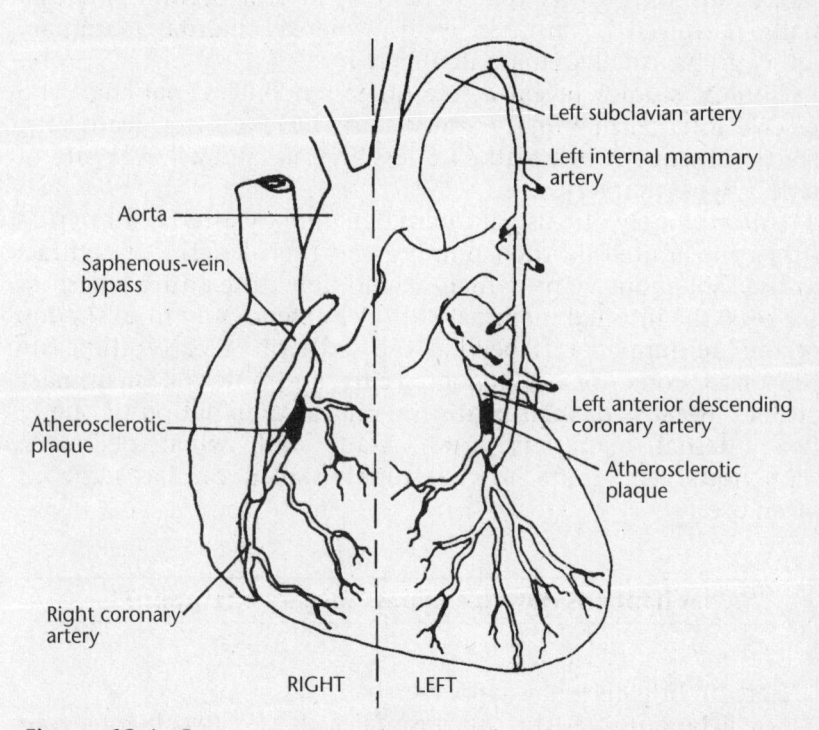

Figure 18-4. Bypass surgery using a saphenous vein and left internal mammary artery. The right side of the diagram shows bypass surgery using the saphenous vein. The left side of the diagram shows bypass surgery using the left internal mammary artery. The saphenous-vein bypass has been sutured to the aorta and to the right coronary artery at a point beyond the obstruction. The left internal mammary artery has been sutured to the left anterior descending coronary artery, also at a point beyond the obstruction. (Adapted from S. A. Price and L. M. Wilson, *Pathophysiology: Clinical Concepts of Disease Processes.* New York: McGraw-Hill, 1978.)

artery (shown in Figure 18-4). In some instances, however, a section of the internal mammary artery is removed and sewn onto both the aorta and the occluded coronary artery, in very much the same way as the saphenous vein.

Which is preferable for bypass surgery—a saphenous vein graft or an internal mammary artery graft?

In contrast to the saphenous vein, the internal mammary artery appears to be a vessel that is relatively resistant to atherosclerotic plaque buildup. Because of this, internal mammary arteries have the potential to remain open longer than saphenous vein grafts. Indeed, ten years after bypass surgery, 95 percent of internal mammary artery grafts are still open, compared with 60 to 70 percent of saphenous vein grafts. Moreover, a third of the saphenous vein grafts that remain open still become substantially narrowed by atherosclerosis, whereas internal mammary artery grafts usually remain unaffected.

Clinical studies reveal a few other tendencies: patients who receive internal mammary artery grafts have a lower death rate, fewer subsequent heart attacks, less angina, and a lower rate of repeat bypass surgery.

Unfortunately, the use of internal mammary arteries for bypass surgery is limited by their number and their length. In contrast to the saphenous veins, which extend down the entire length of the legs, the internal mammary arteries extend only from the top of the sternum to just beyond the sixth rib. Clearly, there are pros and cons for saphenous veins and internal mammary arteries. Because of their relative merits, a combination of one or two internal mammary artery grafts and, when necessary, saphenous vein grafts is what highly-skilled cardiac surgeons often use.

"What happens during a bypass surgery operation?"

Here, in brief, is what happens.

You'll be admitted to the hospital a day or two before your operation. The day before your surgery, the anaesthetist will examine you and ask some medical history questions. The anaesthetist will also explain how you'll be put to sleep before surgery and how your vital bodily functions will be maintained throughout.

The evening beforehand, you'll be shaved from chin to toe. You'll also be scrubbed with an antiseptic surgical solution in the places where incisions will be made on your chest and legs. These procedures reduce your risk for infection. They're important.

If you're very nervous about the operation, it's likely you'll be given a sleeping pill to make sure you get a good night's sleep. The next morning, it's also likely you'll be given a mild sedative about an hour before the surgery.

In the operating room, the anaesthetist administers a general anaesthetic. If you are at all nervous about this or if you have any questions, do not hesitate to ask your doctor before you go into hospital. Before you know it, you'll be asleep—and you'll remain asleep throughout the entire operation. You won't feel a thing!

We've already described what a bypass surgeon does to detour blood around your blocked coronary arteries. It will probably take a surgeon four to six hours to complete the operation, although the length, naturally, will depend on the complexity of your heart problem. The more bypasses that need to be created, the longer the surgery will take. Using the internal mammary artery also lengthens the operating time.

After your operation, you'll be transferred to the cardiac intensive care unit, where you'll eventually wake up. When you do, you'll find a breathing tube—the endotracheal tube—in your mouth. It's connected to a respirator that will continue to supply you with oxygen for the next twelve to twenty-four hours. While the tube isn't painful, it makes it impossible for you to talk. But don't worry. The nursing staff is trained to show patients how to communicate their needs without words.

This tube will also make it impossible for you to eat or swallow liquids. Thus, you'll receive all your sustenance through an IV line and a nasogastric tube which passes from your nose down into your stomach.

You'll also have a variety of other tubes and wires connected to you. These include chest tubes for draining off fluid that builds up inside your chest during and after surgery. Generally, these tubes are removed on the second day after surgery.

If all this sounds unpleasant, keep in mind that you'll be on pain-killing medication and will probably be quite disoriented and hazy throughout it all. Night will flow into day and, because the lights will be on throughout, you won't be able to keep track of time.

You'll be transferred back into your hospital room on the cardiac floor a day or two after the operation. Undoubtedly, you'll feel some discomfort in your chest and, if your saphenous veins were used, in your legs. Most patients don't complain of severe pain, though, for there is always medication available that can help alleviate it.

You should be aware that secretions accumulate in your lungs during surgery and in the period immediately following surgery. These are of considerable concern because they could lead to pneumonia if not removed. Lying on your back for long periods of time without moving worsens this condition. That's why it's best to lie on your side for part of the time and change position every hour or so.

The hospital's physiotherapist will be helping you clear out these lung secretions. The therapist will teach you deep-breathing exercises and ask you to cough frequently. These exercises are essential for your recovery, so pay close attention to what the therapist tells you. Many patients become concerned that they are being asked to move too much so soon after the operation. Although it may feel that your chest is about to burst open when you cough, remember that your sternum is being held together by some ten steel wires which aren't about to break.

Incidentally, it's normal to run a fever for a few days after bypass surgery. Don't let that concern you either.

We urge all our bypass surgery candidates to read a comprehensive book called simply *Bypass* by Dr. Jonathan L. Halperin and Richard Levine, published in 1987 by The Body Press, a division of Price/Stem/Sloan in Los Angeles. It goes into great detail about this operation.

"How should I prepare myself for bypass surgery?"

Because procedures differ from hospital to hospital, we urge you to gather as much information from your doctor as possible before your operation. The following checklist of questions should help you to learn what you need to know:

____ **Medications.** Should I stop taking aspirin and other blood-thinning drugs before hospital admission?

____ **Blood for transfusions, in case it's needed.** Most blood in South Africa is supplied through the blood transfusion services. It is tested for antibodies to the AIDS virus and is therefore very safe.

However, in rare cases people choose one of two other options:

you may either donate your own blood in advance or have someone you trust (such as a spouse or other relative) donate their blood for you.

___ **Admission procedures.** How far ahead of the operation will I be admitted? What tests will I undergo?

___ **Presurgery preparation.** What types of specialists will be preparing me for the operation? What will they do? For example, will I be taught beforehand any special techniques, such as deep-breathing exercises, that I'll need to use after the surgery?

___ **The operation.** We've given you only the broad outlines of what happens during bypass surgery. By all means, get your doctor to describe in detail what will happen in your case, including whether a saphenous vein and/or an internal mammary artery will be used.

___ **Operation's length.**

___ **Postoperative recovery.** What will happen in the cardiac intensive care unit? What tubes and contraptions will I be hooked up to when I wake up? How will I feel? What drugs will I be given, and what possible side effects do they have? How long will I remain there?

___ **Recuperation danger signs.** In a worst-case scenario, what can go wrong during recovery? What symptoms should I be on the lookout for?

___ **Hospital visitation.** When can my family visit? For how long?

___ **Hospital discharge.** If all goes smoothly, how long will I be in the hospital?

CHAPTER 19

CONTROVERSIAL TREATMENTS

Risk factors represent a well-known and well-respected way of approaching the scourge of heart disease. By controlling the risk factors, you stand a good chance of preventing, retarding, or even reversing the progression of CHD. However, in the heart disease puzzle, there's still a missing piece: what triggers the process of atherosclerosis to begin with?

As with arthritis and cancer, the exact trigger that starts the process of atherosclerosis is not yet well understood, and, as with these diseases, there's no single, provable, treatable cause of CHD. Because millions of people suffer from these maladies, "miracle cures" and other dubious remedies crop up all the time. These are controversial and often unsubstantiated forms of therapy that are passed along by word of mouth or appear in popular health publications. Needless to say, in the majority of cases, the scientific underpinnings of these therapies are either lacking entirely or extremely questionable.

The purpose of this chapter is to evaluate the more common—and controversial—of the heart disease cure-alls. We do this based on the best current scientific research on each subject. However, we must offer a disclaimer. We recognize that new medical information could come out the week after this book is published. To be sure, the field of medical research is dynamic, with new theories and hypotheses being tested all the time.

HOW TO EVALUATE HEALTH DATA

We won't merely give you our opinions about each remedy, because you'll learn more if we outline some basic criteria you can apply to any treatment you come across, even those we don't mention here.

In assessing therapies, what you're trying to work out is which are quackery and which have some merit. Here are some tip-offs:

Is the Evidence Based on Studies or Stories? Widely accepted medical treatments are always based on a series of well-designed and well-executed research studies. They're published in medical journals most laypeople never see, although we're sure you could find them, if you're interested, in any good library.

Practising physicians, academic researchers, and other scientists are regular readers of these journals. It is their role to criticize or praise the studies. Indeed, the comments following a study's publication have a great impact on whether a hypothesis will lose its credence or gain further adherents, and maybe even inspire other researchers to check it out further in their own studies.

Proper studies remove the personal bias and try to focus solely on the scientific facts. The studies that finally reach the pages of your local newspaper's science section or a respected popular science magazine are usually those that have wended their way through the medical journals and withstood the test of criticism from other scientists.

Unfortunately, the evidence supporting the controversial grassroots remedies usually consists of anecdotal accounts from people who claim they worked for them. Granted, these are fun to read and certainly easier to understand than arcane medical studies, but they're also riddled with personal biases. And they've seldom been aired in a forum that invites scientific scrutiny.

Admittedly, this personal bias rarely takes the form of intentional distortion. The storytellers sometimes have nothing to gain financially from a wider acceptance of a therapy. But the fact remains that they may well have committed honest errors of observation and become unduly optimistic because of their own desperate circumstances. Often these are people in panic. They're frantic to find a cure to stave off invalidism, or even death.

How Many People Have Tried the Therapy—and Benefited? What's Their Medical Profile? Without scientific research to back a remedy, there are too many glaring, unanswered questions. Among them:

How many people have tried this treatment?

Was heart disease the only health problem these people had, or were they also suffering from a mix of ailments that might throw off the conclusions?

Of those who have tried the remedy, what percentage have really been helped?

How do they know they've been helped—just because they feel better or because objective testing shows there's been an appreciable change in their CHD?

How Effective Is It Compared with Other Treatments? We're back to the question of scientific studies again. Of course, no one can answer this question unless a series of controlled studies has been done with the goal of comparing the effectiveness of different therapies—or the effectiveness of the proposed remedy compared with doing nothing. Without such research, conducted on a large scale, no worthwhile conclusions can be drawn.

How Safe Is It? When you're dealing with medical issues, safety is relative. There is no such thing as absolute safety. After all, as you've learned, even staying in bed involves a degree of risk. Moreover, most medications cause side effects.

So the real question is: is the risk justified when the alternatives are considered? You find out the answer to this question through studies covering a broad spectrum of people over long periods of time.

Be Wary of Overly Enthusiastic Advertising Claims and Unusual Marketing Ploys. Words such as "miracle", "breakthrough", and "cure" in advertising or product literature ought to make you suspicious. Vague allusions to "published research" with no citation, coupled with testimonials from satisfied patients or customers, are dubious proof. The endorsement of experts who are not named or fully identified shouldn't put your mind at ease either.

Some advertising emphasizes the opposition or disapproval of the medical profession. You can take that for what it's worth. Our feeling is: if this remedy is really so wonderful, why would doctors, en masse, be critical of it? The medical community isn't a unified force, a monolith, any more than other professions are. Certainly, if a remedy is credible, its supporters ought to be able to find a certain percentage of doctors who have respectable credentials to support it.

It's a medical truism that the broader the claim of medical effectiveness, the more wary you should be. We're reminded of the snake-oil salesmen of lore who used to sell potions "curing everything that ails you".

Also, watch out for medical products sold only through the mail or door-to-door, or whose packaging does not identify the ingredients. Incidentally, a product whose ingredients are "all natural" may be a product that's some combination of vitamins and minerals, and it might be much cheaper for you to bypass the hype and buy those vitamins and minerals directly. Of course, whether those vitamins and minerals in any form will do what the promoters say they'll do is another matter.

JUST PLAIN ASPIRIN

Many heart attacks occur when a blood clot forms in a narrowed vessel. Since aspirin impedes blood-clot formation, one might assume it would be useful in preventing heart attacks.

Much of the interest in this over-the-counter helpmate was piqued by a study using a large group of American physicians as subjects. The doctors agreed to take 325 milligrams of aspirin—the amount in a standard tablet—every other day during the study to see whether or not it would reduce the risk of dying of cardiovascular disease.

This was a well-controlled, large-scale, double-blind, randomized study featuring placebos. Of 22 000 participating physicians, half were assigned at random to take the aspirin and half to take the placebo, which contained no aspirin whatsoever. Neither the doctors nor the researchers knew who was in which group.

The follow-up on this study was unusually good, with 99,7 percent of the physicians reporting back to researchers and the average length of the follow-up being 4,8 years. The preliminary results were published in the January 1988 issue of the *New England Journal of Medicine*.[1] The conclusion: the group taking the aspirin had a statistically significant reduction in the rate of both fatal and nonfatal heart attacks. In all, the aspirin-takers had 104 infarctions—5 fatal and 99 nonfatal. In contrast, the placebo group had 189 heart attacks—18 fatal and 171 nonfatal. In short, those taking the aspirin were half as likely to suffer a heart attack.

This was welcome news but the benefit was not clear-cut. Overall, the study revealed no significant effect on the incidence of stroke, also a cardiovascular ailment. However, the stroke data were somewhat disturbing. There were thirteen haemorrhagic strokes, a few fatal, in the aspirin group, and only ten in the placebo group. In a haemorrhagic stroke, bleeding occurs in the brain, whereas in the other major type of stroke, called ischaemic, blood is prevented from getting to a part of the brain by atherosclerosis and a blood clot. Perhaps the aspirin prevented the clot type of stroke but increased the bleeding type.

A similar study, using British physicians, showed no definitive positive impact on overall mortality and no difference in the incidence of heart attack.[2] But there was again an excess of haemorrhagic strokes.

Such contradictory findings are disturbing and were enough to make critics go back over the U.S. study results with a fine-toothed comb.

Indeed, there are several puzzling aspects to the American study. The actual number of deaths from all cardiovascular causes, which includes both heart attacks and strokes, in both the aspirin and placebo groups was identical—forty-four versus forty-four. This could be due to an inadequate sample size, but it could also reflect a true lack of impact. While some causes of death—such as heart attack—decreased, others increased with aspirin use.

Furthermore, the physicians who were participants in the United States study were remarkably—almost unbelievably—resistant to cardiovascular disease. There were only 88 deaths of cardiovascular origins, when 733 could have been expected in a group with this age distribution. Thus, the doctor population may not have been representative.

In light of these two studies, we don't think it's wise to take aspirin if you have uncontrolled high blood pressure or any of the following: a history of stroke, cerebral vascular disease, bleeding disorders, platelet deficiency, or a family history of cerebral haemorrhage.

Taking the above restrictions into account, it does appear that aspirin will be beneficial to most readers of this book, although we don't advise any of you to embark on aspirin therapy without discussing it with your doctor.

The effect of aspirin on heart attack patients has also been studied. Indeed, there have been at least two randomized trials on a total of about 18 000 heart attack patients.[3,4] Aspirin was first taken on the day of the infarction and continued for four to five weeks. The aspirin-takers showed a 21 percent reduction in mortality compared with the control group.

Altogether, there have been some ten important studies of aspirin and other anti-platelet agents in which patients started using the medications in the months after their infarction and continued taking them for up to two years. Recently, these trials were reviewed by a distinguished group of scientists, the Anti-Platelet Triallists Collaborative Group.[5] Six of the studies focused on aspirin; two on the combination of aspirin and dipyridamole; and two on sulfinpyrazone.

In all, the collective sample comprised 18 441 patients. The results: taking these various anti-platelet agents reduced the risk of cardiovascular death by 13 percent and the risk for nonfatal heart attacks by 31 percent. The incidence of nonfatal stroke dropped by 42 percent. And there was no appreciable change in deaths from non-cardiovascular causes.

The bottom line was that anti-platelet treatment reduced the risk of suffering from a major cardiovascular problem by 25 percent.

This overview also suggests that aspirin, by itself, may be just as effective to prevent clotting as aspirin plus dipyridamole and sulfinpyrazone, two of the most commonly used prescription drugs. It's also clear that the advantages from aspirin aren't that different when the dosage goes from 160 milligrams a day to as high as 900 to 1 500 milligrams a day. In fact, one study underscores the fact that the lower doses cause fewer gastrointestinal side effects.

We make the following recommendation: starting immediately after an acute heart attack, patients and their physicians might consider a dosage of one 325-milligram aspirin tablet every day, or on alternate days. Take them with meals, never on an empty stomach. We think this minimal amount is sufficient to achieve the desired results.

The issue of taking aspirin during and after angioplasty was tackled in a recent study of 376 patients.[6] The study actually spotlighted two anti-platelet agents—aspirin and dipyridamole. During the first six months after angioplasty, the two medications did not reduce the six-month rate of re-stenosis (the renarrowing of a vessel). But they cut down markedly on the chances of a patient having a heart attack during or soon after an angioplasty. Although to date no clear benefit has been shown to occur with long-term use, taking aspirin and dipyridamole starting twenty-four hours before and continuing until forty-eight hours after the procedure would seem to be a good idea.

In contrast, in bypass surgery patients, aspirin and dipyridamole have been clearly shown to be of both short- and long-term benefit. In particular, research conducted at the Mayo Clinic in Rochester, Minnesota, has demonstrated that combined therapy with these two anti-platelet drugs not only helps prevent the occlusion of bypass vessels during the first month after surgery, but continues to be of substantial benefit for at least one year thereafter.[7,8] In view of this, aspirin and dipyridamole are now commonly prescribed for bypass surgery patients.

THE CHELATION CONTROVERSY

Chelation is not practised in South Africa, but we discuss it here for your interest. Chelation refers to the intravenous administration of EDTA, a synthetic amino acid originally used to treat cases of lead or mercury poisoning. To "chelate" means to naturally seek out and bind to another substance.

The theory behind chelation therapy is that EDTA, injected on a regular schedule, will bind to the calcium in atherosclerotic plaques. Once the calcium is removed, the plaques will disintegrate and relieve the narrowing of the artery. Adherents make the claim that chelation will reverse existing atherosclerosis as well as prevent the formation of new plaque, and that it will remedy a potpourri of other ailments. Patients supposedly require from five to thirty treatments. The major problem with chelation is that scientific studies are lacking. All the evidence supporting chelation is anecdotal or involves uncontrolled trials. This means no group of chelation patients was ever studied under the same conditions, nor was there a comparison control group who got a treatment they thought was chelation but amounted to nothing at all.

One reason the research community hasn't undertaken studies is that the theory itself is so questionable. First, scientists do not see how chelation can remove calcium from the plaques. All available evidence suggests that removing calcium from the bloodstream by chelation—or via any other method—results in calcium being withdrawn from bones, not from atherosclerotic plaques.

Second, the idea that plaques, deprived of calcium, will shrivel away and disappear is hard for biochemists to buy. Calcium is only a small part of the plaque and is incorporated only late in its course. They see no scientifically valid reason why the remaining material should just dissolve away.

Naturally, chelationists have a battery of responses to these objections. Their arguments are often quite vague and sometimes highly improbable.

Even though there is no scientific evidence that chelation is of benefit in CHD, there's no disputing the fact that many people feel better and report less pain after a series of chelation treatments. Whether their blood flow is really improved due to chelation is another matter. However, there is another possible explanation for why chelation patients feel they've got a new lease on life.

Most chelation therapists insist that their patients adopt a healthier life-style while undergoing treatments. That means stopping smoking, losing mass, eating more fresh fruits and vegetables, avoiding high-fat foods, and exercising regularly—all recommendations that are made by doctors like us who represent a more mainstream approach to cardiac therapy. We feel these life-style changes are probably far more responsible for making the patients feel better than are the injections of EDTA. Another explanation is the "placebo effect". People think they're being helped, and that, in and of itself, makes them feel better.

WHAT'S FISHY ABOUT FISH-OIL CAPSULES

Greenland's Eskimos are often favourably compared to North Americans. Much has been made of the fact that they eat a steady diet of fish, with little meat and few vegetables, and have a remarkably low incidence of heart disease. But look at the other aspects of their lives: they don't smoke and they're not prone to hypertension. They also have a shorter life span than Americans, despite all the latter's bad health habits. Compared with Americans, Eskimos have a higher incidence of stroke, and they frequently die of infectious disease or trauma. Given the full facts about Eskimos and their mortality rate, there is no reason to assume that fish oil is a miracle substance.

The oil from fish that populate northerly waters—or whose habitat is deep water, where it's always cold—contains omega-3 polyunsaturated fatty acids with an unsaturated double bond in a specific location in their chemical structure. Because omega-3 fatty acids contain a longer chain of carbon atoms and more unsaturated bonds than the fatty acids in vegetable oils, the body seems to react differently to them.

On the plus side, omega-3 fatty acids tend to lower a person's high triglyceride level when taken in large doses (however, the LDL-lowering effect is far less). There is also some research suggesting that omega-3 fatty acids may play a role in arresting the development of atherosclerotic plaques.

On the minus side, they seem to prevent the blood from clotting by stopping the aggregation of platelets. That's good if it prevents a dangerous thrombus from forming in a narrowed artery. That's bad if it simply makes you bleed excessively when you pierce your skin or get a nosebleed.

You should also know that large doses of fish oil cause the levels of vitamin E in the body to drop well below normal. Taking a 100-milligram vitamin E supplement along with fish-oil capsules may solve the problem.

Many brands of fish-oil supplements now grace the shelves of pharmacies and health food stores. Each capsule usually contains 300 to 500 milligrams of omega-3 fatty acids. Those pushing fish oil as a CHD prevention remedy recommend that you take three to six capsules a day. The amount of omega-3 you get in this dosage is roughly equivalent to that in 170 grams of salmon.

We are hesitant to recommend taking fish-oil capsules because you must take megadoses—perhaps as many as fifty capsules a day—to get the desired effect against CHD. That's what the studies show. But if you take that much, the chances of bleeding or other side effects go up in equal measure. And should you combine large doses of fish oil, which inhibits clotting, with regular doses of an anti-platelet agent such as aspirin, which also retards clotting, just imagine the bleeding problem you could be creating for yourself.

So we say skip the fish-oil supplements and eat the fish instead. Good sources of omega-3 fatty acids are pilchards, mackerel, sardines, salmon, kippers, herring, galjoen and mullet. Eating more fish every week means eating less red meat, all to the good in terms of any cholesterol problem you may have.

LECITHIN: YOU'RE ALREADY GETTING ENOUGH

Lecithin is a fatty substance found in egg yolks, soybeans, organ meats, and whole grains. It is also used as an emulsifier in processed foods. It's sold in health food shops in both powdered and pill form.

Lecithin plays a role in blood cholesterol transport. Cholesterol in the bloodstream attaches to a lecithin molecule and becomes soluble. In this form, the cholesterol stays in circulation and can't be deposited inside an arterial lining.

It is known that lecithin plays a critical role in your body's cholesterol metabolism. Thus, it would seem to follow that extra lecithin, in supplementation form, might help lower the blood level of cholesterol.

Logical as it may seem, there is simply no evidence that extra lecithin makes your body do anything more than it would do without it. Indeed, lecithin may be one of the few substances found in the body that humans are never deficient in. At least, there's never been a reported case of lecithin deficiency.

One researcher, Dr. H. F. Ter Welle, did undertake a study to probe the effects of supplemental lecithin.[9] He fed 2 to 4 grams of soya lecithin to twelve patients with high cholesterol counts. Nothing happened. In fact, Dr. Ter Welle felt that the lecithin administered hadn't even been absorbed. His conclusion: "Large amounts of lecithin, taken as dietary supplements, are an expensive source of additional kilojoules." In short, lecithin does not appear to lower blood cholesterol. And when needed for that purpose, it can be synthesized by the body in amounts sufficient to meet its needs.

VITAMIN E—NO MIRACLE CURE-ALL

Vitamin E has been touted for years as a remedy for everything from skin rashes and schizophrenia to heart disease. It's been shown in laboratory animals that a vitamin E deficiency produces abnormalities in the heart muscle. Moreover, a deficiency of vitamin E is associated with ECG changes, even heart failure. From this, some have concluded that vitamin E certainly has a role in treating heart disease in humans, and they recommend doses that are very high.

We think otherwise based on the best clinical studies to date. No studies have demonstrated any cardiac benefit from taking vitamin E. Thus, we advise against taking it as a therapeutic heart medication.

OTHER VITAMINS

This leads us to the broader issue of vitamin supplementation. How beneficial is it in CHD prevention or reversal?

It is common these days for people to take large doses of vitamins for a wide variety of preventive or curative reasons. There are those who claim that vitamins, because they're essential for good nutrition, must be even better in megadoses. And heart disease is one of the ailments they feel will respond to this the-more-the-merrier approach.

We disagree—although niacin, as discussed in Chapter 12, is an exception—for there's no clear-cut evidence in the medical literature to support this claim. In most cases, taking one or two times the recommended daily allowance of a vitamin is not harmful. However, except in the case of niacin, there is no clear evidence that massive doses will have any beneficial effect on heart disease—and these large doses could even be harmful.

While we caution against all vitamin excesses, we want you to be especially careful not to overdo it with vitamins A, D, and E, which are fat soluble and can accumulate in the body, and B_6, which can cause neurological problems and liver damage. Superabundant amounts of vitamin C, a nutrient that is often taken in excessive doses, can increase the risk of kidney-stone formation.

TRACE MINERALS

Only one trace element is known to play a role in heart disease. Yes, there is evidence that a copper deficiency can cause the degeneration of the heart muscle to the point where tissue dies and there is scarring. Copper deficiency is also associated with hypercholesterolaemia and abnormal electrocardiograms. And there are reports that a deficiency can cause high blood pressure.

Unlike vitamins, which people tend to overdo, minerals such as copper are something that many of us have too little of. The recommended daily intake of copper for adults is 2 to 3 milligrams. Many of us take in as little as 0,8 milligrams per day.

Despite this, cardiac researchers do not feel that copper deficiency is an important cause of heart disease. Still, we feel it wouldn't hurt coronary patients to eat more foods containing copper. These include fish, especially shellfish; nuts; wheat-based cereals; dried fruit; chicken; and vegetables.

You should be aware that large doses of zinc can decrease your body's store of copper. Since vitamin-mineral aficionados, in recent years, have proclaimed zinc a cure-all for such annoying maladies as the common cold, its use has gone up, possibly to the detriment of the copper in people's systems.

HERBAL REMEDIES

Everything from dandelion weeds to garlic has been recommended to cure heart disease. While these herbal remedies may not hurt you, we must report that there's no scientific proof to date that any herb influences CHD.

We grant that there's something very attractive about the notion of a natural home remedy, especially one with a long lineage spanning many centuries and cultures. The claims for certain herbs become even more appealing when someone with an advanced degree in the sciences promotes them based on his own studies. When you encounter this type of come-hither, you should evaluate the assertions based on our advice earlier in this chapter.

We are not against herbs, for they've played a legitimate part in the treatment of certain diseases. In fact, one of the most valuable cardiovascular medications—digitalis—is extracted from a plant called foxglove. Digitalis, of course, must be taken in very carefully controlled doses and should never be ingested in its natural plant form.

In summary, we know of no herb, sold in health food stores or from farm stalls, that has any proven benefit in preventing or treating heart disease. You should also be aware that herbs can, in some instances, be toxic. Many of the chemicals present in herbs have never been tested for safety. Potentially toxic ingredients—for instance, aflatoxin, one of the most potent carcinogens we know of—have been identified in some plant foods.

Some food supplements sold in health food stores also contain some potentially harmful ingredients. For example, there may be an oestrogenic hormone in commercial alfalfa tablets, arsenic in kelp tablets, cadmium in dolomite, and potentially toxic amounts of lead in bonemeal and dolomite. Ginseng, one of the most popular herbs, has been reported to produce an oestrogen-like effect. The 1988 U.S. Surgeon General's Report on Nutrition and Health stated that there have been "occasional poisonings and clinical intoxications" after the use of some herbal tea products, such as jimsonweed and peony root.[10]

AFTERWORD

MEETING THE CHALLENGE OF HEART DISEASE

It wasn't that long ago that heart disease was a medical rarity. Indeed, earlier in this century, it was almost unknown. Heart disease can revert to that status again if people would simply pay more attention to the life-style factors that foster CHD. After all, it wouldn't take that radical a revision in most people's lives to keep heart disease at bay—and peak health in the picture.

Unfortunately, that state of happiness hasn't been reached yet. Each year, literally millions of people around the world still die prematurely of heart disease. And many more millions of patients survive a major heart problem and then hope to slow the progress of the CHD already entrenched in their bodies and prevent a recurrence.

In this book, we have offered you a method for preventing that second heart attack—or the need for bypass surgery or angioplasty. We hope you follow our Heart Points System and make the necessary changes in your life-style, because the quality of your remaining years depends on it.

Our cardiac rehabilitation programme was developed expressly for heart patients in the low- to moderate-risk categories. It is a "medically directed" programme—created by knowledgeable specialists—that can be utilized in a cost-effective way by motivated patients in their own homes.

However, the programme does not remove the need for close supervision by a patient's own doctor, who may want to modify aspects of our protocol. We welcome physicians' input. Indeed, we feel that our programme should be viewed as a draft blueprint by both patients and their doctors. It is up to a patient and his or her doctor to make changes in our blueprint—that is, adapt our programme—to suit the medical realities of the case in question.

Despite the promising reduction in CHD deaths in recent years, the challenge of heart disease remains. We accept the fact that it may take years before the full impact of people's healthier life-styles translates into a further decrease of coronary deaths. In the meantime, we offer our cardiac rehabilitation programme as a means to improve the quality of heart patients' remaining years.

RESOURCES SECTION

APPENDIX A   Formulas for Estimating Your MET Value during Exercise Testing

APPENDIX B   Estimating Your Energy Expenditure during Exercise

APPENDIX C   Sample Initial Cardiac Recovery Exercise Programmes

APPENDIX D   For CHD Patients: The Exercise Safety Quiz

APPENDIX E   The ABCs of Heart Medication

APPENDIX A

FORMULAS FOR ESTIMATING YOUR MET VALUE DURING EXERCISE TESTING

THE following formulas will enable you to calculate METs from your exercise tests.

If you were *walking* at a specific speed and gradient during your treadmill test, use one of the following formulas:

in miles per hour (mph):

$$\frac{\left(2{,}68 \times \text{speed in mph}\right) + \left(48{,}24 \times \text{speed in mph} \times \frac{\%\ \text{incline}}{100}\right) + 3{,}5}{3{,}5} = \text{METs}$$

Example: A person who walks on a treadmill at a speed of 2,5 mph at an incline of 12% is expending 7 METs.

in kilometres per hour (km/h):

$$\frac{\left(1{,}67 \times \text{speed in km/h}\right) + \left(30 \times \text{speed in km/h} \times \frac{\%\ \text{incline}}{100}\right) + 3{,}5}{3{,}5} = \text{METs}$$

Example: A person who walks on a treadmill at a speed of 4 km/h at an incline of 12% is expending 7 METs.

If you were *jogging* at a specific speed and gradient during your treadmill test, use one of the following formulas:

in miles per hour (mph):

$$\frac{\left(5{,}36 \times \text{speed in mph}\right) + \left(24{,}12 \times \text{speed in mph} \times \frac{\%\ \text{incline}}{100}\right) + 3{,}5}{3{,}5} = \text{METs}$$

Example: A person who jogs on a treadmill at a speed of 5,5 mph at an incline of 5% is expending 11,3 METs.

in kilometres per hour (km/h):

$$\frac{\left(3{,}33 \times \text{speed in km/h}\right) + \left(15 \times \text{speed in km/h} \times \frac{\%\ \text{incline}}{100}\right) + 3{,}5}{3{,}5} = \text{METs}$$

Example: A person who jogs on a treadmill at a speed of 8,8 km/h at an incline of 5% is expending 11,3 METs.

If you were doing your exercise test on a *stationary* cycle (legs only) and your work rate is expressed in kilogram-metres per minute, use one of the following formulas:

in mass in pounds:

$$\frac{(2 \times \text{kilogram-metres per min.}) + (1{,}59 \times \text{mass in pounds})}{(1{,}59 \times \text{mass in pounds})} = \text{METs}$$

Example: A person who weighs 165 pounds and cycles at 750 kilogram-metres per minute is expending 6,7 METs.

in mass in kilograms:

$$\frac{(2 \times \text{kilogram-metres per min.}) + (3{,}5 \times \text{mass in kilograms})}{(3{,}5 \times \text{mass in kilograms})} = \text{METs}$$

Example: A person who weighs 75 kilograms and cycles at 750 kilogram-metres per minute is expending 6,7 METs.

If you were doing your exercise test on a *stationary* cycle (legs only) and your work rate is expressed in watts, use one of the following formulas:

in mass in pounds:

$$\frac{(12 \times \text{watts}) + (1{,}59 \times \text{mass in pounds})}{(1{,}59 \times \text{mass in pounds})} = \text{METs}$$

Example: A person who weighs 165 pounds and cycles at 120 watts is expending 6,5 METs.

in mass in kilograms:

$$\frac{(12 \times \text{watts}) + (3,5 \times \text{mass in kilograms})}{(3,5 \times \text{mass in kilograms})} = \text{METs}$$

Example: A person who weighs 75 kilograms and cycles at 120 watts is expending 6,5 METs.

APPENDIX B

ESTIMATING YOUR ENERGY EXPENDITURE DURING EXERCISE

As we emphasized in Part 3 and in Chapter 16, where we introduced our Heart Points System, exercise will help you recover. Your goal is to perform an aerobic exercise for 20 to 60 minutes per workout, 3 to 5 days each week, at an intensity which raises the heart rate above 60 percent of your symptom-limited value. This will result in an energy expenditure that brings about the desired recuperative benefits.

No doubt you're scratching your head over the question of how to go about determining what your energy expenditure (and thus Heart Points total) actually is. The charts and formulas in this section will provide you with the answer.

You can roughly estimate the Heart Points you earn during each exercise session by utilizing the charts that follow. We have Heart Point Charts for walking, jogging, stationary cycling (legs only), the Schwinn Air-Dyne and other activities. It was possible to formulate charts for these forms of exercise because none requires a lot of skill. However, for exercises which do require skill, or which may be influenced by external factors such as the weather or terrain, it's not possible to compile accurate Heart Point Charts. That's one reason to confine yourself to these more elemental forms of exercise during your recovery period.

After the Heart Point Charts, you'll find a section of formulas. These are the actual equations, or formulas, that we used to compile the charts. Those of you who demand more precision and are more mathematically inclined will want to skip the Heart Point Charts and utilize the equations to help you more accurately determine your energy expenditure, and thus Heart Points, after each workout.

In truth, the only way people can get an accurate assessment of their energy expenditure during exercise is through laboratory

Walking

Time (min:sec)	Distance (km)	Heart Points	Time (min:sec)	Distance (km)	Heart Points	Time (min:sec)	Distance (km)	Heart Points
5:00	under 0,16	0,8	**7:30**	under 0,24	1,3	**10:00**	under 0,32	1,7
	0,16-0,23	1,0		0,24-0,31	1,5		0,32-0,39	1,8
	0,24-0,31	1,2		0,32-0,39	1,7		0,40-0,47	2,0
	0,32-0,39	1,4		0,40-0,47	1,9		0,48-0,55	2,2
	0,40-0,47	1,6		0,48-0,55	2,1		0,56-0,63	2,4
	0,48-0,53*	1,8		0,56-0,63	2,3		0,64-0,71	2,6
				0,64-0,71	2,5		0,72-0,79	2,8
				0,72-0,78*	2,7		0,80-0,87	3,0
							0,88-0,95	3,2
							0,96-1,06*	3,6

*For longer distances, use the Jogging tables to calculate **Heart Points**

Time (min:sec)	Distance (km)	Heart Points	Time (min:sec)	Distance (km)	Heart Points	Time (min:sec)	Distance (km)	Heart Points
12:30	under 0,32	1,9	**15:00**	under 0,48	2,5	**17:30**	under 0,48	2,8
	0,32-0,47	2,3		0,48-0,63	2,9		0,48-0,79	3,5
	0,48-0,63	2,7		0,64-0,79	3,3		0,80-1,11	4,3
	0,64-0,79	3,1		0,80-0,95	3,7		1,12-1,43	5,1
	0,80-0,95	3,5		0,96-1,11	4,1		1,44-1,75	5,9
	0,96-1,11	3,9		1,12-1,27	4,5		1,76-1,86*	6,7
	1,12-1,27	4,3		1,28-1,43	4,9			
	1,28-1,33*	4,7		1,44-1,58*	5,3			

*For longer distances, use the Jogging tables to calculate **Heart Points**

Time (min:sec)	Distance (km)	Heart Points	Time (min:sec)	Distance (km)	Heart Points	Time (min:sec)	Distance (km)	Heart Points
20:00	under 0,64	3,4	**22:30**	under 0,64	3,6	**25:00**	under 0,80	4,2
	0,64-0,95	4,1		0,64-0,95	4,4		0,80-1,11	5,0
	0,96-1,27	4,9		0,96-1,27	5,2		1,12-1,43	5,8
	1,28-1,59	5,7		1,28-1,59	6,0		1,44-1,75	6,6
	1,60-1,91	6,5		1,60-1,91	6,8		1,76-2,07	7,4
	1,92-2,13*	7,3		1,92-2,23	7,6		2,08-2,39	8,2
				2,24-2,38*	8,4		2,40-2,66*	9,0

*For longer distances, use the Jogging tables to calculate **Heart Points**

Time (min:sec)	Distance (km)	Heart Points	Time (min:sec)	Distance (km)	Heart Points	Time (min:sec)	Distance (km)	Heart Points
27:30	under 0,80	4,5	**30:00**	under 0,80	4,6	**35:00**	under 1,20	6,1
	0,80-1,11	5,2		0,80-1,19	5,6		1,20-1,59	7,0
	1,12-1,43	6,0		1,20-1,59	6,6		1,60-1,99	8,0
	1,44-1,75	6,8		1,60-1,99	7,6		2,00-2,39	9,0
	1,76-2,07	7,6		2,00-2,39	8,6		2,40-2,79	10,0
	2,08-2,39	8,4		2,40-2,79	9,6		2,80-3,19	11,0
	2,40-2,71	9,2		2,80-3,18*	10,6		3,20-3,59	12,0
	2,72-2,93*	10,0					3,60-3,73*	13,0

*For longer distances, use the Jogging tables to calculate **Heart Points**

testing. There, technicians can utilize sophisticated equipment to measure the exact amount of oxygen the body takes up during a workout. The equations that follow are derived from numerous exercise research studies performed in such laboratories.

To utilize our formulas, you need to know:

Walking

Time (min:sec)	Distance (km)	Heart Points	Time (min:sec)	Distance (km)	Heart Points	Time (min:sec)	Distance (km)	Heart Points
40:00	under 1,60	7,5	**45:00**	under 1,60	7,9	**50:00**	under 1,60	8,4
	1,60-1,99	8,5		1,60-2,39	9,9		1,60-2,39	10,3
	2,00-2,39	9,5		2,40-3,19	11,9		2,40-3,19	12,4
	2,40-2,79	10,5		3,20-3,99	13,9		3,20-3,99	14,4
	2,80-3,19	11,5		4,00-4,78*	15,9		4,00-4,79	16,4
	3,20-3,59	12,5					4,80-5,33*	18,4
	3,60-3,99	13,5						
	4,00-4,26*	14,5						

*For longer distances, use the Jogging tables to calculate **Heart Points**

Time (min:sec)	Distance (km)	Heart Points	Time (min:sec)	Distance (km)	Heart Points
55:00	under 1,60	8,8	**60:00**	under 1,60	9,3
	1,60-2,39	10,8		1,60-2,39	11,2
	2,40-3,19	12,8		2,40-3,19	13,2
	3,20-3,99	14,8		3,20-3,99	15,2
	4,00-4,79	16,8		4,00-4,79	17,2
	4,80-5,59	18,8		4,80-5,59	19,2
	5,60-5,86*	20.8		5,60-6,38*	21,2

*For longer distances, use the Jogging tables to calculate **Heart Points**

1. The type of exercise
2. The distance you cover (i.e., the mileage) or work rate (i.e., the wattage)
3. The time you do it in (i.e., the duration)
4. Your mass in pounds or kilograms

For many activities, such as walking and jogging, you'll need a pedometer or your car's odometer to give you the distance—that is, unless you're lucky enough to have access to a measured running track. You'll also need a stopwatch or timepiece with a second hand to determine the duration.

Beginning on page 392 are the energy expenditure formulas for the seven forms of exercise that are most commonly prescribed for heart patients during their early recuperation, as well as a formula for calculating the energy expenditure for other exercises. (Remember, to convert energy expenditure to Heart Points, you must then use the formula provided in Chapter 16.)

Jogging

Time (min:sec)	Distance (km)	Heart Points	Time (min:sec)	Distance (km)	Heart Points	Time (min:sec)	Distance (km)	Heart Points
5:00	under 0,64	3,6	**7:30**	under 0,80	4,7	**10:00**	under 1,28	7,3
	0,64-0,79	4,4		0,80-0,95	5,4		1,28-1,43	8,0
	0,80-0,95	5,2		0,96-1,11	6,2		1,44-1,59	8,8
	0,96-1,10	6,0		1,12-1,27	7,0		1,60-1,75	9,6
	over 1,10	6,8		1,28-1,43	7,8		1,76-1,91	10,4
				1,44-1,59	8,6		1,92-2,07	11,2
				1,60-1,74	9,4		2,08-2,23	12,0
				over 1,74	10,2		2,24-2,38	12,8
							over 2,38	13,6
12:30	under 1,60	9,2	**15:00**	under 1,92	10,9	**17:30**	under 2,24	12,8
	1,60-1,91	10,7		1,92-2,23	12,5		2,24-2,55	14,3
	1,92-2,23	12,3		2,24-2,55	14,1		2,56-2,87	15,9
	2,24-2,55	13,9		2,56-2,87	15,7		2,88-3,19	17,5
	2,56-2,86	15,5		2,88-3,19	17,3		3,20-3,51	19,1
	over 2,86	17,1		3,20-3,50	18,9		3,52-3,83	20,7
				over 3,50	20,5		3,84-4,14	22,4
							over 4,14	24,0
20:00	under 2,40	13,8	**22:30**	under 2,80	16,0	**25:00**	under 3,20	18,2
	2,40-2,79	15,7		2,80-3,19	18,0		3,20-3,59	20,2
	2,80-3,19	17,7		3,20-3,59	20,0		3,60-3,99	22,2
	3,20-3,59	19,7		3,60-3,99	22,0		4,00-4,39	24,2
	3,60-3,99	21,7		4,00-4,39	24,0		4,40-4,79	26,2
	4,00-4,39	23,7		4,40-4,79	26,0		4,80-5,19	28,2
	4,40-4,78	25,7		4,80-5,18	28,0		5,20-5,59	30,2
	over 4,78	27,7		over 5,18	30,0		5,60-5,98	32,2
							over 5,98	34,2
27:30	under 3,20	18,5	**30:00**	under 4,00	22,7	**35:00**	under 4,40	25,1
	3,20-3,59	20,4		4,00-4,39	24,6		4,40-4,79	27,0
	3,60-3,99	22,4		4,40-4,79	26,6		4,80-5,19	29,1
	4,00-4,39	24,4		4,80-5,19	28,6		5,20-5,59	31,1
	4,40-4,79	26,4		5,20-5,59	30,6		5,60-5,99	33,1
	4,80-5,19	28,4		5,60-5,99	32,6		6,00-6,39	35,1
	5,20-5,59	30,4		6,00-6,39	34,6		6,40-6,79	37,1
	5,60-5,99	32,5		6,40-6,78	36,6		6,80-7,19	39,1
	6,00-6,38	34,5		over 6,78	38,6		7,20-7,59	41,1
	over 6,38	36,5					7,60-7,98	43,1
							over 7,98	45,1

Jogging

Time (min:sec)	Distance (km)	Heart Points	Time (min:sec)	Distance (km)	Heart Points	Time (min:sec)	Distance (km)	Heart Points
40:00	under 4,80	27,6	45:00	under 5,60	32,0	50:00	under 6,40	36,5
	4,80-5,59	31,5		5,60-6,39	35,9		6,40-7,19	40,4
	5,60-6,39	35,5		6,40-7,19	40,0		7,20-7,99	44,4
	6,40-7,19	39,5		7,20-7,99	44,0		8,00-8,79	48,4
	7,20-7,99	43,5		8,00-8,79	48,0		8,80-9,59	52,4
	8,00-8,79	47,5		8,80-9,59	52,0		9,60-10,39	56,4
	8,80-9,58	51,6		9,60-10,38	56,0		10,40-11,19	60,4
	Over 9,58	55,6		over 10,38	60,0		11,20-11,98	64,5
							over 11,98	68,5
55:00	under 7,20	40,9	60:00	under 7,20	41,3			
	7,20-7,99	44,8		7,20-7,99	45,3			
	8,00-8,79	48,9		8,00-8,79	49,3			
	8,80-9,59	52,9		8,80-9,59	53,3			
	9,60-10,39	56,9		9,60-10,39	57,3			
	10,40-11,19	60,9		10,40-11,19	61,3			
	11,20-11,99	64,9		11,20-11,99	65,3			
	12,00-12,78	68,9		12,00-12,79	69,3			
	over 12,78	72,9		12,80-13,59	73,4			
				13,60-14,38	77,4			
				over 14,38	81,4			

Stationary Cycling (Legs Only)

HEART POINTS

Time (min:sec)	Work Rate (watts)	under 45 kg	45 to 55 kg	56 to 67 kg	68 to 78 kg	79 to 89 kg	90 to 100 kg	101 to 112 kg	over 112 kg
5:00	under 25	1,7	1,4	1,2	1,1	1,0	0,9	0,9	0,8
	25-49	2,7	2,2	1,8	1,6	1,4	1,3	1,2	1,1
	50-74	3,8	3,0	2,5	2,1	1,9	1,7	1,6	1,5
	75-99	4,9	3,8	3,1	2,7	2,4	2,1	1,9	1,8
	100-124	6,0	4,6	3,8	3,2	2,8	2,5	2,3	2,1
	125-149	7,1	5,5	4,5	3,8	3,3	2,9	2,7	2,4
	150-174	8,2	6,3	5,1	4,3	3,8	3,4	3,0	2,8
	175-199	9,3	7,1	5,8	4,9	4,2	3,8	3,4	3,1
	200-224	10,4	7,9	6,4	5,4	4,7	4,2	3,8	3,4
	225-249	11,5	8,8	7,1	6,0	5,2	4,6	4,1	3,8
	over 249	12,6	9,6	7,8	6,5	5,7	5,0	4,5	4,1
7:30	under 25	2,5	2,0	1,8	1,6	1,5	1,4	1,3	1,2
	25-49	4,1	3,2	2,7	2,4	2,1	1,9	1,8	1,7
	50-74	5,8	4,5	3,7	3,2	2,8	2,6	2,4	2,2
	75-99	7,4	5,7	4,7	4,0	3,5	3,2	2,9	2,7
	100-124	9,1	7,0	5,7	4,9	4,3	3,8	3,5	3,2
	125-149	10,7	8,2	6,7	5,7	5,0	4,4	4,0	3,7
	150-174	12,4	9,4	7,7	6,5	5,7	5,0	4,6	4,2
	175-199	14,0	10,7	8,7	7,3	6,4	5,7	5,1	4,7
	200-224	15,7	11,9	9,7	8,2	7,1	6,3	5,7	5,2
	225-249	17,3	13,1	10,6	9,0	7,8	6,9	6,2	5,6
	over 249	19,0	14,4	11,6	9,8	8,5	7,5	6,8	6,1
10:00	under 25	3,4	2,7	2,4	2,1	1,9	1,8	1,7	1,6
	25-49	7,0	4,3	3,6	3,2	2,8	2,6	2,4	2,3
	50-74	7,7	6,0	4,9	4,3	3,8	3,4	3,1	2,9
	75-99	9,9	7,6	6,3	5,4	4,7	4,2	3,9	3,6
	100-124	12,1	9,3	7,6	6,5	5,7	5,1	4,6	4,2
	125-149	14,3	10,9	8,9	7,6	6,6	5,9	5,3	4,9
	150-174	16,5	12,6	10,2	8,7	7,6	6,7	6,1	5,6
	175-199	18,7	14,2	11,5	9,8	8,5	7,5	6,8	6,2
	200-224	20,9	15,9	12,9	10,9	9,4	8,4	7,5	6,9
	225-249	23,1	17,5	14,2	12,0	10,4	9,2	8,3	7,5
	over 249	25,3	19,2	15,5	13,1	11,3	10,0	9,0	8,2
12:30	under 25	4,2	3,4	3,0	2,6	2,4	2,3	2,1	2,0
	25-49	6,8	5,4	4,5	4,0	3,6	3,2	3,0	2,8
	50-74	9,6	7,5	6,2	5,3	4,7	4,3	3,9	3,6
	75-99	12,3	9,5	7,8	6,7	5,9	5,3	4,8	4,5
	100-124	15,1	11,6	9,5	8,1	7,1	6,3	5,8	5,3
	125-149	17,8	13,7	11,1	9,5	8,3	7,4	6,7	6,1
	150-174	20,6	15,7	12,8	10,8	9,4	8,4	7,6	6,9
	175-199	23,3	17,8	14,4	12,2	10,6	9,4	8,5	7,8
	200-224	26,1	19,8	16,1	13,6	11,8	10,5	9,4	8,6
	225-249	28,8	21,9	17,7	15,0	13,0	11,5	10,3	9,4
	over 249	31,6	24,0	19,4	16,3	14,2	12,5	11,3	10,2

ESTIMATING YOUR ENERGY EXPENDITURE DURING EXERCISE 381

Stationary Cycling (Legs Only)

HEART POINTS

Time (min:sec)	Work Rate (watts)	under 45 kg	45 to 55 kg	56 to 67 kg	68 to 78 kg	79 to 89 kg	90 to 100 kg	101 to 112 kg	over 112 kg
15:00	under 25	5,0	4,1	3,5	3,2	2,9	2,7	2,6	2,4
	25-49	8,2	6,5	5,4	4,8	4,3	3,9	3,6	3,4
	50-74	11,5	9,0	7,4	6,4	5,7	5,1	4,7	4,4
	75-99	14,8	11,4	9,4	8,1	7,1	6,4	5,8	5,4
	100-124	18,1	13,9	11,4	9,7	8,5	7,6	6,9	6,3
	125-149	21,4	16,4	13,4	11,4	9,9	8,8	8,0	7,3
	150-174	24,7	18,9	15,3	13,0	11,3	10,1	9,1	8,3
	175-199	28,0	21,3	17,3	14,7	12,7	11,3	10,2	9,3
	200-224	31,3	23,8	19,3	16,3	14,2	12,6	11,3	10,3
	225-249	34,6	26,3	21,3	18,0	15,6	13,8	12,4	11,3
	over 249	37,9	28,8	23,3	19,6	17,0	15,0	13,5	12,3
17:30	under 25	5,9	4,8	4,1	3,7	3,4	3,2	3,0	2,8
	25-49	9,6	7,6	6,4	5,6	5,0	4,5	4,2	3,9
	50-74	13,4	10,5	8,7	7,5	6,6	6,0	5,5	5,1
	75-99	17,3	13,3	11,0	9,4	8,3	7,4	6,8	6,3
	100-124	21,1	16,2	13,3	11,3	9,9	8,9	8,1	7,4
	125-149	25,0	19,1	15,6	13,3	11,6	10,3	9,3	8,6
	150-174	29,0	22,0	17,9	15,2	13,2	11,8	10,6	9,7
	175-199	32,7	24,9	20,2	17,1	14,9	13,2	11,9	10,9
	200-224	36,5	27,8	22,5	19,0	16,5	14,7	13,2	12,0
	225-249	40,4	30,7	24,8	21,0	18,2	16,1	14,5	13,2
	over 249	44,2	33,6	27,1	22,9	19,8	17,5	15,8	14,3
20:00	under 25	6,7	5,5	4,7	4,2	3,9	3,6	3,4	3,2
	25-49	11,0	8,6	7,3	6,3	5,7	5,2	4,8	4,5
	50-74	15,4	11,9	9,9	8,5	7,6	6,8	6,3	5,8
	75-99	19,8	15,2	12,5	10,7	9,5	8,5	7,7	7,1
	100-124	24,2	18,5	15,2	12,9	11,3	10,1	9,2	8,5
	125-149	28,6	21,8	17,8	15,1	13,2	11,8	10,7	9,8
	150-174	33,0	25,1	20,5	17,3	15,1	13,4	12,1	11,1
	175-199	37,4	28,4	23,1	19,5	17,0	15,1	13,6	12,4
	200-224	41,8	31,7	25,7	21,7	18,9	16,7	15,1	13,7
	225-249	46,2	35,0	28,4	23,9	20,8	18,4	16,5	15,1
	over 249	50,6	38,3	31,0	26,1	22,7	20,0	18,0	16,4
22:30	under 25	7,6	6,1	5,3	4,8	4,4	4,1	3,8	3,6
	25-49	12,3	9,7	8,2	7,1	6,4	5,8	5,4	5,1
	50-74	17,3	13,4	11,1	9,6	8,5	7,7	7,1	6,6
	75-99	22,2	17,1	14,1	12,1	10,6	9,6	8,7	8,0
	100-124	27,2	20,9	17,1	14,6	12,8	11,4	10,4	9,5
	125-149	32,1	24,6	20,1	17,0	14,9	13,3	12,0	11,0
	150-174	37,1	28,3	23,0	19,5	17,0	15,1	13,7	12,5
	175-199	42,0	32,0	26,0	22,0	19,1	17,0	15,3	14,0
	200-224	47,0	35,7	29,0	24,5	21,2	18,8	17,0	15,5
	225-249	51,9	39,4	31,9	26,9	23,4	20,7	18,6	17,0
	over 249	56,9	43,1	34,9	29,4	25,5	22,6	20,3	18,4

Stationary Cycling (Legs Only)

HEART POINTS

Time (min:sec)	Work Rate (watts)	under 45 kg	45 to 55 kg	56 to 67 kg	68 to 78 kg	79 to 89 kg	90 to 100 kg	101 to 112 kg	over 112 kg
25:00	under 25	8,4	6,8	5,9	5,3	4,8	4,5	4,3	4,0
	25-49	13,7	10,8	9,1	7,9	7,1	6,5	6,0	5,6
	50-74	19,2	14,9	12,4	10,7	9,5	8,6	7,8	7,3
	75-99	24,7	19,0	15,7	13,4	11,8	10,6	9,7	8,9
	100-124	30,2	23,2	19,0	16,2	14,2	12,7	11,5	10,6
	125-149	35,7	27,3	22,3	18,9	16,5	14,7	13,3	12,2
	150-174	41,2	31,4	25,6	21,7	18,9	16,8	15,2	13,9
	175-199	46,7	35,5	28,9	24,4	21,3	18,9	17,0	15,5
	200-224	52,2	39,7	32,2	27,2	23,6	20,9	18,8	17,2
	225-249	57,7	43,8	35,5	29,9	26,0	23,0	20,7	18,8
	over 249	63,2	47,9	38,8	32,7	28,3	25,1	22,5	20,5
27:30	under 25	9,3	7,5	6,5	5,8	5,3	5,0	4,7	4,4
	25-49	15,1	11,9	10,0	8,7	7,8	7,1	6,6	6,2
	50-74	21,1	16,4	13,6	11,7	10,4	9,4	8,6	8,0
	75-99	27,2	21,0	17,2	14,8	13,0	11,7	10,6	9,8
	100-124	33,2	25,5	20,9	17,8	15,6	13,9	12,7	11,6
	125-149	39,3	30,0	24,5	20,8	18,2	16,2	14,7	13,4
	150-174	45,3	34,6	28,1	23,8	20,8	18,5	16,7	15,3
	175-199	51,4	39,1	31,8	26,9	23,4	20,8	18,7	17,1
	200-224	57,4	43,6	35,4	29,9	26,0	23,0	20,7	18,9
	225-249	63,5	48,2	39,0	32,9	28,6	25,3	22,7	20,7
	over 249	69,5	52,7	42,7	35,9	31,2	27,6	24,8	22,5
30:00	under 25	10,1	8,2	7,1	6,3	5,8	5,4	5,1	4,9
	25-49	16,4	12,9	10,9	9,5	8,5	7,8	7,2	6,8
	50-74	23,0	17,9	14,8	12,8	11,4	10,2	9,4	8,7
	75-99	29,6	22,9	18,8	16,1	14,2	12,7	11,6	11,2
	100-124	36,2	27,8	22,8	19,4	17,0	15,2	13,8	12,7
	125-149	42,8	32,8	26,7	22,7	19,8	17,7	16,0	14,7
	150-174	49,4	37,7	30,7	26,0	22,7	20,2	18,2	16,7
	175-199	56,0	42,7	34,6	29,3	25,5	22,6	20,4	18,6
	200-224	62,6	47,6	38,6	32,6	28,3	25,1	22,6	20,6
	225-249	69,2	52,6	42,6	35,9	31,2	27,6	24,8	22,6
	over 249	75,8	57,5	46,5	39,2	34,0	30,1	27,0	24,6
35:00	under 25	11,8	9,6	8,3	7,4	6,8	6,3	6,0	5,7
	25-49	19,2	15,1	12,7	11,1	10,0	9,1	8,4	7,9
	50-74	26,9	20,9	17,3	14,9	13,3	12,0	11,0	10,2
	75-99	34,6	26,7	21,9	18,8	16,6	14,9	13,6	12,5
	100-124	42,3	32,4	26,6	22,6	19,9	17,7	16,1	14,8
	125-149	50,0	38,2	31,2	26,5	23,2	20,6	18,7	17,1
	150-174	57,7	44,0	35,8	30,3	26,5	23,5	21,3	19,4
	175-199	65,4	49,8	40,4	34,2	29,8	26,4	23,8	21,7
	200-224	73,1	55,5	45,0	38,0	30,1	29,3	26,4	24,1
	225-249	80,8	61,3	49,7	41,9	36,4	32,2	29,0	26,4
	over 249	88,5	67,1	54,3	45,7	39,7	35,1	31,5	28,7

ESTIMATING YOUR ENERGY EXPENDITURE DURING EXERCISE

Stationary Cycling (Legs Only)

HEART POINTS

Time (min:sec)	Work Rate (watts)	under 45 kg	45 to 55 kg	56 to 67 kg	68 to 78 kg	79 to 89 kg	90 to 100 kg	101 to 112 kg	over 112 kg
40:00	under 25	13,5	10,9	9,5	8,5	7,8	7,2	6,8	6,5
	25-49	21,9	17,3	14,5	12,7	11,4	10,4	9,6	9,0
	50-74	30,7	23,9	19,8	17,1	15,1	13,7	12,6	11,6
	75-99	39,5	30,5	25,1	21,5	18,9	17,0	15,5	14,3
	100-124	48,3	37,0	30,4	25,9	22,7	20,3	18,4	16,9
	125-149	57,1	43,7	35,6	30,3	26,5	23,6	21,4	19,6
	150-174	65,9	50,3	40,9	34,7	30,2	26,9	24,3	22,2
	175-199	74,7	56,9	46,2	39,1	34,0	30,2	27,2	24,8
	200-224	83,5	63,5	51,5	43,5	37,8	33,5	31,2	27,5
	225-249	92,3	70,1	56,8	47,9	41,5	36,8	33,1	30,1
	over 249	101,1	76,7	62,0	52,3	45,3	40,1	36,0	32,8
45:00	under 25	15,2	12,3	10,6	9,5	8,7	8,1	7,7	7,3
	25-49	24,7	19,4	16,3	14,3	12,8	11,7	10,8	10,1
	50-74	34,6	26,9	22,3	19,2	17,0	15,4	14,1	13,1
	75-99	44,5	34,3	28,2	24,2	21,3	19,1	17,4	16,1
	100-124	54,4	41,7	34,2	29,1	25,5	22,8	20,7	19,0
	125-149	64,3	49,1	40,1	34,1	29,8	26,5	24,0	22,0
	150-174	74,2	56,6	46,0	39,0	34,0	30,2	27,3	25,0
	175-199	84,1	64,0	52,0	44,0	38,2	34,0	30,6	28,0
	200-224	94,0	71,4	57,9	48,9	42,5	37,7	33,9	30,9
	225-249	104,0	78,8	63,9	53,9	46,7	41,4	37,2	33,9
	over 249	113,8	86,3	69,8	58,8	51,0	45,1	40,5	36,9
50:00	under 25	16,8	13,7	11,8	10,6	9,7	9,0	8,5	8,1
	25-49	27,4	21,6	18,2	15,9	14,2	13,0	12,0	11,3
	50-74	38,4	29,8	24,7	21,4	18,9	17,1	15,7	14,6
	75-99	49,4	38,1	31,3	26,9	23,6	22,2	19,4	17,9
	100-124	60,4	46,3	37,9	32,4	28,4	25,4	23,0	21,2
	125-149	71,4	54,6	44,5	37,9	33,1	29,5	26,7	24,5
	150-174	82,4	62,8	51,1	43,4	37,8	33,6	30,4	27,8
	175-199	93,4	71,1	57,7	48,9	42,5	37,7	34,0	31,1
	200-224	104,4	79,3	64,3	54,4	47,2	41,9	37,7	34,4
	225-249	115,4	87,6	70,9	59,9	51,9	46,0	41,4	37,7
	over 249	126,4	95,8	77,5	65,4	56,6	50,1	45,0	41,0
55:00	under 25	18,5	15,0	13,0	11,6	10,7	9,9	9,4	8,9
	25-49	30,1	23,7	19,9	17,4	15,6	14,3	13,2	12,4
	50-74	42,2	32,8	27,2	23,5	20,8	18,8	17,3	16,0
	75-99	54,3	41,9	34,5	29,5	26,0	23,4	21,3	19,6
	100-124	66,4	51,0	41,7	35,6	31,2	27,9	25,3	23,3
	125-149	78,5	60,0	49,0	41,6	36,4	32,4	29,4	26,9
	150-174	90,6	69,1	56,3	47,7	41,6	37,0	33,4	30,5
	175-199	102,7	78,2	63,5	53,7	46,7	41,5	37,4	34,2
	200-224	114,8	87,3	70,8	59,8	52,0	46,1	41,5	37,8
	225-249	126,9	96,3	78,0	65,8	57,1	50,6	45,5	41,4
	over 249	139,0	105,4	85,3	71,9	62,3	55,1	49,5	45,1

Stationary Cycling (Legs Only)

HEART POINTS

Time (min:sec)	Work Rate (watts)	under 45 kg	45 to 55 kg	56 to 67 kg	68 to 78 kg	79 to 89 kg	90 to 100 kg	101 to 112 kg	over 112 kg
60:00	under 25	20,2	16,4	14,2	12,7	11,6	10,8	10,2	9,7
	25-49	32,9	26,0	21,8	19,0	17,0	15,6	14,4	13,5
	50-74	46,1	35,8	29,7	25,6	22,7	20,5	18,8	17,5
	75-99	59,3	45,7	37,6	32,2	28,4	25,5	23,2	21,4
	100-124	72,5	55,6	45,6	38,8	34,0	30,4	27,6	25,4
	125-149	85,7	65,5	53,5	45,4	39,7	35,4	32,0	29,4
	150-174	98,9	75,4	61,4	52,0	45,3	40,3	36,4	33,3
	175-199	112,1	85,3	69,3	58,6	51,0	45,3	40,8	37,3
	200-224	125,3	95,2	77,2	65,2	56,7	50,2	45,2	41,2
	225-249	138,5	105,1	85,1	71,8	62,3	55,1	49,6	45,2
	over 249	151,7	115,0	93,1	78,4	68,0	60,1	54,0	49,2

SCHWINN AIR-DYNE

HEART POINTS

Time (min:sec)	Work Load	under 45 kg	45 to 55 kg	56 to 67 kg	68 to 78 kg	79 to 89 kg	90 to 100 kg	101 to 112 kg	over 112 kg
5:00	under 0,5	1,7	1,4	1,2	1,1	1,0	0,9	0,9	0,8
	0,5-0,9	2,6	2,0	1,7	1,5	1,3	1,2	1,1	1,1
	1,0-1,4	3,7	2,8	2,4	2,0	1,8	1,6	1,5	1,4
	1,5-1,9	4,8	3,7	3,0	2,6	2,3	2,1	1,9	1,7
	2,0-2,4	5,9	4,5	3,7	3,1	2,8	2,5	2,2	2,1
	2,5-2,9	7,0	5,3	4,3	3,7	3,2	2,9	2,6	2,4
	3,0-3,4	8,1	6,1	5,0	4,2	3,7	3,3	3,0	2,7
	3,5-3,9	9,2	7,0	5,7	4,8	4,2	3,7	3,3	3,1
	4,0-4,4	10,3	7,8	6,3	5,3	4,6	4,1	3,7	3,4
	4,5-4,9	11,4	8,6	7,0	5,9	5,1	4,5	4,1	3,7
	over 4,9	12,5	9,4	7,6	6,4	5,6	4,9	4,4	4,0
7:30	under 0,5	2,5	2,0	1,8	1,6	1,5	1,4	1,3	1,2
	0,5-0,9	3,8	3,0	2,6	2,2	2,0	1,8	1,7	1,6
	1,0-1,4	5,5	4,3	3,6	3,1	2,7	2,5	2,3	2,1
	1,5-1,9	7,1	5,5	4,5	3,9	3,4	3,1	2,8	2,6
	2,0-2,4	8,8	6,8	5,5	4,7	4,1	3,7	3,4	3,1
	2,5-2,9	10,4	8,0	6,5	5,5	4,8	4,3	3,9	3,6
	3,0-3,4	12,1	9,2	7,5	6,4	5,6	4,9	4,5	4,1
	3,5-3,9	13,7	10,5	8,5	7,2	6,3	5,6	5,0	4,6
	4,0-4,4	15,4	11,7	9,5	8,0	7,0	6,2	5,6	5,1
	4,5-4,9	17,0	12,9	10,5	8,8	7,7	6,8	6,1	5,6
	over 4,9	18,7	14,2	11,5	9,7	8,4	7,4	6,7	6,1
10:00	under 0,5	3,4	2,7	2,4	2,1	1,9	1,8	1,7	1,6
	0,5-0,9	5,1	4,1	3,4	3,0	2,7	2,5	2,3	2,1
	1,0-1,4	7,3	5,7	4,7	4,1	3,6	3,3	3,0	2,8
	1,5-1,9	9,5	7,4	6,1	5,2	4,6	4,1	3,8	3,5
	2,0-2,4	11,7	9,0	7,4	6,3	5,5	4,9	4,5	4,1
	2,5-2,9	13,9	10,7	8,7	7,4	6,5	5,8	5,2	4,8
	3,0-3,4	16,1	12,3	10,0	8,5	7,4	6,6	6,0	5,4
	3,5-3,9	18,3	14,0	11,3	9,6	8,3	7,4	6,7	6,1
	4,0-4,4	20,5	15,6	12,7	10,7	9,3	8,2	7,4	6,8
	4,5-4,9	22,7	17,3	14,0	11,8	10,2	9,1	8,2	7,4
	over 4,9	24,9	18,9	15,3	12,9	11,1	9,9	8,9	8,1
12:30	under 0,5	4,2	3,4	3,0	2,6	2,4	2,3	2,1	2,0
	0,5-0,9	6,4	5,1	4,3	3,7	3,4	3,1	2,9	2,7
	1,0-1,4	9,2	7,1	5,9	5,1	4,5	4,1	3,8	3,5
	1,5-1,9	11,9	9,2	7,6	6,5	5,7	5,1	4,7	4,3
	2,0-2,4	14,7	11,3	9,2	7,9	6,9	6,2	5,6	5,1
	2,5-2,9	17,4	13,3	10,9	9,2	8,1	7,2	6,5	6,0
	3,0-3,4	20,1	15,4	12,5	10,6	9,3	8,2	7,4	6,8
	3,5-3,9	22,9	17,4	14,2	12,0	10,4	9,3	8,4	7,6
	4,0-4,4	25,7	19,5	15,8	13,4	11,6	9,8	9,3	8,5
	4,5-4,9	28,4	21,6	17,5	14,7	12,8	11,3	10,2	9,3
	over 4,9	31,1	23,6	19,1	16,1	14,0	12,4	11,1	10,1

SCHWINN AIR-DYNE

HEART POINTS

Time (min:sec)	Work Load	under 45 kg	45 to 55 kg	56 to 67 kg	68 to 78 kg	79 to 89 kg	90 to 100 kg	101 to 112 kg	over 112 kg
15:00	under 0,5	5,0	4,1	3,5	3,2	2,9	2,7	2,6	2,4
	0,5-0,9	7,7	6,1	5,1	4,5	4,0	3,7	3,4	3,2
	1,0-1,4	11,0	8,6	7,1	6,1	5,4	4,9	4,5	4,2
	1,5-1,9	14,3	11,0	9,1	7,8	6,9	6,2	5,6	5,2
	2,0-2,4	17,6	13,5	11,1	9,4	8,3	7,4	6,7	6,2
	2,5-2,9	20,9	16,0	13,1	11,1	9,7	8,6	7,8	7,2
	3,0-3,4	24,2	18,5	15,0	12,7	11,1	9,9	8,9	8,2
	3,5-3,9	27,5	20,9	17,0	14,4	12,5	11,1	10,0	9,2
	4,0-4,4	30,8	23,4	19,0	16,0	13,9	12,4	11,1	10,2
	4,5-4,9	34,1	25,9	21,0	17,7	15,3	13,6	12,2	11,1
	over 4,9	37,4	28,4	23,0	19,3	16,8	14,8	13,3	12,1
17:30	under 0,5	5,9	4,8	4,1	3,7	3,4	3,2	3,0	2,8
	0,5-0,9	9,0	7,1	6,0	5,2	4,7	4,3	4,0	3,7
	1,0-1,4	12,8	10,0	8,3	7,2	6,4	5,8	5,3	4,9
	1,5-1,9	16,7	12,9	10,6	9,1	8,0	7,2	6,6	6,1
	2,0-2,4	20,5	15,8	12,9	11,0	9,7	8,6	7,9	7,2
	2,5-2,9	24,4	18,6	15,2	12,9	11,3	10,1	9,1	8,4
	3,0-3,4	28,2	21,5	17,5	14,9	13,0	11,5	10,4	9,5
	3,5-3,9	32,1	24,4	19,8	16,8	14,6	13,0	11,7	10,7
	4,0-4,4	34,9	27,3	22,1	18,7	16,3	14,4	13,0	11,8
	4,5-4,9	39,8	30,2	24,5	20,6	17,9	15,9	14,3	13,0
	over 4,9	43,6	33,1	26,8	22,6	19,6	17,3	15,6	14,2
20:00	under 0,5	6,7	5,5	4,7	4,2	3,9	3,6	3,4	3,2
	0,5-0,9	10,3	8,1	6,8	6,0	5,4	4,9	4,6	4,3
	1,0-1,4	14,7	11,4	9,5	8,2	7,3	6,6	6,0	5,6
	1,5-1,9	19,1	14,7	12,1	10,4	9,2	8,2	7,5	6,9
	2,0-2,4	23,5	18,0	14,8	12,6	11,0	9,9	9,0	8,3
	2,5-2,9	27,9	21,3	17,4	14,8	12,9	11,5	10,4	9,6
	3,0-3,4	32,3	24,6	20,0	17,0	14,8	13,2	11,9	10,9
	3,5-3,9	37,7	27,9	22,7	19,2	16,7	14,8	13,4	12,2
	4,0-4,4	41,1	31,2	25,3	21,4	18,6	16,5	14,8	13,5
	4,5-4,9	45,5	34,5	27,9	23,6	20,5	18,1	16,3	14,9
	over 4,9	49,9	37,8	30,6	25,8	22,4	19,8	17,8	16,2
22:30	under 0,5	7,6	6,2	5,3	4,8	4,4	4,1	3,8	3,6
	0,5-0,9	11,5	9,1	7,7	6,7	6,1	5,5	5,1	4,8
	1,0-1,4	16,5	12,8	10,7	9,2	8,2	7,4	6,8	6,3
	1,5-1,9	21,4	16,5	13,6	11,7	10,3	9,3	8,4	7,8
	2,0-2,4	26,4	20,3	16,6	14,2	12,4	11,1	10,1	9,3
	2,5-2,9	31,3	24,0	19,6	16,6	14,5	13,0	11,7	10,8
	3,0-3,4	32,3	27,7	22,5	19,1	16,7	14,8	13,4	12,3
	3,5-3,9	41,2	31,4	25,5	21,6	18,8	16,7	15,0	13,7
	4,0-4,4	46,2	35,1	28,5	24,1	20,9	18,5	16,7	15,2
	4,5-4,9	51,1	38,8	31,5	26,5	23,0	20,4	18,3	16,7
	over 4,9	56,1	42,5	34,4	29,0	25,1	22,3	20,0	18,2

SCHWINN AIR-DYNE

HEART POINTS

Time (min:sec)	Work Load	under 45 kg	45 to 55 kg	56 to 67 kg	68 to 78 kg	79 to 89 kg	90 to 100 kg	101 to 112 kg	over 112 kg
25:00	under 0,5	8,4	6,8	5,9	5,3	4,8	4,5	4,3	4,0
	0,5-0,9	12,8	10,1	8,5	7,5	6,7	6,2	5,7	5,4
	1,0-1,4	18,3	14,3	11,8	10,2	9,1	8,2	7,6	7,0
	1,5-1,9	23,8	18,4	15,1	13,0	11,4	10,3	9,4	8,7
	2,0-2,4	29,3	22,5	18,4	15,7	13,8	12,3	11,2	10,3
	2,5-2,9	34,8	26,6	21,7	18,5	16,2	14,4	13,1	12,0
	3,0-3,4	40,3	30,8	25,0	21,2	18,5	16,5	14,9	13,6
	3,5-3,9	45,8	34,9	28,3	24,0	20,9	18,5	16,7	15,3
	4,0-4,4	51,3	39,0	31,6	26,7	23,2	20,6	18,6	16,9
	4,5-4,9	56,8	43,1	34,9	29,5	25,6	22,7	20,4	18,6
	over 4,9	62,3	47,3	38,2	32,2	27,9	24,7	22,2	20,2
27:30	under 0,5	9,3	7,5	6,5	5,8	5,3	5,0	4,7	4,5
	0,5-0,9	14,1	11,6	9,4	8,2	7,4	6,8	6,3	5,9
	1,0-1,4	20,2	15,7	13,0	11,3	10,0	9,0	8,3	7,7
	1,5-1,9	26,2	20,2	16,7	14,3	12,6	11,3	10,3	9,5
	2,0-2,4	32,3	24,8	20,3	17,3	15,2	13,6	12,3	11,3
	2,5-2,9	38,3	29,3	23,9	20,3	17,8	15,9	14,4	13,2
	3,0-3,4	44,4	33,8	27,6	23,4	20,4	18,1	16,4	15,0
	3,5-3,9	50,4	38,4	31,2	26,4	23,0	20,4	18,4	16,8
	4,0-4,4	56,5	42,9	34,8	29,4	25,6	22,7	20,4	18,6
	4,5-4,9	62,5	47,5	38,4	32,4	28,1	24,9	22,4	20,4
	over 4,9	68,6	52,0	42,1	35,5	30,7	27,2	24,4	22,2
30:00	under 0,5	10,1	8,2	7,1	6,3	5,8	5,4	5,1	4,9
	0,5-0,9	15,4	12,2	10,3	9,0	8,1	7,4	6,9	6,4
	1,0-1,4	22,0	17,1	14,2	12,3	10,9	9,9	9,1	8,4
	1,5-1,9	28,6	22,1	18,2	15,6	13,7	12,3	11,3	10,4
	2,0-2,4	35,2	27,0	22,1	18,9	16,6	14,8	13,5	12,4
	2,5-2,9	41,8	32,0	26,1	22,2	19,4	17,3	16,6	14,4
	3,0-3,4	48,4	36,9	30,1	25,5	22,2	19,8	17,9	16,4
	3,5-3,9	55,0	41,9	34,0	28,8	25,0	22,2	20,1	18,3
	4,0-4,4	61,6	46,8	38,0	32,1	27,9	24,7	22,3	20,3
	4,5-4,9	68,2	51,8	41,0	35,4	30,7	27,2	24,5	22,2
	over 4,9	74,8	56,7	45,9	38,7	33,5	29,7	26,7	24,2
35:00	under 0,5	11,8	9,6	8,3	7,4	6,8	6,3	6,0	5,7
	0,5-0,9	17,9	14,2	12,0	10,5	9,4	8,6	8,0	7,5
	1,0-1,4	25,6	20,0	16,6	14,3	12,7	11,5	10,6	9,8
	1,5-1,9	33,3	25,7	21,2	18,2	16,2	14,4	13,2	12,1
	2,0-2,4	41,0	31,5	26,0	22,0	19,3	17,3	15,7	14,4
	2,5-2,9	48,7	37,3	30,4	25,9	22,6	20,2	18,3	16,8
	3,0-3,4	56,4	43,1	35,1	29,7	25,9	23,1	20,8	19,1
	3,5-3,9	64,1	48,8	39,7	33,6	29,2	25,9	23,4	21,4
	4,0-4,4	71,8	54,6	44,3	37,4	32,5	28,8	26,0	23,7
	4,5-4,9	79,5	60,4	48,9	41,3	35,8	31,7	28,5	26,0
	over 4,9	87,2	66,2	53,5	45,1	39,1	34,6	30,6	28,3

SCHWINN AIR-DYNE

HEART POINTS

Time (min:sec)	Work Load	under 45 kg	45 to 55 kg	56 to 67 kg	68 to 78 kg	79 to 89 kg	90 to 100 kg	101 to 112 kg	over 112 kg
40:00	under 0,5	13,5	10,9	9,5	8,5	7,8	7,2	6,8	6,5
	0,5-0,9	20,5	16,2	13,7	12,0	10,8	9,9	9,2	8,6
	1,0-1,4	29,3	22,8	19,0	16,4	14,5	13,2	12,1	11,2
	1,5-1,9	38,1	29,4	24,2	20,8	18,3	16,5	15,0	13,9
	2,0-2,4	46,9	36,0	29,5	25,2	22,1	19,8	18,0	16,5
	2,5-2,9	55,7	42,6	34,8	29,6	25,9	23,0	20,9	19,1
	3,0-3,4	64,5	49,2	40,0	34,0	29,6	26,4	23,8	21,8
	3,5-3,9	73,3	55,8	45,4	38,4	33,4	29,7	26,8	24,4
	4,0-4,4	82,1	62,4	50,6	42,8	37,2	33,0	29,7	27,1
	4,5-4,9	90,9	69,0	55,9	47,2	40,9	36,3	32,6	29,7
	over 4,9	99,7	75,6	61,2	51,6	44,7	39,6	35,6	32,3
45:00	under 0,5	15,2	12,3	10,6	9,5	8,7	8,1	7,7	7,3
	0,5-0,9	23,1	18,2	15,4	13,5	12,1	11,1	10,3	9,7
	1,0-1,4	33,0	25,7	21,3	18,4	16,4	14,8	13,6	12,6
	1,5-1,9	42,9	33,1	27,3	23,4	20,6	18,5	16,9	15,6
	2,0-2,4	52,7	40,5	33,2	28,3	24,8	22,2	20,2	18,6
	2,5-2,9	62,7	47,9	39,2	33,3	29,1	25,9	23,5	21,5
	3,0-3,4	72,6	55,4	45,1	38,2	33,3	29,7	26,8	24,5
	3,5-3,9	82,5	62,8	51,0	43,2	37,6	33,4	30,1	27,5
	4,0-4,4	92,4	70,2	57,0	48,1	41,8	37,1	33,4	30,4
	4,5-4,9	102,3	77,6	62,9	53,1	46,1	40,8	36,7	33,4
	over 4,9	112,2	85,1	68,8	58,0	50,3	44,5	40,0	36,4
50:00	under 0,5	16,8	13,7	11,8	10,6	9,7	9,2	8,5	8,1
	0,5-0,9	25,6	20,3	17,1	15,0	13,5	12,3	11,4	10,7
	1,0-1,4	36,6	28,5	23,7	20,5	18,2	16,4	15,1	14,0
	1,5-1,9	47,6	36,8	30,3	26,0	22,9	20,6	18,8	17,3
	2,0-2,4	58,6	45,0	36,7	31,5	27,6	24,7	22,4	20,6
	2,5-2,9	69,6	53,2	43,5	37,0	32,3	28,8	26,1	23,9
	3,0-3,4	80,6	61,5	50,1	42,5	37,0	32,9	29,8	27,2
	3,5-3,9	91,6	69,8	56,7	48,0	41,7	37,1	33,4	30,5
	4,0-4,4	102,6	78,0	63,3	53,5	46,5	41,2	37,1	33,8
	4,5-4,9	113,6	86,3	69,9	58,0	51,2	45,3	40,8	37,1
	over 4,9	124,6	94,5	76,5	64,5	55,9	49,4	44,4	40,4
55:00	under 0,5	18,5	15,0	13,0	11,6	10,7	9,9	9,4	8,9
	0,5-0,9	28,2	22,3	18,8	16,5	14,8	13,6	12,6	11,8
	1,0-1,4	40,3	31,4	26,1	22,5	20,0	18,1	16,6	15,4
	1,5-1,9	52,4	40,4	33,3	28,6	25,2	22,6	20,7	19,1
	2,0-2,4	64,5	49,5	40,6	34,6	30,4	27,2	24,7	22,7
	2,5-2,9	76,6	58,6	47,8	40,7	35,5	31,7	28,7	26,3
	3,0-3,4	88,7	67,7	55,1	46,7	40,7	36,2	32,8	30,0
	3,5-3,9	100,8	76,7	62,4	52,6	45,9	40,8	36,8	33,6
	4,0-4,4	112,9	85,8	69,6	58,8	51,1	45,3	40,8	37,2
	4,5-4,9	125,0	94,9	76,9	64,9	56,3	49,8	44,9	40,8
	over 4,9	137,1	104,0	84,1	70,9	61,5	54,4	48,9	44,5

SCHWINN AIR-DYNE

HEART POINTS

Time (min:sec)	Work Load	under 45 kg	45 to 55 kg	56 to 67 kg	68 to 78 kg	79 to 89 kg	90 to 100 kg	101 to 112 kg	over 112 kg
60:00	under 0,5	20,2	16,4	14,2	12,7	11,6	10,8	10,2	9,7
	0,5-0,9	30,8	24,3	20,5	18,0	16,1	14,8	13,7	12,9
	1,0-1,4	43,9	34,2	28,4	24,6	21,8	19,7	18,1	16,8
	1,5-1,9	57,2	44,1	36,4	31,2	27,5	24,7	22,5	20,8
	2,0-2,4	70,3	54,0	44,3	37,8	33,1	29,6	26,9	24,8
	2,5-2,9	83,6	63,9	52,2	44,4	38,8	34,6	31,3	28,7
	3,0-3,4	96,8	73,8	60,1	51,0	44,4	39,5	35,7	32,7
	3,5-3,9	109,9	83,7	68,0	57,6	50,1	44,5	40,1	36,6
	4,0-4,4	123,2	93,6	75,9	64,2	55,7	49,4	44,5	40,6
	4,5-4,9	136,4	103,5	83,9	70,8	61,4	54,4	48,9	44,6
	over 4,9	149,6	113,4	91,8	77,4	67,1	59,3	53,3	48,5

Other Activities

Time (min:sec)	METs	Heart Points	Time (min:sec)	METs	Heart Points	Time (min:sec)	METs	Heart Points
5:00	under 2,0	0,8	**7:30**	under 2,0	1,3	**10:00**	under 2,0	1,7
	2,0-2,9	1,2		2,0-2,9	1,8		2,0-2,9	2,4
	3,0-3,9	1,6		3,0-3,9	2,4		3,0-3,9	3,2
	4,0-4,9	2,0		4,0-4,9	3,1		4,0-4,9	4,1
	5,0-5,9	2,4		5,0-5,9	3,7		5,0-5,9	4,9
	6,0-6,9	2,9		6,0-6,9	4,3		6,0-6,9	5,8
	7,0-7,9	3,3		7,0-7,9	4,9		7,0-7,9	6,6
	8,0-8,9	3,7		8,0-8,9	5,6		8,0-8,9	7,4
	9,0-9,9	4,1		9,0-9,9	6,2		9,0-9,9	8,3
	10,0-10,9	4,5		10,0-10,9	6,8		10,0-10,9	9,1
	over 10,9	5,0		over 10,9	7,4		over 10,9	9,9
12:30	under 2,0	2,1	**15:00**	under 2,0	2,5	**17:30**	under 2,0	2,9
	2,0-2,9	3,0		2,0-2,9	3,6		2,0-2,9	4,2
	3,0-3,9	4,1		3,0-3,9	4,9		3,0-3,9	5,7
	4,0-4,9	5,1		4,0-4,9	6,1		4,0-4,9	7,2
	5,0-5,9	6,1		5,0-5,9	7,4		5,0-5,9	8,6
	6,0-6,9	7,2		6,0-6,9	8,6		6,0-6,9	10,1
	7,0-7,9	8,2		7,0-7,9	9,9		7,0-7,9	11,5
	8,0-8,9	9,3		8,0-8,9	11,1		8,0-8,9	13,0
	9,0-9,9	10,3		9,0-9,9	12,4		9,0-9,9	14,4
	10,0-10,9	11,4		10,0-10,9	13,6		10,0-10,9	15,9
	over 10,9	12,4		over 10,9	14,9		over 10,9	17,4
20:00	under 2,0	3,3	**22:30**	under 2,0	3,8	**25:00**	under 2,0	4,2
	2,0-2,9	4,8		2,0-2,9	5,4		2,0-2,9	6,0
	3,0-3,9	6,5		3,0-3,9	7,3		3,0-3,9	8,1
	4,0-4,9	8,2		4,0-4,9	9,2		4,0-4,9	10,2
	5,0-5,9	9,8		5,0-5,9	11,1		5,0-5,9	12,3
	6,0-6,9	11,5		6,0-6,9	12,9		6,0-6,9	14,4
	7,0-7,9	13,2		7,0-7,9	14,8		7,0-7,9	16,5
	8,0-8,9	14,8		8,0-8,9	16,7		8,0-8,9	18,5
	9,0-9,9	16,5		9,0-9,9	18,6		9,0-9,9	20,6
	10,0-10,9	18,2		10,0-10,9	20,4		10,0-10,9	22,7
	over 10,9	19,8		over 10,9	22,3		over 10,9	24,8

Other Activities

Time (min:sec)	METs	Heart Points	Time (min:sec)	METs	Heart Points	Time (min:sec)	METs	Heart Points
27:30	under 2,0	4,6	**30:00**	under 2,0	5,0	**35:00**	under 2,0	5,8
	2,0-2,9	6,6		2,0-2,9	7,2		2,0-2,9	8,5
	3,0-3,9	8,9		3,0-3,9	9,7		3,0-3,9	11,4
	4,0-4,9	11,2		4,0-4,9	12,3		4,0-4,9	14,3
	5,0-5,9	13,5		5,0-5,9	14,8		5,0-5,9	17,2
	6,0-6,9	15,8		6,0-6,9	17,3		6,0-6,9	20,1
	7,0-7,9	18,1		7,0-7,9	19,7		7,0-7,9	23,0
	8,0-8,9	20,4		8,0-8,9	22,3		8,0-8,9	26,0
	9,0-9,9	22,7		9,0-9,9	24,8		9,0-9,9	28,9
	10,0-10,9	25,0		10,0-10,9	27,2		10,0-10,9	31,8
	over 10,9	27,3		over 10,9	29,8		over 10,9	34,7
40:00	under 2,0	6,7	**45:00**	under 2,0	7,5	**50:00**	under 2,0	8,3
	2,0-2,9	9,7		2,0-2,9	10,9		2,0-2,9	12,1
	3,0-3,9	13,0		3,0-3,9	14,6		3,0-3,9	16,2
	4,0-4,9	16,3		4,0-4,9	18,4		4,0-4,9	20,4
	5,0-5,9	19,7		5,0-5,9	22,1		5,0-5,9	24,6
	6,0-6,9	23,0		6,0-6,9	25,9		6,0-6,9	28,8
	7,0-7,9	26,3		7,0-7,9	29,6		7,0-7,9	32,9
	8,0-8,9	29,7		8,0-8,9	33,4		8,0-8,9	37,1
	9,0-9,9	33,0		9,0-9,9	37,1		9,0-9,9	41,3
	10,0-10,9	36,3		10,0-10,9	40,9		10,0-10,9	45,4
	over 10,9	39,7		over 10,9	44,6		over 10,9	49,6
55:00	under 2,0	9,2	**60:00**	under 2,0	10,0			
	2,0-2,9	13,3		2,0-2,9	14,5			
	3,0-3,9	17,9		3,0-3,9	19,5			
	4,0-4,9	22,5		4,0-4,9	24,5			
	5,0-5,9	27,0		5,0-5,9	29,5			
	6,0-6,9	31,6		6,0-6,9	34,5			
	7,0-7,9	36,2		7,0-7,9	39,5			
	8,0-8,9	40,8		8,0-8,9	44,5			
	9,0-9,9	45,4		9,0-9,9	49,5			
	10,0-10,9	50,0		10,0-10,9	54,5			
	over 10,9	54,5		over 10,9	59,5			

WALKING
ENERGY EXPENDITURE FORMULA*

in pounds and miles:

$$\left[\left(\frac{160{,}8 \times \text{distance in miles}}{\text{duration in minutes}}\right) + 3{,}5\right] \times \frac{\text{mass in pounds} \times \text{duration in minutes} \times 4{,}2}{440} = \text{kilojoule expenditure (kJ)}$$

Example: A person who has a mass of 165 pounds and walks 3 miles in 45 minutes has an energy expenditure of 1008 kJ.

in kilograms and kilometres:

$$\left[\left(\frac{100 \times \text{distance in kilometres}}{\text{duration in minutes}}\right) + 3{,}5\right] \times \frac{\text{mass in kilograms} \times \text{duration in minutes} \times 4{,}2}{200} = \text{kilojoule expenditure (kJ)}$$

Example: A person who has a mass of 75 kilograms and walks 5 kilometres in 45 minutes has an energy expenditure of 1036 kJ.

*At fast speeds, the energy expenditure for walking approaches that for jogging. Therefore, for speeds of 4 mph (or 6,4 km/h) or faster, we recommend that you use our jogging formulas to calculate your energy expenditure.

TREADMILL WALKING ENERGY EXPENDITURE FORMULA*

in pounds and miles:

$$\left[\left\{\left[0{,}1 + \left(1{,}8 \times \frac{\%\ incline}{100}\right)\right] \times 26{,}8 \times speed\ in\ mph\right\} + 3{,}5\right] \times \frac{mass\ in\ pounds}{2{,}2} \times duration\ in\ minutes \times 0{,}021$$
$$=\ kilojoule\ expenditure\ (kJ)$$

Example: A person who has a mass of 165 pounds and walks 4 mph for 30 minutes at a 5% elevation (or incline) has an energy expenditure of 1128 kJ.

in kilograms and kilometres:

$$\left[\left\{\left[0{,}1 + \left(1{,}8 \times \frac{\%\ incline}{100}\right)\right] \times 16{,}67 \times speed\ in\ km/h\right\} + 3{,}5\right] \times mass\ in\ kilograms \times duration\ in\ minutes \times 0{,}021$$
$$=\ kilojoule\ expenditure\ (kJ)$$

Example: A person who has a mass of 75 kilograms and walks 6 km/h for 30 minutes at a 5% elevation (or incline) has an energy expenditure of 1063 kJ.

*At fast speeds, the energy expenditure for walking approaches that for jogging. Therefore, for speeds of 4 mph (or 6,4 km/h) or faster, we recommend that you use our jogging formulas to calculate your energy expenditure.

JOGGING
ENERGY EXPENDITURE FORMULA

in pounds and miles:

$$\left[\left(\frac{321{,}6 \times \text{distance in miles}}{\text{duration in minutes}}\right) + 3{,}5\right] \times \frac{\text{mass in pounds} \times \text{duration in minutes} \times 4{,}2}{440} = \text{kilojoule expenditure (kJ)}$$

Example: A person who has a mass of 165 pounds and jogs 2 miles in 20 minutes has an energy expenditure of 1123 kJ.

in kilograms and kilometres:

$$\left[\left(\frac{200 \times \text{distance in kilometres}}{\text{duration in minutes}}\right) + 3{,}5\right] \times \frac{\text{mass in kilograms} \times \text{duration in minutes} \times 4{,}2}{200} = \text{kilojoule expenditure (kJ)}$$

Example: A person who has a mass of 75 kilograms and jogs 3 kilometres in 18 minutes has an energy expenditure of 1044 kJ.

TREADMILL JOGGING ENERGY EXPENDITURE FORMULA

in pounds and miles:

$$\left[\left\{\left[0{,}2 + \left(0{,}9 \times \frac{\% \text{ incline}}{100}\right)\right] \times 26{,}8 \times \text{speed in mph}\right\} + 3{,}5\right] \times \frac{\text{mass in pounds}}{2{,}2} \times \text{duration in minutes} \times 0{,}021$$
$$= \text{kilojoule expenditure (kJ)}$$

Example: A person who weighs 165 pounds and jogs at 5 mph for 20 minutes at a 5% elevation (or incline) has an energy expenditure of 1144 kJ.

in kilograms and kilometres:

$$\left[\left\{\left[0{,}2 + \left(0{,}9 \times \frac{\% \text{ incline}}{100}\right)\right] \times 16{,}67 \times \text{speed in km/h}\right\} + 3{,}5\right] \times \text{mass in kilograms} \times \text{duration in minutes} \times 0{,}021$$
$$= \text{kilojoule expenditure (kJ)}$$

Example: A person who weighs 75 kilograms and jogs at 8 km/h for 20 minutes at an elevation (or incline) of 5% has an energy expenditure of 1139 kJ.

STATIONARY CYCLING (LEGS ONLY) ENERGY EXPENDITURE FORMULA

in pounds:

$$\left[\left(12 \times \text{work rate in watts*}\right) + \left(1{,}59 \times \text{mass in pounds}\right)\right] \times \text{duration in minutes} \times 0{,}021 = \text{kilojoule expenditure (kJ)}$$

Example: A person who has a mass of 165 pounds and cycles for 30 minutes at a work rate of 120 watts has an energy expenditure of 1072 kJ.

in kilograms:

$$\left[\left(12 \times \text{work rate in watts*}\right) + \left(3{,}5 \times \text{mass in kilograms}\right)\right] \times \text{duration in minutes} \times 0{,}021 = \text{kilojoule expenditure (kJ)}$$

Example: A person who has a mass of 75 kilograms and cycles for 30 minutes at a work rate of 120 watts has an energy expenditure of 1073 kJ.

*For the Monarch cycle ergometer, work rate in watts = revolutions per minute × work load in kilograms. For the Tunturi cycle ergometer, work rate in watts = revolutions per minute × work load in kilograms × 0,5.

SCHWINN AIR-DYNE
ENERGY EXPENDITURE FORMULA

in pounds:

$$\left[\left(600 \times \text{work load}\right) + \left(1{,}59 \times \text{mass in pounds}\right)\right] \times \text{duration in minutes} \times 0{,}021 = \text{kilojoule expenditure (kJ)}$$

Example: A person who has a mass of 165 pounds and cycles for 40 minutes at a work load of 2 has an energy expenditure of 1228 kJ.

in kilograms:

$$\left[\left(600 \times \text{work load}\right) + \left(3{,}5 \times \text{mass in kilograms}\right)\right] \times \text{duration in minutes} \times 0{,}021 = \text{kilojoule expenditure (kJ)}$$

Example: A person who has a mass of 75 kilograms and cycles for 40 minutes at a work load of 2 has an energy expenditure of 1229 kJ.

ARM-CYCLE ERGOMETRY
ENERGY EXPENDITURE FORMULA

in pounds:

$$[(18 \times \text{work rate in watts}) + (1,59 \times \text{mass in pounds})] \times \text{duration in minutes} \times 0,021 = \text{kilojoule expenditure (kJ)}$$

Example: A person who has a mass of 165 pounds and cycles for 30 minutes at a work rate of 60 watts has an energy expenditure of 846 kJ.

in kilograms:

$$[(18 \times \text{work rate in watts}) + (3,5 \times \text{mass in kilograms})] \times \text{duration in minutes} \times 0,021 = \text{kilojoule expenditure (kJ)}$$

Example: A person who has a mass of 75 kilograms and cycles for 30 minutes at a work rate of 60 watts has an energy expenditure of 846 kJ.

OTHER ACTIVITIES
ENERGY EXPENDITURE FORMULA

If you know the MET requirement of an activity—see Tables 6-1 and 6-2—then you can calculate your energy expenditure using the following formulas:

in pounds:

$$\frac{\text{METs} \times \text{mass in pounds} \times \text{duration in minutes} \times 4.2}{132} = \text{kilojoule expenditure (kJ)}$$

Example: A person who has a mass of 165 pounds and performs an activity requiring 5 METs for 45 minutes has an energy expenditure of 1181 kJ.

in kilograms:

$$\frac{\text{METs} \times \text{mass in kilograms} \times \text{duration in minutes} \times 4.2}{60} = \text{kilojoule expenditure (kJ)}$$

Example: A person who has a mass of 75 kilograms and performs an activity requiring 5 METs for 45 minutes has an energy expenditure of 1181 kJ.

APPENDIX C

SAMPLE INITIAL CARDIAC RECOVERY EXERCISE PROGRAMMES

Here we offer you guidelines on initiating a walking or stationary cycling exercise programme—or a combination of the two. We recommend these forms of exercise to cardiac patients because they're a good way to slowly ease into the routine of regular exercise over an 8-week period. Later, you may want to try some of the other forms of exercise we talked about earlier.

After you've completed an introductory 8 weeks or so following one of the programmes below, you'll be ready to start trying to earn the 100 exercise Heart Points we discussed in Chapter 16.

BEGINNING WALKING PROGRAMME (INITIAL 8 WEEKS)

Walking is a wonderful way for CHD patients to get moving down the road to recovery.

Before you begin, you should know your symptom-limited MET value (refer to the reply to Question 4 or, in the absence of any abnormalities, Question 2a of Table 5-6). Then follow these guidelines.

Use this formula to estimate the speed (in mph or km/h) at which you should walk during the first 8 weeks:

in miles:

$$\frac{(\text{symptom-limited METs} \times 2{,}1) - 3{,}5}{2{,}68} = \text{estimated walking speed}$$

Example: A person with a symptom-limited MET value of 5 should walk at a speed of about 2,6 mph.

in kilometres:

$$\frac{(\text{symptom-limited METs} \times 2{,}1) - 3{,}5}{1{,}67} = \text{estimated walking speed}$$

Example: A person with a symptom-limited MET value of 5 should walk at the target speed of about 4,2 km/h.

Should it turn out that your estimated speed exceeds 3,5 mph (or 5,6 km/h), stay with 3,5 mph (or 5,6 km/h) as your target speed for the first 8 weeks of your walking programme. In the event that you do not know your symptom-limited MET value, we recommend that you err on the side of caution and start out at a comfortable speed of no more than 3 mph (or 5 km/h).

If you are not in a medically supervised rehabilitation programme, do not exceed a Borg RPE of 13 (see Table 5-1) or 80 percent of your symptom-limited heart rate during the first 8 weeks.

Warm up and cool down adequately, devoting 5 minutes to each.

Warm up by walking slowly at first, gradually building up to your estimated walking speed and heart rate over 5 minutes. Cool down by reversing the process—gradually reducing your speed and, thus, your heart rate.

Here's what the first 8 weeks of your walking programme will look like in terms of each workout's duration and frequency:

Week	Duration Per Session	Frequency Per Week
1	10 minutes	3–5 times
2	15 minutes	3–5 times
3	20 minutes	3–5 times
4	25 minutes	3–5 times
5	30 minutes	3–5 times
6	35 minutes	3–5 times
7	40 minutes	3–5 times
8	45 minutes	3–5 times
9 and onward	Keep your exercise time at 45 minutes per session and gradually increase your speed until you exceed 60% of your symptom-limited heart rate (if you are not doing so yet). If this does not result in the desired weekly energy expenditure (or Heart Points) using the formula (or charts) we cited earlier in Appendix B, do one or more of the following: try exercising within the upper range of your target heart rate zone; exercise more frequently; or increase the duration of each exercise session.	

A Follow-up Walk-Jog Programme (12 Weeks)

Don't try jogging until you've followed a walking regimen for at least 6 weeks, ideally 12. You should be walking at speeds in excess of 4 mph (6,4 km/h) just before you graduate to jogging. If you're walking at a slower rate, you might as well stay with walking.

When you start to jog, you should do so at a speed no faster than that at which you currently walk.

As always, warm up and cool down—each for 5 minutes.

For the warm-up phase, walk briskly and try to gradually raise your heart rate to within at least 20 beats per minute of your target heart rate. On completing your jog, gradually reduce your speed to a slow walk over a 5-minute period.

Week	Duration Per Session	Frequency Per Week
1	*20 minutes total*—walk 4,5 min ... jog 0,5 min ... walk 4,5 min ... jog 0,5 min ... walk 4,5 min ... jog 0,5 min ... walk 4,5 min ... jog 0,5 min.*	3-5 times
2	*20 minutes total*—walk 4 min ... jog 1 min ... walk 4 min ... jog 1 min ... walk 4 min ... jog 1 min ... walk 4 min ... jog 1 min.*	3-5 times
3	*20 minutes total*—walk 3 min ... jog 2 min ... walk 3 min ... jog 2 min ... walk 3 min ... jog 2 min ... walk 3 min ... jog 2 min.*	3-5 times
4	*20 minutes total*—walk 2 min ... jog 3 min ... walk 2 min ... jog 3 min ... walk 2 min ... jog 3 min ... walk 2 min ... jog 3 min.*	3-5 times
5	*20 minutes total*—walk 5 min ... jog 5 min ... walk 5 min ... jog 5 min.*	3-5 times
6	*20 minutes total*—walk 4 min ... jog 6 min ... walk 4 min ... jog 6 min.*	3-5 times
7	*20 minutes total*—walk 3 min ... jog 7 min ... walk 3 min ... jog 7 min.*	3-5 times
8	*20 minutes total*—jog 10 min ... walk 10 min.*	3-5 times
9	*20 minutes total*—jog 12 min ... walk 8 min.*	3-5 times
10	*20 minutes total*—jog 15 min ... walk 5 min.*	3-5 times
11	*20 minutes total*—jog 17 min ... walk 3 min.*	3-5 times
12	*20 minutes total*—jog 20 min.*	3-5 times

Week	Duration Per Session	Frequency Per Week
13 and onward	By the time you reach this point, you are likely to have exceeded 60% of your symptom-limited heart rate, and you've possibly attained your desired weekly energy expenditure (or Heart Points) using the formula (or charts) cited earlier in Appendix B. If so, just keep following Week 12's regimen. If, on the other hand, you haven't been able to exceed 60% of your symptom-limited heart rate, increase your speed. If that does not result in the desired weekly energy expenditure (or Heart Points), do one or more of the following: try exercising within the upper range of your target heart rate zone; exercise more frequently; or increase the duration of each exercise session.	

*You may find that you are below your desired weekly energy expenditure (or Heart Points) during the early weeks of this walk-jog effort. You can compensate by walking longer at the end of the jogging phase, before starting your cool-down. Use the jogging formulas and charts in Appendix B when calculating your kilojoules and Heart Points for your walk-jog programme.

BEGINNING STATIONARY CYCLING PROGRAMME (INITIAL 8 WEEKS)

If indoor cycling is more to your liking than walking, that's fine. It's an excellent form of exercise.

Before you begin, you should know your symptom-limited MET value (refer to the reply to Question 4 or, in the absence of any abnormalities, Question 2a of Table 5-6) as well as your mass in either pounds or kilograms. Then follow these guidelines.

To estimate your cycling work rate (in watts) for the first 8 weeks, the formula is:

in pounds:

$$\frac{(\text{symptom-limited METs} \times 2{,}1 \times \text{body mass in pounds}) - (3{,}5 \times \text{body mass in pounds})}{26{,}4} = \text{estimated work rate (in watts)}$$

Example: A person who has a mass of 165 pounds with a symptom-limited MET value of 7 should cycle at a work rate of 70 watts. The calculation looks like this:

$$\frac{(7 \times 2{,}1 \times 165) - (3{,}5 \times 165)}{26{,}4} = 70 \text{ watts}$$

in kilograms:

$$\frac{(\text{symptom-limited METs} \times 2{,}1 \times \text{body mass in kilograms}) - (3{,}5 \times \text{body mass in kilograms})}{12} = \begin{array}{l}\text{estimated}\\ \text{work rate}\\ \text{(in watts)}\end{array}$$

Example: A person who has a mass of 75 kilograms with a symptom-limited MET value of 7 should cycle at a work rate of 70 watts.

Should it turn out that your estimated work rate exceeds 90 watts, stay with 90 watts anyway as your target work rate for the first 8 weeks of your cycling programme. In the event that you do not know your symptom-limited MET value, we recommend that you err on the side of caution and start out at a comfortable work rate that does not exceed that suitable for a symptom-limited MET value of 5.

If you are not part of a medically supervised rehabilitation programme, do not exceed a Borg RPE of 13 (see Table 5-1) or 80 percent of your symptom-limited heart rate during the first 8 weeks.

Warm up and cool down for 5 minutes each at the opening and close of your session.

Warm up by building up to your target work rate and heart rate over a 5-minute period. Cool down for at least 5 minutes by reversing the process.

Here are duration and frequency recommendations for the first 8 weeks of your cycling programme:

Week	Duration Per Session	Frequency Per Week
1	7,5 minutes	3–5 times
2	10,0 minutes	3–5 times
3	12,5 minutes	3–5 times
4	15,0 minutes	3–5 times
5	17,5 minutes	3–5 times
6	20,0 minutes	3–5 times
7	25,0 minutes	3–5 times
8	30,0 minutes	3–5 times
9 and onward	Keep your exercise time at 30 minutes per session and gradually increase your work rate until you exceed 60% of your symptom-limited heart rate (if you are not doing so yet). If this does not result in the desired weekly energy expenditure (or Heart Points) using the formula (or charts) we cited earlier in Appendix B, do one or more of the following: try exercising within the upper range of your target heart rate zone; exercise more frequently; or increase the duration of each exercise session.	

BEGINNING SCHWINN AIR-DYNE CYCLING PROGRAMME (INITIAL 8 WEEKS)

A second form of indoor cycling, which works both your arms and legs, is the Schwinn Air-Dyne. The machine is not found at all rehabilitation centres in South Africa, but we discuss it here for those of you who have access to it or to similar cycles.

Again, you should know your symptom-limited MET value (refer to the reply to Question 4 or, in the absence of any abnormalities, Question 2a of Table 5-6) as well as your mass in either pounds or kilograms. The formula for estimating your work load for the first 8 weeks is:

in pounds:

$$\frac{(\text{symptom-limited METs} \times 2,1 \times \text{body mass in pounds}) - (3,5 \times \text{body mass in pounds})}{1320} = \text{estimated work load}$$

Example: A person who has a mass of 165 pounds with a symptom-limited MET value of 7 should cycle at a work load of 1,4.

in kilograms:

$$\frac{(\text{symptom-limited METs} \times 2,1 \times \text{body mass in kilograms}) - (3,5 \times \text{body mass in kilograms})}{600} = \text{estimated work load}$$

Example: A person who has a mass of 75 kilograms with a symptom-limited MET value of 7 should cycle at a work load of 1,4.

Should it turn out that your estimated work load exceeds 1,8, stay with 1,8 anyway as your work load ceiling for the first 8 weeks of your Schwinn Air-Dyne programme. In the event that you do not know your symptom-limited MET value, we recommend that you err on the side of caution and start out at a comfortable work load that does not exceed that suitable for a symptom-limited MET value of 5.

If you are not in a medically supervised rehabilitation programme, do not exceed a Borg RPE of 13 (see Table 5-1) or 80 percent of your symptom-limited heart rate during the first 8 weeks.

Warm up and cool down for 5 minutes each. Warm up by building up to your target work load and heart rate gradually, over 5 full minutes. Cool down for at least 5 minutes by reversing the process.

Here are duration and frequency recommendations for your Schwinn Air-Dyne routine:

Week	Duration Per Session	Frequency Per Week
1	7,5 minutes	3–5 times
2	10,0 minutes	3–5 times
3	12,5 minutes	3–5 times
4	15,0 minutes	3–5 times
5	17,5 minutes	3–5 times
6	20,0 minutes	3–5 times
7	25,0 minutes	3–5 times
8	30,0 minutes	3–5 times
9 and onward	Keep your exercise time at 30 minutes per session and gradually increase your work load until you exceed 60% of your symptom-limited heart rate (if you're not doing so yet). If this does not result in the desired weekly energy expenditure (or Heart Points) using the formula (or charts) we cited earlier in Appendix B, do one or more of the following: try exercising within the upper range of your target heart rate zone; exercise more frequently; or increase the duration of each exercise session.	

BEGINNING PROGRAMME OF COMBINED WALKING AND STATIONARY CYCLING (INITIAL 8 WEEKS)

Some people get bored doing the same exercise day after day. For such people, we've devised an 8-week regimen that combines walking with stationary cycling. This combination will also help reduce your risk of injury.

Our aforementioned guidelines for walking and stationary cycling apply. Estimate your starting walking speed and stationary cycling work rate for the first 8 weeks of this programme using the formulas above.

We repeat: if you are not in a medically supervised rehabilitation programme, do not exceed a Borg RPE of 13 (see Table 5-1) or 80 percent of your symptom-limited heart rate during the first 8 weeks.

You may start with either activity. As always, warm up for 5 minutes. After completing the first activity, proceed immediately to the other one—another warm-up is not needed. Upon completion of the second activity, cool down for 5 minutes.

Week	Duration Per Session Walking	Stationary cycling	Frequency Per Week
1	5,0 minutes	5,0 minutes	3–5 times
2	7,5 minutes	7,5 minutes	3–5 times
3	10,0 minutes	10,0 minutes	3–5 times
4	12,5 minutes	12,5 minutes	3–5 times
5	15,0 minutes	15,0 minutes	3–5 times
6	17,5 minutes	17,5 minutes	3–5 times
7	20,0 minutes	20,0 minutes	3–5 times
8	22,5 minutes	22,5 minutes	3–5 times
9 and onward	Keep the combined exercise time at 45 minutes per session and gradually increase the intensity until you exceed 60% of your symptom-limited heart rate (if you're not doing so yet). If this does not result in the desired weekly energy expenditure (or Heart Points) using the formula (or charts) we cited earlier in Appendix B, do one or more of the following: try exercising within the upper range of your target heart rate zone; exercise more frequently; or increase the duration of each exercise session.		

APPENDIX D

FOR CHD PATIENTS:
The Exercise Safety Quiz

As a simple way of reviewing how much you've learned about your condition and exercise safety from reading this book, we've devised the following quiz. It's a 50-question multiple-choice test. There are no trick questions.

Perhaps you'll want to spend 20 minutes or so with the quiz as a way to gauge how much of the most essential information you've retained. It's also a way to further educate yourself. Note the questions you get wrong and pay special attention to the right answers.

There is no correct or passing score. But, ideally, you should aim to get all your answers right.

Directions: Read each item carefully and decide which choice best completes the statement or answers the question. Indicate your answer by placing the appropriate letter next to the appropriate number on a sheet numbered from 1 to 50. Don't simply try to guess the correct answer to a question; if you do not know the answer, place a (d) next to the question number. Each correct answer is worth 2 points. For an incorrect answer, 1 point is subtracted; if you marked (d), no points are subtracted.

1. Coronary heart disease is a disease in which:
   (a) the coronary arteries die and are unable to supply the heart with blood and oxygen.
   (b) the coronary arteries, which supply the heart muscle with blood and oxygen, become narrowed as a result of atherosclerotic plaque buildup.
   (c) the heart muscle is unable to remove adequate amounts of oxygen from the blood flowing through the heart's chambers.
   (d) I don't know.

2. coronary heart disease results in:
   (a) an inadequate supply of carbon dioxide to the heart muscle.
   (b) an inadequate supply of oxygen to the valves of the heart.
   (c) an inadequate supply of oxygen to the heart muscle.
   (d) I don't know.
3. coronary heart disease may cause:
   (a) no symptoms whatsoever, a condition known as silent ischaemia.
   (b) chest discomfort, a condition known as angina pectoris.
   (c) both silent ischaemia and angina pectoris.
   (d) I don't know.
4. A heart attack generally occurs when the heart muscle is deprived of an adequate oxygen supply for longer than:
   (a) 24 hours.
   (b) 1 hour.
   (c) 30 minutes.
   (d) I don't know.
5. Fatal heart rhythm disturbances may occur if the heart muscle is deprived of an adequate oxygen supply for:
   (a) even only a few minutes.
   (b) more than 20 minutes.
   (c) more than 30 minutes.
   (d) I don't know.
6. The heart muscle's oxygen requirements increase when the:
   (a) heart rate slows down.
   (b) systolic blood pressure decreases.
   (c) heart rate speeds up.
   (d) I don't know.
7. During exercise the heart muscle's oxygen requirements:
   (a) remain the same as always.
   (b) decrease in direct proportion to the intensity of effort.
   (c) increase in direct proportion to the intensity of effort.
   (d) I don't know.
8. The heart rate at which myocardial ischaemia (an inadequate oxygen supply to the heart muscle) occurs during exercise generally:
   (a) varies from day to day.
   (b) can be determined during an exercise test and remains the same from day to day.
   (c) remains the same from day to day but can only be determined during coronary angiography.
   (d) I don't know.

9. After a heart attack, the damaged area of heart muscle:
   (a) heals by the process of scar tissue formation and never regains its function again.
   (b) heals by the process of scar tissue formation and is soon capable of functioning normally.
   (c) heals by the process of blood-clot formation and never regains its function again.
   (d) I don't know.
10. How long does the process by which the heart muscle heals after a heart attack usually take before it is completed?
    (a) 1 to 3 weeks.
    (b) 6 to 8 weeks.
    (c) 16 to 18 weeks.
    (d) I don't know.
11. During the period after a heart attack when heart muscle healing is still taking place:
    (a) strenuous exercise is generally very safe and beneficial.
    (b) regular exercise is beneficial, but strenuous exercise should be avoided.
    (c) even light exercise is dangerous and should be avoided.
    (d) I don't know.
12. Before embarking on an exercise programme, persons with coronary heart disease must:
    (a) obtain clearance from their physician.
    (b) read a book about exercise written by physicians for persons with heart disease.
    (c) join a health club.
    (d) I don't know.
13. When you are starting an exercise programme, your training heart rate limit (the heart rate not to be exceeded during exercise) must be based on:
    (a) your maximum heart rate, which can be calculated by subtracting your age (in years) from 220.
    (b) the results of an exercise test performed within the last 2 years.
    (c) the results of an exercise test performed within the last 3 months.
    (d) I don't know.
14. If you are participating in an exercise programme and there is a change in your condition—another heart attack or major cardiac procedure, new symptoms, or a change in medication—you must:
    (a) continue with your programme as usual.

(b) take it easy for a few weeks and then continue with your programme where you left off.
(c) under no circumstances undertake another workout until you've consulted your doctor.
(d) I don't know.
15. Once involved in an exercise programme, you should have a repeat exercise test:
(a) at least once a year, even if all seems well.
(b) only if you experience symptoms during exercise.
(c) only if you experience symptoms either at rest or during exercise.
(d) I don't know.
16. During exercise, you should never exceed:
(a) 85% of your symptom-limited heart rate.
(b) 60% of your symptom-limited heart rate.
(c) your symptom-limited heart rate.
(d) I don't know.
17. If you exercise above your training heart rate limit you are:
(a) likely to derive more benefit from your workouts.
(b) likely to speed up your recovery process.
(c) placing yourself at greater risk of experiencing an exercise-related cardiac complication.
(d) I don't know.
18. When taking your pulse during exercise you must be sure to:
(a) keep very still so that you can obtain an accurate reading.
(b) keep moving the active muscles, even if it means simply walking on the spot.
(c) lie down to prevent yourself from fainting.
(d) I don't know.
19. For how long should you count your pulse when calculating your *resting* heart rate?
(a) at least 30 seconds.
(b) 10 seconds.
(c) 6 seconds.
(d) I don't know.
20. For how long should you count your pulse when calculating your heart rate *during exercise?*
(a) 30 seconds.
(b) 20 seconds.
(c) 10 seconds.
(d) I don't know.
21. To get the most accurate pulse count during exercise, it is best to:
(a) use the pulse in your wrist (your radial pulse) and start

counting immediately on stopping.
- (b) use the pulse in your neck (your carotid pulse) and start counting immediately on stopping.
- (c) use either your radial or carotid pulse and wait for at least 10 seconds before starting to count after stopping.
- (d) I don't know.

22. If you experience mild chest discomfort during exercise you should:
    - (a) slow down immediately and stop if it does not subside within 2 to 3 minutes.
    - (b) continue exercising at the same intensity and slow down only if the discomfort worsens.
    - (c) slow down immediately and stop if it does not subside within 10 to 15 minutes.
    - (d) I don't know.

23. If you are exercising without supervision and chest discomfort persists for more than 2 to 3 minutes after stopping exercise, you should:
    - (a) lie down until the discomfort subsides.
    - (b) continue with your workout.
    - (c) take a nitroglycerin tablet.
    - (d) I don't know.

24. If chest discomfort is not relieved by 3 nitroglycerin tablets, taken 5 minutes apart, you should:
    - (a) lie down until the discomfort subsides.
    - (b) take another nitroglycerin tablet and wait another 5 minutes to see what happens.
    - (c) contact your doctor or the emergency medical system immediately.
    - (d) I don't know.

25. Warning symptoms of a possible exercise-related cardiac complication include:
    - (a) a nauseous sensation during or after exercise.
    - (b) dizziness during exercise.
    - (c) both (a) and (b).
    - (d) I don't know.

26. If you were *previously capable* of walking 3 miles (4,8 km) in 45 minutes without any problems, but now suddenly find you become short of breath when doing so:
    - (a) you need to train harder because you are unfit.
    - (b) your heart condition may have worsened, and you should notify your doctor as soon as possible.
    - (c) you should switch from walking to cycling, because you

may be getting stale.
(d) I don't know.

27. If your pulse was *previously regular* but you now notice what appear to be extra heartbeats or missed beats:
    (a) you need to train harder because you are unfit.
    (b) your heart condition may have worsened, and you should notify your doctor as soon as possible.
    (c) you should continue to exercise as normal, because this occurs frequently in persons with heart disease.
    (d) I don't know.

28. The majority of exercise-related cardiac complications occur:
    (a) during the middle of a workout.
    (b) the day after a workout.
    (c) either at the beginning or at the end of a workout.
    (d) I don't know.

29. An adequate warm-up is of vital importance to persons with coronary heart disease because it:
    (a) increases their body temperature and reduces their risk of developing an infection.
    (b) makes their workout last longer and therefore increases their energy expenditure.
    (c) provides their circulation sufficient time to adjust to the increased oxygen requirements of the heart muscle.
    (d) I don't know.

30. The warm-up should last at least 5 minutes and serve to:
    (a) gradually increase your heart rate to within at least 20 beats per minute of your target heart rate.
    (b) gradually increase your heart rate to within at least 40 beats per minute of your target heart rate.
    (c) rapidly increase your heart rate to within at least 30 beats per minute of your target heart rate.
    (d) I don't know.

31. What is the best way for persons with coronary heart disease to cool down after exercise?
    (a) take a cold shower.
    (b) stop exercising and lie flat on their back.
    (c) gradually slow down in order to allow their heart rate to return to near resting values.
    (d) I don't know.

32. To avoid dehydration when working out on hot and humid days, you should:
    (a) drink a cup of water every 5 minutes during exercise.

(b) drink a cup of water every 20 minutes during exercise.
   (c) drink a cup of water every 60 minutes during exercise.
   (d) I don't know.
33. Four of the *most important* steps to prevent your body temperature from rising excessively during outdoor warm-weather workouts are:
   (a) take a cold shower before you exercise; acclimatize adequately; drink water during exercise; and wear a cap during exercise.
   (b) limit your outdoor exercise on very hot days; acclimatize adequately; drink water during exercise; and dress appropriately.
   (c) limit outdoor exercise on very hot days; acclimatize adequately; drink water during exercise; ask your doctor to prescribe a beta-blocker for you.
   (d) I don't know.
34. Exercising while you've got the flu is dangerous and you should therefore:
   (a) wait until your temperature has been normal for at least 24 hours and then return to your usual level of activity gradually over the course of a week or two.
   (b) wait until your temperature has been normal for at least 24 hours and then return to your usual level of activity gradually over the course of a day or two.
   (c) continue exercising, but at a lower intensity.
   (d) I don't know.
35. A key factor for cold-weather workouts is to:
   (a) wear thick clothing.
   (b) wear a good pair of shoes.
   (c) wear multiple layers of clothing.
   (d) I don't know.
36. To reduce their risk of being exposed to high concentrations of carbon monoxide, persons with coronary heart disease should:
   (a) exercise only late in the afternoon.
   (b) avoid working out along heavily travelled roadways at rush hour and try to stay at least 20 metres away from exhaust fumes.
   (c) avoid working out along heavily travelled roadways at rush hour and try to stay at least 5 metres away from exhaust fumes.
   (d) I don't know.
37. When exercising at higher than normal altitudes, you should:

(a) reduce the pace of your workouts and take more frequent pulse counts.
(b) reduce the pace of your workouts and take less frequent pulse counts.
(c) increase the pace of your workouts and take more frequent pulse counts.
(d) I don't know.

38. During the first 6 months after a heart attack, bypass surgery, or angioplasty, competitive exercise:
    (a) should generally be avoided because it may place you at greater risk for an exercise-related cardiac complication.
    (b) is especially good for you because it makes your heart work harder.
    (c) should be undertaken no more than once each week.
    (d) I don't know.

39. In order to derive the optimum health-related benefits from exercise training with the minimum of risk, you should:
    (a) make use of high-intensity anaerobic exercise such as sprinting.
    (b) make use of moderate-intensity aerobic exercise such as brisk walking and jogging.
    (c) both (a) and (b).
    (d) I don't know.

40. Once you have been in a medically supervised cardiac rehabilitation programme for more than 12 weeks and are cleared for *unsupervised* exercise, it is best to:
    (a) continue exercising under the direction of your physician and work out at the rehabilitation facility at least once every 3 months.
    (b) continue exercising at a local health club because you no longer require direction from your physician and other cardiac rehabilitation health professionals.
    (c) continue exercising at home because you no longer require direction from your physician and other cardiac rehabilitation health professionals.
    (d) I don't know.

41. Two factors that increase your risk of experiencing a cardiac problem during exercise are:
    (a) exceeding your training heart rate limit and infrequent (less than 3 times per week) exercise training.
    (b) staying below your training heart rate limit and frequent (3 or more times per week) exercise training.
    (c) exercising for longer than 30 minutes and staying below your training heart rate limit.

(d) I don't know.
42. Isometric exercise (in which a muscle remains contracted for more than a few seconds without relaxing) and exercises using heavy weights are not recommended for persons with coronary heart disease because they:
   (a) cause you to become muscle-bound.
   (b) sometimes elicit adverse cardiac responses in certain individuals.
   (c) increase your risk of sustaining a musculoskeletal injury.
   (d) I don't know.
43. Persons with coronary heart disease should generally embark on a serious strength-training programme only if they:
   (a) have been a regular participant in a cardiac rehabilitation programme for at least 12 weeks.
   (b) have an exercise capacity of at least 4 METs.
   (c) are not receiving therapy with beta-blockers.
   (d) I don't know.
44. After a workout it is best for persons with coronary heart disease to:
   (a) wait 5 minutes before taking a sauna.
   (b) wait 10 minutes before taking a sauna.
   (c) not take a sauna at all.
   (d) I don't know.
45. If you exercise for at least 45 minutes on at least 5 days each week at the correct intensity you:
   (a) must still pay careful attention to your diet and other coronary heart disease risk factors.
   (b) do not have to worry too much about your diet.
   (c) do not have to worry too much about other coronary heart disease risk factors besides your diet.
   (d) I don't know.
46. Which of the following activities are most suitable for persons with coronary heart disease?
   (a) basketball and water-skiing.
   (b) weight lifting, push-ups, and sprinting.
   (c) walking, jogging, and cycling.
   (d) I don't know.
47. If you experienced chest discomfort typical of angina on the weekend and you have not had any angina in recent months, you should:
   (a) work out on Monday and if you experience angina, consult your doctor.
   (b) work out on Monday and if you do not experience

angina, do not consult your doctor.
(c) consult your doctor before your Monday workout.
(d) I don't know.

48. To derive *major* benefits from your exercise programme, you should do aerobic exercise for:
    (a) 20 to 60 minutes per workout 3 to 5 days each week at an intensity which raises your heart rate above 60% of your symptom-limited value.
    (b) 20 to 60 minutes per workout 1 to 2 days each week at an intensity which raises your heart rate above 80% of your symptom-limited value.
    (c) 5 to 10 minutes per workout 3 to 5 days each week at an intensity which raises your heart rate above 80% of your symptom-limited value.
    (d) I don't know.

49. (To be answered only by persons who have undergone open-heart surgery. All other persons automatically score 2 points for this question.)
    After open-heart surgery, you should not lift weights in excess of 4,5 kg during the first:
    (a) 2 weeks.
    (b) 4 weeks.
    (c) 6 weeks.
    (d) I don't know.

50. The most important cause of exercise-related injuries is
    (a) exceeding 60% of your symptom-limited heart rate.
    (b) attempting to do too much exercise too soon.
    (c) performing moderate-intensity aerobic exercise such as brisk walking.
    (d) I don't know.

Answers—a correct answer = 2 points; if you did not mark (d) and your answer is incorrect, subtract 1 point:

1.	(b)	11.	(b)	21.	(a)	31.	(c)	41.	(a)
2.	(c)	12.	(a)	22.	(a)	32.	(b)	42.	(b)
3.	(c)	13.	(c)	23.	(c)	33.	(b)	43.	(a)
4.	(c)	14.	(c)	24.	(c)	34.	(a)	44.	(c)
5.	(a)	15.	(a)	25.	(c)	35.	(c)	45.	(a)
6.	(c)	16.	(a)	26.	(b)	36.	(b)	46.	(c)
7.	(c)	17.	(c)	27.	(b)	37.	(a)	47.	(c)
8.	(b)	18.	(b)	28.	(c)	38.	(a)	48.	(a)
9.	(a)	19.	(a)	29.	(c)	39.	(b)	49.	(c)
10.	(b)	20.	(c)	30.	(a)	40.	(a)	50.	(b)

APPENDIX E

THE ABCs OF HEART MEDICATION

A GENERATION ago, many physicians prescribed medications with a condescending attitude. Their internal monologue went something like this: "As long as I understand why a medication is needed, I see no reason to bother the patient with this information. Besides, it takes a considerable degree of medical knowledge to comprehend how a drug does its job. Also, I don't want to be drawn into a discussion of side effects since that might plant suggestions in the patient's mind. If I don't talk about possible problems, there'll be less chance of autosuggestion."

Fortunately, this attitude is dying out, although there are still a few doctors of the old school in practice. We think this point of view is not only incorrect but foolish.

In our experience, patients are much more likely to follow through with medication and take it correctly if they understand why drugs are necessary in lieu of other therapies, the drug's purpose, and the side effects they should be on the lookout for.

If a patient knows which side effects are likely to occur, he or she can be a much better helper to the physician in monitoring them and making sure things don't progress to the regrettable point where the negatives outweigh the positives. There's a certain risk-to-benefit ratio that accompanies every drug. If patients' experience with a medication isn't sufficiently weighted toward the benefit side, why should they continue to take it?

Besides, we're strong proponents of the idea that patients have a right to know about a therapy, be it drug treatment or a surgical procedure. When it comes to a medication, they certainly should be told, for example, how long it is anticipated they must stay on it.

THE PROS AND CONS OF CORONARY DRUG THERAPY

Nobody wants to take medications. Many patients, in moments of truth, admit that the mere fact that they require prescription drugs makes them feel dependent. It's a constant reminder that they're in less than optimal health.

Actually, this notion on the part of patients is about as outmoded as the doctors' attitude we just mentioned. In recent years, there have been tremendous scientific advances in cardiac pharmacology. As a consequence, it is now possible for many recovering heart disease patients to feel better faster through the judicious use of drugs. Be happy you're living in the l990s, a time when medications have become wonderfully targeted and sophisticated in what they can accomplish.

On the other hand, we admit there's always some risk when you take a drug. Despite the great benefits that most patients realize from various heart medications, every drug has some potential side effect, no matter how small.

Drugs are nothing to be meek about. If your doctor starts writing out a prescription with little or no explanation about why, speak up. See the first box at the end of this appendix, which lists the eight questions you must get answered before you pop that first pill or down that first swallow of some medicinal liquid.

Even after you've been given a thorough explanation by your physician, there's still no law that says you must agree to a specific drug therapy. If you're adamantly opposed to it, say so.

No, we're not trying to foment revolt in cardiologists' offices around the country or around the world. Conversely, neither are we on the side of doctors who absentmindedly dictate a regimen without taking patients' life-style needs and concerns into account.

Use the following cardiac drug charts to check what your doctor says about a medication he or she is prescribing. If there's a discrepancy, by all means point it out and ask for an explanation.

Before having your prescription filled, go over the hints and tips in the second box at the end of this appendix. Prescription drug labelling and storage are more important than you may think.

WHAT YOU NEED TO KNOW ABOUT SOME COMMON CARDIAC DRUGS

These charts will introduce you to the major categories of drugs prescribed after a heart attack, bypass surgery, or angioplasty. In them, we outline the dosages, side effects, and any additional things you should know before you take a drug. Drugs are a serious matter. Never hesitate to call your doctor if you have questions about any medication you've been given.

Diuretics

Diuretics help to eliminate excess water from the body. In cardiac patients, this is often necessary because of a tendency toward ankle swelling (oedema). Excess water can also contribute to heart failure and high blood pressure.

Your total body salt content is about 0,3 kilograms. Every day, your kidneys work hard filtering and refiltering salt. Over a 24-hour period, your kidneys filter about 1,5 kilograms' worth, or five times the total amount in your body. About 99 percent of this salt is placed back in circulation.

Diuretics block some of your body's reabsorption of salt, causing more of it, along with some of your body's fluids, to be excreted as urine. For sufferers of hypertension and for some heart patients, it's beneficial to reduce the total amount of body fluid in this fashion because it sets off a welcome chain reaction. Less fluid means a lower blood volume, which in turn decreases the load on your heart and lowers elevated blood pressures.

Some diuretics cause the body to lose potassium, making potassium supplements necessary.

Diuretics

Type of Drug	Dosage Range (mg/day)	Selected Side Effects[a]	Precautions and Special Considerations
Thiazides and related diuretics		Low potassium, high uric acid, elevated blood sugar, elevated LDL cholesterol, elevated triglycerides, sexual dysfunction, muscle fatigue, weakness.	Low potassium increases the risk of digitalis toxicity and heart rhythm disturbances; may precipitate gout by increasing uric acid levels.
Bendroflumethiazide (ingredient of Corgaretic)	2,5–5		
Chlorthalidone (Hygroton)	12,5–50		

Diuretics *(continued)*

Type of Drug	Dosage Range (mg/day)	Selected Side Effects	Precautions and Special Considerations
Hydrochlorothiazide (ingredient of Aldoretic, Amiluretic, Dyazide, Moduretic)	12,5–50		
Hydroflumethiazide (ingredient of Rautrax, Serenol, Protensin, Hydravern)			
Indapamide (Natrilix)	2,5–5		
Metolazone (Zaroxlyn)	1,25–10		
Loop diuretics		Low potassium, elevated uric acid	
Bumetanide (Burinex)	0,5–5		
Furosemide (Lasix)	20–320		
Potassium-sparing agents		High blood potassium, high uric acid, elevated blood glucose, elevated LDL cholesterol, elevated triglycerides, sexual dysfunction, weakness and muscle fatigue.	Danger of high blood potassium level or renal failure in patients treated with an ACE inhibitor or a non-steroidal anti-inflammatory drug.
Amiloride (ingredient of Aldoretic, Amiluretic, Moduretic)	5–10		
Spironolactone (Aldactone)	25–100	Enlarged breasts and breast pain.	Interferes with digoxin assay. Danger of kidney
Triamterene (ingredient of Dyazide)[b]	50–150		

[a] Side effects are possible occurrences, but generally affect only a minority of patients.
[b] Dyazide also contains hydrochlorothiazide.
Source: Some of this material is drawn from the 1988 report of the Joint National Committee on the Detection, Evaluation and Treatment of High Blood Pressure.

Nitrates

Yes, nitrates—or nitroglycerin—are used in explosives. But don't worry. When nitrates are made into medication, their effects may be dynamic, but they won't mirror dynamite.

Nitrates are a class of drugs which dilate the veins in your body, thus decreasing the amount of blood that returns to your heart. Net effect: they reduce the heart's work load. Nitrates also have a similar effect on arteries, but to a lesser degree. Their purpose is to give rapid temporary relief from angina. However, long-acting forms, such as Isordil, aren't as effective in terminating angina pain once it's begun, although they do seem to be helpful in preventing an attack before it gets under way.

Nitrate compounds, generally inexpensive, can be absorbed through the skin, which is a more effective way to administer them to some patients. A problem with nitrates (especially those applied on the skin) is that their frequent use can cause your body to develop a tolerance, thus nullifying much of their effect. That's why many doctors warn patients not to overdo it. They recommend moderation, even abstention for a period of time (that is, overnight), in most patients.

Nitrates

Type of Drug	Dosage Range (mg/day)	Selected Side Effects	Precautions and Special Considerations
Nitroglycerin sublingual (Angised)	0,15–0,6, as needed	Increase in heart rate, headache, drop in blood pressure with a change in posture, dizziness, flushing.	Becomes outdated more quickly than other medications (approximately 6 months); tolerance may develop (in other words, it may not be as effective after it is used for a while).

Nitrates (continued)

Type of Drug	Dosage Range (mg/day)	Selected Side Effects	Precautions and Special Considerations
Long-acting nitroglycerin–isosorbide dinitrate (Isordil, Ismo)	2,5–80 sublingual 10–20 oral	Same as above.	A significant drop in blood pressure may occur; this drop in blood pressure may be more likely if calcium channel blockers are also being taken; tolerance may develop.
Nitroglycerin ointment	1/2–4 inches ointment	Same as above.	
Nitroglycerin patch (Transderm nitro, Nitroderm, Nitradisc)	10–60 cm^2	Same as above.	Easy to apply; steady or too frequent use may lead to tolerance.

Beta-Blockers

Beta-blockers lower the heart muscle's demand for oxygen. Studies show that beta-blockers may reduce the frequency of repeat heart attacks and death after an initial infarction. Most of this benefit occurs in the first three years after that initial heart attack, which is why many experts feel that after this period, beta-blockers may not be necessary for some patients.

The *Harvard Medical School Health Letter,* in its January 1984 issue, published a particularly lucid explanation of how beta-blockers work. The article was called "Putting the Squeeze on Angina":

> The heart is largely under the control of the autonomic, or involuntary, nervous system, which sends its instructions through several different kinds of nerves. One set of these nerves sends its messages to sites in the heart muscle known as beta-receptors. When beta-receptors are stimulated, they invariably respond by making the heart beat faster and faster.
>
> You can think of beta-receptors as tiny telegraph receivers that sit waiting for a signal to come down the wire. When it comes, the receivers automatically activate the heart. As a result, the heart

demands more blood, and if blood is in short supply because of coronary artery disease, angina results.

Beta-blockers, then, are like a little wad of paper slipped under the telegraph key to prevent it from clicking. The nerve sends its signal, but now the heart can't "hear" it. The problem with beta-blockers is that they can also interfere with signals elsewhere in the body, and uncomfortable symptoms may result. The airways in the lungs, for example, depend on beta stimulation to stay wide open; thus, beta blockage may lead to asthma-like symptoms in some people.

Fortunately, it turns out that beta-receptors are not all alike. Those in the lungs are subtly different from those in the heart, and so it has been possible to design drugs which act mainly in the heart and have little effect on the lungs. Metoprolol (Lopressor) and atenolol (Tenormin) are two agents that were designed to work in the heart and leave the lungs alone.

In short, beta-blockers slow down your heart rate, reduce your systolic blood pressure, and consequently reduce the oxygen requirements of the heart muscle, which makes them effective drugs for controlling angina and preventing silent ischaemia. They are also helpful for controlling certain types of heart rhythm disturbances.

However, as this explanation made clear, not all beta-blockers are identical in their action. Thus, determining which beta-blocking drug to prescribe for each patient requires a doctor's careful judgment.

Atenolol and metoprolol are cardioselective beta-blockers. "Cardioselectivity" refers to a beta-blocker's effect on beta-receptors found in the heart versus beta-receptors found in the lungs and vessels. Theoretically, as the newsletter copy points out, this ability to block special receptors often results in fewer side effects.

Acebutolol and pindolol are beta-blocking drugs which do not slow the heart rate as much, so they are sometimes helpful in treating patients in whom a slow heart rate would otherwise limit the use of beta-blockers.

A beta-blocker's duration of action depends on its lipid (fat) solubility—the lower the solubility, the longer the action. Atenolol and nadolol are the longest-acting beta-blockers, lasting approximately 24 hours. Because of their low lipid solubility, they are also the least likely to cause central nervous system side effects such as depression and nightmares. From a biochemical standpoint, they're metabolized by the liver at slow rates, are excreted primarily via the kidneys, and do not cross the blood-brain barrier—hence the absence of negative psychological effects.

Labetalol acts primarily as a beta-blocker. However, it also blocks another type of receptor (called an alpha-receptor) located in the muscular walls of the arteries. This additional effect is useful mostly for lowering high blood pressure.

Beta-Adrenergic Blockers (Beta-Blockers)

Type of Drug	Dosage Range (mg/day)	Selected Side Effects	Precautions and Special Considerations
Acebutolol (Sectral)	200–1 200	Shortness of breath, particularly in those with a tendency toward asthma or upper respiratory allergy, peripheral arterial insufficiency, fatigue, insomnia, sexual dysfunction, worsening of congestive heart failure, high triglycerides, a decrease in HDL cholesterol (except for pindolol and acebutolol), slow heart rate.	Should not be used by those with a history of asthma, chronic obstructive pulmonary disease (COPD), congestive heart failure, certain ECG abnormalities such as heart block (greater than first degree), and sick sinus syndrome; beta-blockers should be used with caution in insulin-dependant diabetics and patients with peripheral vascular disease; beta-blockers should not be discontinued abruptly (do not run out).
Atenolol (Tenormin)	25–150		
Metoprolol (Lopressor)	50–200		
Nadolol (Corgard)	40–320		
Pindolol (Visken)	10–60		
Propranolol (Inderal)	40–320		
Propranolol long-acting (Inderal LA)	60–320		
Timolol (Blocadren)	20–80		

Other Adrenergic Blocking Drugs

Besides beta-blockers, there are drugs that block other receptors at different places in the body. They're grouped into such broad classifications as centrally acting adrenergic inhibitors, peripheral-acting adrenergic inhibitors, and alpha-1 adrenergic blockers. These drugs block certain of the effects of adrenaline-like compounds that carry messages to the body's small arteries, telling them to tighten up and increase their resistance to blood flow. Drugs like clonidine, for example, block receptors in the brain which control blood pressure signals. Prazosin, for example, acts on a similar type of message centre, but it's located in the body, away from the brain.

Other Adrenergic Blocking Drugs

Type of Drug	Dosage Range (mg/day)	Selected Side Effects	Precautions and Special Considerations
Centrally acting adrenergic inhibitors			
Clonidine (Catapres)	0,1–1,2	Drowsiness, sedation, dry mouth, fatigue, sexual dysfunction.	Rebound hypertension may occur with abrupt discontinuance, especially when taken in high doses or when combined with beta-blocker therapy.
Guanethidine (Ismelin, Normoten)	10	Diarrhoea, hypotension, sexual dysfunction.	Withdraw before an operation
Methyldopa (Aldomet)	250–2 000	Drowsiness, sedation, dry mouth, fatigue, sexual dysfunction.	May cause liver damage and one type of anaemia; should be used cautiously in elderly patients because of a tendency to cause dizziness on standing.
Peripheral-acting adrenergic inhibitors			
Reserpine (Serpasil)	0,1–0,25	Lethargy, nasal congestion, depression.	Should not be used in individuals with a history of mental depression. Should be used with caution in individuals with a history of peptic ulcer disease.
Alpha-1 adrenergic blockers			
Prazosin (Minipress)	1–20	First-dose fainting episodes, drop in blood pressure on standing, weakness, palpitations	Should be used cautiously in elderly patients because of a tendency to cause low blood pressure on standing.

Combined Alpha- and Beta-Adrenergic Blockers

Type of Drug	Dosage Range (mg/day)	Selected Side Effects	Precautions and Special Considerations
Labetalol (Trandate)	200–1 800	Shortness of breath in those with a history of asthma or upper respiratory allergies, peripheral vascular insufficiency, drop in blood pressure on standing.	Should not be used in patients with a history of asthma, chronic obstructive pulmonary disease, congestive heart failure, heart block (greater than first degree), and sick sinus syndrome; should be used with caution in insulin-treated diabetics and patients with peripheral vascular disease.

Calcium Antagonists

Beta-blockers and calcium antagonists are polar opposites in the way they help patients, but both are effective. Calcium antagonists act to keep blood flowing to the heart muscle, while beta-blockers lower the heart muscle's demand for blood. Calcium is a mineral present in your blood and body fluids. Calcium antagonists block the entry of dissolved calcium into your heart muscle's cells as well as into the cells in the muscular walls of your arteries. This is beneficial because it relaxes the arteries and also prevents them from going into spasm. A spasm of a coronary artery, of course, could cut off the supply of blood flowing to the heart, a dangerous ischaemic condition.

Calcium antagonists help prevent chest pain, especially due to coronary artery spasm. They can also lower blood pressure, and may be useful in treating certain types of heart rhythm disturbances.

ACE Inhibitors

This is a new class of medications used mostly to treat hypertension and heart failure. They're relatively free of side effects compared with some predecessor drugs.

"ACE" stands for "angiotensin-converting enzyme." This is an enzyme found mainly in the lungs. It's responsible for activating angiotensin II, a hormone which is one of the body's major

Calcium Antagonists

Type of Drug	Dosage Range (mg/day)	Selected Side Effects	Precautions and Special Considerations
All calcium antagonists		Oedema, headache.	Use with caution in patients with congestive heart failure; contra-indicated in patients with second- or third-degree heart block.
Verapamil (Isoptin)	120–480	Constipation.	May cause liver dysfunction.
Diltiazem (Tilazem)	60–360	Constipation, but usually less severe than that associated with verapamil.	May cause liver dysfunction.
Nifedipine (Adalat)	30–180	Tachycardia (rapid heart rate), flushing, dizziness, fatigue.	

ACE Inhibitors

Type of Drug	Dosage Range (mg/day)	Selected Side Effects	Precautions and Special Considerations
Captopril (Capoten)	25–300	Rash, cough, localized welts on the skin, high potassium, change in taste.	Protein in the urine (rare at recommended doses); high serum potassium, particularly in patients with kidney disease; can induce a low white blood cell count; low blood pressure at initiation of treatment, especially in patients already taking diuretics.
Enalapril (Renitec)	2,5–40		
Lisinopril (Zestril)	5–40		
Quinapril (Accupril)	5–40		

signals to increase blood pressure. When an ACE-inhibiting drug is taken, the enzyme is inhibited; thus no signal to increase blood pressure is sent via angiotensin II. End result: the blood vessels stay dilated rather than constricting. The load on the heart is reduced. And left ventricular function is improved. The latter effect is important in patients with the serious problem of depressed left ventricular function.

Digitalis

Digitalis enhances the ability of the heart muscle to contract, allowing it to beat more vigorously and effectively. This may be needed when a heart is hampered by scar tissue from a heart attack.

Digitalis can also be helpful in treating certain arrhythmias. The drug interacts in a complex way with the heart's electrical conduction system. Its net effect is to slow the conduction of electricity through the heart's electrical system.

ACE Inhibitors

Type of Drug	Dosage Range (mg/day)	Selected Side Effects	Precautions and Special Considerations
Digitalis (Lanoxin)	0,125–0,5	Virtually none if the dose is right; otherwise anorexia, nausea and visual disturbances	If serum levels are too high, arrhythmias and visual changes may result; be careful to make sure that the potassium level is right if diuretics are being taken along with the digitalis; may cause a false-positive exercise test.

Anti-Arrhythmic Drugs

There are a vast number of drugs to control heart rhythm disturbances. In general, these drugs do their job by making heart muscle cells less excitable. Like digitalis, they also slow the conduction of electricity through the heart's electrical system.

Unfortunately, this class of drugs often is known to cause bothersome side effects. This is why it is extremely important for doctors prescribing these medications to make certain that the dosages are right—and that patients adhere strictly to dosage instructions.

Anti-Arrhythmia Drugs

Type of Drug	Dosage Range (mg/day)	Selected Side Effects	Precautions and Special Considerations
Quinidine (Quinaglute)	600–2 400	Diarrhoea, nausea, and vomiting; gastrointestinal disturbance; ringing in ears; visual blurring; dizziness; drop in platelet count	In patients with atrial fibrillation or flutter this medication should be prescribed only after digitalis therapy has been instituted; may prolong the QT interval on the electrocardiogram.
Procainamide (Pronestyl, Procan SR)	1 500–4 000	Rash, difficulty sleeping, gastrointestinal disturbance, drop in blood pressure, altered blood counts.	Lupus syndrome may result; this drug should be used with caution in patients with heart failure.
Disopyramide (Norpace)	400–800	Dry mouth, blurred vision, urinary hesitancy, dizziness, hypoglycaemia, constipation.	Use with caution in patients with heart failure because may cause arrhythmias.
Mexiletine (Mexitil)	600–1 200	Gastrointestinal distress, tremor, co-ordination difficulties, light-headedness, dizziness.	Can cause or worsen arrhythmias.

Anti-Arrhythmia Drugs (continued)

Type of Drug	Dosage Range (mg/day)	Selected Side Effects	Precautions and Special Considerations
Amiodarone (Cordarone)	400–600	Pulmonary inflammation, sensitivity to sunlight, nausea and vomiting, liver disease, malaise, fatigue, tremor, poor co-ordination, small deposits in the corneas.	May cause or worsen existing arrhythmias; drug interactions are common with Coumadin and digitalis; takes a long time to become effective (10 days to 3 weeks).

Vasodilators

Only a few drugs fall into the category of vasodilators. All dilate your arteries, which makes them very useful in controlling blood pressure. Minoxidil also has the effect of making hair grow in some people, which came as a pleasant, commercially viable surprise to the drug's developer.

Vasodilators

Type of Drug	Dosage Range (mg/day)	Selected Side Effects	Precautions and Special Considerations
All vasodilators		Headache, tachycardia (rapid heart rate), ankle swelling.	May precipitate angina.
Hydralazine (Apresoline)	50–300	Positive blood test for lupus syndrome.	Lupus syndrome may occur (rare at recommended doses).
Minoxidil (Loniten)	2,5–80	Excessive hair growth.	May cause or aggravate fluid accumulation along the lining of the lungs or of the heart; may precipitate angina.

Anti-Clotting Medication

Anticoagulants. Warfarin is a medication that inhibits prothrombin and other substances in the body that help form blood clots. Thus, it is prescribed to reduce the body's ability to form a thrombus (clot), which can be the final ingredient of an MI.

Anti-Platelet Drugs. Platelets are tiny particles in the blood that are the building blocks of a blood clot. These drugs help prevent clots from forming by acting against platelets. Dipyridamole may also act as a dilator of coronary vessels. Sulfinpyrazone may also help prevent gout.

Anticoagulants

Type of Drug	Dosage Range (mg/day)	Selected Side Effects	Precautions and Special Considerations
Warfarin (Coumadin)	2–10	Bruising, small areas of skin may undergo degeneration.	Many drugs change the effectiveness of Coumadin—be sure that your physician knows of any other medications that you may be taking; surgery cannot be performed while patient is on this medication; degree of anticoagulation must be checked regularly; may cause bleeding.

Anti-Platelet Drugs

Type of Drug	Dosage Range (mg/day)	Selected Side Effects	Precautions and Special Considerations
Dipyridamole (Persantin)	100–400	Headache, flushing.	None.
Sulphinpyrazone (Anturan)	400–800		May interact with Coumadin and oral hypoglycaemics (oral drugs to lower blood glucose); patient must maintain a high urine output to avoid a buildup of uric acid.

MEDICATION MATTERS: 8 QUESTIONS TO ASK YOUR DOCTOR BEFORE YOU AGREE TO TAKE A DRUG

Medications are a serious matter—and you should understand them fully before you agree to take them.

Many doctors make it a policy to explain the implications of drug therapy before writing out a prescription. If yours does, you needn't read any further.

However, if your physician is quick to prescribe drugs but hesitant to offer a rationale, the following queries will safeguard your body as well as afford you peace of mind. Ask your physician these 8 questions—before you reach out to take that prescription that's being handed to you:

1. What's the generic as well as the trade name of this drug?
2. What is its strength?
3. Why do you think I should take this drug?
4. Are you sure it will interact positively with the other medications I'm taking? (Be prepared to list everything you're taking, from other prescription drugs to over-the-counter medications, even vitamins.)
5. How do you recommend I take this drug? (For example, with meals or on an empty stomach? With water or juice?)
6. What side effects should I be watching out for? Should I report them to you right away or wait until our next visit?
7. Are there any activities—such as driving a car or operating machinery—that I should not do under the influence of this drug?
8. For how long do you foresee me taking this drug?

Source: American Heart Association.

MEDICATION LABELLING AND STORAGE TIPS

Before leaving a pharmacy, make sure that a prescription's label contains the following:

- The pharmacy's name, address, and phone number
- Your name, spelled correctly
- The prescription number
- The name of the medication, and whether it's a trade name or generic
- Directions about how much of the drug to take, and when
- Expiry date, if applicable
- Your prescribing doctor's name
- The current date
- Any special storage instructions

Proper storage is important because medications that aren't handled correctly can lose their potency—which is the whole point of taking them, after all. In addition to heeding the drug manufacturer's or your pharmacist's instructions, keep in mind these storage tips:

- Bathrooms are humid places—which is why you shouldn't store medications there. Instead of using your bathroom's medicine cabinet, find a storage place in a room where the humidity is low and the temperature is fairly constant.
- Store all medications in their original containers with the labels securely affixed.
- Never combine different tablets or capsules in the same container, even to make it easier to carry them in your pocket or purse, or when you're travelling. You never know when you may become incapacitated and someone else will have to give you your medication. That's when the right labelling information becomes especially crucial.
- If necessary, ask your pharmacist for smaller containers that are easier to carry around.
- Don't put medicines in your car's glove compartment or leave them on a windowsill or anywhere else where they would get direct sunlight. Excessive heat or cold can sometimes affect the ingredients.
- By this time, we hope it goes without saying that all medicine should be kept well out of children's reach.

Source: American Heart Association.

GLOSSARY

ACE inhibitor (angiotensin-converting enzyme inhibitor) a type of heart drug used to treat high blood pressure and heart failure.
adrenaline a natural stimulant hormone produced by the adrenal gland; also called "epinephrine."
aerobic exercise physical exercise that relies on oxygen for energy production and can be sustained for prolonged periods of time.
anaerobic exercise physical exercise that does not rely on oxygen for energy production and therefore can be sustained only for short periods of time.
aneurysm a bulging out of the muscular wall of a blood vessel or heart chamber, due to weakness of the wall resulting from disease or injury.
angina chest discomfort or pain resulting from an inadequate supply of blood and oxygen to the heart muscle; also called "angina pectoris."
angiography see *coronary angiography*.
angioplasty a procedure used to dilate the coronary arteries at the sites where they have become narrowed by plaque buildup; also called "percutaneous transluminal coronary angioplasty" or "PTCA."
aorta main artery in the body that carries blood away from the left ventricle.
aortic valve the heart valve between the left ventricle and the aorta.
arrhythmia irregularity of the heartbeat.
arteries blood vessels that transport blood away from the heart to the rest of the body; arteries transport oxygenated blood (with the exception of the pulmonary artery).
atherosclerosis buildup of fatty deposits (plaques) on the inner walls of the coronary or other arteries, resulting in obstruction of the normal flow of blood.
atrium upper chamber of the heart (left and right).
Balke protocol a specific treadmill protocol used for exercise testing; it is usually used only after hospital discharge.
beta-blocker a type of heart drug used to treat angina, high blood pressure, and other heart disorders.

blood pressure the force that blood exerts against the walls of the arteries when it is pumped out of the left ventricle to the rest of the body; the systolic blood pressure reflects the highest and the diastolic blood pressure the lowest amount of pressure in the arteries at any given time.

blood vessel an artery or vein.

Borg RPE (rating of perceived exertion) a system for rating physical exertion which consists of a scale running from (equal to exertion at rest) to 20 (extreme effort) or from 0 (equal to exertion at rest) to 10 (extreme effort).

Bruce protocol a specific treadmill protocol used for exercise testing; it is usually not used on hospitalized patients recovering from a heart attack.

bypass surgery a surgical technique by which blood is detoured around a blocked coronary artery with the use of a vein or an artery from another part of the body.

CHD (coronary heart disease) a progressive disease resulting from the narrowing of the coronary arteries and resultant lack of an adequate oxygen supply to the heart muscle.

calcium antagonists (calcium blockers) a type of heart drug used to treat coronary spasm, angina, high blood pressure, and other heart disorders; also called "calcium channel blockers."

cardiac related to the heart.

cardiac rehabilitation the sum of activities required to ensure cardiac patients the best possible physical, mental, and social conditions so that they may by their own efforts regain as normal as possible a place in the community and lead an active, productive life.

cardiogenic shock a severe form of heart failure, manifested by a falling systolic blood pressure and an inadequate blood supply to many parts of the body.

catheter a thin plastic tube that can be inserted into an artery and then directed toward the heart.

catheterization procedure during which a catheter is inserted into an artery and directed toward the heart for the purpose of assessing the functioning of the heart.

coronary intensive care unit special section of a hospital with intensive medical care and equipment for heart patients.

cholesterol a fatlike substance in the blood that predisposes to atherosclerotic plaque buildup in the coronary arteries.

cholesterol ratio ratio of total cholesterol to HDL cholesterol in the blood; the lower the ratio, the lower is one's risk for CHD.

collaterals a network of reserve blood vessels that branch off from nearby coronary arteries in order to provide the heart muscle that is supplied by an obstructed coronary artery with adequate blood and oxygen.

complex PVCs PVCs that are associated with an adverse prognosis; see PVC on page 442 of glossary.

cool-down the all-important final phase of an exercise training session, during which the exercise intensity is gradually decreased.

coronary angiography a diagnostic X-ray technique that involves the injection of radiopaque dye (for contrast) into the coronary arteries and left ventricle.

coronary arteries arteries that supply the heart muscle with blood and oxygen.

coronary artery spasm spasm of the muscular walls of a coronary artery that clamps off the lumen of the coronary artery.

CPR (cardiopulmonary resuscitation) the procedure by which the heartbeat and/or breathing are restored to a person who is threatened with death.

diabetes disease related to an excessively high level of sugar in the blood; also called "diabetes mellitus."

diastole in each heartbeat, the period during which the heart muscle relaxes and the chambers fill with blood.

diastolic blood pressure see *blood pressure*.

dilate to make wider.

diuretic a type of heart drug used to treat heart failure, high blood pressure, and other heart disorders.

echocardiogram a "picture" of the heart taken by bouncing sound waves off the heart muscle and valves.

ejection fraction percentage of blood in the left ventricle that is pumped out, or "ejected," during each heartbeat.

electrocardiogram tracings on special graph paper that record the heart's electrical activity; also called an "ECG" or "EKG."

epidemiology the study of the distribution and determinants of disease in a population.

epinephrine see *adrenaline*.

ergometer an instrument used to measure work and power output during exercise.

ergometry measurement of work and power; utilizing standard equipment to measure work and power output during exercise.

fibrinogen a substance which circulates in the blood that is a factor in blood clotting.

Framingham Study epidemiological study of the health status of residents in Framingham, Massachusetts, to identify the risk factors for heart disease.

heart attack irreversible damage to an area of the heart muscle caused by an insufficient oxygen supply; also called "myocardial infarction" or "MI".

heart failure a condition in which the heart muscle is unable to pump enough blood to maintain normal circulation; this results

440 GLOSSARY

in buildup of fluid in the body (especially in the feet, ankles, and lungs); also called "congestive heart failure."

heart rate number of contractions (beats) of the heart per minute.

high-density lipoprotein a blood cholesterol component which limits the buildup of atherosclerotic plaques in the coronary arteries; also called "HDL."

Holter monitor a procedure involving the recording on magnetic tape of the heart's electrical signals as they are emitted during an ECG taken over a period of 24 hours; the signals are replayed to detect changes that might go unnoticed in the short time of an ordinary ECG recording; also "ambulatory ECG monitoring."

hypertension higher than normal blood pressure.

hyperthermia an excessive rise in body temperature.

hypotension lower than normal blood pressure

hypothermia an excessive drop in body temperature.

infarction death of living cells as a result of an insufficient supply of blood and oxygen; see *heart attack*.

internal mammary artery artery (left and right) located just under the ribs and running down the chest near the margin of the sternum, commonly used during bypass surgery.

ischaemia local, usually temporary deficiency in the supply of oxygen to some part of the body; see *myocardial ischaemia* and *residual myocardial ischaemia*.

isometric muscle contraction during which the length of the muscle does not change and joint movement does not occur.

kilojoule a basic unit of energy measurement; it is also commonly used as a measure of energy expenditure.

laser device emitting an intense narrow beam of light which can be used to vaporize atherosclerotic plaques.

left main coronary artery the major coronary artery supplying the left ventricle with blood and oxygen.

left ventricular dysfunction an impairment in the normal functioning of the left ventricle.

lipid fatty substance in the blood.

lipoprotein the fat-protein complexes that are used to transport cholesterol and related substances in the blood; LDL and HDL are lipoproteins.

low-density lipoprotein a blood cholesterol component which predisposes to the buildup of atherosclerotic plaques in the coronary arteries; also called "LDL."

lumen central channel of a blood vessel, through which the blood flows.

MET (metabolic equivalent unit) a quantitative measure of human energy output; 1 MET equals the amount of energy expended at rest.

mitral valve the heart valve between the left atrium and left ventricle.
modified Bruce protocol a specific treadmill protocol used for exercise testing; often used for predischarge exercise testing.
monocytes type of blood cells that play an important role in the formation of atherosclerotic plaque buildup.
monounsaturated fats a type of fat derived from certain plants, such as olives, which does not elevate blood cholesterol levels and may, in fact, actually work to lower cholesterol levels.
myocardial infarction see *heart attack*.
myocardial ischaemia lack of an adequate supply of oxygen to the heart muscle; see *residual myocardial ischaemia*.
myocardium heart muscle.
Naughton protocol a specific treadmill protocol used for exercise testing; often used for predischarge exercise testing.
nitrates a type of heart drug used mainly for the treatment of angina; these drugs relax the walls of blood vessels, causing them to dilate.
nitroglycerin a rapidly acting nitrate drug which can be placed under the tongue for immediate relief of angina.
norepinephrine a natural stimulant hormone produced by the adrenal gland; also called "noradrenaline".
oedema swelling of body tissue caused by fluid buildup.
pacemaker an electronic device that delivers electrical stimuli to the heart and can substitute for a defective natural pacemaker; see *S-A node*.
pericardium thin membranous sac that surrounds the heart.
placebo inactive medication that is commonly used during medical research.
plaque fatty deposits that build up on the inner walls of the coronary arteries, resulting in obstruction of the normal flow of blood to the heart muscle.
platelets type of blood cells that play an important role in the formation of blood clots and atherosclerotic plaque buildup.
polyunsaturated fats a type of fat derived from plants, such as vegetables, which does not elevate blood cholesterol levels.
predischarge exercise test exercise test performed before hospital discharge.
prognosis forecast or prediction of the probable outcome of a disease.
pulmonary artery major artery that carries blood from the right ventricle to the lungs.
pulmonary oedema severe form of heart failure in which fluid moves into the breathing spaces in the lungs and causes shortness of breath.
pulmonary valve the heart valve between the right ventricle and the pulmonary artery.

pulse pulsation of an artery which may be felt with the fingers and used to determine the heart rate; the "radial" pulse is felt in the wrist and the "carotid" pulse in the neck.

PVC (premature ventricular contraction) irregular heartbeat that arises from the ventricles; also called "VEB" or "VPB."

radionuclide ventriculography specialized nuclear cardiology test which can be used to assess the functioning of the left ventricle.

rales abnormal breath sounds that result from fluid buildup in the lungs and can be heard in patients with heart failure by listening to their chest with a stethoscope.

rate-pressure product heart rate multiplied by the systolic blood pressure; an indicator of the heart muscle's oxygen requirements.

residual myocardial ischaemia myocardial ischaemia that is still present after a heart attack.

resuscitation restoration of the heartbeat and/or breathing to a person who is threatened with death; see *CPR*.

risk factors habits or conditions that increase one's likelihood of developing CHD.

S-A node the heart's natural pacemaker, which generates the electrical impulses that cause the chambers of the heart to beat rhythmically in the correct sequence.

saphenous vein leg vein commonly used during bypass surgery to detour blood around an occluded coronary artery.

saturated fats a type of fat derived mainly from animal products that causes an elevation in blood cholesterol levels.

septum the wall that separates the left and right sides of the heart.

silent ischaemia myocardial ischaemia that is not accompanied by chest discomfort or other symptoms.

ST segment portion of the ECG tracing between the S and T waves that is of key importance in detecting myocardial ischaemia during exercise testing.

stroke brain damage resulting from an interruption of blood flow to the brain.

symptom-limited heart rate heart rate at which significant cardiac-related abnormalities first begin to appear during exercise testing or, in the absence of any abnormalities, the highest heart rate achieved during exercise testing.

systole in each heartbeat, the period during which the heart muscle contracts and pumps blood out of the heart's chambers.

systolic blood pressure see *blood pressure*.

target heart rate desired heart rate during exercise training; usually 60% to 85% of the symptom-limited heart rate.

thallium scan a nuclear medicine test in which thallium, a radioactive isotope, is injected into a vein during exercise and then scanned with a special instrument in an effort to detect myocardial ischaemia.

thrombus a clot of blood that partially or completely blocks off a blood vessel.

t-PA (tissue-type plasminogen activator) a drug which can be infused to dissolve blood clots in a coronary artery.

tricuspid valve the heart valve between the right atrium and the right ventricle.

triglycerides fatty substances found in the blood.

unstable angina a worsening of angina which may herald a heart attack.

Valsalva manoeuvre an attempt to exhale forcibly with the glottis closed (that is, without letting the air out of the lungs).

veins blood vessels that transport blood to the heart; veins carry unoxygenated blood (with the exception of the pulmonary veins).

ventricle lower chamber of the heart (left and right).

ventricular fibrillation irregular and ineffective contractions of the ventricles, which, if uninterrupted, result in death.

ventricular tachycardia three or more consecutive PVCs.

warm-up the all-important beginning phase of an exercise training session, during which the exercise intensity is gradually increased.

ACKNOWLEDGEMENTS

Working together on this book has been an extremely pleasurable and gratifying experience. To prepare a book as detailed and complex as *The Cooper Clinic Cardiac Rehabilitation Programme,* we have required the assistance and cooperation of many talented people. To adequately acknowledge all would be impossible. However, we would be remiss not to recognize a few special contributions.

Jacqueline Thompson, an exceptionally talented writer based in Staten Island, New York, provided outstanding editorial assistance on the American edition. Her recommendations and overall contributions to the book were invaluable.

Ken Cooper, M.D., M.P.H., chairman and founder of the Cooper Clinic, was of immense assistance in initiating this book. In addition to writing the Introduction reviewing the book, and providing many useful suggestions, he also served as an excellent role model for us in this adventure of writing our first book.

Our editor at Simon and Schuster, Fred Hills, provided guidance that greatly enhanced the practical value of the book. Our literary agent, Herb Katz, was extremely helpful in expediting the business arrangements for the book.

Two world-renowned authorities, Bill Kannel, M.D., M.P.H. (Professor of Medicine and Public Health, Boston University School of Medicine, Boston Massachusetts) and Kent Smith, M.D., M.P.H. (Medical Director, Cardiac Rehabilitation and Preventive Medicine Programmes, Arizona Heart Institute, Phoenix, Arizona), reviewed earlier drafts of our book and provided many excellent suggestions.

Our outstanding secretaries, Linda Robbins, Cynthia Krug, and Stacey Spain, helped with the typing of the manuscript, the compilation of many of the figures and charts, and much more. Bruce Peschel and Irving Perkins Associates were responsible for many of the drawings and figures that are included in our book.

Our colleagues at the Cooper Clinic and Institute for Aerobics Research provided us with much scientific guidance, feedback, and support. Steve Blair, P.E.D., Ruth Carpenter, M.S., R.D., John Duncan, Ph.D., Georgia Kostas, M.P.H., R.D., Chris Scott, M.S.S., M.S., Charles Sterling, Ed.D., and Jody Wilkinson, M.S., were particularly helpful. Many of our student interns assisted with the photocopying of research materials and the checking of our tables and charts.

Twenty-one North American cardiac rehabilitation experts completed a survey of ours on guidelines for returning to various activities after a cardiac event. Their response to this survey will undoubtedly benefit the readers of our book.

A special word of thanks to the Cooper Clinic patients who allowed us to tell their stories. In addition to adding clarity to certain issues discussed in the book, their stories have enabled us to give the book a more human and personal touch. And, last but not least, we wish to thank our many patients, from whom we have learned so much about the practice of medicine over the years.

To all these people—and many others far too numerous to list—many thanks for helping to make this book a reality and in so doing benefiting cardiac patients around the world.

Our grateful thanks to the following for their tremendous help in preparing the South African edition: Prof Tim Noakes; Cecily Fuller of the Heart Foundation of Southern Africa; Dr Dave Marais of the Lipid Clinic at Groote Schuur...

...and also: Dr Krisela Steyn; Prof Harry Seftel; Prof L. Schlebusch; Prof Weich; Dr Rocky Gordon; Dr Y. Salojee of the Council of Smoking and Health; Mrs M. Langenhoven of the Medical Research Council; Vicky Lambert; the Dairy Services Organization in Pretoria.

CHAPTER NOTES

CHAPTER 2

1. E. J. Topol, K. Burek, W. W. O'Neill et al., "A Randomized Controlled Trial of Hospital Discharge Three Days after Myocardial Infarction in the Era of Reperfusion". *New England Journal of Medicine,* 318 (1988):1083–1088.
2. D. C. Renshaw and A. Karstaedt, "Is There (Sex) Life after Coronary Bypass?" *Comprehensive Therapy,* 14 (1988):61–66.
3. H. K. Hellerstein and E. H. Friedman, "Sexual Activity and the Postcoronary Patient". *Archives of Internal Medicine,* 125 (1970): 987–999.
4. M. Ueno, "The So-Called Coition Death". *Japanese Journal of Legal Medicine,* 17 (1963):333–340.
5. Lipid Research Clinic's Program, "The Lipid Research Clinic's Coronary Primary Prevention Trial Results". *Journal of the American Medical Association,* 251 (1984):351–364.
6. V. Manninen, M. H. Frick, K. Haapa et al., "Lipid Alterations and Decline in the Incidence of Coronary Heart Disease in the Helsinki Heart Study". *Journal of the American Medical Association,* 260 (1988):641–651.
7. The nationwide Coronary Drug Project, sponsored by the National Heart, Lung and Blood Institute in Bethesda, Maryland, used a sample of 8 341 men, thirty to sixty-four years old, who had suffered one or more heart attacks. They were treated with the cholesterol-lowering drug niacin. During the follow-up period, their chances of dying from heart disease were compared with those of a control group of similar heart attack patients who did not receive the niacin therapy. Conclusion: the treated patients had a 12 percent lower risk of death from heart disease. See P. L. Canner, K. G. Berge, N. K. Wenger et al., "Fifteen-Year Mortality in Coronary Drug Project Patients: Long-Term Benefit with Niacin". *Journal of the American College of Cardiology,* 8 (1986):1245–1255.

   A second study, sponsored by the same organization, followed 116 men and women with heart disease for five years to determine the effect of lowering cholesterol on the progression of their disease. The results were in agreement with those of the above study. The individuals who had coupled a decreased blood cholesterol level with an increase in the HDL component found that they had reduced significantly the progression of their heart disease. The fortunate individuals did it by switching to a low-cholesterol diet and taking a cholesterol-lowering drug called cholestyramine. See K. M. Detre, R. I. Levy, S. F. Kelsey et al., "Secondary Prevention and Lipid Lowering: Results and Implications". *American Heart Journal*, 110 (1985):1123–1127.

One final study makes our case complete. It's the Cholesterol-Lowering Atherosclerosis Study, conducted at the University of Southern California School of Medicine in Los Angeles. This time coronary angiograms were performed on 162 non-smoking men, forty to fifty-nine years old, who had all undergone bypass surgery. A follow-up angiogram was performed two years later. In the interim, study participants had been treated with either a placebo (inactive medication) or a combination of two cholesterol-lowering drugs, colestipol and niacin. Results: the men treated with the drugs had a 26 percent reduction in blood cholesterol levels and a 37 percent elevation in their good HDL cholesterol. In turn, their favourable blood lipid changes were manifest in less deterioration in their bypass vessels and in their natural coronary arteries. In addition, the researchers observed a visible improvement in the condition of the coronary arteries of 16 percent of the men who had taken colestipol and niacin. Thus, this is the first study to show that lowering cholesterol not only slows the deterioration which normally occurs with time, but may also reduce somewhat any coronary artery blockage that is already present. See D. H. Blankenhorn, S. A. Nessim, R. L. Johnson et al., "Beneficial Effects of Combined Colestipol-Niacin Therapy on Coronary Atherosclerosis and Coronary Venous Bypass Grafts". *Journal of the American Medical Association*, 257 (1987):3233–3240.

8. J. E. Rossouw, B. Lewis and B. M. Rifkind, "The Value of Lowering Cholesterol after Myocardial Infarction". *New England Journal of Medicine*, 323 (16) (1990):1112-9.
9. K. E. Powell, P. D. Thompson, C. J. Caspersen et al., "Physical Activity and the Incidence of Coronary Heart Disease". *Annual Review of Public Health*, 8 (1987):253–287.
10. S. N. Blair, H. W. Kohl, R. S. Paffenbarger, Jr., et al., "Physical Fitness and All-Cause Mortality: A Prospective Study of Healthy Men and Women". *Journal of the American Medical Association*, 262 (1989):2395–2401.
11. A. S. Leon, J. Connett, D. R. Jacobs et al., "Leisure-Time Physical Activity Levels and the Risk of Coronary Heart Disease and Death". *Journal of the American Medical Association*, 258 (1987): 2388–2395.
12. J. M. Rippe, A. Ward, J. P. Porcari et al., "Walking for Health and

Fitness". *Journal of the American Medical Association*, 259 (1988):2720–2724.
13. J. L. Goldstein and M. S. Brown, "Broader Perspectives on Heart Disease and Cardiologic Practice", in E. Braunwald, ed., *Heart Disease: A Textbook of Cardiovascular Medicine*, 3rd ed. Philadelphia: W. B. Saunders Co., 1988, pp. 1617–1649.
14. K.-T. Khaw and E. Barrett-Connor, "Family History of Heart Attack: A Modifiable Risk Factor?" *Circulation*, 74 (1986):239–244.
15. L. P. ten Kate, H. Boman, S. P. Daiger et al., "Increased Frequency of Coronary Heart Disease in Relatives of Wives of Myocardial Infarct Survivors: Assortative Mating for Lifestyle and Risk Factors?" *American Journal of Cardiology*, 53 (1984):399–403.
16. W. B. Kannel and R. D. Abbott, "Incidence and Prognosis of Unrecognized Myocardial Infarction". *New England Journal of Medicine*, 311 (1984):1144–1147.
17. L. Campeau, M. Enjalbert, J. Lesperance et al., "The Relation of Risk Factors to the Development of Atherosclerosis in Saphenous Vein Bypass Grafts and the Progression of Disease in the Native Circulation". *New England Journal of Medicine*, 311 (1984):1329–1332.
18. A. Wiseman, D. D. Waters, A. Walling et al., "Long-Term Prognosis after Myocardial Infarction in Patients with Previous Coronary Artery Bypass Surgery". *Journal of the American College of Cardiology*, 12 (1988):873–880.
19. K. Chatterjee, "Is There Any Long-Term Benefit from Coronary Artery Bypass Surgery?" *Journal of the American College of Cardiology*, 12 (1988):881–882.
20. American College of Cardiology/American Heart Association Special Task Force Report, "Guidelines for Percutaneous Transluminal Coronary Angioplasty". *Circulation*, 78 (1988):486–502.
21. C. L. Jajich, A. M. Ostfeld, and D. H. Freeman, "Smoking and Coronary Heart Disease Mortality in the Elderly". *Journal of the American Medical Association*, 252 (1984):2831–2834.
22. B. Hermanson, G. S. Omenn, R. A. Kronmal et al., "Beneficial Six-Year Outcome of Smoking Cessation in Older Men and Women with Coronary Artery Disease". *New England Journal of Medicine*, 319 (1988):1365–1369.

CHAPTER 3

1. R. Ross, "The Pathogenesis of Atherosclerosis—An Update". *New England Journal of Medicine*, 314 (1986):488–500.
2. Quoted in D. Brand, "Searching for Life's Elixir". *Time*, December 12, 1988, pp. 62-66.
3. Quoted in J. D. Rutherford, E. Braunwald, and P. F. Cohn, "Chronic Ischemic Heart Disease", in E. Braunwald, ed., *Heart Disease: A*

Textbook of Cardiovascular Medicine, 3rd ed. Philadelphia: W. B. Saunders Co., 1988, pp. 1314–1378.
4. M. Prinzmetal, R. Kennamer, R. Merliss et al., "Angina Pectoris I: A Variant Form of Angina Pectoris". *American Journal of Medicine*, 27 (1959):375–388.
5. N. O. Fowler, " 'Preinfarctional' Angina: A Need for an Objective Definition and for a Controlled Clinical Trial of Its Management". *Circulation*, 44 (1971):755–758.

CHAPTER 4

1. R. Mayou, "Psychological Aspects of the Treatment of Myocardial Infarction", in C. T. Kappagoda and D. V. Greenwood, eds., *Long-Term Management of Patients after Myocardial Infarction*. Boston: Martinus Nijhoff Publishing, 1988.
2. T. P. Hackett and N. H. Cassem, "Psychologic Aspects of Rehabilitation after Myocardial Infarction and Coronary Artery Bypass Surgery", in N. K. Wenger and H. K. Hellerstein, eds., *Rehabilitation of the Coronary Patient*, 2nd ed. New York: John Wiley & Sons, 1984.
3. J. Runions, "A Program for Psychological and Social Enhancement during Rehabilitation after Myocardial Infarction". *Heart and Lung*, 14 (1985):117–125.
4. M. J. Stern, "Psychosocial Rehabilitation Following Myocardial Infarction and Coronary Artery Bypass Surgery", in N. K. Wenger and H. K. Hellerstein, eds., *Rehabilitation of the Coronary Patient*, 2nd ed. New York: John Wiley & Sons, 1984.
5. C. Rabiner, A. Willner, and J. Fishman, "Psychiatric Complications Following Coronary Bypass Surgery". *Journal of Nervous and Mental Disorders*, 160 (1975):342–348.

CHAPTER 5

1. M. A. Hlatky, H. E. Cotugno, D. B. Mark et al., "Trends in Physician Management of Uncomplicated Acute Myocardial Infarction, 1970 to 1987". *American Journal of Cardiology*, 61 (1988):515–518 .
2. S. H. Rahimtoola, "The Hibernating Myocardium". *American Heart Journal*, 117 (1989):211–219.
3. R. F. DeBusk, C. G. Blomquist, N. T. Kouchoukos et al., "Identification and Treatment of Low-Risk Patients after Acute Myocardial Infarction and Coronary-Artery Bypass Graft Surgery". *New England Journal of Medicine*, 314 (1986):161–166.
4. American College of Cardiology/American Heart Association Special Task Force Report, "Guidelines for Coronary Angiography". *Journal of the American College of Cardiology*, 76 (1987):963A–977A.
5. J. Ross, Jr., E. Gilpin, E. B. Madsen et al., "A Decision Scheme for

Coronary Angiography after Acute Myocardial Infarction". *Circulation*, 79 (1989):292–303.
6. ACC/AHA Task Force, "Guidelines for Coronary Angiography".
7. Hlatky et al., "Trends in Physician Management".
8. S. O. Gottlieb, S. H. Gottlieb, S. C. Achuff et al., "Silent Ischemia on Holter Monitoring Predicts Mortality in High-Risk Postinfarction Patients". *Journal of the American Medical Association*, 259 (1988): 1030–1035.
9. J. M. Stang and R. P. Lewis, "Early Exercise Tests after Myocardial Infarction". *Annals of Internal Medicine*, 94 (1981):814–815.
10. C. K. Ewart, C. B. Taylor, L. B. Reese et al., "Effects of Early Postmyocardial Infarction Exercise Testing on Self-Perception and Subsequent Physical Activity". *American Journal of Cardiology*, 51 (1983):1076–1080.
11. C. B. Taylor, A. Bandura, C. K. Ewart et al., "Exercise Testing to Enhance Wives' Confidence in Their Husbands' Cardiac Capability Soon after Clinically Uncomplicated Acute Myocardial Infarction". *American Journal of Cardiology*, 55 (1985):635–638.
12. A. Pedersen, P. Grande, and K. Schaadt, "Letter to the Editor", *New England Journal of Medicine*, 302 (1980):174.
13. R. F. DeBusk and W. L. Haskell, "Symptom-Limited vs. Heart-Rate-Limited Exercise Testing Soon after Myocardial Infarction". *Circulation*, 61 (1980):738–743.
14. M. P. J. Senaratne, L. Hsu, R. E. Rossall et al., "Exercise Testing after Myocardial Infarction: Relative Values of the Low Level Predischarge and Postdischarge Exercise Test". *Journal of the American College of Cardiology*, 12 (1988):1416–1422.
15. K. H. Cooper, *Running Without Fear*. New York: M. Evans & Co., 1985.
16. Hlatky et al., "Trends in Physician Management".

CHAPTER 6

1. G. K. Mallory, P. D. White, and J. Salcedo-Salgar, "The Speed of Healing of Myocardial Infarction". *American Heart Journal*, 18 (1939):647–671.
2. S. A. Levine and B. Lown, " 'Armchair' Treatment of Acute Coronary Thrombosis". *Journal of the American Medical Association*, 148 (1952):1365-1369.
3. E. J. Topol, K. Burek, W. W. O'Neill et al. "A Randomized Controlled Trial of Hospital Discharge Three Days after Myocardial Infarction in the Era of Reperfusion". *New England Journal of Medicine*, 318 (1988):1083-1088.
4. R. F. Levin, *Heart-Mates: A Survival Guide for the Cardiac Spouse*. Englewood Cliffs, NJ: Prentice Hall, 1987.
5. R. A. Kloner and J. A. Kloner, "The Effect of Early Exercise on

Myocardial Infarct Scar Formation". *American Heart Journal,* 106 (1983):1009–1013.
6. B. I. Jugdutt, B. L. Michorowski, and C. T. Kappagoda, "Exercise Training after Anterior Q Wave Myocardial Infarction: Importance of Regional Left Ventricular Function and Topography". *Journal of the American College of Cardiology,* 12 (1988):362–372.
7. D. E. Haines, G. A. Beller, D. D. Watson et al., "Exercise-Induced ST Segment Elevation Two Weeks after Uncomplicated Myocardial Infarction: Contributing Factors and Prognostic Significance". *Journal of the American College of Cardiology,* 9 (1987):996–1003.
8. H. K. Hellerstein and E. H. Friedman, "Sexual Activity and the Postcoronary Patient". *Archives of Internal Medicine,* 125 (1970): 987–999.
9. S. Cambre, *The Sensuous Heart.* Atlanta: Pritchett & Hull Associates, 1978.
10. C. Dennis, N. Houston-Miller, R. R. Schwartz et al., "Early Return to Work after Uncomplicated Myocardial Infarction". *Journal of the American Medical Association,* 260 (1988):214–220.
11. Ibid.
12. W. L. Haskell, "Restoration and Maintenance of Physical and Psychologic Function in Patients with Ischemic Heart Disease". *Journal of the American College of Cardiology,* 12 (1988):1117–1119.

CHAPTER 7

1. J. N. Morris, J. A. Raffle, C. G. Roberts et al., "Coronary Heart Disease and Physical Activity of Work". *Lancet,* 2 (1953):1053–1057.
2. J. N. Morris, M. G. Everitt, R. Pollard et al., "Vigorous Exercise in Leisure-Time: Protection Against Coronary Heart Disease". *Lancet,* 2 (1980):1207–1210.
3. Paffenbarger's first important cardiac study, published in 1975, looked at the role of regular exercise in reducing death from heart disease in 6 351 San Francisco Bay Area longshoremen. When the study commenced, the men ranged in age from thirty-five to seventy-four. Paffenbarger followed them for twenty-two years or until they died or reached seventy-five. Those workers who had jobs requiring low energy expenditure had almost twice the risk of dying from CHD as those with high-energy jobs. Physical activity's protective effect was especially marked when it came to sudden death. The workers with the light jobs were at nearly three times greater risk than those with the physically demanding ones. These differences in risk held even after the researchers took other CHD risk factors into consideration. See R. S. Paffenbarger, Jr., and W. Hale, "Work Activity and Coronary Heart Disease Mortality". *New England Journal of Medicine,* 292 (1975):545–550.
4. R. S. Paffenbarger, Jr., R. T. Hyde, A. L. Wing et al., "Physical

Activity, All-Cause Mortality, and Longevity in College Alumni". *New England Journal of Medicine*, 314 (1986):605–613.
5. S. N. Blair, H. W. Kohl, R. S. Paffenbarger, Jr., et al., "Physical Fitness and All-Cause Mortality: A Prospective Study of Healthy Men and Women". *Journal of the American Medical Association*, 262 (1989): 2395–2401.
6. L. G. Ekelund, W. L. Haskell, J. L. Johnson et al., "Physical Fitness as a Predictor of Cardiovascular Mortality in Asymptomatic North American Men". *New England Journal of Medicine*, 319 (1988): 1379–1384.
7. A. S. Leon, J. Connett, D. R. Jacobs et al., "Leisure-Time Physical Activity Levels and Risk of Coronary Heart Disease and Death". *Journal of the American Medical Association*, 258 (1987):2388–2395.
8. M. L. Slattery, D. R. Jacobs, and M. Z. Nichaman, "Leisure Time Physical Activity and Coronary Heart Disease Death: The U.S. Railroad Study". *Circulation*, 79 (1989):304–311.
9. N. B. Oldridge, G. H. Guyatt, M. E. Fischer et al., "Cardiac Rehabilitation after Myocardial Infarction". *Journal of the American Medical Association*, 260 (1988):945–950.
10. "Questions and Answers" column, "Diagnostic and Therapeutic Technology Assessment". *Journal of the American Medical Association*, 258 (1987):1959–1962.
11. P. D. Thompson, "The Benefits and Risks of Exercise Training in Patients with Chronic Coronary Artery Disease". *Journal of the American Medical Association*, 259 (1988):1537–1540.
12. T. Kavanagh, "Does Exercise Improve Coronary Collateralization? A New Look at an Old Belief". *The Physician and Sports Medicine*, 17 (1989):96–114.
13. R. Rauramaa, J. T. Salonen, K. Seppanen et al., "Inhibition of Platelet Aggregability by Moderate-Intensity Physical Exercise: A Randomized Clinical Trial in Overweight Men". *Circulation*, 74 (1986): 939–944.
14. E. R. Eichner, "Coagulability and Rheology: Hematologic Benefits from Exercise, Fish, and Aspirin. Implications for Athletes and Nonathletes". *The Physician and Sports Medicine*, 14 (1986) 102–110.
15. T. D. Noakes, L. Higginson, and L. H. Opie, "Physical Training Increases Ventricular Fibrillation Thresholds of Isolated Rat Hearts during Normoxia, Hypoxia and Regional Ischaemia". *Circulation*, 67 (1983):24–30.
16. U.S. National Exercise and Heart Disease Project, "Effects of Prescribed Supervised Exercise Program on Mortality and Cardiovascular Morbidity in Patients after a Myocardial Infarction". American Journal of Cardiology, 48 (1981):39–46.
17. This is so true that it led Tim Noakes to comment, "The major aspect of any medical intervention is whether or not it improves the

quality of life". Thus, it may be that "these psychological benefits (of exercise) are so important that they nullify concerns of whether or not exercise training prolongs life or prevents reinfarction in cardiac patients". See T. D. Noakes, "Criticisms of Exercise after Heart Attack: Variations on an Old Theme?" *South African Medical Journal,* 62 (1982):238–240.

After many years of clinical experience, we agree. Like Dr. Noakes, we are convinced that a better quality of life is one of the principal benefits cardiac patients receive from a physically active life-style.

18. J. F. Fixx, *The Complete Book of Running.* New York: Random House, 1977.
19. T. D. Noakes, L. H. Opie, A. G. Rose et al., "Autopsy-Proved Coronary Atherosclerosis in Marathon Runners". *New England Journal of Medicine,* 301 (1979):86–89.
20. D. Rennie and N. K. Hollenberg, "Cardiomythology and Marathons" (editorial). *New England Journal of Medicine,* 301 (1979):86–89.
21. G. Schuler, G. Schlierf, A. Wirth et al., "Low-fat diet and regular, supervised physical exercise in patients with symptomatic coronary artery disease: reduction of stress-induced myocardial ischemia". *Circulation,* 77 (1988):172–181.
22. World Health Organization, *Rehabilitation of Patients with Cardiovascular Disease: Report of a W.H.O. Expert Committee,* Technical Report Series, no. 270. Geneva: World Health Organization, 1964.
23. See Note 3 to this chapter.
24. G. Prosser, P. Carson, and R. Phillips, "Exercise after Myocardial Infarction: Long-Term Rehabilitation Effects". *Journal of Psychosomatic Research,* 29 (1985):535–540.

CHAPTER 8

1. D. S. Siscovick, N. S. Weiss, R. H. Fletcher et al., "The Incidence of Primary Cardiac Arrest during Vigorous Exercise". *New England Journal of Medicine,* 311 (1984):874–877.
2. P. D. Thompson, E. J. Funk, R. A. Carleton et al., "Incidence of Death during Jogging in Rhode Island from 1975 through 1980". *Journal of the American Medical Association,* 247 (1982):2535–2538.
3. S. P. Van Camp and R. A. Peterson, "Cardiovascular Complications of Outpatient Cardiac Rehabilitation Programs". *Journal of the American Medical Association,* 256 (1986):1160–1163.
4. R. F. DeBusk, W. L. Haskell, N. H. Miller et al., "Medically Directed At-Home Rehabilitation Soon after Clinically Uncomplicated Acute Myocardial Infarction: A New Model for Patient Care". *American Journal of Cardiology,* 55 (1985):251–257.

5. "Questions and Answers" column, "Diagnostic and Therapeutic Technology Assessment". *Journal of the American Medical Association*, 258 (1987):1959–1962.
6. P. Greenland and P. V. Pomilla, "ECG Monitoring in Cardiac Rehabilitation: Is It Needed?" *The Physician and Sports Medicine*, 17 (1989):75–82.
7. K. F. Hossack and R. Hartwig, "Cardiac Arrest Associated with Supervised Cardiac Rehabilitation". *Journal of Cardiac Rehabilitation*, 2 (1982):402–408.
8. T. D. Noakes, "Heart Disease in Marathon Runners: A Review". *Medicine and Science in Sports and Exercise*, 19 (1987):187–194.
9. W. L. Haskell, "Cardiovascular Complications during Exercise Training of Cardiac Patients". *Circulation*, 57 (1978):920–924.
10. R. J. Barnard, G. W. Gardner, N. V. Diaco et al., "Cardiovascular Responses to Sudden Strenuous Exercise—Heart Rate, Blood Pressure, and ECG". *Journal of Applied Physiology*, 34 (1973):833–837.
11. J. E. Dimsdale, L. H. Hartley, T. Guiney et al., "Postexercise Peril". *Journal of the American Medical Association*, 251 (1984):630–632.
12. B. G. Gatmaitan, J. L. Chason, and A. M. Lemer, "Augmentation of the Virulence of Murine Coxsackie-Virus B-3 Myocardiopathy by Exercise". *Journal of Experimental Medicine*, 131 (1970):1120–1136.
13. N. F. Gordon, "Effect of Selective and Nonselective Beta-Adrenoceptor Blockade on Thermoregulation during Prolonged Exercise in Heat". *American Journal of Cardiology*, 55 (1985):74D–78D. Also, N. F. Gordon, D. P. Myburgh, M. P. Schwellnus et al., "Effect of Beta-Blockade on Exercise Core Temperature in Coronary Artery Disease Patients". *Medicine and Science in Sports and Exercise*, 19 (1987):591–596.
14. B. R. Londeree and S. W. Mittelstadt, "Upper Body Attire for Running in Heat". *Medicine and Science in Sports and Exercise*, 20 (1988):S69.
15. C. F. Brown and N. B. Oldridge, "Exercise-Induced Angina in the Cold". *Medicine and Science in Sports and Exercise*, 17 (1985):607–612.
16. M. Juneau, M. Johnstone, L. Larivee et al., "Effect of Cold upon Ischemic Threshold in Patients with Stable Angina: Magnitude and Mechanism". *Journal of the American College of Cardiology* (annual meeting report), 13 (1989):184A.
17. T. Kavanagh, *The Healthy Heart Program*. Toronto: Van Nostrand Reinhold, Ltd., 1980.
18. W. S. Aronow, C. N. Harris, M. W. Isbell et al., "Effect of Freeway Travel on Angina Pectoris". *Annals of Internal Medicine*, 77 (1972):669–676.
19. B. Balke, "Altitude and Cold: The Cardiac Patient", in M. L. Pollock, D. H. Schmidt, and D. T. Mason, eds., *Heart Disease and Rehabilitation*, 2nd ed. New York: John Wiley & Sons, 1986, pp. 537–547.

20. R. W. Squires, "Moderate Altitude Exposure and the Cardiac Patient". *Journal of Cardiopulmonary Rehabilitation,* 5 (1985):421–426.
21. L. W. Gibbons, K. H. Cooper, B. M. Meyer et al., "The Acute Cardiac Risk of Strenuous Exercise". *Journal of the American Medical Association,* 244 (1980):1799–1801.
22. J. H. Mitchell, B. J. Maron, and S. E. Epstein, "16th Bethesda Conference: Cardiovascular Abnormalities in the Athlete: Recommendations Regarding Eligibility for Competition". *Journal of the American College of Cardiology,* 6 (1985):1222–1224.
23. Siscovick, "The Incidence of Primary Cardiac Arrest".
24. Gibbons, "The Acute Cardiac Risk of Strenuous Exercise".
25. K. H. Cooper, *The Aerobics Program for Total Well-Being.* New York: Bantam Books, 1982. Also, K. H. Cooper and M. Cooper, *The New Aerobics for Women,* rev. ed. New York: Bantam Books, 1988.

CHAPTER 9

1. S. N. Blair, D. G. Clark, K. J. Cureton et al., "Exercise and Fitness in Childhood: Implications for a Lifetime of Health", in C. V. Gisolfi and D. R. Lamb, eds., *Perspectives in Exercise Science and Sports Medicine,* Vol. 2: Youth, Exercise and Sport. Indianapolis: Benchmark Press, 1989, pp. 401–430.
2. W. L. Haskell, H. J. Montoye, and D. Orenstein, "Physical Activity and Exercise to Achieve Health-Related Physical Fitness Components". *Public Health Reports,* 100 (1985):202–212.
3. J. A. Blumenthal, J. Rejeski, M. Walsh-Riddle et al., "Comparison of High- and Low-Intensity Exercise Training Early after Acute Myocardial Infarction". *American Journal of Cardiology,* 61 (1988):26–30.

CHAPTER 10

1. K. H. Cooper, *Aerobics.* New York: Bantam Books, 1968.
2. J. M. Rippe, A. Ward, J. P. Porcari et al., "Walking for Health and Fitness". *Journal of the American Medical Association,* 259 (198): 2720–2724.
3. T. R. Thomas and B. R. Londeree, "Energy Cost during Prolonged Walking vs. Jogging Exercise". *The Physician and Sports Medicine,* 17 (1989):93–102.
4. T. E. Auble, L. Schwartz, and R. J. Robertson, "Aerobic Requirements for Moving Handweights Through Various Ranges of Motion while Walking". *The Physician and Sports Medicine,* 15 (1987):133–140.
5. R. J. Shephard, T. Kavanagh, J. Tuck et al., "Marathon Jogging in Post-Myocardial Infarction Patients". Journal of Cardiac Rehabilitation, 3 (1983):321–329.

6. T. Kavanagh, *The Healthy Heart Program*. Toronto: Van Nostrand Reinhold, 1980.
7. T. Noakes, *The Lore of Running*. Cape Town, South Africa: Oxford University Press, 1986.
8. P. B. Sparling and J. D. Cantwell, "Strength Training Guidelines for Cardiac Patients". *The Physician and Sports Medicine*, 17 (1989): 190–197.
9. R. H. Superko, "Effects of Cardiac Rehabilitation in Permanently Paced Patients with Third-Degree Heart Block". *Journal of Cardiac Rehabilitation*, 3 (1983):561–568.
10. T. Kavanagh, M. H. Yacoub, D. J. Mertens et al., "Cardiorespiratory Responses to Exercise Training after Orthotopic Cardiac Transplantation". *Circulation*, 77 (1988):162–171.
11. N. R. Banner, M. H. Lloyd, R. D. Hamilton et al., "Cardiopulmonary Response to Dynamic Exercise after Heart and Combined Heart-Lung Transplantation". *British Heart Journal*, 61 (1989):215–223.

CHAPTER 11

1. J. F. Fixx, *The Complete Book of Running*. New York: Random House, 1977.
2. K. H. Cooper, *Aerobics*. New York: Bantam Books, 1968.
3. K. H. Cooper, *Running Without Fear*. New York: M. Evans & Co., 1985.
4. American Heart Association booklets: *Coronary Risk Factor Statement for the American Public* (1987) and *Risk Factors and Coronary Disease: A Statement for Physicians* (1980).
5. W. B. Kannel, "New Perspectives on Cardiovascular Risk Factors". *American Heart Journal*, 114 (1987):213–219.
6. J. E. Brody, "Countering the Myth that Women Have Little to Fear from Heart Disease". *New York Times*, February 2, 1989, p. B7.

CHAPTER 12

1. J. C. Piscatella, *Choices for a Healthy Heart*. New York: Workman Publishing Co., 1987.
2. National Cholesterol Education Program, *Report of the Expert Panel on Detection, Evaluation, and Treatment of High Blood Cholesterol in Adults*. National Institutes of Health Publication No. 88–2925, January 1988.
3. J. L. Goldstein and M. S. Brown, "The Low Density Lipoprotein Pathway and Its Relation to Atherosclerosis". *Annual Review of Biochemistry*, 46 (1977):897–930.
4. W. P. Castelli, M. S. Garrison, P. W. Wilson et al., "Incidence of Coronary Heart Disease and Lipoprotein Cholesterol Levels—The

Framingham Study". *Journal of the American Medical Association,* 256 (1986):2835–2838.
5. Piscatella, *Choices for a Healthy Heart.*
6. A. Bonanome and S. M. Grundy, "Effect of Dietary Stearic Acid on Plasma Cholesterol and Lipoprotein Levels". *New England Journal of Medicine,* 318 (1988):1244–1248.
7. D. Kromhout, E. B. Bosschieter, and C. de Lezenne Coulander, "The Inverse Relation Between Fish Consumption and 20-Year Mortality from Coronary Heart Disease". *New England Journal of Medicine,* 312 (1985):1205–1209.
8. S. M. Grundy, "Comparison of Monounsaturated Fatty Acids and Carbohydrates for Lowering Plasma Cholesterol". *New England Journal of Medicine,* 314 (1986):745–748.
9. J. W. Anderson, "Dietary Fibre, Lipids and Atherosclerosis". *American Journal of Cardiology,* 60 (1987):17–22G. Also, J. W. Anderson, L. Story, B. Sieling et al., "Hypocholesterolemic Effects of Oat-Bran or Bean Intake for Hypercholesterolemic Men". *American Journal of Clinical Nutrition,* 40 (1984):1146–1155
10. W. Hotz, "Nicotinic Acid and Its Derivatives: A Short Survey", in *Advances in Lipid Research,* Vol. 20. San Diego: Academic Press, 1983, pp. 195–217.
11. Coronary Drug Project Research Group, "The Coronary Drug Project: Clofibrate and Niacin in Coronary Heart Disease". *Journal of the American Medical Association,* 231 (1975):360–381.
12. D. H. Blankenhorn, S. A. Nessim, R. L. Johnson et al., "Beneficial Effects of Combined Colestipol-Niacin Therapy on Coronary Atherosclerosis and Coronary Venous Bypass Grafts". *Journal of the American Medical Association,* 257 (1987):3233–3240.
13. *Family Practice News,* 16 (1986):65.
14. V. Manninen, O. Elo, M. H. Frick et al., "Lipid Alterations and Decline in the Incidence of Coronary Heart Disease in the Helsinki Heart Study". *Journal of the American Medical Association,* 260 (1988): 641–651.

CHAPTER 13

1. "Dear Abby" column, "Man's Excess Weight Brings Early Death". *Dallas Times Herald,* December 5, 1988.
2. B. M. Hannon and T. G. Lohman, "The Energy Cost of Overweight in the United States". *American Journal of Public Health,* 68 (1978): 765–767.
3. R. P. Donahue, R. D. Abbott, E. Bloom et al., "Central Obesity and Coronary Heart Disease in Men". *Lancet,* 8537 (1987):821–824.
4. J. C. Piscatella, *Choices for a Healthy Heart.* New York: Workman Publishing Co., 1987, p. 67.
5. I. Romieu, W. C. Willet, and M. J. Stampler, "Energy Intake and Other

Determinants of Relative Weight". *American Journal of Clinical Nutrition*, 47 (1988):406–412.
6. A. P. Simopoulos, "Questions and Answers—Diet, Exercise, and Calorie Balance". *Journal of the American Medical Association*, 260 (1988):1953.
7. K. D. Brownell, M. R. C. Greenwood, E. Stellar et al., "The Effect of Repeated Cycles of Weight Loss and Regain in Rats". *Physiology and Behavior*, 38 (1986):459–464.
8. Council on Scientific Affairs, "Treatment of Obesity in Adults". *Journal of the American Medical Association*, 260 (1988):2547–2551.

CHAPTER 14

1. M. Friedman and R. H. Rosenman, *Type A Behavior and Your Heart*. New York: Alfred A. Knopf, 1974.
2. B. K. Houston and K. E. Kelly, "Type A Behavior in Housewives and Its Relation to Work, Marital Adjustment, Stress, Tension, Health, Fear of Failure, and Self-Esteem". *Journal of Psychosomatic Research*, 31 (1987):55–61.
3. J. E. Dimsdale, "A Perspective on Type A Behavior and Coronary Disease" (editorial). *New England Journal of Medicine*, 318 (1988): 110–112.
4. J. Bishop, "Hostility, Distrust May Put Type A's at Coronary Risk". *Wall Street Journal*, January 17, 1989.
5. Ibid.
6. R. Williams, "Refining the Type A Hypothesis: Emergence of the Hostility Complex". *American Journal of Cardiology*, 60 (1987): 27J–32J.
7. H. Selye, *Stress Without Distress*. New York: J. B. Lippincott, 1974.
8. W. B. Cannon, *The Wisdom of the Body*. New York: W. W. Norton, 1932.
9. L. Freeman, G. F. Nixon, P. Sallabank et al., "Psychological Stress and Silent Myocardial Ischemia". *American Heart Journal*, 114 (1987):477–482.
10. A. Rozanski, C. N. Bairey, D. Krantz et al., "Mental Stress and the Induction of Silent Myocardial Ischemia in Patients with Coronary Artery Disease". *New England Journal of Medicine*, 318 (1988): 1008–1012.
11. M. Follick, L. Gorkin, R. Capone et al., "Psychological Distress as a Predictor of Ventricular Arrhythmias in a Post-Myocardial Infarction Population". *American Heart Journal*, 116 (1988):32–37.
12. T. Paula, P. D. Thomas, J. M. Gordon et al., "Effect of Social Support on Stress-Related Changes in Cholesterol Level, Uric Acid Level, and Immune Function in an Elderly Sample". *American Journal of Psychiatry*, 142 (1985):735–737
13. R. Eliot, *Is It Worth Dying For?* New York: Bantam Books, 1989.
14. C. Thoresen, M. Friedman, L. Powell et al., "Altering the Type A

Behaviour Pattern in Postinfarction Patients". *Journal of Cardiopulmonary Rehabilitation,* 5 (1985):258–266.
15. N. Cousins, *Anatomy of an Illness.* New York: W. W. Norton & Co., 1979.
16. H. Benson, *The Relaxation Response.* New York: Avon Books, 1976. Also, the same author's *Beyond the Relaxation Response.* New York: Berkley, 1985.
17. L. Schlebusch (ed.), *Clinical Health Psychology: A Behavioural Medicine Perspective.* Johannesburg: Southern Book Publishers, 1990.

CHAPTER 15

1. J. Barry, K. Mead, E. Nabel et al., "Effect of Smoking on the Activity of Ischemic Heart Disease". *Journal of the American Medical Association,* 261 (1989):398–402.
2. B. Hermanson, G. S. Omenn, R. A. Kronmal et al., "Beneficial Six-Year Outcome of Smoking Cessation in Older Men and Women with Coronary Artery Disease". *New England Journal of Medicine,* 319 (1988):1365–1369.
3. C. L. Jajich, A. Ostfeld, and D. H. Freeman, Jr., "Smoking and Coronary Heart Disease in the Elderly". *Journal of the American Medical Association,* 252 (1984):2831–2834.
4. F. B. Stem, W. E. Halperin, R. W. Hornung et al., "Heart Disease among Bridge and Tunnel Officers Exposed to Carbon Monoxide". *American Journal of Epidemiology,* 128 (1988):1276–1288.
5. W. B. Kannel, P. Wolf, W. Castelli et al., "Fibrinogen and Risk of Cardiovascular Disease". *Journal of the American Medical Association,* 258 (1987):1183–1186.
6. J. Urtel and S. Runtz, "Tangled Roles: A Nurse Practitioner's Experience as a Cardiac Surgery Patient". *Cardiovascular Nursing,* 24 (1988):19–23.
7. T. Kottke, R. Battista, G. DeFriese et al., "Attributes of Successful Smoking Cessation Interventions in Medical Practice". *Journal of the American Medical Association,* 259 (1988):2883–2889.
8. P. Tonnesen, V. Fryd, M. Hansen et al., "Effect of Nicotine Chewing Gum in Combination with Group Counseling on the Cessation of Smoking". *New England Journal of Medicine,* 318 (1988):15–18.
9. U.S. Public Health Service/National Institutes of Health, *1988 Report on the Detection, Evaluation, and Treatment of High Blood Pressure,* National Institutes of Health Publication No. 88-1088, May 1988.
10. American Heart Association, *1988 Heart Facts,* p. 9. Chart, "Hypertension Prevalence by Race and Sex—U.S. Adults Age 18–74", statistics compiled by the National Health and Nutrition Examination Survey II, 1976–1980.
11. S. N. Blair, N. Goodyear, L. W. Gibbons et al., "Physical Fitness and the Incidence of Hypertension in Healthy Normotensive Men and

Women". *Journal of the American Medical Association*, 252 (1984):487–490.
12. S. Weiss, "Stress Management in the Treatment of Hypertension". *American Heart Journal*, 116 (1988):645–649.
13. N. Sasaki, "High Blood Pressure and Salt Intake of the Japanese". *Japanese Heart Journal*, 3 (1962):313–324.
14. "Lowering the Risk for High Blood Pressure". *Tufts University Diet and Nutrition Letter*, 5 (1987):3–6.

CHAPTER 18

1. D. A. Cooley, "A Brief History of Cardiac Surgery". *Journal of Applied Cardiology*, 3 (1988):89–99.
2. P. C. Block, I. Ockene, R. J. Goldberg et al., "A Prospective Randomized Trial of Outpatient versus Inpatient Cardiac Catheterization". *New England Journal of Medicine*, 319 (1988):1251–1255.
3. D. S. Baim and E. J. Ignatius, "Use of Percutaneous Transluminal Coronary Angioplasty: Results of a Current Survey". *American Journal of Cardiology*, 61 (1988):3G-8G.
4. J. W. Hurst, "The Value of Coronary Bypass Surgery Compared with Medical Therapy" (editorial). *Journal of the American Medical Association*, 261 (1989):2118.
5. R. M. Califf, F. E. Harrell, K. L. Lee et al., "The Evolution of Medical and Surgical Therapy for Coronary Artery Disease: A 15-Year Perspective". *Journal of the American Medical Association*, 261 (1989):2077–2086.
6. J. W. Hurst, "The Value of Coronary Bypass Surgery Compared with Medical Therapy" (editorial). *Journal of the American Medical Association*, 261 (1989):2118.

CHAPTER 19

1. Steering Committee of the Physicians' Health Study Research Group, "Preliminary Report: Findings from the Aspirin Component of the Ongoing Physicians Health Study". *New England Journal of Medicine*, 318 (1988):262–264.
2. R. Peto, R. Gray, R. Collins et al., "Randomized Trial of Prophylactic Daily Aspirin in British Male Doctors". *British Medical Journal*, 296 (1988):313–316.
3. ISIS-2 Collaborative Group, "Randomized Trial of IV Streptokinase, Oral Aspirin, Both, or Neither among 17 187 Cases of Suspected Acute Myocardial Infarction". *Lancet*, 2 (1988):349–360.
4. ISIS Pilot Study Investigators, "Randomized Factorial Trial of High Dose IV Streptokinase, of Oral Aspirin and of IV Aspirin in Acute Myocardial Infarction". *European Heart Journal*, 8 (1987):634–642.
5. Anti-Platelet Trialists Collaboration, "Secondary Prevention of

Vascular Disease by Prolonged Treatment". *British Medical Journal,* 296 (1988):320–331.
6. L. Schwartz, M. G. Bourassa, and J. Lesperance, "The Prevention of Restenosis after Percutaneous Transluminal Coronary Angioplasty". *New England Journal of Medicine,* 318 (1988):1714–1719.
7. J. H. Chesebro, I. P. Clements, V. Fuster et al., "A Platelet Inhibitor Drug Trial in Coronary Heart Disease Bypass Operations: Benefit of Perioperative Dipyridamole and Aspirin Therapy on Early Postoperative Vein-Graft Patency". *New England Journal of Medicine,* 307 (1982):73–78.
8. J. H. Chesebro, V. Fuster, L. Elveback et al., "Effect of Dipyridamole and Aspirin on Late Vein-Graft Patency after Coronary Bypass Operations". *New England Journal of Medicine,* 310 (1984):209–214.
9. H.F. Ter Welle, "The Effect of Soya Lecithin on Serum Lipid Values in Type II Hyperlipoproteinemia". *Acta Medica Scandinavica,* 195 (1974):267–271.
10. U.S. Department of Health and Human Services, *The Surgeon General's Report on Nutrition and Health,* Department of Health and Human Services (Public Health Service) Publication No. 88–50210, 1988.

INDEX

abdomen:
 fat on, 255–56
 pain in, 159, 249
 sit-ups myth and, 263
 strength training routine for, 194
ACE inhibitors, 315–16, 428–30
activity, *see* physical activity
acupuncture, stopping smoking and, 299
adipose tissue, 253
 see also fat, body
adrenergic inhibitors, 315, 424–28
 beta-, see beta-blockers
 other, 426–28
aerobic exercise, 15, 178–85
 defined, 178–79
 getting started on, 184–85
 ideal, characteristics of, 179–80
 pros and cons of, 180–84
Aerobics (Cooper), 15, 178–79
Aerobics Activity Centre, 17n
Aerobics Centre, 17, 35, 148, 164, 172, 282
Aerobics Centre Longitudinal Study, 131, 173–74
Aerobics Programme for Total Well Being, The (Cooper), 172
affection, 118
age:
 heart attacks and, 43
 as risk factor, 206, 207
AIDS, 352–53
Alberta, University of, 82
alcohol, 32, 122
 HDL levels and, 247
 hypertension and, 305
 sexual intercourse and, 119
aflatoxin, 365

American Association of Cardiovascular and Pulmonary Rehabilitation, 112, 143
American Cancer Society, 299
American College of Cardiology, 75, 78, 171
American College of Sports Medicine, 201–2
American Dietetic Association, 223
American Heart Association, 17, 75, 78, 104, 218–19, 301
American Heart Journal, 99–100
American Journal of Medicine, 56
American Lung Association, 299
American Medical Association, 72, 132, 151, 153
American Rheumatism Association, 200
amino acid, synthetic, EDTA as, 360–61
amphetamines, 121
amyl nitrite, 121
anaerobic exercise, defined, 179
Anatomy of an Illness (Cousins), 286
aneurysm, defined, 75, 99–100
anger, stress and, 275–76
angina, 27, 56–57, 74
 drugs for, 422–23
 exercise tests and, 88, 89
 patient stratification and, 30
 Prinzmetal's (rest angina; variant angina), 56–57
 sexual intercourse and, 121
 silent ischaemia and, 38
 symptoms of, 56, 113
 unstable, 57
angina scale, 89

angiography (angiograms), 26, 74, 75, 338–41
  goal of, 77, 338
  hospital procedures for, 338–41
  need for, 338
  risk of, 341
angioplasty, 26, 30, 74, 75, 337–346
  activity after, 104, 106, 125
  aspirin and, 359
  benefits of, 39–40
  as "cure," myth of, 39–41
  decision to perform, 341–42
  emotional aftermath of, 67 69
  exercise programme after, 139–40
  follow-up studies of, 40
  hospital stay for, 343–46
  incidence of, 39
  return to work after, 125
  risks of, 343
  risk stratification for, 95, 98
angiotensin II, 316, 428, 430
animal studies:
  cholesterol in, 213
  kilojoules in, 259
  yo–yo syndrome in, 264
ankles, swollen, 114
Annals of Internal Medicine, 80
anti-arrhythmic drugs, 430–32
anti-clotting drugs, 40, 58, 433–434
  anticoagulants, 433, 434
  anti-platelet drugs, 359–60, 433, 434
  aspirin, 40, 357–60
anticoagulants, 433, 434
antidepressants, 121
anti-platelet drugs, 359–60, 433, 434
Anti-Platelet Triallists Collaborative Group, 359
anxiety and tension:
  reduction of, 36
  see also stress
aorta, 46, 350
aortic valve, 46
appetite, loss of, 170
arm-cycle ergometry, 182, 200
  energy expenditure formula for, 398
arms:
  pain in, 159
  strength training routines for, 192, 193
arrhythmias, 26, 79, 158, 244
  drugs for, 430–32
  stress and, 278–79
arteries, 48–52
  blood detoured around, 348–50
  in blood transport network, 45
  circumflex coronary, 49, 50
  dilation of, 422
  endothelium of, 51, 52
  hardening of, *see* atherosclerosis
  internal mammary, 349–50
  laser techniques for, 346–47
  myocardial oxygenation and, 49
  number of, 49
  physiology of, 48–50
  Prinzmetal's angina and, 56–57
  pulmonary, 45, 46
  reduction of blockage in, 32–33
  residual myocardial ischaemia and, 74
  silent ischaemia and, 38
  see also coronary heart disease
arthritis, exercise and, 182, 200
aspirin, 244, 294–95
  blood clot prevention and, 40, 357–60
  dipyridamole combined with, 359–60
atherosclerosis, 28, 40, 51–52, 207
  in animals, 213
  start of, 51
  see also plaque
atrium, 44, 46, 47
atropine, 166
attitudes, toward personal health, 23
autopsy studies, 52

back:
  exercise and, 182, 187, 188, 191, 194
  pain in, 159, 182, 277
  strength training routines for, 191, 194
  stretching exercises for, 187, 188
Balke, Bruno, 170
Balke protocol, 87
Barnard, Christiaan, 15, 197
Barrett-Conner, Elizabeth, 37
Bassler, Thomas J., 135

bed rest, prolonged, 99–101, 133–134
Bensen, Herbert, 286
bent-over shoulder raise, 191
beta-blockers, 121, 132, 245, 424–426
  cardioselective, 425
  exercise and, 166, 198–99
  exercise tests and, 84
  hypertension and, 315
Beyond the Relaxation Response (Benson), 286
biceps curl, 192
bile acids, 54
bile acid sequestrants, 245, 249
bio–electric impedance method, 255
biofeedback techniques, 306
birth control pills, 118
blacks:
  hypertension in, 304, 315
Blair, Steven N., 35, 173–74, 175
blood:
  for bypass surgery, 352–53
  functions of, 44
  transport network of, 44–47, 161–62, 167
blood clots, 26, 58
  drugs in prevention of, 40, 58, 357–60, 433–34
  exercise effects on, 133–34
  small (thrombosis), 28, 293, 294
  symptoms of, 114
  thrombus, 58
blood pressure, 138
  alcohol and, 247
  anger and, 275–76
  defined, 47
  diastolic, 47, 134
  exercise and, 134
  Heart Points System and, 321–322, 327–28
  high, *see* hypertension
  stress and, 275–76
  systolic, 47, 49, 88, 89, 110, 134
blood vessels, 44–46
  effect of smoking on, 291–94
  see also arteries; veins
body:
  stress effects on, 276–79
  see also specific organs
Bonanome, Andrea, 228–29

Borg, Gunnar, 83
Borg perceived exertion scale, 83, 84, 88, 112, 138, 197, 198, 199
  revised, 83, 85
Bowman Gray School of Medicine, 176–77
breath, shortness of, 113–14, 159, 201
bronchitis, 200
Brown, Michael S., 37, 54, 214
Brownell, Kelly, 264
butter, 227–28
buttocks, strength training routine for, 195
Bypass (Halperin and Levine), 352
bypass surgery, 26–27, 30, 74, 75, 337–42, 347–53
  activity after, 104–5, 106, 125
  aspirin and, 359–60
  benefits of, 39–46, 347–48
  blood detours around arteries in, 348–50
  as "cure," myth of, 39–41
  decision to perform, 341–42
  emotional aftermath of, 67–69
  exercise programme after, 139, 140, 182
  goal of, 338
  hospital procedures for, 350–52
  incidence of, 39
  preparations for, 352–53
  return to work after, 125
  risks of, 347, 348
  risk stratification for, 95, 98
  symptoms to watch for after, 114

CHD, *see* coronary heart disease
caffeine, 122
calcium, 428
  chelation controversy and, 360–361
  hypertension and, 312
calcium antagonists (calcium channel blockers), 316, 428, 429
  exercise tests and, 84
calf pain, swelling, redness, or "heat" in, 114
calf raise, 195
calf stretch, 188
Califf, Robert M., 347

Campeau, Lucien, 40
cancer, 253, 290
Cannon, Walter B., 276
Cantwell, John D., 189
carbohydrates, 234, 239–41
   complex, 234, 239–41, 260, 263
   eating suggestions for, 241
   metabolism of, 134
   simple, 234, 259—60
   in slimming diets, 262–63
carbon dioxide, 44–47
carbon monoxide, 169–70, 293–94
cardiac catheterization laboratory (cath lab), 26
"cardiac cripples," 30
cardiac rehabiliation, *see* rehabilitation, cardiac
cardiogenic shock, 77
cardiologists, 72–73
   criticism of, 30
cardiopulmonary resuscitation (CPR), 104
cardiovascular system, 48
   see also arteries; blood vessels; heart
Castelli, William, 215
cataracts, 246
catecholamines, 161, 171
catheterization, heart, 75, 78
Cedars–Sinai Medical Centre, 277–78
cellulose, 239
Centres for Disease Control, Lipid Standardization Programme of, 216
Charing Cross Hospital, stress study at, 277
Chatterjee, Kanu, 40
cheese 224
chelation controversy, 360–61
chest, strength training routines for, 193–94
chest pain, 25–27, 57
   in angina, 56
   during exercise, 159
   myths about, 38–39
children, CHD in, 213
chills, 114
chocolate, 229
cholesterol, 34, 212–49, 317
   acceptable levels of, 215
   animal sources of, 233–34
   borderline high, 214
   CHD and, 51–55, 212–18
   carbohydrates and, 234, 239–41
   diet solution to, 217–19
   exercise and, 134, 247
   HDLs and, *see* high-density lipoproteins
   high, 214
   high consumption of, 218
   hypertriglyceridaemia and, 246, 249
   LDLs and, *see* low-density lipoproteins
   lecithin and, 362–63
   lowering of, 32–33, 243, 244, 246, 361
   measurement of, 214–17
   in shellfish, 233, 234
   stearic acid and, 229
   testing of, 24
   total, 134, 214, 215, 243
cholesterol-free food, 33–34
cholesterol-lowering drugs, 33, 40, 241–49
   combining of, 247
   drawbacks of, 242–46
   niacin as, 243–44, 249
   summary of, 247, 248
cholesterol ratio, 55
chronic obstructive pulmonary disease (COPD), 200–201
Churchill, Winston, 285
chylomicrons, 53, 249
cigar smoking, 296
circuit resistance training, 184
circulatory system, physiology of, 44–50
circumflex coronary artery, 49, 50
cirrhosis, 244
clothing, exercise and, 162, 166–169
cocaine, 121
cocoa butter, 228
coconut oil, 33–34, 228
College of American Pathologists, 216
Commentary on the History and Cure of Diseases (Heberden), 132–33
community-based programmes, 140–141, 149–50
competition:
   exercise and, 171–72
   sports and, 109

Complete Book of Running, The
  (Fixx), 135–36, 205
contraception, 118
contraindication:
  defined, 244
  for niacin, 244
cooling down, 160–62, 198
Cooper, Kenneth, 87, 172,
  178–179, 183, 205–6, 282
COPD (chronic obstructive
  pulmonary disease), 200–201
copper deficiency, 365
corn oil, 231
coronary arteries, *see* arteries
coronary heart disease (CHD), 43,
  48, 50–58
  autopsy studies of, 52
  cholesterol's role in, 51–55,
    212–18
  death rates for, 13–15, 43,
    302–303
  definition and causes of, 50–52
  fatty-streak formation and, 51
  as hazard, 55–57
  oestrogen use and, 118
  risk factors for, 52, 60, 134–36,
    205–11; *see also* cholesterol;
    diabetes melitus; hyper-
    tension; obesity; sedentary
    lifestyle; smoking; stress
  see also angina; heart attacks;
    myocardial ischaemia; silent
    ischaemia
Coronary Artery Surgery Study,
  41
coronary intensive care unit,
  27, 6365, 72, 77, 138, 346
coronary collaterals, 55
Coronary Drug Project, 243
coronary spasm, 55, 59
coronary thrombosis, 28, 293,
  294
  use of term, 58
  see also heart attacks
cottonseed oil, 228
counselling:
  dietary, 223
  psychiatric, 67
  sexual, 122
Cousins, Norman, 286
CPR (cardiopulmonary
  resuscitation), 104
crash dieting, myth of, 264–65

cravings, psychology of, 261
cross-country skiing, 183
cyanosis of the lips, 297
Cybex Metabolic Systems, 182
cycling:
  outdoor, 182
  Schwinn Air–Dyne, 375,
    385–389, 397, 406–8
  stationary, 181–82, 185, 375,
    380–84, 396, 404–8

dairy products, fat in, 224–28
dancing, aerobic, 183–84
death, death rates:
  for bypass surgery, 348
  for coronary artery disease,
    13–15, 43, 302–3
  exercise and, 136, 146–48,
    158–159, 161–62, 205
  during exercise testing, 81
  fear of, 64
  in first year after heart attack,
    76–77
  from heart attacks, 17
  from heart disease, 15–17, 37
  in high-risk category, 29
  in low-risk category, 29
  in moderate-risk category, 30
  obesity and, 250–51
  post-exercise, 161–62
  during sexual intercourse,
    31–32,115
  smoking and, 41, 290
  of tunnel toll-takers, 293–94
DeBusk, Robert F., 82, 148
deep muscle relaxation, 287–88
dehydration, 163
denial, 64–65
depression, after heart attack, 30,
  65–66, 67, 69–70
diabetes mellitus, 244, 249,
  316–317
  exercise and, 134, 164, 201–2,
    317
  Heart Points System and, 322
  LDL cholesterol and, 210
  obesity and, 253
  Type I, 201–2, 316
  Type II, 201–2, 316
diaries:
  exercise training, 192, 196
  smoking-cessation, 301
diastole state, 46, 47

diastolic blood pressure, 47, 134
diet, 217–41
  cholesterol lowered by, 217–19
  fat in, *see* fat, dietary
  fibre in, 239–41
  food facts and, 220–41
  high-protein/low-carbohydrate, 262–63
  improvement of, 17, 219–20
  low-fat, 32–33, 249
  myths about, 32–34
  Step 1 Eating Plan and, 219–23, 234
  Step 2 Eating Plan and, 220, 223
dieter's dilemma (yo–yo syndrome), 264–65
dietitians, registered, 223
dieting, *see* mass loss
digitalis, 365, 430
disaccharides, 239
disquiet, hospital, 63–65
diuretics, 121, 245, 315, 421–22
dizziness, 114, 159, 314
doctors:
  criticism of, 30
  denial of need for, 23
  exercise test and, 88–92, 112
  medical clearance for exercise and, 149, 150
  recovery instructions from, 102
Donahue, Richard, 255–56
drugs, 419–36
  ACE inhibitors, 315–16, 428–430
  addiction fears and, 64
  adrenergic inhibitors, 315, 424–428; *see also* beta-blockers
  anti-arrhythmia, 430–32
  beta-blockers, *see* beta blockers
  blood clots prevented by, 40, 58, 357–60, 433–34
  bypass-surgery preparations and, 352
calcium antagonists, 84, 316, 428, 429
cholesterol-lowering, 33, 40, 241–49
  digitalis, 365, 430
  diuretics, 121, 245, 315, 421–22
  exercise and, 164–66
  exercise tests and, 84–85
  for hypertension, 304–5,
  311–312, 314–16, 421, 426
  labelling and storage tips for, 436
  nitrates (nitroglycerin), 25–26, 113, 121, 422–24
  pros and cons of, 419–20
  questions to ask about, 435
  sexual intercourse and, 121
  stress management and, 286, 289
  vasodilators, 315, 433
Duke University Medical Centre, 176–77
  Cardiology Division of, 72–73, 78

ECG, *see* electrocardiogram
echocardiogram, 78
ectopic beats, 90
EDTA, 360—61
education, stress management and, 280
egg yolks, 233, 234
Eichner, Edward R., 133–34
Eisenhower, Dwight D., 99
ejection fraction, 78
elderly, exercise and, 199
electrical system, of heart, 48
electrocardiogram (ECG), 39, 48, 74,79,138
  copper deficiency and, 364
  exercise monitored by, 151, 153–54
  exercise testing and, 80, 85–87, 90–91
  sexual activity monitored by, 115
  vitamin E and, 363
  work monitored by, 124
Eliot, Robert, 284, 285
E–LOG, 377
emotions, *see* feelings, in recovery; feelings, in stress management
emphysema, 200
employment, *see* work
endothelium, 51, 52
energy expenditures:
  for cardiovascular benefits, 174–75
  estimating of, 375–99
  formulas for, 375–77, 392–99
  for physical activities, 107–8

for sporting activities, 110
Environmental Protection
    Agency, U.S., 169
Eskimos, 231, 361
exercise, 24, 127–202
    aerobic, *see* aerobic exercise
    amount of, 173–77
    anaerobic, 179
    benefits of, 34–36, 132–36, 142, 143, 258
    choice of, 143–44, 178–84
    cholesterol and, 134, 247
    clothing and, 162, 166–69
    conditions precluding use of, 150
    in context of cardiac rehabilitation, 136–42
    cooling down and, 160–62, 198
    diabetes and, 134, 164, 201–2, 317
    discomfort during, 25
    drugs and, 164–66
    elimination of risk factors of, 160–72
    estimation of energy expenditure during, 375–79
    FIT concept and, 175–77
    goals of, 173–77
    heart and, 48
    Heart Points System and, 321–324
    high-altitude, 170–71
    hypertension and, 36, 134, 305
    hyperthermia and, 16–63, 164
    during illness, 164–66
    increase in, 15
    infrequent, 172
    intensity of, 175, 176–77
    isometric, 120, 186–87
    mass loss and, 257, 258
    see also cycling; jogging; running; walking
    medical clearance for, 149, 150
    myths about, 34–36, 135–36, 206
    on-site medical supervision and, 149–54
    past experiences with, 144
    pollution and, 169–70
    post-infarct patient and, 132–36
    as preventive measure, 34–35
    risk of death during, 146–48
    safety guidelines for, 148–72
    safety quiz for, 409–18
    special cardiac conditions and, 196–202
    strenuous vs. moderate, 35–36
    stress and, 134, 282–83
    stretching and strength training, 185–96
    training heart rate and, 154–58
    upper-body, 105, 197
    warm-ups for, 120, 160–62, 198
    warning signs during, 25, 158–160
    weather conditions and, 163–164, 167–69
"exercise hypothesis," 129–31
exercise programmes, 137–45, 401–8
    combined walking and stationary cycling, 407–8
    persevering in, 142–45
    phases of, 137–42, 151
    progress in, 143
    Schwinn Air-Dyne, 406–8
    special occasions and, 144–45
    stationary cycling, 404–8
    support for, 144
    walking, 401–4, 407–8
exercise training log, 192, 196
exercise tests, 73, 75, 79–98, 155
    abnormal ST segment and, 88, 90–91, 92, 160
    angina and, 88, 89
    appropriate use of, 81–82
    blood pressure aberrations and 88, 89
    Borg scale and, 83, 84, 88
    complex PVCs and, 88, 90
    doctor's perspective on, 88–92, 112
    ECG and, 80, 85–87, 90–91
    excessive fatigue and, 88, 91–92
    formulas for estimation of MET during, 371–73
    interpreting results of, 92
    machine for, 87–88
    nuclear medicine techniques during, 92–93
    patients excluded from, 77–79
    patients excluded from, question about prognosis for, 92, 94–95
    before returning to work,

123–124
    safety of, 79–83
    submaximal vs. symptom-limited maximal, 82, 124
    subsequent, 93, 95–98
    typical, 83–85
exercise training log, 192, 196
Exersentry heart rate monitor, 158
extramarital affairs, health risk of, 32

fainting, 159
family:
    feelings of, 102–3
    as risk factor, 206, 208–9
    stress management and, 280
fat, body:
    acceptable percentages for, 255
    distribution of, 255–56, 263
    measuring of, 253–55
fat, dietary, 28, 223–34
    in dairy products, 224–28
    in ideal diet, 34
    mass loss and, 259, 262
    monounsaturated, 33, 229, 232, 233
    omega–3, 231, 361–62
    omega–6, 231
    per serving, calculating of, 227
    polyunsaturated, 33, 228, 230–233, 361–62
    in red meats, 228–30
    saturated, see saturated fats
fatigue:
    excessive, exercise tests and, 88, 91–92
    after heart attacks, 30–31 fatty-streak formation, 51
fears:
    post-heart attack, 64, 103, 119
    of spouses, 103, 119
Federal Drug Administration (FDA), 300
feelings, in recovery:
    after bypass surgery or angioplasty, 67–69
    depression, 30, 65–66, 67, 69–70
    of family members, 102–3
    hospital disquiet and, 63–65
    normalization of, 66–67
feelings, in stress management, 280–82

acknowledgment of, 280–81
constructive release of, 281–82
feet, swollen, 114
fever, 114
fibre, dietary, 239–41
    insoluble, 239
    soluble, 239–41
    sources of, 239, 240
fibrinogen, 291, 294–95
fidelity, marital, 32
fight-or-flight reaction, 171, 276
fish, 230, 231, 361, 362
fish oils, 231, 233
    capsules of, 361–62
FIT (Frequency, Intensity, and Time), 175–77
Fixx, Jim, 135–36, 205–6
flu, exercise and, 164, 166
follow-up heart attacks, 367–68
    prevention of, 17, 34–35, 424–426
    risk of, 29–30
food, 220–41
    cholesterol-free, 33–34
    cholesterol in, see cholesterol
    labelling of, see labels, food
    low-fat, 34
    processed, 230, 306–7
    shopping for, 262
    sodium content of, 308–11
    special, mass-loss myth of, 263
    see also specific foods and food groups
food intake, timing of, 263
food rewards, replacements for, 261–62
foreplay, 119–20
formulas:
    for energy expenditure, 375–77, 392–99
    for MET estimation, 371–73
    for target heart rate, 155
Fowler, Noble O., 57
foxglove, 365
Framingham Study, 39, 43, 60, 294
Frances Scott Key Medical Centre, 79
Freedom from Smoking for You and Your Family (American Lung Association), 299
Friedman, Ernest H., 31, 115
Friedman, Meyer, 272–74, 284

friends:
  recovery reactions of, 103–4
  stress management and, 280
  front shoulder raise, 190

gallbladder disease, 253
Gallup poll, 15
GAS (general adaptation syndrome), 276–77
gastroenteritis, 164
gastrointestinal upsets, 244, 245, 246, 277
gender, as risk factor, 206, 207–8
general adaptation syndrome (GAS), 276–77
genetic factors:
  in cholesterol levels, 53
  in heart disease, 27, 36–38, 208
  myths about, 36–38
  in mass problem, 252
Germany, Federal Republic of (West Germany), 136
Gibbons, Larry (co-author), background of, 18
ginseng, 365
glucose intolerance:
  impaired, 253
  see also diabetes mellitus
Goldstein, Joseph L., 37, 54, 214
Gold Life, The (American Heart Association), 301
Gordon, Neil (co-author), background of, 18–19
gout, 244
Great Britain:
  cardiac rehabilitation studies in, 143, 174, 198
  stress study in, 277
Greeks, ancient, 129, 161,162
Greenland, Philip, 153
grief, 70
grilling food, 230
Grundy, Scott, 228–29
Gruntzig, Andreas R., 337
Guest Lodge, 17*n*
gum, nicotine (Nicorette), 300–301

habits:
  eating, 261–62, 265
  inheritance of, 37, 209
haemorrhagic stroke, 357–58
Halperin, Jonathan L., 352

hamstrings, stretching exercise for, 188
Haresfield Hospital, Cardiothoracic Unit of, 198
Harvard Medical School Health Letter, 424–25
Harvard School of Public Health, 259
Harvard study, 131, 142, 174
Haskell, William L., 82, 174–75
HDLs, *see* high-density lipoproteins
headaches, 170, 277
Health and Human Services Department, U.S., 212
health care, costs of, 367–68
health data, evaluation of, 354–57
Healthy Heart Programme, The (Kavanagh), 181
heart:
  chambers of, 44, 48
  electrical system of, 48
  irregular beating of, *see* arrhythmias
  left side of, 47
  oxygen needs of, 49–50, 132–33
  palpitations of, 114
  physiology of, 44–48
  transplantation of, 197–98
  valves of, 46, 47
heart attacks, 43–60
  age and, 43
  aspirin's role in prevention of, 357–60
  case study of, 23–28
  causes of, 58–59
  cholesterol index of risk of, 215
  damage of, 47, 58, 59–60
  exercise programme after, 140
  follow-up, see follow-up heart attacks incidence of, 17, 43
  left ventricle in, 47
  recovering from, *see* recovering from a heart attack or surgery
  severity of, 71–99; *see also* risk stratification
  stress and, 269–71
  timetable for, 59
  undetected, 39, 57
  warning signs of, 25, 57
heart catheterization, 75, 78
Heart Corps, 143

heart disease:
  asymptomatic, 38, 43
  decline in incidence of, 15–17
  genetic factors in, 27, 36–38, 208
  myths about, 29–42
  myths about "curing" of, 39–41
  risk factors for, 205–11, *see also* cholesterol; diabetes mellitus; hypertension; obesity; sedentary lifestyle; smoking; stress
  as self-inflicted, 13–15
  understanding, 21–60
  in women, 37, 207–8
  see also specific topics
Heart-Mates (Levin), 103
Heart Points Exercise Charts, 185, 375–91
  formulas for, 325–77, 392–99
  for jogging, 375, 378–79
  for other activities, 390–91
  for Schwinn Air-Dyne, 375, 385–89
  for stationary cycling, 375, 380–84
  for walking, 375, 376, 377
Heart Points Scorecard, 333–34
Heart Points System, 19, 185, 210, 211, 217, 321–32
  blood pressure and, 321–22, 327–28
  diabetes and, 322
  exercise and, 321–24
  HDL cholesterol and, 322
  LDL cholesterol and, 321–22, 325–26
  mass control and, 321–22, 329–30
  stress management and, 321–322, 331–32
heart rate:
  exercise and, 154–58
  per minute, calculating of, 155, 157
  portable monitors of, 158
  resting, 156
  symptom-limited, 112, 176–77
  training, 154–58, 175, 177
"heat," in calf, 114
Heberden, William, 56, 132–33
Heidelberg study, 136
Hellerstein, Herman K., 31, 115

helplessness, feeling of, 270–71
Helsinki Heart Study, 32
hepatitis, 244
herbal remedies, 365
heredity, *see* genetic factors
hibernating myocardium, 75
high-altitude exercise, 170–71
high blood pressure, *see* hypertension
high-density lipoproteins (HDLs), 53, 214–17, 253
  anti-hypertensive drugs and, 314, 315
  benefits of, 54–55
  gender and, 207
  Heart Points System and, 322
  increase of, 32, 33, 55, 134, 243, 244, 246, 247, 249
  low levels of, 206, 242
  niacin and, 243, 244
  smoking and, 291, 293
high-risk category, 30, 104, 367
  death rates for, 29
  fatigue and, 31
  first-year risk of, 76–77
  sexual activity and, 119–20
  stratification methods for, 77–79
Hippocrates, 129
hips, fat on, 256
HMG CoA reductase inhibitors, 246
Holmes-Rahe scale, 271
Holter monitoring, 79, 115, 124, 277
homecoming letdown, 65–66
hormones:
  angiotension II, 316, 428, 430
  catecholamines, 161, 171
hospital disquiet, 63–65
hostility, stress and, 272, 275–276
Houston, B. Kent, 275
Hurst, J. Willis, 348
hydrogenation, 228
hypercholesterolaemia, 213, 364
hyperkalaemia, 311–12
hypertension (high blood pressure), 15, 24, 27, 34, 52, 206, 207, 302–16
  alcohol and, 305
  calcium and, 312
  causes and treatment of, 304–313

defined, 303–4
drugs for, 304–5, 311–12, 314–316, 421, 426
exercise and, 36, 134, 305
mass loss and, 305
obesity and, 253, 305
potassium intake and, 307, 311–12
relaxation and, 306
salt and sodium and, 306–13
smoking and, 305
hyperthermia, 162–63
warning signs of, 163, 164
hypertriglyceridaemia, 246, 249
hypnosis, giving up smoking and, 299
hypothyroidism, 249

ice cream, 227
illness:
exercise during 164–66
obesity and, 253
see also specific illnesses
immune system, 277
Index Medicus, 129
infection, exercise and, 164–65
influenza, 164
inner thigh stretch, 188
inpatient programme, 137–39
insomnia, 170, 277
Institute for Aerobics Research, 17n, 377
insurance:
life, 24
medical, 367
intellectual dysfunction, 69
intensive care unit (ICU), 138
intermittent claudication, 199–200
internal mammary arteries, 349–350
invulnerability, myth of, 135–36, 206
ischaemia:
heart attack vs., 58
myocardial, 55–56, 73–74; *see also* heart attacks
silent, 38, 57, 277–78
ischaemic stroke, 358
isometric exercise, 120, 186–87

Japan, heart disease study in, 31–32

jaw pain, 159
"Jim Fixx syndrome," 206
jobs, *see* work
jogging, 146, 147
energy expenditure formulas for, 394–95
exercise programme for, 403–4
Heart Point Charts for, 375, 378–79
pros and cons of, 181
shoes for, 167
treadmill, 395
Johns Hopkins Hospital, 79
Journal of Cardiopulmonary Rehabilitation, 112
Journal of the American College of Cardiology, 40
Journal of the American Medical Association, 100

Kavanagh, Terence, 169, 181
Kerr, Katherine, 251
Khaw, Kay-Tee, 37
kidneys, 249, 312, 364
kilojoule, 174, 218–19, 234, 256–60
kilojoule, packaging, 257
Korean War, autopsy evidence from, 52
Kuopio, University of, 133

labels, drug, 436
labels, food, 241
fat content on, 227
myths about, 33–34
lasers, use of, 346–47
laughter, importance of, 285–286
LDLs, *see* low-density lipoproteins
lecithin, 362–63
left anterior descending coronary artery (LAD), 49, 50
left ventriculography, 339–40
legs:
intermittent claudication and, 199–200
swollen, 114
Leiden, University of, 231
lettuce, 239
Levin, Rhoda F., 103
Levine, Richard, 352
Levine, Samuel A., 100
lidocaine, 26
life insurance, medical exams

472 INDEX

required for, 24
life-style factors, 125, 206
 beneficial trends in, 15, 17
 controllable, 206, 207
 in coronary heart disease, 13,
  15, 130–31, 206
 marriage and, 37
 obesity and, 252
 sedentary, 130–31, 206
 in stress, 271–72
 see also diet; exercise; hypertension; smoking
light-headedness, 114
linoleic acid (omega-6 fatty acid),
 231
Lipid Research Centre:
 Coronary Primary Prevention
  Trial results of, 32
 Mortality Follow-up Study of,
  131
lipoprotein lipase, 53, 54
lipoproteins, 53–55
 defined, 53
 HDLs, *see* high-density
  lipoproteins
 LDLs, *see* low-density
  lipoproteins
 VLDLs, *see* very-low-density
  lipoproteins
liver, 364
 bile acid sequestrants and, 245,
  249
 cholesterol and, 53, 54
 niacin and, 244
liver disease, 249
Long Beach Veterans
 Administration Hospital, 169
long-term, community-based
 programme, 140–41
Lore of Running, The (Noakes),
 181, 167
low-density lipoproteins (LDLs),
 53–54, 55, 212–20, 253
 anti-hypertensive drugs and,
  314
 complex carbohydrates and, 239
 diabetes and, 210
 Heart Points System and,
  321–322, 325–26
 high levels of, 206, 207
 lowering of, 243, 244, 246, 361
 niacin and, 243, 244
 optimum levels for, 242

 reduced number of receptors
  for, 213
 saturated fats and, 224
"low–fat," on food labels, 34
Lown, Bernard, 100
low-risk category, 29, 31, 367
 activity recommendations for,
  104
 exercise programmes for, 140
 first-year risk of, 76–77
lumen, 51, 52
lung cancer, 290
lunges, 195
lungs, 45, 46
 as oxygen filling station, 46–47
Luthe, W., 287

McMaster University, 167 *Mad*,
146
maintenance programme,
 unsupervised, 141–42,
 149–51
Mallory, G. Kenneth, 99–100
marathon running, 181
 sudden death in, 158–59, 161
margarine, 227–28, 229
marijuana, 121
marriage:
 deterioration of, 66
 life–style and, 37
 sexual intercourse and, 31–32
mass control, Heart Points System
 and, 321–22, 329–30
mass gain:
 stopping smoking and, 296
 without change in eating
  habits, 114
 see also obesity
mass loss (dieting), 27, 256–68
 changes in eating habits and,
  261–62, 265
 diabetes and, 316–17
 exercise and, 36, 257, 258
 fast, 264–65
 high-protein/low-carbohydrate
  diets and, 262–63
 hypertension and, 305
 kilojoule-exercise relationship
  in, 257, 258
 myths about, 262–65
 nutritionally dense vs. "empty-
  kilojoule" foods in, 258–60
 permanent, 252

INDEX 473

sit-ups myth and, 263
special foods and, 263
timing of food intake and, 263
mass-loss programmes, 265–68
   guide to, 266–67
Massachusetts, University of,
   exercise study of, 36
Mayo Clinic, 359–60
meat:
   dietary recommendations for, 230
   organ, 233
   red, 228–30, 241
medical insurance, 367
medically-supervised exercise programmes, 149–54
   ECG monitoring and, 151, 153–154
   medically directed exercise programme vs., 151, 152–53
medications, *see* drugs; *specific drugs*
memory loss, 69
mental stress, routine for removal of, 288
metabolic equivalent unit (MET), 83, 91
   activity programme design and, 106–11
   exercise programme and, 138
   formulas for estimation of, 371–73
   sexual intercourse and, 115
metabolism:
   crash dieting and, 264
   exercise and, 258
   resting metabolic rate and, 258, 264
MI (myocardial infarction), 25, 28, 58
Michigan, University of, Medical Centre, 31, 100
milk, 224, 227
   low-fat, 34
   skim, 227
minerals, 357, 364
mitral valve, 46, 47
   malfunctioning of, 75
moderate-risk category, 29, 104
   death rates for, 30
   first-year risk of, 76–77
modified Bruce protocol, 87
monitors, heart rate, portable, 158
monocytes, 51, 52
monosaccharides, 239
monounsaturated fats, 33, 229, 232, 233
Montoye, Henry, 174–75
Montreal Heart Institute, 40, 167
Morris, Jeremy N., 129–31
mountain sickness:
   acute, 170–71
   high-altitude, 171
mourning, 70
Multiple Risk Factor Intervention Trial (MRFIT), 35–36, 131, 174
muscle relaxation, deep, 287–88
myocardial infarction (MI), 25, 28, 58
myocardial ischaemia, 55–56
   residual, 73–74
   see also heart attacks
myocardial oxygenation, 49, 50
myocardial revascularization, goal of, 338
myocardium, 49

National Academy of Sciences, 306
National Cholesterol Education Programme, 212, 214, 216
National Exercise and Heart Discase Project, U.S., 134–35
National Heart, Lung and Blood Institute, 212, 343
Naughton protocol, 87, 109
nausea, 113–14, 159, 170
neck:
   pain in, 159
   strength training routine for, 191
New Aerobics for Women, The (Cooper), 172
New England Journal of Medicine, 136, 357
New Mexico, University of, School of Medicine, 281
niacin (nicotinic acid), 249, 364
   contraindications for, 244
   as LDL-lowering agent, 243–44, 249
niacinamide, 243
nicotine, 293–96
nicotine gum (Nicorette),

300–301
nitrates (nitroglycerin), 25–26, 113, 121, 422–24
  exercise tests and, 84
Noakes, Timothy, 134, 136, 158, 181
"no pain, no gain" myth ("weekend-warrior syndrome"), 35–36
nutrition, 220–41
  see also diet; food; *specific foods and food groups*

oats, 240–41
obesity, 24, 52, 206, 207, 250–268
  CHD and, 252–56
  death and, 250–51
  exercise and, 134, 199
  fuel oil equivalent of, 251
  self-test estimate of, 253–54
Occupational Safety and Health Administration (OSHA), 291, 294
oestrogen, 118, 208
oils:
  fish, 231, 233, 361–62
  with saturated fats, 33–34, 228
  vegetable, 33–34, 228, 231, 233
Oldridge, Neil B., 132
oleic acid, 233
olive oil, 233
Olympic Games, 129, 161
omega–3 fatty acid, 231, 361–62
omega–6 fatty acids (linoleic acid), 231
Orenstein, Diane, 174–75
orgasm, heart rate and, 115
osteoarthritis, exercise and, 200
osteoporosis, 36
outpatient, early-convalescence programme, 139–40
overeating, stress and, 281–82
overmass, *see* obesity
Oxford English Dictionary, 179
oxygen, 44–50
  beta-blockers and, 424
  exercise and need for, 132–33
  heart's need for, under pressure, 49–50
  in lungs, 46–47
  myocardium and, 49, 50
  smoking and, 291, 293
  temporary shortage of, 38

pacemakers, exercise and, 197
Paffenbarger, Ralph S., Jr., 130–131, 134, 142
pain:
  abdominal, 159, 249
  angina, 27
  back, 159, 182, 277
  in calf, 114
  chest, 25–27, 38–39, 56, 57, 159
  during exercise, 159
  of heart attack, 25–27
palm kernel oil, 33–34, 228
palm oil, 33–34, 228
pancreatitis, 246, 249
paraplegics, 182
patient stratification, 29–30
  see also high-risk category; low-risk category; moderate-risk category
peanut oil, 233
peptic ulcer, 244
pericardium, 44
peripheral vascular disease, 199–200
Peterson, Richard A., 147
Pheidippides, 161, 162
physical activity, 99–125
  assessment of, 105–9
  dangers of excess in, 104–5
  energy expenditures for, 107–8
  poll of experts' on, 112, 115, 116–17
  returning to work and, 122–25
  symptoms and signs to watch for during, 112, 113–14
  see also exercise; exercise tests; sexuality, sexual intercourse; sports
physicians, *see* doctors
pipes, smoking of, 296
placebo effect, 361
plaque:
  buildup of, 51–52, 58, 60, 207
  chelation controversy and, 360–361
  defined, 28 HDL
  cholesterol and, 32
  omega-3 fatty acids and, 362
  residual myocardial ischaemia and, 74
platelets, 51, 58
  anti–platelet drugs and, 359–60,

433, 434
exercise effects on, 133
pollution, exercise and, 169–70
polyunsaturated fats, 33, 228, 230–33
  drawbacks of, 231
  omega-3, 231, 361–62
Pomilla, Paul V., 153
postcardiotomy psychosis, 69
potassium, 421
  hyperkalaemia and, 311–12
  increase of, 307, 311–12
Powell, Kenneth E., 34
premature ventricular contractions (PVCs), 78–79, 160
  complex, 88, 90
  probucol and, 246
prevention, 13
  "primary," 17
  "secondary," 17
preventive medicine, inadequate, 23
Prinzmetal, Myron, 56
Prinzmetal's angina (rest angina; variant angina), 56–57
processed foods, 230, 306–7
protein, 241 in slimming diets, 262–63
  see also specific sources of protein
psychological factors:
  in cravings, 261
  exercise tests and, 124
  in heart disease, 36
  in stress, 276–79
psychosis, postcardiotomy, 69
pullover, 194
pulmonary artery, 45, 46
pulmonary valve, 46
pulmonary veins, 45
pulse:
  irregular, 159
  monitoring of, 110–11
  taking of, 155, 156–57
PVCs, see premature ventricular contractions

radionuclide ventriculography, 78, 92, 93
Rahimtoola, Shahbudin H., 75
Railroad Study, U.S., 131
rales, 77
rate-pressure product, 49

rating of preceived exertion (RPE), 83, 138, 197, 198, 199
rats, yo-yo syndrome in, 264
Reagan, Ronald, 346
realism, in dieting, 262
rebounding, 183
recovering from a heart attack or surgery, 17–18, 61–125
  activity in, see physical activity
  bed rest and, 99–101
  feelings during, 63–70
  transition from hospital to home in, 101–4
  see also risk stratification
Recurrent Coronary Prevention Project, 284–85
redness, in calf, 114
registered dietitians (R.D.'s), 223
rehabilitation, cardiac:
  advantages of, 149
  defined, 136
  exercise and, 129, 136–43
  programmes for, 101–2, 105, 367
relaxation:
  hypertension and, 306
  therapy for, 286–89
Relaxation Response, The (Benson), 286
resting heart rate, 156
resting metabolic rate (RMR), 258, 264
reversibility concept, 142
rheumatoid arthritis, 200
Rippe, James M., 36
risk factors, 205–11, 253
  biological (uncontrollable), 206–9
  defined, 206
  exercise and, 160–72
  exercise effects on, 134–36
  exponential addition of, 210
  interrelatedness of, 209–10
  cholesterol; diabetes mellitus; hypertension; obesity; sedentary lifestyle; smoking; stress
risk stratification, 71–98
  see high-risk category; low-risk category; moderate-risk category
  for bypass and angioplasty patients, 95, 98

concept of, 71–73
Cooper Clinic guidelines for, 75–77, 82–83
exercise testing and, *see* exercise tests
left ventricular dysfunction and, 73, 74–75, 78–79
residual myocardial ischaemia and, 73–74
summary of, 98
see also high-risk category; low-risk category; moderate-risk category
RMR (resting metabolic rate), 258, 264
role models, 144
Roosevelt, Franklin D., 302
rope skipping, 183
Rosenman, Ray, 272–74
Ross, John, Jr., 75
Ross, Russell, 51, 52
RPE (rating of peceived exertion), 83, 138, 197, 198, 199
running, 205–6
death and, 136, 158–59, 161, 205
pros and cons of, 181
Running Injuries (Noakes and Granger), 167
Running Without Fear (Cooper), 87, 205

S-A (sinoatrial) node, 48, 197
safety:
of cholesterol-lowering drugs, 245
exercise and, 146–77, 409–18
of exercise test, 79–83
health data evaluation and, 356
mass loss and, 265
Salcedo-Salgar, Jorge, 99–100
salt:
dietary tips for reduction of, 313
diuretics and, 421
hypertension and, 306–13
reduction of use of, 306–7
see also sodium
saphenous vein, 349, 350
saturated fats, 33–34, 218, 224–30
in dairy products, 224–28
in oils, 33–34, 228
stearic acid, 228–30

Schultz, V. H., 287
Swart, Robert, 282–83
Schwinn Air-Dyne, 182
energy expenditure formula for, 397
exercise programmes for, 406–8
Heart Point Charts for, 375, 385–89
sedentary life-style, 130–31, 206
Selye, Hans, 276
Sender, Peter, 68–69
Sensuous Heart, The (Cambre), 122
septum, 44
"set point" hypothesis, 252
sex (gender), as risk factor, 206, 207–8
sexual expectations, 118–19
sexuality, sexual intercourse:
guidelines for, 115, 118–22
heart disease and, 31–32, 115–122
sudden death and, 31–32, 115
shellfish, as meat substitute, 233, 234
shoes, 167, 202
shopping, food, 262
shoulder and back stretch, 187
shoulders, strength training routines for, 190–91
side shoulder raise, 190
silent ischaemia, 38, 57, 277–78
sinoatrial node (S-A node), 48, 197
Siscovick, David S., 146–47, 172
sit-ups, 194
myth about, 263
skiing, cross-country, 183
skinfold measurements, 254–55
"smoker's face," 297
smoking, 27, 34, 52, 206, 207, 290–302
as addiction, 295, 298–99
blood vessels and, 291–94
carbon monoxide and, 169, 170, 293–94
death rates and, 41, 290
decline in, 15
exercise and, 134–35
fibrinogen and, 291, 294–95
hypertension and, 305
incidence of, 41, 290
"inheritance" of, 37
myths about, 41–42

nicotine and, 293–96
smoking, giving up, 295–97, 299–302
  comparing methods for, 299–302
  excuses about, 296–97
  willpower for, 295–96
sodium:
  hypertension and, 306–13
  substitutes for, 312
  in various foods, 308–11
Sones, F. Mason, 338, 341
Sparling, Phillip B., 189
special occasions, exercise and, 144–45
sports:
  competitive, 109
  energy expenditures for, 110
  recreational, 109, 184
spot-reducing, myth about, 263
spouses:
  exercise test effects on, 81
  fears of, 103, 119
sprinting, 179
Squires, Ray W., 170
Stanford Centre for Research in Disease Prevention, 287
Stanford University, exercise test studies by, 80–81
starches, 239
stationary cycling, 181–82, 185
  energy expenditure formula for, 396
  exercise programmes for, 404–8
  Heart Point Charts for, 375, 380–84
  walking combined with, 182, 185, 407–8
  see also Schwinn Air–Dyne
stearic acid, 228–30
Step 1 Eating Plan, 219–23, 234
Step 2 Eating Plan, 220, 223
Stern, Frank, 294
stethoscopes, use of, 46, 77
Stop Smoking (American Lung Association), 299
strength training:
  pros and cons of, 186–87
  recommendations for, 189, 192
  routines for, 189–95
stress, 17, 52, 269–89
  body's reaction to, 276–79
  exercise and, 134, 282–83

family members and, 102–3, 280
feeling of helplessness and, 270–71
GAS and, 276–77
job, 24–25, 123, 269, 270
positive vs. negative, 279
sources of (stressors), 271
Type A behaviour and, 134, 206, 269, 272–77, 284–85
as unavoidable, 271–72
stress management, 271–74
  assessment of, 272, 273, 274
  drugs and, 286, 289
  exercise and, 282–83
  family and friends and, 280
  feelings and, 280–82
  Heart Points System and, 321–322, 331–32
  laughter and, 285–86
  prioritizing and, 283–84
  relaxation therapy and, 286–89
  self-education and, 280
  techniques for, 279–89
  Type A traits modification and, 284–85
Stress Without Distress (Selye), 276
stretching, 185–88
  benefits of, 185–86
  exercises for, 187–88
stroke, 293, 302
  in Eskimos, 361
  haemorrhagic, 357–58
  ischaemic, 358
ST segment, abnormal, 88, 90–91, 92, 160
submaximal exercise tests, 82–92, 124
sugars, simple, 239, 259–60
sunburn, 164
sunflower seed oil, 231, 233
Superko, Robert, 197
supine fly, 193
support, for exercise programme, 144
Surgeon General, U.S., 290
Surgeon General's Report on Nutrition and Health, 365
surgery:
  bypass, *see* bypass surgery
  recovering from, *see* recovering from a heart attack or surgery
swelling:

in calf, 114
of feet, ankles, or legs, 114
swimming, 182–83
symptom-limited heart rate, 176
  defined, 112
symptom-limited maximal exercise test, 82, 124
  community-based programmes and, 140–41
systole state, 46, 47
systolic blood pressure, 47, 49, 110
  exercise and, 134
  exercise tests and, 88, 89

teenagers, 103
telemetry, 151
tension, *see* anxiety and tension; stress
Ter Welle, H. F., 363
tests:
  angiograms, *see* angiography
  of cholesterol levels, 214–17
  exercise, *see* exercise tests
  of stress management, 272, 273, 274
thallium scans, 92–93
therapy, 67
thighs:
  fat on, 256
  strength training routine for, 195
  stretching exercises for, 188
Thompson, Paul D., 147
Thoresen, Carl E., 284
thrombosis, 28, 58, 293, 294
thrombus, 58
thyroid gland, overactive, 164
Time, 54
toll-takers, tunnel, death rates of, 293–94
Topol, Eric J., 31
t–PA (tissue-type plasminogen activator), 26, 58, 133–34
training heart rate, 175, 177
  determining of, 154–58
tranquillizers, 64, 121
transplants, heart, 197–98
Travelstead, Michael, 269–71, 283–84
treadmills, 87–88
  jogging on, 395
  walking on, 181, 393

triceps extension, 193
tricuspid valve, 46
triglycerides, 53–54, 134, 245
  alcohol and, 247
  hypertriglyceridaemia, 246, 249
  lowering of, 246, 361
Type A Behaviour and Your Heart (Friedman and Rosenman), 273
Type A personality, 134, 206, 269
  GAS and, 276–77
  modification of, 284–85
  myth of, 272–76
Type B personality, 275, 276, 277, 285

UCLA School of Medicine, 160–161
ulcer, peptic, 244
underwater weighing, 254
upper-body exercises, 105, 197
  see also specific exercises and body parts
upright row, 191
urination, excessive nighttime, 114

Valsalva maneouvre, 187
valves, heart, 46, 47
Van Camp, Steven P., 147
vasodilators, 315, 433
vegetable oils, 228, 231, 233
  saturated fats in, 33–34, 228
veins, 45
  dilation of, 422
  saphenous, 349, 350
venae cavae, 46
Venter, John:
  case history of heart attack of, 23–28
  early convalescence regimen of, 109–15
  homecoming letdown of, 65–66
  hospital disquiet of, 63–65
  as moderate-risk patient, 30
ventricles, 44, 46, 47, 48
  left, dysfunction of, 73, 74–75, 78–79
  left, importance of, 47
  PVCs and, 78–79, 88, 90, 160, 246
ventricular fibrillation, 56, 90, 293, 341

exercise effects and, 134
ventricular septal defect, 75
ventricular tachycardia, 293
very-low-density lipoproteins (VLDLs), 53–54, 216, 249, 253
  bile acid sequestrants and, 245, 249
Vietnam War, autopsy evidence from, 52
viral myocarditis, 165–66
vision problems, cholesterol-lowering drugs and, 244, 246
Visken (pindolol), 425
vitamin A, 364
vitamin B6, 364
vitamin C, 364
vitamin D, 364
vitamin E, 362, 363, 364
vitamins, 357, 363–64
  absorption of, 245
  fat-soluble, 245, 364
  see also niacin
VLDLs, *see* very-low-density lipoproteins

walking, 35, 36, 166–67
  energy expenditure formulas for, 392–93
  exercise programmes for, 401–4, 407–8
  Heart Point Charts for, 375, 376, 377
  with light hand-held weights, 180
  pros and cons of, 180
  sexual intercourse compared with, 31, 115
  stationary cycling combined with, 182, 185, 407–8
  treadmill, 181, 393
warm-ups, 120, 160–62, 198
Washington, University of:
  Centre for Inherited Diseases at, 37

heart rate study of, 157–58
"water weight," 263
Wayne State University, 312
weather, exercise and:
  cold, 167–69
  hot and humid, 163–64, 165
"weekend-warrior syndrome" ("no pain, no gain" myth), 35–36
weights, walking with, 180
Weiss, Stephen, 306
Westernized nations, incidence of coronary heart disease in, 13–15
wheat bran, 239
White, Paul Dudley, 30, 99–100
Williams, Redford B., 275–76
windchill index, 167–69
women:
  body fat of, 256
  heart attacks in, 39
  heart disease in, 37, 207–8
  hypertension in, 304
  premenopausal, HDL cholesterol in, 207
  premenopausal, sexual activity and, 118
  Type A behaviour in, 274–75
work:
  returning to, 122–25
  stress of, 24–25, 123, 269, 270
World Health Organization, 15, 136
wound infection, symptoms of, 114

X-rays, in angiograms, 26, 338–340

Yale University School of Medicine study, 4
yo–yo syndrome (dieter's dilemma), 264–65

zinc, 364